AF477748

About the Author

Mack W. Borgen is a graduate of Harvard Law School and a national award-winning author. He is a native of Montana and was raised in the Pacific Northwest and the Midwest. Upon graduation from the University of California at Berkeley with Honors in Economics, he delivered one of the last University-wide Commencement Addresses. Then, after graduating from law school, he served more than four years in the U.S. Army.

He lived in Europe for a short period before returning to California and Montana where for years he has practiced business law and continued to write about various economic, political, and social matters.

In 2008, he partly withdrew from both business and his law practice in order to devote himself to the writing of a long-planned series of books about the current American condition and about how we, as a country, can do better.

His first two books, *The Relevance of Reason—The Hard Facts and Real Data About the State of Current America* ((*Volume 1—Business and Politics*) (407 pp) and (*Volume 2—Society and Culture*) (437 pp)) were released in 2013. Each of the books won multiple national book awards.

Mack W. Borgen's blogs and excerpts from his other writings may be viewed at *mackwborgen.com*.

The author lives with his wife and son in Santa Barbara, California.

DEAD SERIOUS
and LIGHTHEARTED

DEAD SERIOUS

and LIGHTHEARTED

VOLUME I (1957-1976)

The Memorable Words
of Modern America

MACK W. BORGEN

NATIONAL AWARD-WINNING AUTHOR

The Relevance of Reason, Vols I and II

Santa Barbara, CA

Schmitt & Brody Publishers
Schmitt & Brody Publishers
3655 Montalvo Way
Santa Barbara, California 93105

First Edition

Schmitt & Brody books may be purchased for educational and business purposes. For information, please write, Schmitt & Brody—Special Markets, 3655 Montalvo Way, Santa Barbara, California 93105.

Printed in the United States of America.

ISBN: 978-0-9997299-0-8 Hardcover
       978-0-9997299-1-5 Paperback
       978-0-9997299-2-2 ebook
LCCN: 2018900338

Publisher's Cataloging-In-Publication Data

Names: Borgen, Mack W. | Borgen, Mack W. Chance of a lifetime series.
Title: Dead serious and lighthearted. Volume I (1957-1976) : the memorable words of
    modern America / Mack W. Borgen.
Description: First edition. | Santa Barbara, CA : Schmitt & Brody Publishers, [2018] |
    Includes bibliographical references and index.
Identifiers: ISBN 9780999729908 (hardcover) | ISBN 9780999729915 (paperback) |
    ISBN 9780999729922 (ebook)
Subjects: LCSH: United States--History--1945- | United States--Civilization--1945- |
    United States--Intellectual life--20th century. | Popular culture--United States--
    History--20th century.
Classification: LCC E839 .B67 2018 (print) | LCC E839 (ebook) | DDC 973.92--dc23

For Shawna
For sharing my journeys.

For Brody
For reminding me, each day, of all that is good.

And

For My Close Friends and Mentors
Who over many years,
Have displayed to me their goodness,
Have offered to me their inspiration,
And
At times and when so needed,
Have shared with me their wisdom and
Have offered me their guidance.
They have given me more than I can repay;
They have taught me more than I can learn;
But, I have tried.
And
I am, to them each day, thankful.

NOTE TO READERS

This book, *Dead Serious and Lighthearted—The Memorable Words of Modern America—1957–1976,* is the first of three volumes in this *Dead Serious and Lighthearted* series. In these books, the author seeks to identify, present and contextually explain those words, those memorable words, through which we may, together and depending upon our age, remember or learn about our country. The good, the humorous, and the touching are here, along with the sobering, the horrific, and the consequential. This first volume presents the memorable words of the dawning period of Modern America from 1957 to 1976. The second volume presents the memorable words from 1977 to 1993. The third and last volume presents the memorable words from 1994 to 2015.

Thus, the chronologically presented Memorable Words sections of each of the three volumes are unique to each book. However, the genesis, purposes, assumptions, and underlying methodologies of each volume, as presented in Chapters 1 through 6 are largely the same in each book. Therefore, the Preface, Introduction, and Chapters 1 through 6 are largely unchanged in all three volumes—excepting, if and as applicable, some minor modifications and period-specific updates.

Table of Contents

PART II

THE MEMORABLE WORDS OF MODERN AMERICA
(1957–1976)

Appendices

Preface

This book is offered with great humility, but whether written by this author or by others, this book—the collected "Memorable Words" of Modern America—is needed. Now more than ever.

These Memorable Words of Modern America are offered as a new way, depending upon one's age, to remember or to learn our country's recent history.

But the task of selecting the Memorable Words is, at the least, daunting because words are one of the core currencies of our society. The subjects of our society are many and varied—economics, race, education, immigration, international relations, and on and on, but it is the words which are the means by which these subjects are learned and addressed. It is words by which movements are started and changes are made. It is words by which we alternatively revere, honor, dismiss, or insult both ideas and people. But despite their importance, words are a terribly imperfect currency.

Words get exchanged, borrowed, and stolen. Words get forgotten and lost amidst the shuffle and cacophony of our country's 2015 population of 319,500,000 people[1]—all with their own ideas, hopes, dreams *and words;* all with their own thoughts, understandings, perspectives *and words.*

Words get twisted in furtherance of agendas. Words become dated or distorted through the relentless occurrence of intervening events. Their meaning can be lost or their importance elevated or diminished, whether by the mere passage of time or by the reckless or intentional misquoting of others.

Yet words remain the real currency of our country—our primary tools of communication and rally; our tools of encouragement and persuasion; our tools of observation and critique. Even giving every deserved deference to the power of photos, movies, and imagery in especially the later years of our now-viral Modern America, words remain the text of our history, and for all their faults, it is the words which can reveal truth—about the speaker, the subject, and the circumstance. With context, they can even reveal insights about a period or age in our country's history.

One of the frailties of words is that they vary greatly in their shelf lives. Sometimes, words have lasting meaning and resonance. Sometimes, they are wrapped in passion and delivered with excitement. Sometimes, they reflect only a passing joy or an unchecked rage. Sometimes, they are thick with meaning but reveal the cold distance of the academic. Sometimes, they emanate importance at the moment of utterance, but become deservedly lost in the shuffle of new events or with the arrival of new voices.

Collectively, though, words—and especially the "memorable words"— are almost definitionally an integral component of our nation's narrative. They are not the only part of the binding fabric of our national community, but they are an integral part of it.

Words can help us struggle through the linear continuum of our past, present, and future. We therefore need to record and reflect upon our nation's words for three reasons: the past is hard to remember; the present is hard to understand; and the future is hard to see.

In the phrasing of Nate Silver, it is hard for each of us to sort the signals from the noise, but it is axiomatic that some words matter. Some words can further a cause, clarify a meaning, reveal a belief, foretell that which may be coming, or explain that which has occurred.

Certainly, each reader would have his or her own selection of memorable words, but there are also some shared and objective bases for consensus. Some words, for example, are remembered by collective America. Some words become etched into the very DNA of the successive generations. Those who were alive when they were spoken, remember hearing them, and younger Americans remember reading about them. We remember where we were. Exactly. What they meant. Exactly. Who said or wrote them and why. And in these ways, the words, the Memorable Words, for better or worse, bind us together as a nation.

This book and its associated volumes present this author's careful selection of America's "Memorable Words" from the period 1957 to 2015. The sole purpose of these books is to try to assemble, in one place, the Memorable Words of Modern America.

These books present two types of "Memorable Words"

The first type of Memorable Words are the titles of books, movies, television shows along with, in some cases, the best movie lines of the respective years of Modern America. Included amongst these titles and lines are the 63 Seminal Books of Modern America; the 166 Pulitzer Prize-winning books in Fiction, General Nonfiction, and History; and the 125 best-selling books of Modern America. Each book is presented chronologically based on its year of initial publication. Also included are the titles of the award-winning movies and nearly 175 of the most famous and impactful movie lines of Modern America together with the titles and stars of and viewership information about those television shows that, each for its own reason, have defined or encapsulated American society. Lastly, this grouping of titles and lines includes a careful selection of the 60 most dominant commercial advertising campaigns and slogans that, by virtue of either their cleverness or raw repetition, have become a part of our American life.

The true core of this book lies is in the second type of included words—the more than 675 selections of those Memorable Words that, in the opinion of the author, have best defined, exemplified, or explained our country, or that have captured—even if briefly—our passions, fears, joys, ideas, or ideals over the course of the 58 years of Modern America. The selections are not limited to the heavy, important, and "dead serious" words. Also included are those "lighthearted" words that also reveal the truth about our country.

Following each of these selected Memorable Words, both the "dead serious" and the "lighthearted," is a summary explanation of the words' context, meaning, and impact. In some cases, an explanation of the triggering event or circumstance underlying the speaker's or writer's words is also included. Lastly and in order to reflect the electoral and political shifts that have occurred over the course of Modern America, the nearly 160 campaign slogans used by candidates of major political parties during the fourteen Presidential elections are included along with the results of those elections.

As is evident and obvious, for any one author to accurately select all the Memorable Words of a vast period of American life is far too great a task to perfectly achieve. But I have tried.

Hopefully, the honor of this task will not merely be in the effort. Despite the admitted risk that this type of book may be a fool's errand, the task remains to be done—especially in an America which, for the first time in its history, is now crowded with four generations.

As e.e. cummings famously noted, "each of us shall do foolish things in our lives, but do such things with enthusiasm." It is with cummings' remark in mind that this collection of our history is offered. *With enthusiasm.*

One last comment is necessary. America is in an edgy era. Our people are routinely subjected to fear, verbosity, and bluster. With that in mind, it is hoped that this book, at this uneasy time in our history, may help in a small way to bring our country together again. Possibly, this book can help us lower our voices in honor and remembrance of those who have spoken or written before. Possibly, this book can help us raise our spirits and renew our hopes by reflecting upon whence we came as a nation. Possibly, this book can help us better remember that which has been achieved, so that, in turn, we may be able to better find, accept and embrace what now must be done.

Thus, before more words are thrown into the ether, it may be useful, comforting, and in certain contexts, even amusing to remember where we have been; what has been said; by whom; and when and why. Possibly, it is important to remember both the "dead serious" and the "lighthearted" words which have been a part of our common past.

PART I

The Purposes of History,
Its Relevance to Our National Community,
and
The Concept of Memorable Words

Author's Note

Part I of this book, consisting of the first six chapters, is common to all three volumes of Dead Serious and Lighthearted—The Memorable Words of Modern America (Volume I (1957–1976); Volume II (1977–1993); and Volume III (1994–2015)). *Thus, in this Part I, there are multiple references to "these books," and, in a few instances, examples of Memorable Words are drawn from all of the years of Modern America—from 1957 through 2015.*

One of the primary purposes of these books is to present a new way of studying our nation's recent history. In these books, the Memorable Words of Modern America have been carefully selected and set forth chronologically, oftentimes with a short explanation of the meaning, implications, and immediate context of such words. It is hoped that the orderly presentation of these Memorable Words may help lift the otherwise burdensome weight of studying and recalling the major events of our nation's recent history. As more thoroughly discussed in Chapter 3 ("The Purposes of These Books and the Concept of Memorable Words"), this presentation is expansive and detailed, but it is not thick with theory or weighed down by extensive analysis. As suggested by the title, the selection of Memorable Words includes two distinct dimensions of our country's recent history—both the "dead serious" and the "lighthearted" words of America's modern era. Depending upon the reader's age, the words may trigger memories of the events surrounding the words or statement. Younger Americans, meanwhile, may discover for the first time, what was actually said, by whom, and why.

There are, however, two threshold subjects that must be addressed at the outset. First, the very meaning and utility of history; and second, the need for and certain unique realities of our national community.

CHAPTER 1

The Purposes and Challenges of History and Community in the Age of Modern America

Introduction

"Poorly taught and rarely learned"

For most Americans, history is poorly taught and rarely learned. Despite the dedication and competence of our teachers, academics, and professors; despite the brilliant writings of our modern historians and —from Manchester to Durant, from McCullough to Meacham, from Goodwin to Beschloss, from Schlesinger to Caro, from Burns and Brinkley, from Ambrose to Halberstam, and on and on[2]—too often, the stubborn truth remains the same—excepting at our country's colleges and universities, history is poorly taught and rarely learned. And even when learned, history and its many lessons are too often forgotten or discarded as irrelevant—as mere anecdotes from another time; from a different circumstance.

Part of the problem is that history is too often taught as a boring lineage of dates and places; a tired recitation of time-worn stories; the rote learning of distant wars and forgotten battles. With such presentation, history comes to be viewed merely as the dusty study of long-ago events—empty stories about dead white men speaking in the cadence and parlance of another era.

In addition, history is too often presented in seeming isolation from contemporary life. It is presented as an almost detached subject matter; an independent field of study without obvious, or at least emphasized, contemporary relevance other than perhaps the obligatory recitation of George Santayana's warning that those who cannot remember the past are condemned to repeat it.[3] Unsurprisingly, the lessons of history get lost amidst the drone of too many words, and history's constant relevance to our lives gets lost amidst the dry monotone of the heavy words and thick tomes of academics.

Certainly some allowances have to be made. History is arguably less fun and more difficult to teach than some other subjects. For most younger students, it is certainly not as fun as recess. History's outcomes are rarely as definitive as those of sports. For some students, math seems just simpler. Math offers tight precision and correct answers; 2 plus 2 equals 4—always has and always will. And for some students, other subjects are just less challenging than history—less challenging, at least, in that good-grade, kind of way.

Consider the simplicity of geography, for example. It has always there for measurement. Except for an occasional earthquake or a Mount St. Helens eruption, it almost never changes. Mount Everest has barely budged an inch since the first Sherpa looked up. On the other hand, while music may demand more creativity, Beethoven and Beyonce, Mozart and Madonna, Tchaikovsky and Macklemore all wrote in the same language. They all used the same bar lines. They all heard the same C Major.

And it doesn't help that history, by its very nature, is *not* tidy. History, just like life, comes at us jumbled and tangled. It comes in drip by drip. First, it arrives in the form of news—the "first drafts of history"—written and compiled amidst a stir of oftentimes incomplete and inaccurate information. The initial reports are, nearly always, clouded by confusion and emotion. Then comes the commentary. And then, but only over time and after much analysis, does a semblance of thoughtful history appear. But even then, the narratives are constantly re-packaged in books and other writings. Sometimes consensus is achieved. Oftentimes, it is not—and the decades of debates and interpretations begin.

Complicating matters, history is oftentimes composed of an almost endless series of largely unforeseeable events. Such unforeseen occurrences are not just commonplace—they are the very narrative of history. Even anticipated events arrive at their leisure unburdened by any sense of punctuality. Epochs, periods, and movements sneak upon us, arriving without announcements, without media rollouts or celebratory parades, without press releases, and without tidy explanations.

Lastly, the very nature of history presents unique challenges for its learning. One must accept the need for patience and reflection because history is a definitionally cumulative and unending subject. Every day, there is more of it. Every week, there are more chapters. Every month, there are more books. In addition, because events of historical importance must be placed in the context of time and place, one must accept the need for inference and for constant reevaluation and elaboration.

Nevertheless and even though it can be difficult to teach and frustratingly slow to learn, history is there to be embraced. It cannot be ignored. As Jon Meacham wisely said several years ago, "history cannot be dismissed with a nod."[4] Whether we like it or not, history haunts us with its importance. We ignore its lessons at our own risk. We forget its warnings at our own cost. Indeed, "history is strapped to our backs. We do not have to see it; we can always feel it."[5]

As noted above, these books seek to present the history of Modern America in an entirely new manner—in a more engaging, "Dead Serious and Lighthearted" manner. But before we get into the concept and definition of Memorable Words, the place to begin is a detailed look at some of the more important uses and some of the more specific purposes of history which can themselves be elusive. And different uses can take us to different places; different purposes can be seeds of misunderstanding.

The Purposes of History and The New Realities of Our National Community

The Traditional Purposes of History: Learning from Our Past, Adding Color to Our Lives, and Honoring Our Heritage

"Understanding and Honoring Our Common Past"

One of the most commonly accepted purposes of the study of history is to help us understand and learn from the past so that we, as individuals, families, groups, or nations, can more wisely see our choices, chart our courses, make our decisions, and respond to challenges as they arise.

Partly because of these weighty, utilitarian purposes, history is often seen as an academic subject requiring sober study and steady diligence. The problem is that such utilitarian aspects of history are just too simplistic. They only represent a small piece of a much larger picture. The study of history has many other purposes. History is much more than the narrative collection and study of the memories and experiences of one generation stacked all wobbly upon those who came before.

For example, history can add color, dimension, and understanding to our life and travels. There is a reason that thousands of Americans travel each year to see Plymouth Rock southeast of Boston. There is a reason the Alamo remains protected and revered in the center of San Antonio. There is a reason that Gettysburg is so much more than a small town in southeast Pennsylvania. There is a reason men broke treaties and stole their access to the Black Hills. There is a reason people still trek out to see that lonely spot in Utah known as Promontory Point. And on it goes.

History also represents one of the few means by which we best honor our forefathers and recognize their sacrifices. A visit to Arlington National Cemetery is fully embraced only with the knowledge of who and why so many died. Walking the sacred grounds of Ellis Island is fully appreciated only with remembrance of the nearly 12 million people who passed through its gates in the 60 years between 1892 and 1954. It is just such pieces of our history that can help us to better understand and appreciate our country.

But apart from adding color to our lives through deeper understanding of our country and apart from enabling us to better honor our heritage and our forefathers by knowing what they did, history has several other purposes of even greater importance and relevance to our daily lives.

The Additional Purposes of History: Comfort, Perspective and National Community
"History is a quiet medicine."

One of those additional purposes of history is its utility as a source of comfort and perspective about our country—something sorely needed amidst the anger and acrimony that have come to so characterize these last several decades of Modern America.

History is a quiet medicine, but it can allow us, individually and as a nation, to better remember our accomplishments. It can reinforce our patience with one another.

Studying our shared history allows us to better remember where we have been as a nation—what we or our forefathers have together witnessed, viewed, pondered, read, and collectively endured. Viewing the present through the lens of history, we can more easily appreciate, and sometimes better understand, the radically variant perceptions of our country that are held by different sectors of our society.

Studying our history also allows us to better understand the challenges ahead. For example, whether amidst the labyrinth of international relations, the demagoguery of contemporary politics, or the complexities of racial and ethnic integration, history can serve as a reminder, a guide, and, when necessary, even a goalpost.

Studying our history allows us to tighten the ever-loosening strands of our national community. By helping us to better remember the many and varied components of our shared past, history allows us to remember our country's purposes, standards, objectives, and aspirations.

In these ways, history is almost unique. For example, with all due and deserved respect for our U.S. Constitution and all of the treaties, laws, and court opinions that document America's official past, it is our history and our shared aspirations that are the real glue of our society.

Matters of economics, politics, and culture may routinely dominate the news, but it is our history that serves as the quiet bond holding together our regional and national communities. It is the good, the bad, the ups, the downs, the successes, the failures, and even the absurdities of our collective and shared history that are the indispensable components necessary for the orderly functioning of our society and—albeit very roughly—for the acceptance of our rules of law and our social codes of ethics, behavior, and morals.

It is beyond the scope of these books to argue for the role and necessity of community, but the subject of community must be at least briefly addressed. This is because there is a growing perception among some Americans that a sense of community, and especially a national community, is both unachievable and unnecessary. In the opinion of this author, this is both dangerous and wrong.

In this context, the interplay of history and community must be understood. First, the interplay must be understood because the tightening of our sense of community is one of the purposes of history. Second, the interplay must be understood because the hard fact that America remains unalterably one community is one of the most obvious lessons of history. This relationship between our knowledge of our national history and our sense of community is too rarely acknowledged. It is too rarely discussed. But it is significant. It is real.

To further these understandings, our teachers must be encouraged to teach the *relevance of history* as a topic almost separate from the teaching of history itself. As will be discussed below, this is especially true in today's highly-accelerated world where more and more younger Americans question the contemporary relevance of all but the most recent events. Adding the teaching of the relevance of history to the American school curriculum is an admitted, but necessary, burden. No one needs more homework, but our country's children (and, for that matter, our country's distracted and busy adults) must embrace the idea that learning our history, just like voting (and, in this writer's opinion and in a more perfect union, public service), is one of the duties of citizenship—not a requirement of citizenship, but a duty of citizenship.

Certainly many factors—race, ethnicity, religiosity, linguistic homogeneity, aspirational hopes, and shared values—affect the strength of our national community. Certainly many forces challenge that strength. Our nation has not admitted a new state since Hawaii and Alaska in 1959, but 50 states is still a lot more than 13 colonies. America's current 3.8 million square miles is nearly nine times that of those lonely original 13 colonies which hugged the Eastern seaboard. Even more important, the population and diversity of our nation's population has continued to grow exponentially. We all have more neighbors than we will ever meet.

But apart from these splintering influences upon our sense of national community and apart from our oftentimes shared *lack* of knowledge about our country's history, there are three other new, distinct factors which have arisen in the era of Modern America and which deserve particular note because they directly affect our understanding and acceptance of national community.

The New Factors Affecting Our National Community

The three new factors affecting our understanding and acceptance of national community are (i) the blunt reality that withdrawal from the national community is rarely a realistic alternative; (ii) the dangerous consequences that have resulted from the growing separation and distancing of America's wealthy from the broader American community; and (iii) the unique, unavoidable, but powerful impact of multi-generational ignorance.

The Impossibility of Isolation and Withdrawal

*"The need, if not the presence,
of a strong American community remains"*

To a certain extent, the very concept of community grates against America's passionate tradition of and respect for individualism. Such individualism in American life does not in itself connote, let alone require, retreat from the American community, but extreme individualism characterized by isolation and withdrawal is sometimes sought. In the right place and with sufficient resources and resourcefulness, such a life can still be achieved. But rarely.

This writer was born in Montana and has lived there, on and off, for many years. There are good families there who, for their many and varied reasons, live deep down the road, back in the woods, and off the grid. Similar families can be found in the woods of Maine or in the Great Smokies of Tennessee and North Carolina or, for that matter, amidst the solitude and isolation which can be found in the American Southwest or along the county roads of the Great Plains. Some of these people are self-described survivalists and preppers, but most are not. But while such social and geographic isolation is desired and possible for a few Americans, it is unrealistic for and undesired by a great majority of America's now largely urbanized population. For most Americans, the blunt reality is that isolation and withdrawal are not realistic alternatives. Short of expatriation,[6] the American community is our only home. And that is a good thing.

Most Americans, in fact, want to be a part of a community however defined. Most Americans enjoy the nearby presence of friends and family. Most Americans need a grocery store, a gas station, and a power grid. Most Americans need their radio, their television, and their Internet. Even in an age of ever-advancing technology, most Americans still want a human voice at the other end of their 9-1-1 calls. Most Americans want their streets plowed in the winter. They want their schools accessible and open. They want emergency rooms to be ready. They want their food to be safely prepared. They want America's elderly to be cared for and America's workers to be protected. They want, indeed expect, our country's national defenses to be strong and our environment to be preserved. And on and on.

The point here is simple—for all of these reasons and for better or worse, the first new factor to be understood about the American community is the nearly universal impossibility of isolation and withdrawal. They are rarely realistic alternatives. Thus, the need, if not the presence, of a strong American community remains.

The Distancing of the Wealthy
"The cold fact is that … even wealth-based isolation
from the national community is rarely feasible."

Certainly, the wealthy have always lived differently. This is not news. To a degree, this is not wrong. The wealthy have always had their enclaves. Free from many of the financial burdens and insecurities of normal

American life, the wealthy have always had privileged lifestyles and expectations. Again, this is not wrong.

But standing in the lobby of any five-star hotel, it is easy to understand how Americans can readily self-divide themselves as "us" and "them;" as "we" and "they." The resources and opportunities available to the wealthy are to be both envied and applauded. It is a stubborn statistical reality that an overwhelming majority of the present-day wealthy came to their status through the circumstances of their birth and through an inheritance of wealth or privilege, but certainly some fortunes have been hard- and well-earned—the result of their effort, diligence, and wisdom.

But even though it is of little news that the lives of the extremely wealthy are different from those of most Americans, lately those differences have grown. Lately, the extent and degree of their detachment and withdrawal from our national community has become more severe. It has become more dangerous to the broad and public good.

Thus, the second new factor relating to our national community is the increasing degree to which America's wealthy naively believe that they can distance themselves from the broader national community. This distancing differs from the deep-in-the-wood isolation and withdrawal discussed above. This factor is a dimension of America's growing income and wealth inequality. It results from the increasingly widespread, but mistaken, belief held by many wealthy Americans that they can somehow immunize themselves from the challenges of their national community; that they can somehow not be at risk; that as a result of their wealth, they can be protected from the vagaries and condition of their fellow citizens.

Over the course of especially the last several decades, income and wealth inequality have been accentuated. More and more wealthy Americans have come to quietly, almost unconsciously, believe that they can withdraw from the broader national community; that they can live and remain safely within a rarefied community; that they are entitled (an admittedly loaded phrase) to live within their own separate, rarefied communities. These communities are composed almost exclusively of people of similar wealth, education, race, and ethnicity. Increasingly in our politicized, password America, a component of admission to such exclusivity is the expectation that such persons also hold similar political beliefs and belong to aligned associations.

There are many examples of such withdrawal. There is a growing sense among the wealthy that the problems of public schools need not afflict their families—they can afford private schools. There is a sense that health care debates are largely irrelevant—they can afford health insurance, absorb health costs, and have ready access to concierge medicine. There is a sense that the condition of public parks has little relevance to the care and feeding of the lawns within their gated communities and private clubs. There is a sense that their children do not need to serve in our Armed Forces —there is a "voluntary" army for that purpose. And the list goes on and on. But these perceptions are misguided. One cannot be an American and buy one's way out of the American community. The edgy, survival-of-the-fittest Darwinism of our American economy does not absolve the wealthy from a needed rebalancing of their private interests and the broad public good.

To many Americans, it seems that the wealthy have almost monetized their relationship with the national community. It seems that citizenship is now defined by the frequency and size of political contributions, and as honorable as these acts may be, it is awkwardly important to also recognize the growing hostility in our country. In other words, while political donations may constitute acts of political participation, it is also true that one's relationship with the American community cannot be built solely upon such donations. Our communities demand more. Our communities deserve more.

It is certainly not the intention of this author to stir anger or spread insults, and this author, a humble student of history, is well aware that messengers are often shot. But the words must be written. The wealthy must understand, if not accept, a reality. Many Americans now perceive political contributions as nothing more than pay-to-play tickets. They do not see the political contributions of the wealthy as rooted in any sense of public good. Instead, these contributions are seen as flowing merely from one's own sense of self-interest.

Even acts of philanthropy are sometimes harshly perceived. Such perceptions may not be fair, but they must be recognized. Unless the sense of a broad national community is tight and unless the wealthy are honorably and deeply invested in that community, even philanthropic acts will be dismissed by large segments of the community. With the bonds of our national community weakening over the recent decades and with acrimony and cynicism increasingly clouding our vision and judgment, the cold reality is that even genuinely altruistic acts on the part of the wealthy are often seen as nothing more than methodologies. The perceived methodologies have variant forms—the wealthy merely reaping the advantages of tax deductions for charitable donations; the wealthy merely abating their consciences and only doing that what they deem to be expected; and, especially after the financial crisis of 2008, the wealthy merely giving back to society a portion of that which they had previously and wrongly taken through their exploitation of a slanted tax code, their receipt of undue and unearned salaries and bonuses, their access to advantaged stock trades, and through other forms of self-serving, "soft" work.

Obviously, many aspects of the relationship between the wealthy and the rest of America must change. In the opinion of some, the American dream of opportunity must be reinstated or some other accommodations must be achieved. There will always be a degree of tension between the classes of society, but the hostility must be lessened. More Americans, and very bluntly, especially the wealthy, must come to recognize the importance that the long-term interests of all classes stay on roughly parallel tracks.

This belief is not rooted in any naïve, sophomoric, egalitarian dream. It is based solely upon a cold reality. That reality is that wealth-based isolation from the national community is rarely feasible. Just as with the deep-in-the-woods isolation discussed above, isolation and withdrawal from our national community through wealth is unrealistic. Though it is sometimes not apparent, the fortunes of all Americans are closely interconnected and the lives of all Americans are closely intertwined. It is wrong for any American to believe that the rest of America is not close by. No doors are thick enough; no locks are secure enough; no walls are high enough. This statement is *not* meant to be harsh or threatening. It is simply reality.

The proximity of the rest of America is true in the context of economics, politics, and geography. The distances are just not that great—from the skylines of Chicago's Miracle Mile to the open fields of Kansas; from the estates in the Hamptons to the apartments in the Bronx; from the brilliance of Silicon Valley to the horrors of Columbine; from the wealth of Wall Street to the poverty of Appalachia; from the Rust Belt to the Sun Belt; and on and on.

Similarly, the distance from the rewards of industry to the efforts of workers is not that far. America is a big country, but it is a country of mutual interdependence. As it should be. The successes and failures of its people are commonly shared. Both our good and our bad are widely seen around the world. Both our words and acts of encouragement are felt by all. Contrariwise, anyone's disengagement—however passing or passive—is felt by all. Thus, once again, isolation and withdrawal are rarely feasible.

For that reason, each of us must reach out. Too many Americans already know their computers better than their neighbors. That must change. Too many Americans define "their community" tightly. That must change. The definition of "neighbors" must extend far beyond our immediate peers, our like kind, and our immediate surroundings.

This author well-recognizes how banal and trite these words may, at first blush, appear. But they are neither banal nor trite. And so it is like all marriages. America is our nation for better or worse; in sickness and in health. As such, America must be seen and accepted as a national community. Individualism and wealth can be encouraged and even honored, but withdrawal is nearly impossible. More Americans must willingly accept that the public good will at times conflict with their private interests and that sometimes, the public good must be allowed to prevail.

This brings us back to the one of the roles of history itself because the best way to rekindle our sense of community is through the study of our history—the shared history whence we came; the shared future to which we go.

But before proceeding, there is one more new and powerful factor affecting our national community that must be recognized. Unlike desires for isolation or the elective, but dangerous, withdrawal of the wealthy, this last factor is unique to our times. It is also unavoidable. This is the factor of multi-generational ignorance.

The Impact of Multi-Generational Ignorance
"Both a blessing and burden … It has changed everything.
It has complicated everything."

The third new factor affecting our acceptance and understanding of national community is the impact of multi-generational ignorance.

In 1900, the average life expectancy in the United States was about 40 years. As a result, on any given day, our nation was shared by only two generations. Now, the average life expectancy in the United States is about 79.8 years. Life expectancy has roughly doubled in the last 125 years.

As a result, our country is, for the first time, both blessed and burdened by the simultaneous presence of four generations. What has changed in America is the presence of multiple generations—in 1900, two generations; in 1960, three generations; in 2015, four generations.

The extension of life expectancy and the presence of four generations in our country are wonderful but they bring with them many new challenges. They haven't just made things far more crowded. They have changed *everything*. It has complicated *everything* … including our sense of community. As important, this new reality has complicated the understanding of our own nation's history because the first thing to remember about the nearly six decades of Modern America, from 1957 to 2015, is that most of "us" were not there.

A great majority of Americans have not lived the duration of Modern America. While some memories, like the horror of 9/11, are widely shared, most memories have not been shared.

Consider just a few examples.

For most Americans, Vietnam is now a long-ago war. In fairness to the younger generations and even though many Americans properly view our nation as a peaceful nation, there have been too many wars to keep them all straight—ISIS, Iraq and Afghanistan (2002–Present), First Gulf War (1990–1991), Grenada invasion (1983), Vietnam (1955–1975), Korean War (1950–1953), World War II (1941–1945). And then there is the omnipresence of the Cold War. It is not easy to explain the Cold War reality of classroom "duck-n-cover" drills to younger Americans.

Nor is it easy to explain military service and the draft. The current median age of the U.S. population is about 37.8 years. Since the military draft ended in 1975, nearly half of all Americans have *always* viewed military service as a matter of choice rather than a matter of duty. There is no fault to be assigned. However, using just this example, the impact of a military draft upon the two older generations of Americans are not easily understood, let alone shared, by the two younger generations.

Consider also the duel events of President Kennedy's assassination and the moon landing. The 1963 assassination of President Kennedy is now as historically distant to younger Americans as the 1901 assassination of President McKinley was to today's older Americans when the Kennedy assassination occurred. Older Americans remember their sense of awe when they viewed the 1969 moon landing. Younger Americans have devoted their awe to the technological revolutions represented by Facebook and Google The Internet is their moon landing.

In the context of American economics, younger Americans have a rough grasp of the Great Recession of 2008, but they know little about the breadth, the depth, or the pain of the Great Depression of the 1930s. And the very nature of our economy and employment has changed. Younger Americans have grown up in a highly mobile and Darwinian economic environment in which life-time employment with the same company, common among prior generations, is now a nearly unheard of rarity.

Lastly, and especially in light of the 2016 national political election, consider the acrimony and polarization of our political system and the style and tone of our public discourse. Only older Americans remember the exuberant hopefulness of Kennedy, the oratory of King, and the "drinks-after-5" camaraderie shared by Republican President Reagan and Democratic Speaker of the House Tip O'Neill. Now the very concept of compromise is seen by some as appeasement and by others as surrender. However, it was less than three decades ago—i.e. *recently*—when compromise was seen as a matter of obligation amongst politicians; as one of the definitional requisites of political life.

Just a few decades ago, passion was commonplace, but (excepting in the context of the Vietnam War and the urban riots of the 1960s) anger was rarely the starting place. Ideological rigidity was rarely expected or insisted upon by the voters. Far more commonly, there was an expectation of cooperation; honest negotiation, and, as noted above, compromise.

But for at least the last two generations of Americans, these statements are matters of history not matters of memory. Thus, it is understandably hard for younger generations to comprehend that American politics has not always been hostile. By the dates of their birth, by the very laws of nature, they cannot know—let alone remember—that things have not always been this way.

Multi-generational ignorance inherently escalates the risks of misunderstandings because America is now seen through the radically different lenses of our four distinct generations. Every good and every bad, every idea and every invention, every "why" and every "why not," every election and every leader, are viewed uniquely through the layered perspectives of these different generations. The old don't understand the young. The young don't understand the old. And the middle generations play referee. The risks of national disunity are heightened, and without a re-emphasis upon history, each generation will continue to live largely in ignorance, confusion or disbelief about the perspectives of the other generations.

The obvious, but under-discussed, reality is that each generation is born of ignorance all its own. Absent a study of history, each generation remains mired in its own generational ignorance. Each generation joins our national community with what is here referred to as its own "multi-generational ignorance." And each generation's ignorance is stacked one upon the other. The issue is simple to understand but hard to remedy.

Only the patient studying of history can limit the impact of this third new dominant factor in Modern America. For this reason as well, the study of history is more essential than ever in order to shorten the distance—*the literal foreignness*—separating the four generations of Americans now sharing the terra firma of our country.

The study of history may be one of the few tools by which to minimize the impact of our multi-generational ignorance. Understanding our history may help to avoid requiring each generation to blindly carve its own narrative. Our shared history, one of the few glues holding us together, may help re-establish the bonds between our American generations and our now disparate communities.

However, as will be seen in the next chapter, the challenges of history and the complexities of our national community lie not just in appreciating the uses of history. History itself has to overcome its own issues—such as those of accuracy and relevance.

CHAPTER 2

The Issues of Accuracy, Reception, Teaching, Undue Deference, and Relevance

This chapter addresses issues relating to the degree to which history, as a practical matter, may assist us in understanding (and better enjoying and appreciating) our own country.

There are at least four distinguishable, but interrelated, sets of issues which must be considered. Those issues are as follows:

Firstly, the issues of reporting, accuracy, and perception—how well and how accurately can history be reported and to what extent do the predispositions of the readers block their acceptance of the truth and the message of history?

Secondly, the issue of teaching—to what extent has America's seeming elevation of experiential knowledge over more traditional, formal learning (and the concurrent degrading of broad liberal arts curricula) diminished the practical availability of the learning of history?

Thirdly, the issue of deference—to what extent in our hyper-complicated, -accelerated, and -specialized world have our personal desires for the learning of history been willingly subordinated and deferred to others? and

Fourthly, the issue of relevance—to what extent has history in Modern America come to be deemed irrelevant in America's high-speed, rapidly-changing Age of Now?

Issues of Reporting, Accuracy, and Reception
The Reporting and Receipt of History
"Sometimes it takes years ... to get the story right."

The reporting of history is, at best, challenging, and the accuracy of history itself sometimes diminishes over time. These realities are regrettable, but unavoidable for many reasons.

Witness accounts vary. The narratives get twisted by interpretation and perspective. The stories become molded by the writers and burdened by the words and sometimes the agendas of commentators. Facts become blurred. Details are lost. Exaggerations are made. Memories fade and details become forever lost. In other instances, new materials are found. New recordings are discovered. And for all of these reasons, sometimes it takes years for historians to get the story right. Sometimes the whole truth never emerges.

Sometimes, like barnacles on a ship, urban legends form, grow, and slowly cover over the truth. Also, and possibly worst of all, as the cold words of history books—each written in the style and words of the writer—are delivered from one generation to the next, they rarely catch the full emotion, tone, passion, and color of the moment. As the last witnesses pass away, the passion and vividness of their memories goes with them.

Even when every effort is made to remain objective and open-minded to new facts, events, interpretations, and theories, other factors come into play that further complicate our capacity to study and learn from history as well.

For example, we each contribute barriers of our own. Our willingness to accept any narration of history is, to a degree, self-constrained. Each of us is influenced by the latitude and longitude of our birth; by our age and generational association; by our race, ethnicity, gender, and religion; by our raw intelligence and level of education; by the nature of our profession and the extent of our wealth or our poverty; by the breadth of our life experiences; by our immediate circumstances such as our health or the level of our own familial, social and financial security; by the nature of our associations and our choices in study and reading; and by the extent of our personal interests and curiosities. Collectively, these factors are referred to as issues of perception and reception.

In addition, just like history's witnesses, our own memories fade. Our grasp of facts and our recollection of events become muddled and lost over time. Previously disassociated facts are blended and bent in order to fit into our desired narrative or sense of the world. Former truths do not necessarily become lies—they just become misplaced; forgotten or contorted amidst the millions of intervening pieces of our personal and societal lives. Thus, even those who have lived through or witnessed an historical event, do not necessarily share a common vision or understanding of that event.

Possibly the most important factor affecting our very willingness to study history is simply a matter of time and timing. We are busy. Even our own lives are rarely organized. We spend our days amidst the pressures and demands of work and families. We bear the brunt of illnesses and poverty and depression and elation. On any given day, we have a headache, our coworker phoned in sick, the markets are down, and we're out of milk. By the end of the day, we are out of energy, and the study of history is way down on any of our lists.

And even if we're not out of energy, we may be out of time. At any given moment, some people are searching for the perfect gumbo, some are obsessed with their painting, some are working on a new screenplay, others are still celebrating the Chicago Cubs' first championship in 108 years, others are counting their winter money or waiting for deer season... and on it goes ....

For all of these reasons, it is only natural that the "study" of history is conveniently deferred. The only immediate civic "duties" are to comply with the laws, answer jury duty notices, and every once in a while vote — and even this last one is optional. There are no quizzes after dinner, and in the lazy parlance of civic debate, we're all entitled to our own opinion.

History is sometimes poorly received for still other reasons. It may be poorly received merely because of the disorganization of its delivery. As noted above, exactly because it usually takes years for history to get the story "right," most of current and recent history is, at best, clumsily delivered.

Consider, for example, the very manner in which that delivery of history is made. It usually first arrives as a disorganized collage of incomplete information. The initial drafts of history are delivered as "news"

—snippets of quick writings and assessments. Except in those rare instances of shared national unity born of tragedy or glory—Kennedy's and Martin Luther King's assassinations, the moon landing, 9/11, Hurricane Katrina, and for many Americans, Superbowls and Presidential elections, information is delivered without prioritization. It is left for each of us to sort out, but it is both hard and tedious for each of us to separate the important from the interesting; the consequential from the merely curious.

Thus, through no fault of anyone, history is itself hard to find. In the jargon of Modern America, history (and news) almost always requires deciphering and separating of the "signal" from the "noise."[7] And even that task has gotten more challenging in recent years.

Who to Trust and Who to Believe
A Defense of Truth and A Cautious Defense of "The Media"

In the early years of Modern America, there was some unity at least in the context of the reporting of the news. Partly this was simply because there were relatively few news sources. Americans read their local papers. A great majority of Americans selected their television news from one of just three choices—ABC, NBC, or CBS. Although somewhat unimaginable in today's environment, in the early years of Modern America, most Americans were comfortable with the commonness of their news. Most Americans willingly allowed (Uncle Walt) Cronkite to tell us "… and that's the way it is….." Americans certainly drew different conclusions depending upon their predispositions or their various interpretations of the news, but, for better or worse, the news (and our history) were drawn at least initially from the same sets of reported facts.

In recent decades, however, this has changed. Information is now both delivered and received differently. Roughly paralleling the rise of cynicism in American life, information is now received with an expectation of spin and bias, if not hard distortion. At least two generations of Americans have now been raised with the specter of stranger-danger, and in a variant thereof, Americans no longer know who to trust; who to believe.

But with both reluctance and a degree of assured correctness, this author accepts that Americans live in that highly cynical, brevity-obsessed, bottom-line society. For exactly these reasons, these books seek to locate a certain objectivity by identifying the exact and precise Memorable Words of Modern America from numerous perspectives and in many contexts.

There is an admitted fear that the goal may be nobler than the result. However, this approach is the only way to grasp a more accurate understanding of America. We cannot see America from our front porches, by talking with friends, or watching through the portals of our televisions and laptops. However, because of the wide attacks upon the truth of the "news" and widespread skepticism of the "media," these subjects require special note and attention.

No matter how narrowly or widely one wishes to define the media —newspapers, periodicals, opinion journals, wire services, television news, talk radio, or Internet bloggers—the media should be relied upon with appropriate, but not undue, caution. Its reporting certainly needs to be evaluated, and over especially the last several decades, some aspects of reporting have become unquestionably diminished and some parts of the media have been unquestionably compromised.

In part, this diminishment and compromise are the result of the media's competitive desire for attention and audience and of the raw demands of commercialism. Nevertheless, unalterably—and excepting only those few individuals who actually see and live the events or who are at the center of the story—it is still the media that speaks first and regularly to the American people. Enhanced by its omnipresence and its power of digital repetition (and in the case of political elections it seems, repetition *ad nauseum*), the media retains a critical and commanding role in informing the public, in defining the issues, and in framing the perceptions, beliefs, and opinions of the American people.

And in a more honorable sense, the media presents the initial drafts of history. Rarely are reporters, columnists, broadcasters, or bloggers able to present the thoughtful styles or the researched thoroughness of historians. Rarely do they even purport to present all of the multiple perspectives of each story. But at least in the context of the more responsible members of the media, these first drafts of history *are* written with some informed knowledge. The better articles, columns, and broadcasts do try to honor the truth as it is then understood, even though "the drafts" are released after only a certain degree of proofing, fact checking, and dutiful confirmations; even though they are always, almost by definition, contemporary in nature and influenced by the commercialism of the media.

Thus, the initial drafts of history are always the result of a relentless back and forth. The news is oftentimes written or broadcast with relentless speed and under the pressures of mandated tight deadlines. Even the better investigative reporting is rarely presented with the clarity or precision that comes from the discovery, assemblage, or analysis of all of the relevant facts or all of the distanced and informed perspectives. Admittedly, the media's reporting rarely resembles—either in substance or in style—anything approaching the detailed thoroughness of academic writings. But it should not be dismissed.

The media oftentimes does have knowledge about its subjects. The media does write about the Modern America in which we live. But the media is under continuous assault—justified or otherwise. It is far beyond the purposes of these books or the intent of this author to defend the state of the American media, and of journalism in particular. But some of the overly broad-brush criticisms of the media have gone too far. Some criticisms and dismissals are both naïve and wrong.

Very bluntly, by any measure, some publications *are* better than others. Some *are* even good. Regardless of one's political beliefs or social persuasions, some publications, writers and broadcasters are deserving of our respect—begrudging or otherwise. When the base standards of accuracy, thoroughness, and objectivity are combined with clarity of reasoning and quality of articulation, it also becomes obvious that certain writers, columnists, and broadcasters are better than others; some are good; and few are even excellent.

Speaking that which should almost be obvious, *The Wall Street Journal* is not the *National Inquirer. The New York Times* is not the *American Spectator.* The *National Review* is not *The Nation.* Dennis Miller is not Don Imus. NPR is not Howard Stern. The Associated Press is not the Drudge Report. NBC is not the Christian Broadcasting Network. Even the late great Peter Jennings was never Ann Coulter. George Will is not

Glenn Beck. *Field & Stream* is not *Hustler*. With even the utmost respect for editorials in local papers, they are still not the same as the thoughtful and more detailed reporting of *The Economist*. The self-serving babble of many bloggers writing from the comfort of their home is not the same as the information that can be gleaned from on-the-scene reporters or from war correspondents overseas.

The influences of perspective, predisposition, and even bias in the media are oftentimes difficult to isolate and evaluate. But certainly newspapers and magazines do exhibit differing perspectives and biases. Sometimes they do so unabashedly. Sometimes their perspectives and biases bleed far beyond the editorial pages. Sometimes the influences determine which writers are hired, whose writings are printed, and what stories are reported. Thus, these matters govern the selection of subjects and dictate the tone of reporting, but once again, the application of broad-brush thinking in the evaluation of the media is just too simplistic.

And on and on. It could be suggested that this is all obvious—except for the fact that many Americans think otherwise as they shuffle around in the hyper-state of American life, and especially its political life. These books present the Memorable Words of Modern America, and many of these words are taken from the reporting of the media. Martin Luther King *did* "have a dream," Neil Armstrong *did* take a "giant leap for mankind," and Yogi Berra *did* announce, as only he could, that "it ain't over till it's over." These quotations are not "fake news" or "alternative facts." These statements were made. They are and will remain the true words of actual people. They cannot be dismissed as unworthy statements made by the "mainstream, drive-by media," the "talking heads," or the "tabloid press."

As noted above, it is beyond the scope of this book to delve into America's current disdain for the media, the Fourth Estate of our nation. But the fact that many Americans do not discern the good from the bad, the objective from the biased, and the experienced from the novice is both wrong and dangerous. Many of the Memorable Words contained in this book were first reported on the scene and at the very moment when those words were first spoken. This reliance upon the media is not misplaced, and it is hoped that in the less feverish moments of America's future,

Americans will, once again, step back from the overly casual dismissal of all news sources; to do otherwise is to shadowbox blindfolded. In sum, while a certain level of scrutiny and consideration is always appropriate, too many American's dismiss the media far too readily and far too often.

One last note of caution should be offered. Even when stories are exaggerated or over-reported, the networks, the cable stations, the "mass media," the "drive-by" media, and the commentators should not be too readily blamed in isolation. There are other reasons for both our country's and our own cynicism and paranoia. Americans, at varying times, have both reveled and suffered in our own shared history. The media, like all of us, suffered from the years of misinformation about the Vietnam War and soon thereafter from the lies and insults of Watergate. Technology changed, and with that change America and "the media" are still learning how to best live in our new age. In the early 1980s, cable television arrived with its scores of stations. The broadcast media splintered into hundreds of pieces. The 24-hour news cycle was born. More and more news became 'breaking news" with hyped passion and false alarm—oftentimes delivered with weak facts written under the pressures of deadline journalism. At about this same time, in the early 1980s, other factors came into play with respect to the role and identity of the media as well. First, to varying degrees, news and entertainment were merged too much in the attempt to feed America's newfound obsession with all things celebrity. Second, beginning in the 1990s and accelerating with the rise of social media in the 2000s, the Internet allowed all voices to have access to the microphone—or, more precisely, all fingers to have access to keyboards and social media. Last, the burgeoning independent press allowed almost anyone and everything to get into publication and print. The cacophony and the volume grew. Focus became nearly impossible because new and many voices kept coming.

Another result of these developments was that it became easier and easier for each of us to find our own news; our own versions of history which fit comfortably in reinforcing our personal beliefs and predispositions. But for this, we too must accept part of the responsibility. Americans themselves far too readily seek out and then accept historical narratives that fit their beliefs or preconceptions. And with the splintering of the news media and the growth of the Internet, such reinforcing news and history can readily be found. It is itself not "news" that our predispositions can now be readily reinforced; or, in the case of some, our conspiracy theories proven and our paranoias fed. Worn down, we almost willingly accept that our news is not "fair and balanced," and we listen to only "our" part of the story.

By the turn of the millennium, the delivery of news became constant. It was never over. And we were never done. We could never catch up. We found ourselves living in an even more complex world—cluttered with truths, falsities, facts, data, statements, numbers, words, and pictures—and, as referred to above, emerging protestations of "fake news" and "alternative facts." It is, at best, curious that many Americans disparaged the relativity of ethics as a damaging component of the 1960s. Now, however, this relativity has morphed into the far more troublesome negotiability of facts. American cynicism has become too much imbued as a part of American thought. But the role of facts and the role of the media remain critical.

This observation is far distant from the timeworn criticism of history that it is merely "written by the victors." This observation is based upon the new reality that there are now enough facts for everyone to have their own. There is enough history for everyone to have their own. In exhaustion, we accept and tolerate the conspicuous and costly absence of neutral arbiters.

By reading the *Memorable Words of Modern America*—who said exactly what and when they exactly said or wrote it, possibly we can slowly start regaining our trust of information; our trust in the truth of history itself.

Lastly, there is one more dimension of this subject that should be addressed. It is not directly a function of the media, but instead it involves the concept of literary license in general and movies in particular. History has also been compromised through the expanded use of literary license and the explosion of certain genres of movies. Regrettably, the absence of wrongful intent in this instance does not alter the consequences.

The standard disclaimers offered in certain types of movies are not enough. The disclaimers of a movie being a "docudrama" or merely "based upon actual events" are not enough to contain the damage. The disclaimers, even though dutifully made, do not change the reality that for many Americans, their knowledge of major historical events too often rests with the story as presented in the movie. For many Americans, especially younger Americans, their knowledge of the 1962 missile crisis has been forever formulated by Stanley Greenberg and Anthony Page's 1974 movie *The Missiles of October.* For many Americans, their understanding of the Apollo 13 mission has been forever frozen into their memories by Ron Howard and Brian Grazer's unforgettable 1995 movie of the same name. More recently, Americans were introduced to an abbreviated—and some say, factually compromised—version of the events surrounding the civil rights movement as portrayed in Ava DuVernay's 2014 "historical drama" movie, *Selma.* Sometimes the audience rejects the pushed thesis of a director as was the case with Oliver Stone's 1991 *JFK,* but more commonly the movie, not history, wins.

And so the stubborn problem remains—in most cases, we weren't there. Without our own research, we'll never know the truth. Just like we can't take a pill to learn math, we shouldn't watch movies to learn history. But we do. Time is tight. Brevity wins. The gist of the story is enough.

Too often and too readily, like a guilty pleasure, we accept the movie's compaction of history. Most Americans cannot wait for Ken Burns to give us the color, narrative, and detail that is necessary to understand any complicated event. Burns did it in, for example, his series on baseball and the Civil War—but it took him nine episodes each.

These issues of literary license and incompleteness are slightly different than issues of accuracy, but they too cloud the accurate presentation of history. In this sense, literary license and incompleteness must themselves be seen as mere variant forms of inaccuracy.

And for all of these reasons, it can appear that little is to be believed, that nothing is as it appears, and that there is always more to the story. But these books believe otherwise.

These books suggest that even amidst the cacophony of American life, history still remains. Truth still exists. It is hoped that with the presentation of America's Memorable Words—all carefully quoted and cited with precision as to the time, place and context of such words, some objectivity of honest history can prevail. Possibly this manner of studying history can allay some of the problems of reporting, accuracy, and reception. Possibly the presentation of the exact Memorable Words of our American life, as more expansively explained in the next chapter, will help diminish our skepticism and will help each of us to know exactly who said what, when.

But wholly apart from issues of reporting, accuracy, and reception, there are also issues of teaching and learning and the nature of our current norms and expectations of education. These are addressed in the following section.

Issues of Teaching, Learning and Education

"History is too often viewed as an academic subject."

. . .

"At best, a curiosity; at worst, a burden."

There are at least two realities of teaching, learning, and education in Modern America that must be addressed. The first reality relates to the perceived value in Modern America of formal education vis-à-vis experiential education. The second reality relates to the demise of what has historically been referred to as a broad-based, "liberal" or "liberal arts" education.

These subjects are here addressed, albeit briefly, because there is a close correlation between the quality of our educational system and our society's knowledge of history. The quality of our educational system, of course, impacts our citizens' capacities to intelligently assimilate new information and to understand the meaning of statements, events, trends, and discoveries. However, over the course of Modern America, there has also been a potentially dangerous social and economic elevation of the value of experience over knowledge.

Simply stated, this elevation of experiential knowledge derives from the dual beliefs that (i) time is tight and (ii) wisdom comes best from living rather than from learning. In our highly-accelerated, -specialized, and -economically-driven world, the time-consuming tedium of formalized education is more and more frequently questioned.

As a result, many Americans now value experience over knowledge. The legends of famous and successful college drop-outs are enticing. They always have been. But now daydreaming and risk-taking are more and more openly encouraged. The subtext is that classes are for losers, and now too many young Americans believe that they are one new app, one new patent, one new idea away from the big life.

It is *not* this author's intent to diminish the value of experience, work, and hands-on life lessons, but without an organized, formalized, and —to a degree—broad education, citizens have dangerous gaps in their knowledge. Over time, these gaps are accentuated. These gaps can be dangerous because a narrowed, employment-directed education does not provide the minimum knowledge necessary to respond to the plethora of life occurrences and to the challenges that America, as a society, needs to confront.

The shift in the perceived importance of a formal education parallels a second reality that many Americans now hold a narrow view of the very purpose of education. This second reality rests upon the belief that the dominant, if not almost sole, reason for education is to improve one's career options and to increase the likelihood of one's financial security and success.

Under this reasoning, there may remain a begrudging respect for a broad education but only to some degree and only in subservience to education as a basis for career options and employability. Under this reasoning, the entire concept of the "Renaissance Man" seems to be properly identified and properly named—a relic from another age with little direct utility in our age of nano-focus and specialization.

To be sure, most Americans believe that broadly educated persons are good to know. They can be great friends. They can enliven dinner parties. But their commercial value is held in doubt. Such well-rounded and broadly educated persons are deemed, almost by definition, to be unfocused; to possess unduly dispersed minds lacking the laser-beam focus of specialization needed in today's Darwinian society.

This reasoning is of particular importance in the context of teaching and learning history because history is too often viewed solely as a component of the loaded phrase "liberal education." History is too often viewed as an academic subject. Its thick tomes are seen as, at best, a curiosity; at worst, a burden. And so the thick tomes adorn the shelves of libraries and remain there—largely unread and unbothered.

In the highly politicized world of education—from "no-child-left-behind" to STEM and "common core"—the entire concept of "liberal arts" has been shuffled to the sidelines—the province of beardy professors and, well, "liberals" still stuck in another age. The loss of a broadly based education is seen as a mere cost to be paid in exchange for job skills and employment opportunities.

The expansive subject of the alternative purposes of education is far beyond the scope of this writing, but the supplanting of a formal education has societal consequences. The rise of definitionally more limited experiential knowledge and the demise of broad-based education affects America's collective capacity to draw upon history; to understand events; and to independently and wisely choose from among alternative courses of action.

One immediate result of the narrowing of our education and the highly compartmentalized nature of our society in which specialization is so honored and rewarded, is that Americans have become dangerously willing to subordinate their own instincts, knowledge, and beliefs to others. There has been a quiet loss of independent thought. As discussed in the next section, citizens have started to grant undue deference to spokesmen, party leaders, and in some cases well-connected and highly articulate experts. And we all know that, to a degree, history is nothing more than the collected writings of a long sequence of experts—who have been dead wrong.

Issues of Subordination and Deference— The Subordination of Our Knowledge, and the Undue Deference to Experts and Political Leaders

"A growing and dangerous willingness for Americans to unduly defer to the supposed wisdom of others."

One of the consequences of the elusiveness of truth, the complexity of issues, the narrowing of education, and the 21st century's demand for brevity is a growing and dangerous willingness for Americans to unduly defer to the supposed wisdom of others—to the arcane talk of experts; to the eloquence, intimidation, or passions of our political leaders; or to the platforms and positions of one's chosen political party.

The result of this undue deference is that too many Americans, in confusion, exhaustion, or both, have outsourced the task of finding the truth to experts or political leaders or to like-minded commentators, paid spokespersons, or trusted allies. Oftentimes, these parties are buttressed by think tanks, by paid (and monetarily compromised) researchers and other experts. Names are dropped. Data is assembled. Reports are written. Charts are prepared. Graphs are made. And in this variant search for the truth and use of history, one set of experts testifies against the others. In the end, the truth often remains buried and nestled somewhere in the middle.

Another consequence of such undue deference to experts and political leaders is the resultant minimization of each citizen's responsibility to evaluate available information on their own. In Modern America, independent judgment is rarely demanded and even more rarely appreciated.

Certainly it is reasonable and prudent to defer to experts in certain circumstances. Doctors sometimes do know best. Lawyers know the law. Accountants know the taxes. Arborists know trees. The list is endless. What is new, however, is the increasing willingness to grant blind and blanket deference to others about things which are inherently more "social"—what is best politically, what is best culturally; what is best in the context of education and child-rearing. Here, the extent of deference is new.

Less than 100 years ago, the radio was still a novelty. Now radio talk shows go on for hours. Less than 50 years ago, journalism—at least in this country—was distinguishable from propaganda. Less than 25 years ago, most people happily lived in appropriate silence without accessing or responding to their social media at their every moment. It is neither possible nor suggested that we go back. However, it is possible and suggested that we reassert ourselves in the search for truth. We need to think more independently. We need to seek a collage of opinions. We need to build upon the knowledge that we have obtained from our own education and experiences. We need to reassert ourselves with independence, self-confidence, and honesty of thought.

These comments are intended to be passionately apolitical, but consider the following examples. Few of us have the charm of Kennedy, the drive of Johnson, the eloquence of King, the optimism of Reagan, the campaign skills of Bill Clinton, the non-reflective confidence of George W. Bush, or the innovative brazenness of Trump. However, each of us possesses and must assert our own individual wisdom.

It is almost a tautology that a political candidate cannot accept millions of dollars in donations or speaking fees without being subjected to other's expectations of access or influence. Political candidates cannot be allowed to pander without admission of these realities, and when they do, their statements need to be so characterized. We know that we cannot allow ignorance to be buried in bluster and that verbal intimidation should, at a minimum, be viewed askance.

The corrections that are necessary to redirect our country and remold our national community may best come from "us" on the outside rather than from "them" on the inside. Very bluntly, we should not so routinely and blindly defer to experts or other leaders. Bertrand Russell's definition of democracy as a society in which 51 percent of the people are right, 51 percent of the time, is a horrendously low bar. But it is preferable to the inside decision-making that has come to characterize so much of American life.

Possibly remembering or learning the Memorable Words of our country's recent past will help us reassert the powerful collective intellect of the American people. But, there is one more barrier that we must overcome in our use of history. That last barrier is that we must also believe that history itself is useful and relevant. As will be discussed in the next and last section of this chapter, for a multitude of reasons some Americans believe that history, even if accurately reported and even if understood, is burdened by irrelevance—especially so in the context of our new, high-speed, rapidly changing Age of Now.

The Perceived Irrelevance of History in Modern America's Age of Now

"History seems to have lost its place in the Age of Now."

History has always been dismissed by some as a subject of limited relevance—a subject of academic study, ancestral interest, or mere curiosity. However, such dismissals are vastly overstated. They are far too lacking in precision.

First and admittedly, any one particular aspect of history may or may not be relevant to our contemporary world depending upon the subject of history about which one is talking—for there are many dimensions and categories of history. For example, the broad divisions of history, sometimes referred to as "subfields" of history, may be by period (e.g. ancient history, medieval history, the Middle Ages, the Renaissance and Reformation); by century (e.g. the years of exploration and discovery during the 15th, 16th, and 17th centuries, the years of colonization during the 18th and 19th centuries); by region or culture (e.g. Egyptian, Roman, Inca, Aztec, Gaelic, European, and Middle or Far Eastern); or by subject matter (e.g. political history, diplomatic history, social history, economic history, and intellectual history[8]).

Second, when discussing contemporary matters, there is a direct and important correlation based upon the intervening number of years (decades, or centuries) between the subject's historical reference and Modern America. The social and cultural history of ancient Mesopotamia and the traffic patterns along the Hindu Kush have limited relevance to Modern America. Even within the context of our shorter American history, there are boundaries of relevance. Despite how well and appropriately our children are taught about our nation's founding and how frequently the words of our Founding Fathers are scrutinized, there are issues of relevance when comparing matters pertinent to 17th and 18th century agrarian-based America to those of 21st century America's advanced industrial and technological age.

But even within these limitations, many aspects of history remain relevant. Many aspects of history, and especially our more recent American history, remain relevant to guiding our path and evaluating our alternative futures. This seemingly obvious statement is, however, now at risk for the reasons set forth below.

At any given moment, and including any given moment in Modern America, we live in a thousand different ages—the Age of Globalism; the Age of Technology; the Age of the Internet; the Age of Brevity and Speed; the Age of Anger; the Age of Bush or Obama or now Trump; the Age of Terrorism; the Age of ISIS; and on and on. Certainly one of the proper names to describe Modern America, as that phrase is defined in detail in Chapter 4 below, would be the Age of Now.

And one of the dominant characteristics of our Age of Now is that there are few rules. Another such characteristic is that if it's not "Now," then it is by definition "(oh, so) yesterday." Some Americans go further. If it's not digitized, it's not there. If it can't be googled, then it can't be important. And on it goes.

Thus, even if we Americans can get past the issues of accuracy, teaching, and deference as discussed in the sections above, history may still be perceived as having little utility. For in the Age of Now, the Age of Yesterday is dangerously ignored. In Modern America's high-speed, technology-driven society, history is of interest to only those few time-bypassed citizens who, by the circumstances of their age or life, are somehow immune from the pressing realities of families, jobs, careers, and financial success.

But most Americans are not immune from those pressing realities. As a result, most Americans have felt themselves pushed to accept the need for brevity and the importance of speed. In such a context, history and even reflection are seen as almost impediments to action, as almost undue burdens upon the fast decision-making deemed necessary in Modern America. Nuance, thought, understanding, context, and patience are lost arts from another era.

To these Modern Americans, and especially to these younger Americans, the words and teachings of history have little place in their git-'er-done, caffeinated lives where they read as they walk; where multi-tasking is rewarded; and where social interaction is viewed as an almost awkward, time-filler pastime. In this Age of Now, there is an almost palpable disdain for the tedious tasks of reflection and nuance. Planning, precision, and analysis are for the number crunchers and underlings. The unspoken subtext is that the world can't wait for the homework to be done. And besides, by the time you finish your homework, the world will have changed. Again. And again. And again.

In the Age of Now, it is only the immediate results that matter. Corners can be cut. Truth can be rounded. Relationships can be twisted. Facts and data, numbers and phrases, formulas and algorithms are not components of some higher knowledge or thought. They are merely cold tools to action and success. They are not a piece of some larger picture. They are far different in nature and far distant from the arcane, dusty subjects such as history.

George Santayana's over-quoted mantra about "those who fail to remember the past are condemned to repeat it" is cute and clever, but it may have little meaning in the Age of Now which is driven by acceleration and pace.

A related belief is that history almost definitionally cannot repeat itself because everything is changed. Everything is new. Everything is different. There is only pre-industrial and post-industrial. There is only pre-tech and post-tech. There is now only an Internet-connected and ever-changing world. Everything that came before is perceived as from another world—arguably interesting, but unavoidably irrelevant. History seems to have lost its place in the Age of Now.

Consider the awkward fit of history within Modern America's ever more Darwinistic economy. To understand our economy and to operate in business, Americans don't feel any need to read Halberstam's *The Best and the Brightest*, Manchester's *The Glory and the Dream*, or Durant's *Lessons of History*—because Gordon Gecko told us all we needed to know 30 years ago in the 1987 movie *Wall Street*—that "greed...is good." To understand Gecko, one certainly does not need to assess the wisdom of the plutocratic candidates. Instead, we have become too willing to let a candidate's wealth speak for his or her skills; for his or her supposed wisdom; for his or her leadership and capabilities.

In a sense, balance sheets are the resumes in the Darwinian Age of Now. By the time any books are written, the actors have changed. The stories have changed. The players have moved on. The deal has closed, and the monies are safe—sometimes here, sometimes offshore.

The entire logic of the Age of Now is admittedly exciting; even alluring. It fits well in the short-run, get-it-while-you-can, world of hustle. But it is still wrong. It is still dangerous. Not always—but usually.

Thus, the study of history and the reflection upon this country's Memorable Words arguably do not fit easily into the Age of Now. As discussed above, the study of history requires commitment, patience, and interpretation, and these words are, in some respects, the very opposite of action.

But it is humbly suggested that some aspects of history have a compelling relevance to Modern America. This is especially true in the context of establishing and binding our national community. This is especially true in the context of understanding our political-economic system—history can show us that which we have already tried; history can reveal to us various alternatives; history can show us where we could go; and, possibly most importantly, history can remind us how quickly things can change.

The careful selection and detailed presentation of the Memorable Words of Modern America are just one way to study history. It is an admittedly abbreviated way, and it is offered, almost with a degree of embarrassment, as an accepting admission that thick reads and tedious study no longer fit the Age of Now reality of Modern America.

Closing

This chapter has addressed broad issues: the purposes of history; the nature and new realities of our national community; the issues of reporting, accuracy, and reception; the issues of subordination and deference; and the perceived irrelevance of history in Modern America's Age of Now.

It is now time to turn to a more specific subject—the purposes of these books and the concept of "Memorable Words." As will be seen in the next chapter, it is suggested that the history of Modern America may be presented through the careful identification of the powerful, triggering words of Modern America and by identifying when, where, and by whom and in what context they were first spoken or written.

Depending upon the prudence of this author's selection of Modern America's Memorable Words, these words may, in some small part, help to memorialize our nation's recent history. For the older generations of living Americans, these Memorable Words may help remind us of where we were, what we heard, and how we once felt so many years ago. For the younger generations of Americans, they may promote a better understanding of whence "we" all came. And they may assist us all in better knowing how to proceed, grow, and thrive as the national community that we are.

CHAPTER 3

The Purposes of These Books and the Concept and Selection of Memorable Words

The Purposes of These Books

"Both the dead serious and the lighthearted
may help us tie together our national community. Once again."
(But sometimes)
"Our anger runs so deep that reason cannot reach our logic."

There are three primary and closely related purposes of these books. The first purpose of these books is to lighten the load of learning the history of Modern America by introducing our history in a new way. This is done through the careful selection and chronological presentation of the Memorable Words of Modern America. This volume presents the Memorable Words of the initial years of Modern America—from 1957 to 1976. The Memorable Words of the remaining years of Modern America are presented in Volume II (1977–1993) and Volume III (1994–2015), respectively.

The types of Memorable Words fall into one of two categories. The first category of Memorable Words consist of titles, names, and lines—those certain words that can uniquely trigger each of us back to a place or point in time. Included within this category are the titles of seminal, award-winning, and bestselling books; the names and sometimes lines from award-winning movies or the most popular, innovative, or consequential television shows; and major commercial advertising campaigns and slogans. The second category of Memorable Words comprises those words of speakers or writers or those chants and slogans of crowds and protestors—both the dead serious and the lighthearted words—that best and most fully encapsulate the events of the respective years. The selection of these written or spoken words is based upon criteria explained in more detail below. The selected Memorable Words of speakers and writers are followed by a brief narrative about the circumstances, context, and implications of those words in order to, depending upon the age of the reader—refresh our memories or introduce such Memorable Words in a manner that is simultaneously engaging and enlightening.

The second purpose of these books is to encourage a better understanding of the many common threads of the history of Modern America. In the process of reading the literal words which comprise a part of that history, it is hoped that we may, together, (i) better remember or understand the words and events that molded our perceptions and, for better or worse, the perceptions of our nation's current political, economic, and social leaders, and (ii) better remember or understand that which Americans have seen, shared, or lived through. It is hoped that through this collection of Memorable Words we can be reminded of the tight proximity that we all have to our national community.

For older readers, these Memorable Words may trigger long-forgotten memories and may encourage a remembering of our shared Modern American history. For younger readers, these Memorable Words may help explain—in the exact words of the time—what was said and what happened. For all readers, it is hoped that these Memorable Words will help us know whence we came. Presented in an accessible and readable manner, this careful selection of both the dead serious and the lighthearted words may help us tie together our national community. Once again.

The third purpose of these books is to provide a needed lift to the spirit of American life. Too many parts of our American life have become embroiled in acrimony. Too many aspects of our lives have become politicized. Too many of our beliefs have become tightly wrapped. As seen from especially the 2016 national elections, our national conversations have become characterized by hostility. For too many Americans, their anger now runs so deep that reason can no longer reach their logic. Our judgmentalism toward one another has replaced our own sense of assuredness. Our scowls have replaced our smiles. We expend our energy listening for code words from our leaders, and too many teams have been formed —each clawing for their day in the sun.

Many of the Memorable Words are, by their context and subject matter, serious and sobering. But "lighthearted" words are included as well so that these books may remind us of the many other pieces of American life that were well received and widely enjoyed. Laughter, too, has a place in our public life. Despite the implications of the headlines, most of our American life is neither good nor bad. Instead, most of our living takes place in the middle, and the pleasant truth is that not everything matters. Through the inclusion of the "lighthearted" alongside the "dead serious," these books are humbly offered as a means by which we might start to reclaim our better sides, to reestablish our better sense of priorities, and even to reassert the confidence that we Americans have earned. The politicization of America can be contained. We, as a people, can try to achieve a better balance. America can remain a place where there is more to be shared than there is to be coveted; more to be enjoyed than to be debated.

But enough. Let's proceed. Let's have some fun.

The Concept of Memorable Words

"The good, the bad, and the ugly; the heavy and the light;
the hurtful and the heartfelt; the inspirational and the ominous;
and the joyous and the somber."

Certain words, the Memorable Words of Modern America, have a special place in our recent American history. These words have the capacity to help us better know our past, appreciate our country, and bind our national community. For various reasons, these words are special, powerful, and meaningful. These words have survived the passage of time. These words have made an impact. These words matter.

These words have the capacity to take us back over the distance of time; to trigger our emotions; to refresh our memories; and, even many years later, to inflame our passions and move us to action. And since America, just like its people, has aged, it is not always easy to remember what happened. By reading our country's Memorable Words, we can, depending upon one's age, together remember or learn what, when, where, and by whom in what context the Memorable Words of Modern America were first said or written; first heard or read.

As noted in the Preface to these books, the concept of Memorable Words includes two distinct categories of such words: first, the memorable titles and lines; and second, the memorable words of American speakers and writers.

The first category of Memorable Words is composed of the titles of books, movies, television shows and the best movie lines of the respective years of Modern America. Included amongst such titles are the 63 here-selected Seminal Books of Modern America; the 166 Pulitzer Prize-winning books in Fiction, General Nonfiction, and History; and the 125 bestselling books of Modern America—presented chronologically based on their respective year of initial publication. Also included within this category are the titles of the award-winning movies and nearly 175 of the most famous and impactful movie lines of Modern America together with the titles, stars of, and viewership information about those television shows that again, each for its own reason, have defined or encapsulated a part of Modern America. Lastly included within this category of titles and lines is a careful selection of the 60 most dominant commercial advertising campaigns and slogans that by a combination of their cleverness and repetition have become a part of our Modern American life.

The true core of this book is in the second category of Memorable Words—the nearly 675 selections of those Memorable Words that have best defined, exemplified, or explained our country or that have captured—even if briefly—our passions, fears, joys, ideas, or ideals over the course of the 58 years of Modern America. Once again, this book is not limited to the heavy, important, and "dead serious" words. Also included are some of the "lighthearted" words that reveal our country. As noted in the Preface to these books, the author's personal reflections are included in those few instances where the author was present at the first speaking of these words or was otherwise involved in the subject circumstance or event.

Following each of these selected Memorable Words, both the "dead serious" and the "lighthearted," is a summary explanation of the words' context, meaning, and impact. In some cases, an explanation of the triggering events, circumstances, or even probable motives underlying the speaker's or writer's words are also included. Lastly, and in order to reflect the electoral and political shifts that have occurred over the course of Modern America, the nearly 160 campaign slogans that have been used by candidates of major political parties during the fourteen Presidential elections of Modern America are included together with the results of those Presidential elections.

As is evident and obvious, for any one author to correctly select the Memorable Words is admittedly far too great a task to perfectly achieve. But I have tried.

In the opinion of this author, the soul of our country is sometimes better revealed by the lesser known words of America's speakers or writers. The following examples of included Memorable Words are presented in order to give a quick sense of the reach and breadth of the Memorable Words included within these books—from the "dead serious" to the "lighthearted."

In the context of our entertainment—from Desi' iconic *"Lucy, I'm home"* (1957) to Walter Cronkite's nightly closing of *"And that's the way it is …"* (1962); from Ed McMahon's *"Heeeeere's, Johnny!"* (1962) to Flip Wilson's *"The Devil made me do it!"* (1970); from the single words of *"Motown"* (1959) and *"Woodstock"* (1969) to the *"6,000 pounds of turkey"* for The Band's Last Waltz (1976); from Johnny Carson's quiet departing of *"I bid you a very heartfelt goodnight"* (1992) to Donald Trump's weekly desk-pounding of *"You're fired"* (2004);

In the context of sports—from Lombardi's *"football's not a contact sport"* (1970) to Ron Blomberg's *"the day I screwed up baseball"* (1973); from

Ali's "*floating like a butterfly and stinging like a bee*" (1974) to Joe Frazier's plea in the 14th round that "*I want him, boss*" (1975); from Al Michael's screaming "*do you believe in Miracles*" countdown at the Lake Placid Olympics (1980) to McEnroe's whiny taunts of "*you can't be serious!*" (1980);

In the context of fun and good spirits—from Berra's "*the future ain't what it used to be*" (1972) and Trevino's "*the older I get, the better I used to be*" (1990) to Mickey Mantle's "*if I knew I was going to live this long, I'd have taken better care of myself*" (1995); from Chris Rock's clever observation that "*the three most powerful men in America are named Bush, Dick, and Colin*" (2005) to the CIA's teasing disclaimer that "*we can neither confirm nor deny that this is our first tweet*" (2014);

In the context of politics, elections, governance, and the media and the news—from JFK's "*ask not*" (1961) to Goldwater "*extremism in the defense of liberty*" (1964); from "Johnson's "*I shall not seek, and I will not accept the nomination of my party*" (1968) to Nixon's "*enemies list*" (1971) and Deep Throat's admonition to "*follow the money*" (1972); from Sam Ervin's just being "*an old country lawyer*" (1973) to the Watergate mantra of "*what did he know and when did he know it*" (1973); from the "*Saturday night massacre*" (1973) to the empty Nixonian assurance that "*I am not a crook*" (1973"); from Ford's assurance that "*our long national nightmare is over*" (1974) to his humble admission that he was "*a Ford, not a Lincoln*" (1973); from Reagan's disarming "*there you go again*" (1980) to Mondale's "*where's the beef?*" (1984); from Ann Richards' "*Poor George, he just can't help himself*" (1988) to Rush Limbaugh's "*ditto-heads*" and self-description as the "*Maha Rushi*" (1988); from the Republicans' "*Contract with America*" (1994) to Bush's "*compassionate conservative;*" from Obama's "*change you can believe in*" (2008) to Palin's chiding "*how's that hopey-changey stuff working out for you?*" (2010); from Rick Perry's "*Oops*" (2011) to Obama's "*You didn't build that*" (2012); from Romney's "*Corporations are people, my friend*" (2012) to Chris Christie's reminder that "*politics ain't beanbag*" (2014); from Hillary Clinton's "'*don't do stupid stuff*' *is not an organizing principle*" (2014) to Carly Fiorina's "*I think women … very clearly heard what Mr. Trump said*" (2015);

In the context of economics, taxation, and employment—from the first round of "*too big to fail*" (1971) to Nixon's "*work ethics*" and "*welfare ethics*" (1972); from "*voodoo economics*" to "*Reaganomics*"(1981); from Reagan's "*are you better off than you were four years ago*" (1980) to Leona Helmsley's insulting "*only little people pay taxes*" (1982); from Alan Greenspan's skills of "*mumbling with great incoherence*" (1987) to George H.W. Bush's "*Read my lips. No new taxes*" (1988) and the crowds chant of "*we are the 99%*" (2011);

In the context of our social culture, protests, and marches—from Helen Gurley Brown's teasing reminder that "*good girls go to heaven….*" (1962) to Betty Friedan's "*problem with no name*" (1963) from the 1960s' chants of "*tune in, turn on, drop out*" to "*if it feels good, do it;*" from "*hell no, I won't go*" and "*Hey, Hey, LBJ …*" to "*the world is watching*" (1968); from Carter's "*crisis of confidence*" (1977) to Sid Vicious' "*live fast (and) die young*" (1978); from Nancy Reagan's "*just say no*" (1982) to Vidal's sarcastic "*where are the readers?*" (2008); from Jason Collins' "*I'm a 35-year-old NBA center. I'm black, And I'm gay*" (2013) to Bruce Jenner's "*Call me Caitlyn*" (2015); from the Texas bar/shooting range owner's "*bullets first, then beer*" (2014) to Tim Murphey's "*we have replaced the hospital bed with the jail cell* "(2014);

In the context of race and civil rights—from Rev. King's "*I have a dream* " (1963) and the "*arc of the moral universe is long*" (1965) to George Wallace's chilling "*segregation now, segregation tomorrow, segregation forever*" (1963); from the chants of "*power to the people*" to Rodney King's "*can't we all just get along*" (1991); from "*Hands up! Don't Shoot!*" (2014) to Tavis Smiley's observation that "*we are still two America's. Still separate, still unequal*" (2014);

In the context of the passing of generations, our national tragedies, social justice, and famous last words—from MacArthur's "Farewell Address" at West Point (1962) to Lyndon Johnson's "*I ask for your help … and God's*" (1963); from Malcolm X's "*Let's cool it, brothers*" (1965) to Bobby Kennedy's "*Is everybody o.k.?*" (1968); from the reminder words of "*Wounded Knee*" (1973) to Haig's empty assurance that "*I am in charge*" (1980); from Clinton's "*Don't ask, Don't tell*" (1994) to Daniel Pearl's "My father is Jewish. My mother is Jewish. I am Jewish" (2003);

In the context of international relations, wars and terrorism—from JFK's "*Ich bin ein Berliner*" (1963) to Johnson's "*we seek no wider* *war*" (1964); from the chant of "*Let's win or get out*" (1970) to Nixon's "*all-out limited war*" and Kissinger's "*peace is at hand*" (1972); from Reagan's denunciation of the "*Evil Empire*" (1983) to Irangate's "*arms for hostages*" (1987); from Reagan's "*tear down that wall*" (1987) to Tsongas' "*The Cold War is over (and) Japan has won*" (1992); from the horror of the very number and date "*9/11*" to Colin Powell's "*if you break it you own it;*" from the claims of "*weapons of mass destruction*" to George Tenet's "*don't worry, it's a slam dunk;*" from Elie Weisel's reminder that "*indifference is not a beginning...*" (1999) to the displays of "*shock and awe*" (2003); from the premature "*Mission Accomplished*" (2003) to Obama's announcement that "*justice has been done*" (2011);

In the context of law, justice and individual rights, cases, and crimes—from the "*right to counsel*" (1963) to the "*right to remain silent*" (1966); from "*one man, one vote*" (1964) to "*saving the life of the mother*" (1973); from the chilling word of "*Guilty*" to the relief of "*Acquitted;*" from Charles Manson's twisted "*helter skelter*" (1969) to the quieter terror of D.B. Cooper's note—"*Miss, ... I have a bomb*" (1971); from Jim Jones' "*just drink the Kool-Aid*" (1978) to Johnny Cochran's "*if the glove doesn't fit, you must acquit*" (1995) and Florida Sheriff Judd's wise admonition to parents "*to quit being [your children's] best friends and be their best parent*" (2013);

In the context of human failings and public disgraces—from Elizabeth Ray's "*I can't type*" (1976) to Carter's "*I've committed adultery in my heart*" (1976); from Gary Hart's self-destructive " *follow me around. I don't care*" (1988) to Jimmy Swaggert's tearful "*I have sinned against You, my Lord*" (1989) to Bill Clinton's silly "*I didn't inhale*" (1992) and "*I did not have sexual relations with that woman*" (1998); and

In the context of space, science, energy, technology, and the environment—from Neil Armstrong's "*one small step for man*" (1969) to Jack Swigert's chilling words that "*Houston, we've had a problem*" (1970); from the chant of "*drill, baby, drill*" (2008) to Bruce Schmeier's observation that "*surveillance is the business model of the Internet*" (2013) and Senator Inhofe's condescending advice that "*the Pope ought to stay with his job, and we'll stay with ours*" (2015).

As is evident, the original scripting, release, and use of such Memorable Words and the reasons for their historic import vary greatly. Some words were carefully written, thoroughly edited, and carefully presented. Others were emotive and spontaneous. But regardless of the planned or spontaneous nature of their origin, these words have become (or it will be argued below, deserve to become) a part of the recognized history of Modern America. Collectively, these words reveal much about our country—where we have been, where we were, and where we (thought we) were going.

However, the concept of Memorable Words is very different from a mere assemblage of "great quotes." Great quotes are normally chosen due to their wit, wisdom, humor, or insightfulness or merely in recognition of the speaker or writer. But the concept of Memorable Words is very different. It is more complicated.

As suggested by the title of each volume of these books, *Dead Serious and Lighthearted*, these words come in all varieties—the good, the bad, and the ugly; the heavy and the light; the hurtful and the heartfelt; the inspirational and the ominous; and the joyous and the somber.

In one sense, it's unsurprising that certain words would have such a powerful call upon our memories or our education since words are our primary means of expression, inquiry, communication, and explanation. As such, words are among the strongest pieces of our history. Words are one of the primary component bricks by which we build our own story, although admittedly we build our story in other ways as well—by how we behave and what we do; by what we choose to see and what we choose to ignore; and by what we remember and what we forget. More subtly, but no less importantly, our story is also told by the manner in which we measure our accomplishments and acknowledge our shortcomings, allocate our resources, and teach our young and care for our elderly.

But any assemblage of such Memorable Words has its limits. It is impossible to know a nation merely through a study of the words of its people and its leaders. No assemblage of words can begin to portray the full pain of war, the joy of peace, or the evil of 9/11. No assemblage of words can fully articulate the awe of the first moon landing, the beauty of art, or even, in some cases, the emotive powers of a movie. On the "lighthearted" side, no assemblage of words will ever allow us to fully understand Andy Warhol's art, grasp the egotism of some of our leaders, fully comprehend the eccentricities of America's celebrities, or even begin to get a handle on our crazy uncle or the weird guy down the street. But Memorable Words can help because, eventually, we get back to the words. Even in our wide-screen, technicolor, visual, and viral age complete with Dolby sound, eventually we get back to the words. They are a huge part of our legacy, and, as will be seen in these books, the words always linger longer than the voices.

Older Americans, who were alive at the time these words were first spoken or written, may recall many of the words. However, if younger Americans have heard or read these words before, they definitionally did so only by listening to their parents or grandparents or in the cold (and tiring) context of their education and schooling. But whatever the basis of one's recall, these words have, each for their own reasons, become long remembered. Each for different reasons, they have pierced the ether. They have outlasted thousands of news cycles and decades of American life. They have etched their way into the record of our history.

The primary criteria for the inclusion of the Memorable Words are discussed below, but for now let the obvious be noted—a careful narrowing has been necessary since there are too many words in our life and since not all words are the same. In fact, very bluntly, most words don't matter.

Most words are hellos and goodbyes, sidewalk greetings and elevator chitchat; sweet nothings and social pleasantries; celebrity babble and bosses' orders; and all of the rest of the gibberish of American life. Nothing to be long remembered. No notes to be taken.[9] Regrettably, it is also a fact of life that even most of the thoughtfully written, carefully chosen words of experts and analysts remain buried deep in the texts of reports, analyses, journals, and books.

But unlike the generic, talky words of our daily lives, an orderly presentation of the Memorable Words of Modern America can, it is humbly suggested, achieve the three purposes of these books—to lighten the load of learning our history, to better understand the common threads of our shared Modern American history, and to lift our spirits.

The Selection of Memorable Words
Sources and Neutrality
"…No intended political or social objectives"

…

"No intended suggestions of good or evil or right or wrong."

The sources of these Memorable Words are intentionally diverse and varied. The selections with respect to speakers and writers have been made primarily from press reports, articles, commentaries, transcripts, magazines, books, and various Internet sources that are widely and generally deemed responsible.

The Memorable Words of speakers and writers are not derived exclusively from what are commonly known as "primary" sources — original letters and writings, authentic transcripts and ancient texts, and raw data painstakingly assembled and scrupulously reviewed by devoted researchers and specialists boring deeply into their target subjects.[10] Instead, these books come from a different direction and present an entirely new approach. While these books have taken a painful four years to write, no tedious, dusty-book, hunch-back reading was done in their preparation. Instead, these books largely rest upon a careful selection, analysis, and use of both primary and secondary sources.

The author has sought to be politically and socially neutral and balanced in the selection of these Memorable Words even though, as will be discussed below, the author recognizes that with any such assemblage, there are risks of exclusion, oversight, and an unavoidable degree of subjectivity. But again, there are no intended political or social objectives. Except in certain notes instances, there are normally no intended suggestions of good or evil or right or wrong. Instead, the Memorable Words have been selected for the reasons outlined in detail below—their brilliance, prescience, passion, resonance or impact upon our Modern America. Beating the dead horse, these words are not presented in furtherance of any agenda of the author other than to try to memorialize and recognize those words that have, for whatever reason and from whatever source, had a direct impact upon our American conversation

At first blush, this approach may seem shallow, short-cutty, and even unprincipled. However, there is a method to the madness. There is a logic to the approach. Researchers and specialists are commendable. We need them. Their research is conducted with precision. Their works are written with detail. They bore deeply into each subject. But the problem is, as was discussed above, we Americans live in an accelerated, brevity-obsessed, bottom-line society. This is not necessarily an issue of commitment; it is also a matter of time. Even if an individual wants to become informed and well-read—a possibly somewhat wide and even dangerous assumption, time does not permit. There are too many books, too many subjects, too many developments, too many opinions, and too many perspectives. Complicating the whole issue is the fact that most Americans believe that our country is in trouble—that there is much to do, and that the only place to begin is *everywhere.*

Except in a few rare instances where specific attribution is impossible, the identity of the speaker or writer of each of the Memorable Words is presented together with a summary explanation of the context or meaning of the Memorable Words. With a few noted exceptions, the summaries are normally not intended to present criticism or critique, and they are written with intended objectivity and neutrality of presentation.

This author is aware that America has become a scorecard nation, and thus it is hoped that the reader will be pleased to find that both the subjects and the sources of these Memorable Words are—like our country—wide and disparate even if it is also true that all lists, regardless of their purpose or nature, can be dangerous.

The Allure and Danger of Lists
"The dangers of definition, omission, and subjectivity"

These books are assemblages of the Memorable Words of Modern America. And, as we know, all lists have a certain allure. Like a guilty pleasure, most of us can't resist knowing who or what is on this list or that list—the 100 Richest Americans, the FBI's 10 Most Wanted, the Highest Paid

Athletes, the 10 Best Retirement Towns, the 25 Best Destination Resorts, the 37 Most Dog-Friendly States, the 5 Warning Signs of a Heart Attack, the 10 Biggest Tax Traps, and the 25 Best Airline Deals. And on it goes.

But nearly all lists are subject to the same dangers—the dangers of definition, omission, and subjectivity.

The dangers of definition relate to determining the most objective and meaningful criteria for inclusion on any list. In the context of Memorable Words, such determination is unavoidably subjective. The criteria of importance, revelation, wisdom, emotion, impact, or summation are objective in their pronouncement, but indisputably, subjective in their application.

The dangers of omission are that some words of meaning or brilliance are inadvertently omitted due to sheer oversight or the need for brevity. Conversely, some words are easily included—The Reverend Dr. Martin Luther King's *"I Have A Dream"* speech, Neil Armstrong's *"one small step for man,"* and President Nixon's resignation announcement. But one of the keys to these books is the author's attempt to also identify the touching, emotive, revealing or prescient words in American history—including those that at the time of their pronouncement may not have been widely heard or appreciated or at the time of their writing may not have been widely read or understood.

The dangers of subjectivity are closely related to the dangers of definition and omission. It has been the committed intent of this author to present our American history in an accurate and balanced manner, but realizing such intent is almost impossible. Whether by the selection of the sources or by the selection of the words, personal bias—the true demon of all historians—creeps in. Furthermore, additional and deserving Memorable Words are later remembered. With the blessing of further reflection and with the suggestions and comments of readers like yourself, other words are rediscovered, and sometimes old statements or writings take on new meanings. For all of these reasons, the risk of exclusion of deserving Memorable Words remains a constant companion to the author, and books like these can never really be complete or finished.

It may not be enough for the reader to know that this author has tried to be objective and consistent in his selection of the Memorable Words of Modern America, but this humble offering is all that can be tendered. Ultimately, it is for you, the reader, to determine how closely this author may have come to achieving these dual goals of objectivity and consistency.

Additional Criteria for Selection of Memorable Words— Words of Historical Importance or Societal Impact
"Multiple and overlapping sets of reasons"

Most entries in these books have been selected for multiple and overlapping sets of reasons. The reasons generally fall into two categories.

The first set of reasons for inclusion center upon the words' historical significance—the words' resonance, impact, importance, eloquence, prescience, or brilliance. These Memorable Words are sometimes referred to below as words of "political or historical importance." The second set of reasons relate to the inclusion of words such as titles of seminal, award-winning, or bestselling books, the titles of movies and the most-watched television shows, and the major commercial campaigns and slogans. These words are included not because of their resonance or brilliance, but because they may help us remember or understand who we once were and whence we came. These Memorable Words are sometimes referred to below as words of "societal impact."

Collectively, these two categories of words reflect the dual purposes of history itself—first, to help us remember, understand and learn from the past in order to more wisely chart our course, make our decisions, and respond to rising challenges; and second, to help us tighten our sense of community by recognizing the many times and trials and events we have shared and using that common history to strengthen and bind the otherwise and always loosening strands of our national community

Words of Political or Historical Importance

One of the most common basis for selection of the Memorable Words rests upon the words' political or historical importance. These are words that draw their significance from the identity of speaker or writer, the historical time, place, and context of the words or the accuracy or prescience of the words—albeit now judged with the benefit of hindsight.

In order to assist the reader in remembering or learning about the identity of the speaker or writer and the historical context of the excerpted Memorable Words, a brief explanatory summary is set forth immediately below each of these selected Memorable Words. Such summary is also included because in many instances the historical context of the words—who said them and where or why they were spoken—is the core basis for their inclusion.

There are many other reasons why any particular words, phrases, chants, slogans, title, or writings are included in these books. As noted above, there are oftentimes multiple reasons for including any particular words. Some of the reasons for including words in this assemblage of Memorable Words of political or historical impact include the following:

(1) Identity of or the Unique Revelation about the Speaker or Writer. The identity of the speaker or writer or the unique revelations offered by the words about the nature, intelligence, aspirations, or motives of the speaker or writer;

(2) Resonance, Impact, Timeliness, Influence, Context, or Circumstances. The nature and extent of the words' resonance, impact, timeliness and, in some cases, the unique, deserved or otherwise, level of attention the words received or the level of influence the words had upon society or a significant sector thereof;

(3) Place, Setting, Encapsulation of Thought, Emotion, Reaction, and Passion. The place or setting in which the words were first spoken or written or the encapsulation of a widely-shared thought, emotion, or reaction thereby achieving a certain timeliness and long-echoing impact or the raw (and oftentimes almost touching) passion revealed by the words such as Joe Frazier's famous statement at the end of the 1975 Frazier-Ali fight in Manila—*"I want him, boss;"*

(4) Originality of Thought or Observation. The originality of thought or observation behind the words that caught our attention or captured our imagination. Within this basis for inclusion are some authors and commentators who have been identified as having broken new ground with a truly novel idea or insight;

(5) Grace, Style, or Eloquence. The uniqueness of the words' oratory, grace, style, eloquence, passion such as Dr. Martin Luther King's "*I Have a Dream*" speech;

(6) Accuracy, Precision of Thought, Truth, Prescience, Description, Summation, or Clarity of Articulation. The accuracy, conciseness, or truth of the words or, in some few instances, the prescience of words that has been revealed with the passage of time. These considerations may also include the precision and brilliance of the speaker's phrasing of thought such as Jane Leavy's "*(even) his aura had an aura*" description of the reach and breadth of Mickey Mantle's influence as one symbol of Americana;[11]

(7) Meaningfulness or Resonance. The manner in which the words allowed us to open our minds and sometimes our hearts and how meaningful the words were in building understanding or even national consensus about a given subject or because, in the opinion of many Americans, the words, at a given point in time, seemed to "say it all," "get it right," or "reveal the truth;"

(8) Texture, Excitement, or Color. The extent to which the words added humor, texture, excitement, and color to our lives;

(9) Repetition and Durability of Statement. The power of the mere repetition. While such words are arguably undeserving, these words, like the words of a favorite song, can bring back memories from years ago; and/or

(10) Impactful Cleverness or Raw Bluntness. The impactful cleverness or even raw and uniquely memorable bluntness of a statement.

Even with these criteria, decisions about the inclusion or exclusion of certain words are difficult. For example, words extracted from the political campaigns raise peculiar complexities. The inclusion of these Memorable Words is arguably unfair due to the uniquely onerous scrutiny and reporting of every utterance made by candidates during the course of their long and grueling campaigns. In addition, the impact can be disproportionately enhanced by the level of media repetition given to any single statement. Nevertheless, some such statements are included because whether fair or unfair, they had a significant and lasting impact upon political discussions and upon the success or failure of a given candidate, party, or movement. For example, one sub-category of such words of political importance, the Presidential Campaign Themes and Identification Slogans of the major political party candidates, are included in the year of the subject campaign.

Such inclusions are rarely based upon the brilliance of the words. Instead, these words are included because of their revelations about the respective candidates and campaigns, because they were driven into the American subconscious by constant repetition of use, and because, as a consequence, they are indisputably "memorable." Arguably, however, they may reveal little about the candidates or their campaigns since nearly all candidates use variant twists of many of the same words. For example, based upon an analysis of all campaign slogans since 1960, there are only slight variations between the parties. An analysis of all Presidential campaigns from 1960 through 2012 shows that the six most commonly used words in Republican campaign slogans since 1960, in order of frequency of use, are "America(n)," "Leader/Leadership," "Experience," "Change/Reform," "Win," and "Peace." The six most commonly used (and very similar) words in Democratic campaigns slogans since 1960, again in order of frequency of use, are "America(n)," "Change," "Prosperity," "Leader/Leadership," "Hope," "Future/Tomorrow."[12] As may be expected, "slogans that look forward to the future and a better tomorrow have fared well (as) presidential slogans,"[13] but more negative slogans, such as Robert Dole's 1996 slogan "Where's the Outrage" have "tended to alienate voters and (have come) across as mean, petty, or cynical." But there are exceptions. Ronald Reagan's famous 1980 slogan "Are You Better Off Than You Were Four Years Ago?" was well received as was the "Telling It Like It Is" slogan of 2016 Republican hopeful New Jersey Governor Chris Christie.[14]

Words of Societal Impact

The selection of words of societal impact (as compared with those words of political or historical importance) is challenging for different reasons. Their inclusion is based less upon their meaning and more upon their impact and resonance. However, there is no easy set of criteria for the selection of those magical words that best refresh our memories or best teach us our history. Thus, the words of societal impact—the words of our societal memory, are included not for their brilliance but for their commonality. Taken together, these words are the links in our nation's history—the books we have read, the movies we have seen, the shows we have watched, the chants we have yelled, and the slogans we have read—all in various degrees of *ad nauseum.*

The potential candidates for such words are endless. Respecting the patience of readers and honoring the demands for brevity, selections have had to be made. The categories for these words of societal impact that have been selected and included as Memorable Words in these books are set forth below.

Books Titles

The titles of certain major books are included because they, in and of themselves, are some of the most Memorable Words of Modern America. These titles are included due either to their wide readership or seminal influence upon American political or social thought. The books are referenced in the year of their initial publication.

The following three categories of book titles are included:

(i) Seminal Books. These are the titles of books that have been identified by the author as having been uniquely important in the history of Modern America or that have otherwise achieved a discernable consensus of importance.[15] Included herein are also those 21 books that were published during the years of Modern America (1957–2015) and which were included in The Library of Congress' popular exhibition, "Books That Shaped America." The books identified as seminal are rarely Pulitzer prize-winning books or bestselling books. Nevertheless, they are identified as seminal and included (a) because in retrospect and in the opinion of this author (and including, in some cases, also the opinion of the Library of Congress), they were in their own manner and in the context of their own subjects groundbreaking, thought-provoking, or uniquely innovative and (b) because they strongly influenced later developments, understandings or debates about their subjects. As stated by the Library of Congress with respect to its selection of seminal books, the books so selected by its group of curators and subject experts "were not intended to be the 'best' books published in the United States. Rather, (because these)… books by American authors … had, for a wide variety of reasons, a profound effect on American life."[16] Thus, a book's characterization as *seminal* does not necessarily mean *correct*. It merely implies *impact*. One example is Dr. Paul Ehrlich's neo-Malthusian 1968 book, *Population Bomb*. Ehrlich's book contained numerous dead-wrong predictions due to his underestimation of agricultural productivity changes, but it was widely discussed and had a dramatic impact about the risks attendant to the world's growing population. A compilation listing of all Seminal Books during the subject years of each volume (Volume 1 (1957–1976); Volume II (1977–1993); Volume III (1994–2015), respectively) is attached as Appendix E.

Because such seminal books are oftentimes more academic in nature or less well-known as, for example, the Pulitzer Prize-winning books or *The New York Times* Best Sellers discussed below, the title of each seminal book is followed by a brief description of the theme(s) of the book and the reasons why it has been here selected as one of the seminal books of Modern America.

(ii) Pulitzer Prize-Winning Books. Pulitzer Prizes have a unique history. They have been awarded since 1917 pursuant to the testamentary instructions of Joseph Pulitzer, an American journalist and newspaper publisher. It is interesting to note that Pulitzer was also the first major public figure to call for the formal training of journalists at the university level.[17] His substantial endowment to Columbia University led to the opening of Columbia's Graduate School of Journalism in 1912, and the awarding of Pulitzer Prizes was intended to serve as an incentive for excellence in writing and journalism. Pulitzer Prizes remain, even now, one of the world's most prestigious literary awards. There are numerous award categories, and the categories themselves change periodically as rather recently exemplified by the 2007 addition of a category for online writing. There are six categories in letter and drama alone–Fiction, Drama, History, Biography or Autobiography, Poetry, and General Nonfiction. The recipients of the Pulitzer Prizes in the following categories are included herein in the year of the respective award's announcement, i.e. the year following the year of the book's initial publication and release.

Pulitzer Prize for Fiction (1957–2015). (Excepting the six years in which no award was made—Years 1957, 1964, 1971, 1974, 1977 and 2012). Included within this list is a wide and varied group of authors including only three authors (Booth Tarkington (1919 and 1922), William Faulkner (1955 and 1963 (posthumous)), and John Updike (1982 and 1991)) who received more than one Pulitzer Prize for Fiction.

Pulitzer Prize-Winning Books for General Nonfiction (1962–2015). The titles of the award-winning nonfiction books written by an American author and published in the prior calendar year. The first award in this category was awarded in 1962. Normally, only one book is selected, but in three years (1969, 1973, and 1986) two prizes were awarded.

Pulitzer Prize-Winning Books for History (1957–2015). The title of the award-winning books of history written by an American author in the prior calendar year. Awards in this category have been made since the inception of the Pulitzer Prizes in 1917.

A compilation listing of all Pulitzer Prize-Winning Books for History, General Nonfiction, and Fiction during the subject years of each volume (Volume 1 (1957–1976); Volume II (1977–1993); Volume III (1994–2015), respectively) is attached as Appendix F.

(iii) *The New York Times* **Best Sellers.** Included in this presentation of Memorable Words are the titles of the bestselling American books according to *The New York Times* Best Sellers Lists for Nonfiction and Fiction.

First included are the titles of those two books, by year, that dominated and had the most weeks as Number One on *The New York Times* Best Sellers List for Nonfiction. The names of the authors are included along with the number of weeks each title remained as Number One on the list.

Also included are the titles of those books, by year, that dominated and were Number One on *The New York Times* Best Sellers List for Adult Fiction. The names of the authors are included along with the number of weeks each title remained as Number One on such list.

In addition, an analysis of America's reading based upon all of *The New York Times* Best Sellers for Fiction is included at Appendix G. However, in order to achieve better data sampling for this analysis, it is based upon the entire duration of Modern America, 1957–2015.

Because books are arguably some of the most Memorable Words of any generation or period, it is tempting to include many other book lists as well. However, lines must be drawn and decisions made in order to achieve even a semblance of textual brevity. For that reason, only the following book title lists are included as Appendices:

Appendix H. Book Titles of Modern America—The Best and the Worst during the subject years of each volume (Volume I (1957–1976); Volume II (1977–1993); Volume III (1994–2015), respectively).

Appendix I. The 25 Books Most Widely Held in U.S. Libraries.

Appendix J. The Books Most Frequently Banned or Challenged in Modern America.

Award-Winning Movies and Best Movie Lines of the Year

The American movie industry has been a major part of our history since the industry's inception nearly a century ago. The titles of these movies over the course of Modern America are almost definitionally some of the most powerful and remembered words of each year. During the early years of Modern America (Volume I (1957–1976)) the titles range from such early movies as *Bridge on the River Kwai* (1957) and *Ben Hur* (1959) to still-contemporary classics such as *The Godfather* (1972) and *Rocky* (1976). During the middle years of Modern America (Volume II (1977–1993)), the titles range from such movies as *Annie Hall* (1977) and *Star Wars* (1977) to *Schindler's List* (1993) and *The Fugitive* (1993). In the most recent years of Modern America (Volume III (1994–2015)), the titles range from such movies as *Forrest Gump* (1994) and *Pulp Fiction* (1994) to *The Big Short* (2015) and *The Revenant* (2015). The best movies of Modern America for each year are listed herein in the year of their initial release.

The "best movie" selections are derived from two sources. The first selections are the names of the Academy Award winner and the other nominees for the Best Picture of the Year. The second selections are the best movies as ranked by the lesser known *PrettyFamous*, a multi-source data evaluation and presentation company. The reason for the inclusion of *PrettyFamous'* selections for the best picture is that its selection criteria are theoretically more objective than the selection criteria based merely upon the voting of the members of the Academy of Motion Pictures Arts and Science (the "AMPAS"). The disparity in the two lists is partly evidenced by the fact that over the entire span of the nearly 60 years of Modern America (1957–2015) 78% of *PrettyFamous'* best picture selections are *different* from those of the AMPAS.

Lastly, some of the best and most well-known movie lines from each year have been included. Everyone has their own favorite movie lines, and thus this is an unavoidably subjective listing. However, to exclude any sampling of these immortal words would be to omit some of the most impactful and memorable words of our generations. This selection of movie lines is derived from carefully reviewing some of the most frequently quoted and commonly remembered lines of these years—from *Goldfinger's* "*Shaken. Not stirred*" (1964) to *All the President's Men's* "*Follow the money*" (1976); from *Mary Poppins'* "*Supercalifragillisticexpialidocius*" (1964) to *Rocky's* "*Yo, Adrian*" (1976); from *Star Wars'* "*May the force be with you*" (1974) to *A Few Good Men's* "*You can't handle the truth*" (1992); from *Forrest Gump's* "*Run, Forrest, run*" (1994) to *12 Years a Slave's* "*I want to live.*" Some of these lines have also been included because they have passed intact into and become a part of the common language and jargon of American life.[18]

Television Shows - Most Widely-Viewed, Critically-Acclaimed, and Last Seasons

Like the American movie industry, television has been a staple of American life and conversation throughout all of the years of Modern America. For better or worse, deserving or otherwise and just like American movies, the remembrances of these shows are some of the historical threads that bind large segments of our country. Included herein, by year, are several references to television shows.

First, for each year, the three most widely-viewed television shows are presented together with the estimated audience and that audience as a percentage of the then-current U.S. population. The viewership is presented as a percentage of the U.S. population because that percentage is more meaningful in recognizing the reach, importance, and influence of the show upon our American life.

For example, in 1960 the U.S. population was 180,700,000. The most widely-viewed television show was *Gunsmoke* with an estimated weekly audience of 17,600,000. The size of this audience is obviously very large, but the audience size is far more meaningful when presented as a percentage of the U.S. population—i.e. 9.7% of America watched the show each week. However, compare the size of this audience and this viewership percentage with the most widely-viewed shows of 1976. In just the two decades between 1957 and 1976, the U.S. population increased by 46,000,000 people—roughly equivalent to another twelve Chicagos; another eight-four San Antonios.

While, as noted above, *Gunsmoke* had a 1960 estimated weekly audience of 17,600,000 representing 9.7% of the U.S. population, in the year 1976, *Happy Days,* the year's most widely-viewed television show, had a weekly viewing audience of 22,400,000—more than 27% larger than that of *Gunsmoke* in 1960. However, the audience as a percentage of the U.S. population had hardly changed—from 9.7% for *Gunsmoke* in 1960 to 10.3% for *Happy Days* in 1976.

The dispersal of the American audience became far more pronounced in the later years of Modern America. In such later years, the weekly percentages of the U.S. audience watching the most-widely-viewed show started to substantially decrease. This drop reflected, among other things, (i) the splintering of the major networks' audiences; (ii) the rise of cable television; (iii) the availability of more alternative forms of entertainment; and in later years, (iv) the rise of the Internet as a source of entertainment, news and information; and, as discussed above, (v) the ever-shortening attention span of the American audience.

The significance of this dispersal is that over the course of Modern America substantially fewer and fewer Americans, as a percentage of the population, are sharing and, in a sense, bonding over the same television show. By no means does this alone dissolve the American community, but it is a further dimension of the splintering of our national community.

In addition, an understanding of America can be better achieved by knowing not only those television shows that commenced in a given year but also those television shows that ceased in a given year. Some of these shows are also included. Examples of such shows are referenced both in their first year ("Widely-Viewed or Critically-Acclaimed New Television Show(s)") and their last season ("Last Season Television"). Therefore, with respect to some of the most influential American television shows such as *Leave It to Beaver* (1963), *The Andy Griffith Show* (1968), and even *The Ed Sullivan Show* (1971), information is provided with respect to both the shows original airing and its last airing (exclusive of re-runs, specials, and reunion shows).

Lastly, certain television shows of particular or unique social importance are included in the year of their first airing. Some of these shows evidenced or even contributed to changes in social mores and community standards. Others contribute to our understanding of American history by evidencing changes in the interests of the American viewing audience. Admittedly, the selection of such television shows is, once again, dangerously subjective, but the author has tried to include only those shows that have had a unique impact upon American television or are highly reflective of a substantial segment of the American community. Examples of such show include *American Bandstand* (1957–1987), *Bonanza* (1959–1973), *ABC's Wide World of Sports* (1961–1998), *The Tonight Show with Johnny Carson* (1962–1992), *60 Minutes* (1968–), *All in the Family* (1971–1979), and *Saturday Night Live* (1975–), *Dallas* (1978–1991), and *The Sopranos* (1997–2007).

In a few rare instances, even immortal television lines made the final cut. Included amongst the Memorable Words of Modern America are lines such as the immortal nightly *"Heeeere's Johnny"* introduction by Ed McMahon of *The Johnny Carson Show* and the gentle, nightly *"And that's the way it is, ..."* closing of Walter Cronkite of CBS News.

Major Commercial Advertising Campaigns and Slogans

Some of the most Memorable Words of Modern America are those that have been driven into our American life by the powerful tools of modern-day marketing and advertising. These words, arguably even more than major books, movies, and television shows, must be recognized as some of the Memorable Words of Modern America,

A select few of these major commercial marketing and advertising campaigns and slogans have been included as Memorable Words for two reasons. First, these slogans remind us of what was first marketed in any given year. Second, these slogans serve to underscore the ease with which such advertising words are recalled and can dutifully remind us of the raw power of advertising and the indelible impact of such campaigns. Through the use of clever words and their repetitive presentation, many of these marketing campaigns and slogans—the linguistic component of our American economy—have become a part of our conversation, narrative, and history. As such, they have become a part of the American DNA.

Once again, the included slogans are only those of Modern America, but these types of advertising campaigns and slogans have been an integral part of the American conversation for many decades before the beginning of Modern America. Since 1915 and long before Keurig, it was Maxwell House's coffee that was *good to the last drop.* Since 1917 and thanks to FTD, we've been *saying it with flowers;* since 1921 and long before we knew about the health dangers of smoking, Americans had been walking *a mile for Camel;* since 1932 our Kellogg's Rice Krispies have been *snap, crack, and pop*—ing. Since 1932 Hallmark has been encouraging us to *care enough to send the very best.* Since 1948 our diamonds have been *forever,* and since 1950 we've been in Allstate's *good hands.*

Therefore, in recognition of both the importance and the ingraining of these words into the American conversation, select examples of the words of major commercial advertising campaigns and slogans are entered in the year in which they were first widely presented to the American public. Even in the early years of Modern America this seems appropriate because, for example, since 1958 we have been happy to hear the ringing words of Crest toothpaste assuring *Look, Ma, no cavities.* Since 1962 and long before we started relying on our computer keyboards, Americans *let [our] fingers do the walking* thanks to Yellow Pages. Since 1972, we have all shared in Life Cereal's surprise that *heh, Mikey ... he likes it.* And since 1975, the

American Express card has reminded us to *"not leave to home without it."* The middle years of Modern America had its own campaigns and slogans as well—in 1979 *Forbes* magazine proudly identified itself as a *"Capitalist tool."* In the same year AT&T told us to *"reach out and touch someone."* Ever since 1980 the Army has been encouraging our young men and women *"to be all (they) can be."* But it was not until 1993 that America started wondering whether or not we "got milk," and it wasn't until 2002 that Verizon's *"can (you) hear me now"* worked its way into our American life.

Examples of such advertising campaigns and slogans are included in the years of their initial use, and a fuller and more detailed list of advertising campaigns and slogans for all of the years of Modern America is included at Appendix L.

Catchphrases, Chants, and Slogans

Another category of Memorable Words are those certain catchphrases, chants, and slogans that for various reasons have become ingrained into our American life. These chants are far more than mere parlance. They are more than a way of speaking. They have independent meanings and implications. They connote associations and beliefs.

Most of these chants are associated with one or more social or economic movements. They have been repeated by many persons. They have been repeated loudly and in unison by many crowds, during many marches, and in many cities and towns of our country. In a few instances, they have even come from or later become the bylines of Presidential election campaigns.

With such chants, it is nearly impossible to identify the exact timing or origin of the words or to make specific attributions to any speaker or leader. Therefore, they are included in the approximate year of their first use and are included with brief explanations of their respective meanings and contexts. In those few instances where such chants are more generational in nature—and again, since it is impossible to identify the exact timing or origin of such words, they are included in the pages introducing certain decades such as the 1960s or the 1990s.

Many different types of catchphrases, chants, and slogans are included in these books. For example, while no single catchphrase can sum up the counterculture movement of the Sixties, the mantra of *"tune in, turn on, and drop out"* comes close. And while no single chant of the anti-war protestors can fully encapsulate the anger of those opposed to America's ongoing war in Vietnam, the chant of *"Hell no, I won't go"* was heard on college campuses, in front of draft boards, and at the gates of many military bases throughout America during the later years of the 1960s. Just a few years later, it was the chant of *"Let's win or get out"* which best bespoke the frustrations of the American people and many of its leaders. In another context, no catchphrase better reminds us of the passion and resolve of the Civil Rights protests of the 1960s than the constant reminder of the crowds that *"we shall overcome."* There were a few chants and slogans during the middle years of Modern America, but it was not until the later years of Modern America (1994–2015) that the chants returned to prominence—louder and more challenging. Examples of these later chants are the 2011 chant of *"we are the 1%"* and the angry chant starting in 2014 that *"black lives matter."*

Memorable Words from Speeches, Books, Writings, and Other Sources

The largest and most important collection of Memorable Words are those excerpted from a wide range of speeches, books, writings, and many other sources. These are words of political, historical, or societal importance based upon the criteria described above. Each of the entries identifies, as precisely as possible, the date the words were first spoken or written together with the identity of the speaker or writer. In order to explain the context and import of the words, each entry is followed by a summary narrative and explanation.

More precisely, these Memorable Words are drawn both from famous speeches and writings and from a wide and eclectic, but equally impor-tant, array of lesser known sources as well. In order to try to capture the many overlapping aspects of American life during this period—both the grave and the frivolous—these words intentionally include both the "dead serious" and the "lighthearted" words of these years.

For example, in just the first Volume I (1957–1976), the Memorable Words include everything from the *"ask not what you can do for your country"* words of Presidential Inauguration addresses to the *"I have a dream"* eloquence of the Rev. Dr. Martin Luther King, Jr.; from the *"beep, beep, beep"* of Sputnik to the *"I am not a crook"* speech of President Nixon; from the United States Supreme Court's decision of one's "right to remain silent" to Bobby Kennedy *"Is everyone okay?"* last words; from Neil Armstrong's *"one small step for man"* to Woodstock's *"Three Days of Peace and Music;"* from Lombardi's *"football is a collision sport"* to D.B. Cooper's *"Miss, you'd better look at that note. I have a bomb;"* from Deep Throat's *"follow the money"* to Joe Frazier's *"I want him, boss."*

These Memorable Words also include excerpts from the four U.S. Constitutional Amendments that have been adopted during the course of Modern America, and, in a few instances, words are even excerpted from major United States Supreme Court cases.

Few quotes from judicial decisions are included because most cases before the U.S. Supreme Court (sometimes referred to hereinafter as "USSC") involve matters of statutory interpretation. Few of the civil law cases are widely read or discussed because they primarily affect only the named parties or a relatively small number of other similarly situated parties.

However, other cases are different. A few Supreme Court cases do have both broad legal and social impacts upon our society such as those granting defendants a "right to counsel" or those recognizing a new or materially expanded constitutional rights such as "one man, one vote," the "right of privacy," the "right to die," the "right to remain silent," and a "woman's right to choose." In these few instances, where court pronounce-ments have become matters of wide social discussion (and debate) or where court pronouncements have materially changed the constitutional rights of Americans, the USSC's opinions are quoted because the court's words have become a part of our mainstream national conversation as well as a widely-recognized component of our shared American history.

Additionally, there is a category of Memorable Words where a single word or phrase says it all. For example, the single word of "Guilty" or "Acquitted" seems to say it all. In the context of sports, the single phrase "Banned for Life"[19] says it all. But the basis and criteria for these types of Memorable Word inclusions need to be more fully explained.

Each year thousands of criminal prosecutions are initiated. Each year thousands of convictions and acquittals are announced by our federal and state courts. Just like the civil cases discussed above, most criminal cases do not involve well-known persons. Instead, most prosecutions are of limited interest except to the victims, the accused, and their respective close friends and family members. Furthermore, and even in the context of horrendous crimes and important prosecutions, most cases do not raise novel legal questions. As a result, few such cases grasp the attention or the prolonged focus of any community. They pass quickly through the news cycles almost without notice. Except in their patterns and scope of aggregation, rarely do they get or deserve much attention.

But that is not true of all cases. There are exceptions. Some cases are the subject of broader community, regional, and even national interest. Some cases, such as Enron and WorldCom and Lehman Brothers in the later years of Modern America, directly affected thousands of creditors and terminated the employment and wiped out the retirement savings of whole communities. In addition, there are a few cases that attracted sustained attention for other reasons. They became the subject of media reporting and national interest. Books were written. Movies were made. The very words Charlie Manson, My Lai and Lt. Calley, Abscam, Michael Milliken and Junk Bonds, Charles Keating and the S&L Crisis, O.J., Columbine, Bernie Madoff, Trayvon Martin, and on and on—still reverberate in our shared American history. The trials themselves become historic markers, and for that reason, the crimes are also included in these books under the commonly shared Memorable Words banners of either "Guilty" or "Acquitted."[20]

Closing

While the first defining parameter for the selections in these books is that the words be "memorable," the second and overarching parameter is their limitation to the defined years of Modern America. For the reasons explained in the next chapter, the definition of Modern America is limited to the years 1957 through 2015.

CHAPTER 4

The Definition
of Modern America

Introduction

These books only present the Memorable Words of Modern America—the Years 1957 to 2015. This parameter is, to a degree, a concession made in recognition of the patience of the reader and the need for a degree of brevity. The limitation to the words of America's direct experience and to the words of American speakers and writers is relatively easy to explain and understand, but the concept and definition of Modern America, the years 1957–2015, are more subjective and more deserving of explanation.

The tight adherence to these year boundaries definitionally excludes more words than we can begin to record and more books than we can begin to remember. Some of such excluded books remain classics that, even now and to varying degrees, still seem to be "modern"—from Herbert Croly's *The Promise of American Life* published in 1909 to Dale Carnegie's *How to Win Friends and Influence People* published in 1936; from C. Wright Mills' influential *The Power Elite* published in 1954 to John Kennedy's Pulitzer Prize-winning *Profiles in Courage* published in 1955; and even from George Orwell's duel classics *Animal Farm* and *Nineteen Eighty-Four* published in 1945 and 1949, respectively, to J. D.

Salinger's *Catcher in the Rye* published in 1954. The list is almost endless, but a line must be drawn. A focus must be defined. It is done here by the careful definition of Modern America as the period from 1957 to 2015.

Author's Note:
The balance of this chapter is partly adapted from Chapter 4
of my book The Relevance of Reason: The Hard Facts and Real Data About the State of Current America (Volume 1 (Business and Politics) (2013) *and* Volume II (Society and Culture) (2013)).

The Concept of Ages and Eras

"Ages don't arrive with a parade."

The phrase "Modern America," as used in these books, is defined as the fifty-eight-year period from 1957 to 2015, but such year selections are not universally mandated. To the contrary, there is rarely any wide consensus as to the beginning or even the ending of ages and eras. Their beginnings and endings and their definings and namings remain, at best, an imprecise science for rather obvious reasons.

As noted above, ages don't arrive with a parade. Eras aren't announced with a press release. There is no quick agreement about the proper years or the correct titling of any age or era even though some commentators are relentless in their scurry to define and name-tag them—the Age of Jackson, the Ante- and Post-Bellum Era, the Reconstruction Era, the Industrial Age, the Gilded Age, the Great Depression, the War Years, the Modern Age, the Cold War Era, the Age of Affluence, the Age of Technology, the Computer Age, the Information Age, the Age of Entitlement, the Age of Indifference, the Age of Terrorism, the Age of ISIS, the Age of Trump(ism), and on and on.

Especially in the academic world, the significance of events is the subject of endless scholarly papers and debates. Various alternatives are floated around one after another, and only after intervening decades of reflection, research, and analyses is there ever a reasonable degree of distilling perspective whereby, sometimes—but even then only sometimes—a consensus evolves.

In Modern America, where most of us live and work, it is the same. Some degree of consensus may from time to time evolve, but usually the real dating and naming of an era arrive more by the habit of repetition than by any exacting application of any underlying science or studied history.

Thus, it is willingly recognized that there is no tight academic or scientific implication associated with the use of the phrase "Modern America." It will be argued that 1957 was an extraordinary year, but it is the concept of a reference point that matters more than the associated dates. And to that extent, the year selection, the significance of varying events, and the naming of our eras and ages can remain, usually without problem or consequence, a fun, but notoriously subjective, parlor game.[21]

But there are a few exceptions. Even though history is both endless and patient, with a new page being written each day, occasionally there are special dates. Occasionally, an event of such singularity and consequence occurs that a new age is triggered. Excepting for the prickly academic or stubborn contrarian, these events and their associated dates are recognized by everyone as unique. With memories of joy or sadness, these dates hold special distinction. These dates deserve and oftentimes receive names of their own.

In the early 20th century, before the beginning of Modern America, there were many such events and dates: Black Tuesday,[22] Pearl Harbor Day —the Day of Infamy,[23] D-Day and V-E and V-J Days.[24] More recently, the moon landing would have been a candidate but for the raucous cacophony of the 1960s in which it was buried. The obvious, most recent candidate is the tragedy of 9/11. It is far too early to determine, but a tectonic shift in American politics and life may have occurred, for better or worse, with the surprising election of Donald Trump as this country's 45th President. But, again, it is far too early to know.

Thus, there are a few eras that arguably do begin or end with specificity, but not many. Even though it is hard to determine the beginning of a baseline Modern America and even though 1957 was chosen for the many detailed reasons discussed below, this author humbly acknowledges that there are any number of alternative beginning dates worthy of consideration.

The Many Alternative Beginning Years of Modern America

*"But 1957 was The Year when the old yielded to the new;
when Modern America was birthed; when the America which we still see
and feel today finally began; and when the pace of American life,
for better or worse, began to accelerate."*

Working backwards, some could claim that Modern America began just a few years ago—in 2007–2008, when the U.S. financial collapse exposed the weakness and literal fragility of the American economy. The financial collapse and the Great Recession that followed decimated the corporate balance sheets of thousands of companies and the personal finances of millions of American households. It simultaneously escalated the debate about the proper role and the necessary limits of the federal government. It once again exposed the poor, indeed irresponsible, financial condition of our federal and state governments. Debt ceilings and fiscal cliffs aside, it put the entire construct and logic of Keynesian economics back into play.

Seven years earlier, the attacks of 9/11 revealed a new and different kind of American vulnerability when nineteen terrorists commandeered commercial airlines and caused them to crash—all within 51 minutes of each other—into the World Trade Center in New York, the Pentagon on the outskirts of the District of Columbia, and a lonely field near Shanksville, Pennsylvania. With these attacks, a new and deeper kind of fear was injected into the American psyche. The attacks led directly to the American invasion of Afghanistan and then Iraq. The war in Afghanistan now holds the dubious distinction of being the longest war in American history. More than 6,500 American soldiers have lost their lives in Afghanistan and Iraq, and many tens of thousands more have been injured or impaired for life.[25] The 9/11 attacks, the subsequent failures of our forces to stabilize Afghanistan or Iraq, the resultant rise of ISIS and other terrorist groups, and a seemingly resurgent Russia, all further altered the way many Americans view the world. The succession of events changed our concepts of national security. They redefined the boundaries of our personal privacies. They contributed to the massive increase in the American deficit. They further elevated (at least for a period of years) the influence of American neoconservatism, and for a multitude of interwoven reasons, they strained our nation's relations with many countries both within and outside the Muslim world.

A far weaker, but viable candidate as the beginning of Modern America could be 1992. Its claim is more tepid. It rests largely upon being a year of disproportionate significance because it, better than any other year until at least the Presidential election of 2016, marked the beginning of a more discordant and ideological era in American social and political life. This year signified the closing of the Reagan (and Bush Sr.) Era. Ross Perot had said his piece and left the stage just as cocksure of himself as when he arrived. A then-young former Governor from Arkansas, Bill Clinton, was elected. However, much more than that changed. Both coincidentally and partly resultantly, the major political parties became more ideological. Concepts of bipartisanship seemed to have evaporated. Everything became politicized. The media and especially "talk radio" became harsher, coarser, and less restrained. A new and seemingly emboldened style of intransigence was injected into American politics that, as of this writing, remains unabated.

The year 1989 could also lay claim as the beginning of Modern America. Cuba and North Korea aside, 1989 marked the end of the Cold War. A moderated form of Chinese Communism survived the pro-democracy spring protests, but the world watched in awe and silence as a solitary, young man stood and blocked a tank in Tiananmen Square. Just a few months later and on the other side of the world, the Berlin Wall came down. The dismantling of the Soviet Union began. George H.W. Bush, Sr., who is increasingly and possibly correctly viewed by some as the Second Eisenhower, exercised his Presidency with a certain calmness, steadfastness, decency, and decorum. But to the confusion of many, the peace dividend from the collapse of Communism never arrived, and the bounce didn't last long. Nevertheless, for a brief period there was a nearly universal belief that the virtues of democracy and capitalism had finally prevailed as the political and economic models for the world's nations.

The dawn of the 1980s was also another extraordinary and transformational time. The rise and the power of the Moral Majority was becoming more apparent as the late Rev. Jerry Falwell exhorted Americans to "get in step" with conservatism. Ronald Reagan won the Presidential election in a landslide, and many welcomed the "new day in America" even though this was also the year in which the prime interest rate climbed to 21.5% and a crazy man killed John Lennon outside of the Dakota apartments on the Upper West Side of New York.

The deeper historians might lay a serious, albeit far quieter and less recognized, claim to 1971 as the year of the beginning of Modern America. In 1971, wedged between the 1970 killings at Kent State[26] and the 1972 break-in at the Watergate apartments, *All in the Family* debuted in Hollywood and Disney World opened in Orlando. Although it would be another couple of years until the helicopters would lift the last escapees off the roof of the American Embassy in Saigon,[27] by 1971 America and the world came to know, if not accept, that the Vietnam War was starting to wind down. In addition, the longer-term political and social consequences of that tortuous war—such as a heightened skepticism of both the media and governmental leaders—were also beginning to come into view.

In 1971, close observers of American political and social life recognized the early, nascent signs of the rise of both the size and the potential power of the conservative and the evangelical movements. Possibly even more significant is the fact that 1971 was the beginning of the more thorough, intertwining of the private and public sectors. It was subtle at first. For most Americans, it was unrecognized and off-radar. However, in 1971 Lewis Powell, while still a practicing attorney in Virginia and before his 1972 appointment to the USSC by President Richard Nixon, wrote his now-famous Memorandum challenging businesses to organize and take steps "to change both the policy and political mainstream in Washington."

The significance of Powell's recommendations was both massive and immediate, yet even to this day, the impact of Powell's Memorandum is not widely known or recognized. But the changes that resulted speak for themselves. In 1970, for example, there were only about 200 lobbyists in Washington. Within ten years, the number of business lobbyists in Washington would increase more than tenfold to over 2,400 lobbyists. The membership base of the National Federation of Independent Businesses increased from 300 to over 600,000. A couple of years later, in 1974, the conservative Heritage Foundation (now one of the most influential, right-wing think tanks in Washington, D.C.) was started with $250,000 of seed money from the beer magnate Joseph Coors[28] for a very specific purpose and with a tightly-defined, specific audience—to influence "Congress and congressional staff."[29] Soon thereafter, the Heritage Foundation was generating ten to fifteen page position papers, which it called "Backgrounders," further evidencing that the modern age of focused, organized, targeted, business-influenced, if not business-driven, conservatism had begun. This consolidation of the public and private sectors was the real merger and acquisition of the 20th century. And it began in 1971. Businesses organized. First, they asserted their political influence. Then, in the opinion of many, they asserted their control of many aspects of our public life. Congress was no longer a public house. K Street was no longer just an address. And the trend continues. By 2015, more than half the members of Congress who had left office since 2010 had found lobbying-related jobs. By 2015, corporations spent more money each year lobbying Congress (approximately $2.6 billion) than taxpayers did in funding it (approximately $2.0 billion).[30]

For other writers and historians, 1968 was The Year—The Year of *Boom*,[31] the year of tumult and tragedy; the year of the transformation, if not the unwinding, of America. The Vietnam War waged ferociously. In January 1968, the Viet Cong launched the massive Tet Offensive throughout South Vietnam. Also 1968 was the year of the assassination of the Rev. Dr. Martin Luther King, Jr. on April 4 in Memphis, Tennessee. Both grief and riots besieged the nation for weeks, and just two months later Bobby Kennedy was assassinated on June 6 in Los Angeles—the second Kennedy assassinated in five years. In retrospect, it is almost weirdly appropriate that this was the year in which 911 lines were first installed. But back then, nothing seemed to help calm the storm. President Lyndon Johnson announced that he would not seek a second term, and as a result Hubert Humphrey was nominated in August 1968—albeit at the raucous "whole-world-is-watching" Democratic Party Convention in Chicago. A few months later, both Humphrey and George Wallace were defeated by the again resurgent Richard Nixon, who claimed the Presidency with a margin of a mere 49,257 votes out of 59,403,000 cast—less than 1/10th of

1%. And there were other segments of the population committed to their own, sometimes overlapping causes—student radicals and war protestors, civil rights activists rightly emboldened by the Voting Rights Act of 1965 and other legislation,[32] and hippies who were still coming off of (or down from) the Summer of Love in the Haight-Ashbury District of San Francisco. But neither wild chaos nor horrendous tragedy necessarily signifies change. Modern America had begun earlier.

The year 1964 is another viable and deserving candidate for the beginning of Modern America. During the course of a June graduation speech at the University of Michigan, President Lyndon Johnson had the audacity to suggest that America ought to be as great as it said it was. He then proceeded to lay out his plans for the Great Society and for an end to poverty and racial discrimination. In the same month and with the help of 27 Republicans, the Civil Rights Act was passed and the unraveling of the South's social system was set in motion.

However, the passage of the Civil Rights Bill did not preclude three Freedom Workers from being killed outside of Philadelphia, Mississippi. It was not enough to stop Malcolm X from concluding that civil rights had to be achieved "by any means necessary" especially since many people in the African American community no longer felt like waiting "for some degree of civil rights." The separation of white and black communities was exemplified by the white community's nearly complete misunderstanding of Martha and the Vandellas' popular 1964 song *Dancing in the Street*. To the black community, it was a civil rights song—a call to join; a call for people to rise up. However, most of the white community merely enjoyed the song. They entirely missed or blissfully ignored the meaning of the words—*"It doesn't matter what you wear, just so long as you are there."*

But also less than two months after the Great Society speech of President Johnson, Barry Goldwater was nominated as the Republican candidate for President at the Republican National Convention at the Cow Palace in San Francisco. Goldwater, who many viewed as a "true conservative," was against progressive income taxation, thought that social security should be voluntary, and voted against the Civil Rights Act. With his nomination and with his abhorrence of many aspects of especially the national government, many believed that the Republican Party had (finally) become a conservative party. In their opinion, Goldwater's nomination represented the birth of the modern conservative movement. In the opinion of his followers, his suggestion that "extremism in the defense of liberty is no vice and moderation in the pursuit of justice is no virtue" was far more than a political battle cry. The modern conservative movement may have been merely nascent at the time, but the significance of Goldwater's nomination cannot be overstated. Ronald Reagan gave one of the nominating speeches and charged "Goldwater's Army" and the Young Americans for Freedom to go forth. Even though Goldwater was badly defeated in the November 1964 election, receiving only 39% of the popular vote, the modern conservative movement was launched. The political alignment of the Southern Democrats with the Republicans was cemented. Within less than two decades, Ronald Reagan would himself be elected President.

Even while campuses were starting to stir and America's youth were charting a new style, tone, and direction, the role and feelings of women were changing as well. In 1964, women had started to read about and seriously consider "the problem that has no name"—that set of feelings that had finally started to be put into words with the publication the prior year of Betty Friedan's *The Feminine Mystique*.

But the perspective of 1964 as a turning point is subsumed by the still lingering hopefulness and excitement in the country. Even after the crushing sadness of Kennedy's assassination just a few months earlier, that hopefulness and excitement was on display in February 1964 when Pan Am Flight 101 touched down at the recently renamed JFK Airport in New York. The Beatles arrived to the wild screams of the adoring crowds. The British Invasion had begun. Rock 'n' roll moved to a new level in both decibels and significance. And just two months later, Ford Motor Company put the Mustang on the road, while on the other side of the country, the then unknown Ken Kesey and his Merry Pranksters climbed on their bus and started on their own journey, or more precisely and in their words, on their own *trip*. The raucous decade of the 1960s had begun.

Nevertheless, as powerful and significant as the events of 1964 were, Modern America had—once again in the opinion of this author—begun earlier. The seeds had been laid and the nearly unalterable trajectory of our country had already been set.

In 1962 and although the signs of dissent were on the horizon, they were still hard to see because the spirit of Camelot infused in the country. John F. Kennedy, at the age of 43, was the youngest president ever elected, and the White House was alive with Jackie, John-John and Caroline. There was a certain magic to it all. Many thought of JFK as a "hero-president" whose deliverance was nothing less than "existential" as described by then young and star-struck Norman Mailer. America was, at once, both young and virile. America had no limits; not even the sky.

John Glenn may have been strapped and cramped in his Friendship 7 capsule, but in 1962 he listened to his friend Scott Carpenter whisper a simple "Godspeed, John Glenn" as the rockets of the capsule ignited. On that day in 1962, John Glenn became the first American to orbit the Earth. For NASA, for its astronauts, and for America, going to the moon *was* next.

A little closer to home, Andy Williams was singing his first signature hit, *Moon River,* and he could now be seen in more places thanks to America's launching of Telstar, one of our country's first telecommunications satellites—which, while no longer functional, is still orbiting the Earth, all lonely and only occasionally remembered. Milk cartons were not yet adorned with the faces of abducted children, and supervised "playdates" were still largely unheard of. Words like "crack" and "meth" and "stranger danger" were not yet part of the American vocabulary, but some things had changed.

In 1962, James Bond, a character who arose from Ian Fleming's typewriter ten years earlier in England, finally came to life with the premiere of the first of twenty-three Bond films, *Dr. No,* starring Sean Connery and Ursula Andress.[33] In the same year, two far more serious and real doctors received the Nobel Prize in Physiology or Medicine and launched the field of stem-cell science even though they could not at the time anticipate that 55 years later this science would remain the stubborn subject of both hope and controversy.[34] However, in 1962, all was not perfect. No year ever is.

In 1962, like now, the signs of both threat and change were everywhere. More Americans were starting to pull out their maps and find this place called Vietnam. Dominos was still just a board game in 1962, but some Americans were already wondering why we should be sending more "military advisors" to Vietnam, a place so far, far away. Even with the 1961 Bay of Pigs fiasco still in America's recent memory, in October 1962 the U.S. and the Soviet Union gambled with the future of the world as our navy took blockade positions around Cuba. The world survived, but we all knew that things had gone too far, that the end had been in sight.

Domestically, in 1962, there were early signs of other significant changes as well. James Meredith, accompanied by federal marshals, became the first black man to enroll in Ole Miss University. The USSC banned prayer in school. In Chicago, Robert Taylor Homes, the largest public housing project in the world—with twenty-eight, 16-story high-rise buildings—opened in Chicago as Mayor Richard J. Daley stood proudly under a banner that read "GOOD HOMES BUILDING GOOD CITIZENS."[35]

In the same year, Rachel Carson released her book, *Silent Spring,* "and in the process (lent) inspiration—to the then nascent global environmental movement."[36] Almost concurrently, Michael Harrington released his book, *The Other America,* which helped to reveal the plight of America's poor and helped to set the stage for Lyndon Johnson's War on Poverty.

Closing out a prior era, General Douglas MacArthur, as an aging soldier, delivered his famous and eloquent Farewell Address at West Point.[37] However, other voices—younger and with different, more strident tones— were starting to be heard as well. In Port Huron, Michigan, not that far from the hallowed, sacred halls of West Point, another very different type of society was beginning. With little notice at the time, the recently formed Students for a Democratic Society (the "SDS") ratified what it referred to as the Port Huron Statement calling for "a more egalitarian, horizontal society." The SDS would soon become recognized as one of the most vociferous and radical political organizations of the decade, and its formation was, in the opinion of some, the theoretical beginning of radicalization of U.S. college students.[38]

Society was changing in other ways as well. 40-year-old Helen Gurley Brown published *Sex and the Single Girl* to the shock and dismay—this earlier generation's variation of our "shock and awe"—of "decent society." The book quickly became a 1962 best seller.[39] And for reasons some of us still don't understand, Andy Warhol "vaulted Campbell's red-and-white tomato soup cans to icon status."[40] Meanwhile, in Hollywood, Marilyn Monroe, aka Norma Jean Baker, the last of the Hollywood love goddesses, was found dead by suicide at the age of 36, and Joe DiMaggio, though divorced from her at the time of her death, began his many decades of grief. He would never remarry, and he would live another 37 years.

A hop, skip, and a Central Valley away from Marilyn Monroe's Hollywood, George Lucas was just graduating from high school in Modesto, California. It would still be 15 years until Obi Wan and his crew would be born in 1977 and another several years after that before the real beginning of the age of personal computers, but by 1962 the first wave of video technology—television—had already started to change America dramatically.

By 1962, many American families had televisions. Most of the pictures were grainy, and the televisions usually had "rabbit ear" antennas sitting on top. Most of the shows were in black and white since color television (i.e. "living color" as opposed to, one guesses, the other kind of color) was just starting to become commercially available. But it was still an optional feature. Color televisions were still a luxury. They were owned by the rich people down the street. But even by 1962 televisions had become a part of American life. No one minded that programming still signed off each night and was replaced (usually at midnight) with a test pattern. But that, too, would soon change. In October 1962 late night television was introduced with Tony Bennett, Joan Crawford, and Rudy Vallee being the first guests on Johnny Carson's new "Heeeeere's, Johnny" *Tonight Show* which aired that month—and lasted for another 30 years; another 4,530 shows.[41]

For all of these reasons, 1962 is, among all of the valid candidates, the second-best candidate for defining the beginning of Modern America. But there are multiple reasons to go back a bit further to 1957 in order to find The Year that, in the opinion of this writer, is the unquestioned beginning of Modern America.[42] In was the year 1957 was The Year when the old yielded to the new. It was 1957 when Modern America was birthed. It was 1957 when the America which we still see and feel (and at times endure) began; and when the pace of American life, for better or worse, began to accelerate.

1957 - The Beginning of Modern America

"For most Americans — but not all — it was a time of perceived security and welcome stability."

As precisely as one can measure sea changes and detect epochal shifts, 1957 was the end of one era. And it was the beginning of another. It was in that year that the confusion, the wildness, and the most recent (and so far stubbornly irreversible) set of changes in American life began.

The Fifties were "an older, stiffer world, with Britain just (a few) years removed from food rationing and America still in an era of Kramdens, Eisenhowers, and finned Cadillacs."[43] While World War II was not a distant memory, at least some its horrors had been by then contained.

The dead had been buried. The survivors had come home. Squad by squad and company by company, the American soldiers—our fathers, uncles, grandfathers—were released from the military.[44] For the loved ones at home, the waiting along with the rationing of gas and rubber and nylon were over. The last of the other transitions from the war were over as well. The Nazi concentration camps had long since been shut down. The relocation camps in Europe had been emptied, and the long rebuilding of Europe had started. Even the tragic existence (albeit not the pain) of America's own ten Japanese internment camps had come to an end.[45]

The countries of the world had been divided and become realigned. The new ascendant powers were clear. The modern state of Israel had been founded on the southeastern shore of the Mediterranean. The Marshall Plan had been adopted. The Berlin airlift of 1948 was over. And in 1949 China had been "lost" to Communism.

The wartime alliance between the Soviet Union and the West had long since been dissolved, and "(a) new edgier, political era had begun."[46] America's monopoly of the atomic bomb was short-lived, and any hope of a post-war, unilateral domination by the West evaporated when the Soviet Union tested its own nuclear weapon in early September of 1949. With its own bomb unleashed, the resurgent Soviet Union, over the next decade, continued to impose its forced dominion over Eastern Europe. Especially after the Soviet tanks crushed Hungary's brief 1956 uprising,[47] the Soviet

Union came to be seen—correctly, by all and just as the Soviets wished—as a real threat, as a dominant and imposing world power.

It is not surprising that America had welcomed Eisenhower to the White House in 1953. Americans were busy getting on with their own lives. There was an almost literal need for Eisenhower's calm style and well-earned confidence.

Just a few months after Eisenhower entered the White House, Josef Stalin, after having purged millions of his fellow citizens to their exile and eventual death, finally died himself—further and more finally closing the War Years.[48] In 1956, Nikita Khrushchev had delivered his "Secret Speech" to the Soviet's 20th Congress in which he denounced Stalin's purges and the personality cult that had arisen around Stalin himself. By 1957, the Kremlin shuffle was over with the rigid, square Georgian face of Josef Stalin replaced by the seemingly less intimidating and almost disheveled visage of Nikita Khrushchev. However, in November 1956, just six weeks before the beginning of Modern America, Khrushchev used his now-infamous phrase "we shall bury you" for the first time. Americans were crudely reminded that while the Cold War was closing out its first full decade, the new war was still real. It was still dangerous.

Despite the implications of Khrushchev's statement,[49] both the Soviet Union and even the prospect of nuclear war remained largely outside the view (or at least beyond the focus) of most American families. The decision of the United States to start developing the far more powerful H-Bomb had been made at the beginning of the decade, but it was left to Edward Teller and his team of scientists to move from the atomic bomb to the hydrogen bomb. However, at the time, in 1957, most Americans happily chose to remain largely and almost consciously ignorant of the nuclear threat. The threat seemed distant, and parents were at peace with, or at least accepting of, their children duck-n-covering under their desks at school.

No one was digging bomb shelters in their backyards yet. No one was getting scanned at the airports or patted down at our borders. There were no nuclear missiles in Cuba, and for the most part the Russian Bear seemed a long way away. It was, for some, terrifying when in October 1957 Russia launched the world's first orbiting satellite, Sputnik, across the bow of our terrain and our psyche. But despite the unsettling stir of the "Russian eye in the sky," the Americans of 1957 remained confident and steady in their embrace of willing ignorance and their sense of long-earned bliss. Most Americans only took casual and passing notice of the Treaty of Rome, which was signed that year by six European countries and by which the history-defying European Economic Community came quietly into being.

Americans were happy that many of the prior decade's tensions had seemed to ease. They were happy that both the reality and the paranoia of the House Un-American Activities Committee investigations had long since expired. By 1957, it had been seven years since Joe McCarthy, at the time a deservedly little-known Senator from Wisconsin, had given his now-infamous "I have here in my hand a list" speech in Wheeling, West Virginia. By 1957, the ensuing "circus" and the "carnival-like four-year spree of McCarthy's accusations, charges, and threats" was fading into the past.[50] In almost a pathetic coincidence, McCarthy himself died of acute alcoholism in May of 1957. And while certainly not rejoicing in the passing of even that American, America was happy that his carnival had closed. Americans were pleased that the fears had seemed to lessen; that the pains had started to fade; and that some of the scars had started to heal.

America was happy that World War II and, by 1957, the Korean War had ended. World War II obviously remained etched in the collective memory of the country and the personal memories of all of its citizens grieved at the loss of another 54,200 American soldiers in Korea, the Forgotten War,[51] but Americans were tired of war. By 1957, they wanted to move on. And they did. They had no idea that Vietnam was coming. They had no idea that they were, once again, merely in a brief period of respite.[52]

Thus, for most Americans—but, as will be discussed, not all—it was a time of perceived security and welcome stability. However, these types of historical summaries can be dangerous. They can easily be misread as odes to days gone by, as misplaced, almost nostalgic remembrances of previous (good) times. However, be assured that this description of 1957 is *not* so intended. There is no delusion that 1957 was a perfect year or the beginning of some kind of perfect era. It was not. No year ever is. In fact, in 1957, there were many problems. There was the stench of widespread discriminations and the sadness of poverty—especially rural poverty. But it is also true that by 1957 millions of veterans, with their young families in tow, had taken advantage of the GI Bill. And it cannot be denied that they had survived much, and by 1957 many of them re-emerged—energetic, enthusiastic, and educated.[53]

Americans were holding jobs, building families, buying houses, and mowing lawns. They were making up for lost years. They were enjoying an economy characterized by job security and relative economic equality. The terrors of polio abated with the introduction in 1957 of Jonas Salk's vaccine.

Looking back, it seems that 1957 was also one of the last years in which the traditional systems and allocations of authority were still holding. For most Americans, the nation in 1957 remained a well-ordered society in an orderly era even for young people. The Everly Brothers sang their gentle *Bye Bye Love*, and although the world didn't know it then, it would still be another five years until a rock 'n' roll song even won a Grammy when Chubby Checker's *Let's Twist Again* did so in 1962.

In the late 1950s parents still lived in oblivious comfort, and none of their children "did their own thing" even though *The Wild One* with Marlon Brando had been released in 1953, followed by James Dean's *Rebel Without a Cause* in 1955. But no worry. They were still seen as just movies. The real world for most Americans was still more sedate, more controlled, and more controllable. The concept of "teenagers" had not yet fully come of age, and hardly anyone noticed that Jack Kerouac finally got around to publishing his book *On the Road* which he had written several years earlier. Young people were still "largely accepting of the given social covenants,"[54] and even though many Americans (and especially many American women) knew that it wasn't always so, families sat together, without debate or discord, and watched *Father Knows Best* on TV every week.

Just as the traditional family structures and the authoritarian roles of parents still dominated, the American dream especially in the context of its economic aspects was coming true for many Americans—or at least for many white Americans. These families were beginning to possess a sense of the economic security that had been so cruelly eviscerated by the Great Depression and so long postponed by war.

For many Americans, or at least, once again, for many white Americans, there seemed to be a real chance of having a good life. The bounce of optimism was nearly everywhere, and Henry Luce and others started talking about "the American Century."[55] From today's perspective, from the perch of our hyper-accelerated, attention-deprived, multi-tasking, techno-wired life, the country at the dawn of Modern America was moving at a much slower, so-yesterday, snail-mail pace. But part of the wonder of 1957 is that it wasn't that long ago. Modern America *is* new. Modern America *is* recent.

It was an almost naïve, uninformed, and non-reflective period. But it made sense. It felt good. There were deadly serious exceptions, but overall it was almost an era of general good will, and by 1957 and for many Americans, economic security was morphing into something even better—affluence. Few could see and even fewer would accept the seemingly counterintuitive notion that affluence could have a downside. Few people knew (or cared) that John Kenneth Galbraith up in Massachusetts was writing his soon-to-be-famous book, *The Affluent Society,* outlining the adverse consequences of affluence. Leave it to an ivory tower egghead to ruin the day. Instead, in 1957 and for most Americans, affluence was still both good and uncomplicated. The parents of the late 1950s had no idea that Galbraith's book would soon be read by their children — all warm and ensconced years in their college dorms. They had no idea that conformity was soon to be condemned or that so many aspects of American life were soon to be challenged.

To the contrary, the 1960s hadn't arrived yet. In 1957, young boys were still wearing Davy Crockett coonskin hats. *Leave It to Beaver* premiered on TV. On Sunday nights, families gathered around their new televisions to watch the *Ed Sullivan Show* or to listen to the real-deal Uncle Walt introduce the week's *Wonderful World of Disney.*[56] Sid Caesar was wrapping up his dominance as the King of Comedy but through his incredible crew of writers including Mel Brooks, Woody Allen, Neil Simon, and Carl Reiner—another generation of laughs seemed to be assured and on the way.

Television was watched as a family, and it was watched without the interruptions of cell phones and text messages. Instead, just like their one

TV, most families had only one phone and the phone was almost always in the other room, tethered to the wall.

In 1957, politics had a tarnished, but not buffoonish, history. Like now, politicians were rarely seen as the most honest bunch, but politics was still deemed an honorable profession. They did their jobs and, within limits and with some conspicuous exceptions, they could be believed. The press was not disdained. Reporters wore hats, smoked relentlessly, and drank too much. However, by and large, they too seemed to do their job. They collected the news, and they reported the news.

Thus, the late 1950s was indeed an "era of general good will and expanding affluence, (and) few Americans doubted the essential goodness of their society."[57] Americans weren't all grumpy and entitled or as "pushy and self-aggrandizing"[58] as many believe we are today. Americans were not all frustrated and angry as we are today. Americans were not in-your-face cocky or whatever-dismissive as we are today. Certainly, disagreements were real and tensions existed, but cynicism was not seen as a badge-of-honor virtue. To the contrary, in 1957, motives were not doubted as a matter of practice. There was an almost arrogant, but assuring, comfort in having added the words "under God" to the Pledge of Allegiance a few years earlier. Though some intellectuals look back and see "the early seeds of Christian nationalism,"[59] for most Americans there was an almost happily routinized life. Peace. Order. Finally. And it was back then—in 1957—that, maybe not knowing fully why, Congress ordered with little objection, notice or fanfare, that the words "In God We Trust" be for the first time emblazoned on U.S. Currency.

Sports, like today, were big, but it was a less "professional" era. There was a more personal relationship between the fans and the players. The NBA on television was still in its infancy. The league had made its network television debut during the 1955–1956 season,[60] and it was starting to attract more interest due to the introduction of the game-accelerating 24-second rule and the ascendance of the amazing Boston Celtics when Bill Russell joined Bob Cousy and Coach Red Auerbach in 1957.[61] College football games and rivalries were enjoyed and off-radar legacies were getting started such as when Frank Rose, the newly elected President of the University of Alabama flew to Houston, Texas in order to invite Bear Bryant to "come home." Bryant did so the next year and started his incredible 25 years of coaching.[62] Nevertheless, in terms of national dominance as a sport and especially as a television sport, both college football and the NFL—looking back—were also still in their infancy. The first major NFL television contract wasn't even signed until 1962, and, more importantly, college football teams commanded far greater fan loyalties and interest than did those of the NFL. Interestingly, it would be another 50 years before college football coaches routinely made more than state governors.[63]

Although off-camera and out of the spotlight, 1957 was also a big year for boxing. In that year, Angelo Dundee, while in Louisville, Kentucky with light heavyweight champion Willie Pastrono, got a call from a young man named Cassius Clay, who in 1964 would change his named to Muhammad Ali upon his joining the Nation of Islam. Ali and Dundee were soon to become "one of the most successful pairings of trainer and athlete in modern sport" ever launched.[64] But none of this—basketball, football, the rivalry of Bill Russell and Wilt Chamberlain, the teaming of Dundee and Ali—compared in 1957 with the dominance of baseball.

In 1957, baseball, and only baseball, remained the only real national pastime. Kids from Kansas to New York tracked batting averages. They knew every score. They counted every RBI. Both Pee Wee Reese and Ted Williams were in the sunset of their careers, but in 1957 Pee Wee was still at shortstop and Ted Williams was still at bat hitting an extraordinary .388. Many of the players were idolized, and some of them—especially Mickey Mantle—were gods. It was said of Mantle that "even his aura had an aura."[65] Young singers like Buddy Holly had their fans, and there was the usual gaggle of Hollywood stars. However, for most American boys, baseball players were the real American celebrities. They were the real American heroes. Their partying was not the stuff of scandal. It was the stuff of legend.

Baseball was serious business, but there was an easy fun to it all as well, such as the night in May 1957 when Mickey Mantle, Yogi Berra, Hank Bauer, Whitey Ford, and their wives all went out to celebrate Billy Martin's 29th birthday. They went to see Sammy Davis, Jr. at the Copacabana, which "billed itself as 'the hottest club north of Havana,'" (a place you could travel to back then). Before the night ended, a melee broke out. Noses got broken when a bunch of upper Manhattan guys started in with "little black sambo" catcalls at Sammy. But times were different. No arrests were made. No breaking-news reports were aired. No lawyers got involved. Instead, the players' legends grew.[66] It was just a different era.

Other realities were also in play by 1957. The very nature of transportation was changing. Travel was getting easier. By 1956, construction of the interstate highway system, the "largest public works system since the Pyramids,"[67] had begun. By 1957, the network of roads could finally be imagined even though the project technically wouldn't be finished until 1992 with the completion of I-70 through Glenwood Springs, Colorado. Mass transit was so common and so widely used that it wouldn't be until 2011 that the 1957 ridership number of 10.4 billion trips would again be approached.[68]

And air travel had arrived as well. It was new, easy and friendly. Everyone went directly to the gates to wave goodbye to their loved ones or to greet arriving friends. There were no security checkpoints. No luggage inspections. No personal pat-downs. As of 1957, fewer than 1% of Americans had travelled internationally by air, but non-stop transcontinental air travel was becoming routine. Air travel had not yet kickstarted the destination travel and hospitality business, but it had changed the conduct of American business. The nation had gotten smaller. The East and the West had gotten closer.

Also in 1957, diesel power on U.S. railroads for the first time eclipsed steam power. But because of the burgeoning of air travel, Americans no longer needed to rely upon the slow chug of the trains even if it was a "diesel chug" rather than a "steam-powered" chug.

The ease and speed of travel had other ramifications as well. Although in hindsight it was probably inevitable, it was still a shock when both the New York Giants and the Brooklyn Dodgers moved to California in 1957. The Brooklyn Dodgers played their last game at Ebbets Field on September 24, 1957, and some say that Brooklyn never fully recovered. Three years later, on February 23, 1960, Ebbets Field was demolished to make room for an apartment building.

The Brooklyn Dodgers are but one obituary entry for 1957. Obituaries are tempting, but normally dubious, markers for identifying the end of any era. But 1957 was a peculiar year. Many lives from the prior eras came to an end. Many chapters of American history seemed to close. Bugsy Moran died of lung cancer. Elliot Ness died broken and penniless since his book, *The Untouchables,* was not released until the summer after his death. Oliver Hardy and Humphrey Bogart died. Even the Hudson Bay Company, after 275 years of operation, closed its doors.

And conversely there were births and new beginnings. In 1957 Hanna-Barbera began productions. Both the Marriott and Hyatt hotel chains opened their doors. After five years of trying different motel designs (various room sizes, gift shop, swimming pool, "Kids Free," TVs "In *Every* Room"), Holiday Inns finally went public. Vail Ski Resort opened for the rich—but the rich were envied, not vilified. It would be decades before the rich were derisively referred to as "the 1%."

To the delight of kids and the confusion of parents, a little company named Wham-O Manufacturing introduced the Frisbee. A store named Children's Supermart changed its name to Toys-R-Us and began selling toys. Franchising started to accelerate, and McDonalds was still selling its 15-cent hamburgers. At the time, McDonalds only had 40 restaurants while today it doubles as a Disney cross-marketing store. As of 2015, it had 36,339 restaurants worldwide and 14,339 in the U.S. alone—or 287 per state for anyone who is still counting. Just outside of Minneapolis, Minnesota, America's first covered and heated mall was opened. For better or worse, it was all starting to come together.

And possibly the most important and best remembered of all, the '57 Chevy, the "hot one," was born. With no intended offense to Mustangs or Corvettes, the '57 Chevy still owns American automobile history. It remains "the most popular used car in history."[69]

In Nevada, Merv Adelson's Paradise Homes were selling as fast as they could be built during the booming, early Mob days of Las Vegas.[70] Far away, quietly, without flair, and without any expectation of the Vegas-style bow-downs, Warren Buffett was just getting started. In that year and at the age of 27, he bought a five-bedroom stucco house in Omaha,

Nebraska—where he still lives today. And about 710 miles to the southeast, another young man, but the near antithesis of Buffet, was also buying his first home. He would name his palatial home *Graceland,* and Elvis Presley would call it home until his death 20 years later.

On the West Coast, Bill Gates and Steve Jobs, born within eight months of one another, were still toddlers just hanging around and waiting to excel in pre-school. Sixteen-year-old Bob Zimmerman was up in Hibbing, Minnesota living with his parents. It would be another two years until he started using the name Bob Dylan. On the other side of the water in Liverpool, another sixteen-year-old, John Lennon, met Paul McCarthy. Shortly thereafter they started playing together in their newly-formed band, the Quarrymen.[71] A few years later they would change their name to The Beatles.

The Modern American world was anticipatory, alive, exciting, innovative, and energetic. Americans didn't yet realize how much the world would shrink over the next decades, but in Greenwich, England in 1957 Daniel Day-Lewis, who 55 years later would become America's visual personification of our own Abraham Lincoln, was born. More historically important was the birth of another child. In that same year and many continents away, Osama bin Laden was born in Riyadh, Saudi Arabia, the ninth son of a billionaire construction magnate. Decades later, near the other end of Modern America, this child would bring fear, cause destruction, and introduce the word *jihad* to America. However, in 1957, the birth of Osama bin Laden held little significance. The rise of terrorism couldn't be imagined. Most Americans hadn't even noticed or couldn't come to believe that all was not well. The failure to notice was not, for most Americans, a matter of convenience or an instance of stubborn and willful blindness. The answers were simpler and literally more obvious.

At the beginning of Modern America, in 1957, most Americans—or at least their parents and grandparents—had gone through the Great Depression. They had gone through World War II. They had buried uncles and brothers. Most Americans had already lived through too much. They held too many and too recent memories. It is not even surprising that many

Americans, consciously or otherwise, decided to start anew, and by 1957 the 122.7 births per 1,000 women birth rate among U.S. women was higher than at any time before—or since.[72]

The younger, newer members of the Baby Boomer generation were in their childhoods. They had only heard stories from their parents and from their grandparents. They had not lived them. They were unaware that they were in familial proximity with and blood descendants of what would be later referred to as the Greatest Generation.[73]

Intellectually, most Americans—and certainly the Americans in the Negro communities as they were referred to then—knew that all was not perfect. Americans knew that there were poor people in our country. Americans knew that minorities, especially in the South, were oftentimes ignored or mistreated. They knew that their children were beginning to show signs of insolence, indulgence—and worse yet, independence. They knew about McCarthyism, about the Cold War and the Russkies and the Hungarian Revolution. They knew about the stunning failure of Edsel, and they would eventually find out that the Africanized bee had been released in that year. But, largely, in 1957, at that time and for that brief moment in American history, most Americans were anxiously willing to believe that much was good. From the perspective of those who had lived through the Great Depression and the War Years, it wasn't hard to see, to feel, and to believe that the 1950s were better.

This perception was due to many other factors as well. It was due partly to the fact that communities were tighter. The country was smaller. In 1957 there were (only) 172,000,000 Americans—about 53.9% of America's population as of 2015. But the benevolent and widely shared perception that things were better was also partly due to the fact that a measure of public civility was commonplace. Civility was expected. Manners still mattered. The Age of Frustration and the Politics of Anger, which have so dominated our lives and our culture for the last two decades of Modern America, would have been unthinkable in 1957.

Yet despite the then smaller population, America seemed—to itself— to be in other ways big. In 1957, the world itself was a vastly different place, but America's financial and economic position in the world was unrivaled.

It would be 25 years until it seemed like everything was "Made in Japan," and 50 years until it seemed like everything was "Made in China."

Even though America's GDP in 1957 was a mere $461.0 million (only 2.6% of today's GDP!), America possessed one-half of the world's wealth; more than one-half of its productivity; and two-thirds of the world's machines. "The rest of the world [lay] in the shadow of American industry."[74] Americans welcomed and embraced this long-awaited era of national economic dominance and personal job security. Possibly because they so strongly sensed, correctly, that the nation was both powerful and on the move, Americans neither noticed nor cared about the relative lack of innovation. Americans weren't bothered by the relative absence of booming entrepreneurship. Americans weren't bothered by what would today seem to be poor rates of return. Both America's dreams and its expectations were more modest.

Americans also didn't notice the relative absence of consumer choice. To the contrary, they were enthralled with the multitude of new things that *were* available for the first time and for *them*—houses, cars, dishwashers, washers and dryers, air-conditioning, televisions, and above all—*hope.* In sum, there was a certain, albeit overstated and partly misplaced, contentment and even enthusiasm in America. For all things American.

In 1957, Eugene Burdick and William Lederer were busy writing *The Ugly American.* By 1958, it was a best seller. However, most Americans weren't bothered by the title. Most Americans weren't offended by the thinly veiled condemnation of America's arrogance overseas. Even fewer Americans at the time noticed the prescient setting of the book—Southeast Asia.[75] But the cracks in the wall were there. As in any society as diverse— racially, ethnically, culturally, religiously, educationally, economically—as America, there were problems. Looking back, the problems were there then; just as they are today. Everywhere.

Some of the cracks in the wall were not inherently matters of serious social concern. Instead, they were mere matters of evolution; almost matters of preference and taste. For example, in 1957, the 16-piece Count Basie Band was still playing at the Waldorf-Astoria Hotel in New York, but most of the country was moving (far) beyond and away from Big Bands. On

January 6, 1957 more than 60 million Americans, 82.6% of the American television audience, watched Elvis Presley's third and final performance on *The Ed Sullivan Show* or, more precisely, two-thirds of his performance since he was only shown above his waist in order to conceal his "gyrations." The new American bands were smaller. The band members were younger. They didn't wear tuxedos. They practiced in their parents' garages. The clarinets had been traded in for electric guitars. Presley's top hits in the year were *Jailhouse Rock* and, appropriately named for the emerging teenager generation, *All Shook Up*. The battle between the Big Bands and rock 'n' roll was on. And rock 'n' roll won. There was no easy bridge between Count Basie and Bo Diddley. Folk singers and balladeers put up a fight, and Count Basie, God bless him, performed with his orchestra until his death in 1984. But, again, rock 'n' roll won.

The music was hot, lively, and new. And it was a different kind of music. A respectable young 15-year-old Canadian named Paul Anka had spent most of the 1950s "living a romantic dream—touring with Chuck Berry, Little Richard, (and) Eddie Cochran," and in 1957 he released his first signature hit— "Diana."[76] But for all of the traditional respectability, even if it could be defined, it was obvious that Chuck Berry and Ozzie Nelson were never going to be good friends. They came from different places. They had different interests. More importantly, they were headed in different directions. And by 1957, some parents had started to notice. Some parents had started to (futilely) disapprove. But Modern America still came. It came all at once. And it came from everywhere.

The British invasion of The Beatles wouldn't arrive until the early 1960s, but in 1957 *American Bandstand*[77] was born, and a whole new sub-generation was born. They were called "teenagers." They hadn't yet been radicalized, but they had become identifiable as both a market and almost as a generation unto themselves. Even more importantly for our consideration of Modern America, many of them had tasted relative luxury. They had had an easy life. They had been indulged. The word "affluenza" had been coined as early as 1954, but it gained little attention until PBS' 1997 documentary entitled *Affluenza: The All-Consuming Epidemic.*[78] Even then, however, the word wouldn't enter into common parlance until 2015 when it was used and abused by a defense lawyer in Texas to supposedly explain the behavior of a young man named Ethan Couch who killed four people and injured nine more with his drunk driving. But in 1957, things were simpler, and affluenza was not seen a condition of America's youth. Instead, in 1957, teenagers were merely the first derivative beneficiaries of America's new wealth. They had their own unique characteristics apart from their age. Their expectations weren't tempered by memories. And their hopes and dreams weren't burdened by patience.

Other issues, other cracks in the wall were more serious, far more serious. Other issues were of bigger consequence, and they were not mere matters of familial structure or generational association. They were not mere matters of musical preference or taste. They were matters of right and wrong, good and evil. These issues lay just below the surface of busy, bustling America.

In 1957, even amidst the consumerism, confidence, and enthusiasm for all things American, the ferment of change was starting. The winds of change were everywhere. Collectively, the continuing relevance of many of these issues today is another reason for identifying 1957 as the beginning of Modern America.

In that year, about 60 years ago now, Senator Estes Kefauver held Senate hearings about the activities of American pharmaceutical companies. With far less fanfare but arguably with greater long-term significance, two scientists in La Jolla, California reported that fossil fuels increased atmospheric carbon dioxide. In that year the U.S. Surgeon General for the first time reported a link between smoking and lung cancer. And it is believed by some that it was in 1957 that a young Marine, while stationed near a CIA base in Atsugi, Japan, was recruited as a spy by the Soviet KGB. A mere six years later that former Marine, Lee Harvey Oswald, would scar this nation's history and leave America stricken with grief upon his assassination of JFK.

And then, as now, the issues and moralities of race and civil rights were dominant. On a spring day in April 1947, 28-year-old Jackie Robinson had broken the color line and started at first base for the Brooklyn Dodgers. A year later President Truman by Executive Order had mandated the integration of the U.S. military. In 1954, the USSC in the case of *Brown vs. Board of Education* went far further and tossed out the disingenuous "separate but equal" reasoning of 1896's *Plessy v. Ferguson*. By a powerful vote of 9-0, the USSC ordered American public schools to be integrated. The momentum changed, and the inevitability of the civil rights movement began.

On December 21, 1956, just four days before Christmas and eleven days before the beginning of 1957, the city of Montgomery, Alabama finally agreed to permit the integration of the city's buses. As a result, Montgomery's Negro community agreed to end the year-long boycott that had begun when a 42-year-old married, church-going seamstress named Rosa Parks had refused to yield her seat on city bus to a white man. She had been arrested for that refusal and the long and momentous bus strike led by the young Reverend Dr. Martin Luther King, Jr. began. Shortly thereafter, Rev. King along with Ralph Abernathy, Fred Shuttlesworth, and T.J. Jemison,[79] with little notice outside of the black community, founded the Southern Christian Leadership Conference (the "SCLC"). The SCLC selected the Rev. King as its first President, and within a mere six years, he would be delivering his "I Have a Dream" speech in Washington, D.C. to the gathered hundreds of thousands.

Also in 1957, then Senator Lyndon Johnson, largely for his own political, aspirational reasons, ramrodded a civil rights bill[80] through Congress. While this legislation is almost more famous for the 24 hours, 18-minute filibuster of Senator Strom Thurmond, the longest-filibuster in the history of the U.S. Senate, and while the legislation made little meaningful change in and of itself, it was significant in several respects. First, it was the first civil rights bill since 1875. Second and more important, it presaged the powerful civil rights legislation that would be enacted within the next decade.[81]

As further evidence that things were amiss in 1957, it was in this year that President Eisenhower nationalized 1,000 paratroopers and 10,000 Arkansas National Guard troops in order to force Gov. Orval Faubus to step aside and allow nine brave black children to enter Little Rock Central High School.

There were still many more issues on the horizon that would soon start to be addressed—such as the rights of women, the draft and the anti-war movements of the 1960s, the scourge of drugs, the rise of crime, and the waves of alternative and counterculture lifestyles that would soon be introduced into American life. And all of these reasons, 1957 has been selected by this author as the good and right place to begin our understanding of Modern America. For it was then that things started to become astir.

Closing

*"We tend to learn more easily from that which is,
or at last seems, closer to our today."*

It is hoped by this author that the logic and reasoning of the concept of Modern America as an identifiable period in America's history may be, at least for a moment, accepted by you, the reader. The limitation of these books to including only the Memorable Words of Modern America as so defined from 1957 to 2015 is, to an extent, risky and arbitrary, but it is needed to achieve even a degree of brevity.

The concept of Modern America also reflects the reality and necessity of relevance. In other words, there is some point, some date, some year in our nation's history that is so far back in time that the relevance of that time—and the Memorable Words of that time—are too distant and too weak. Memorable Words, if too far distant in time, become matters of curiosity more than matters of utility.

But there are obvious, even looming, exceptions. The placement of the Modern America time boundaries as used in these books is not intended to dismiss the import of the 4,400 words of the Constitution or the passion of Lincoln's Gettysburg Address or FDR's "day in infamy" speech. Of course, this country still draws from such words. This country still struggles with the meaning of "free speech," "the right to bear arms," "due process," and "equal protection."

This country still has much to learn from the words of our early leaders and commentators, but we do live more in the present. There is a cold, almost unfair, reality in acknowledging that Bill Gates and Steve Jobs feel much closer to our lives than Thomas Edison or Eli Whitney. But it is true.

We tend to learn more easily from that which is, or at last seems, closer to our today. It is in that spirit and for those reasons that these books present the words of Modern America—the words that are "closer to our today."

CHAPTER 5

Attribution, Limitations and Exclusions

Attribution, Citations, Context and Explanation

Precision of attribution and the inclusion of citations, context and explanation of the Memorable Words in these books are critical, indeed uniquely important in 21st century America. As discussed above, we live in an age of caution, distrust, and skepticism. Truth is elusive, and facts themselves are seen by some as being almost negotiable. It is neither this author nor, in all likelihood, you, the reader, who has introduced the concepts of "fake news" and "alternative facts" into our national conversation. But these phrases, too, are now a component of our history, an influence upon that which we know or think we know and upon that which we believe or think we believe.

As a result, our history has become harder to learn, harder to remember. It is hoped that a review of the Memorable Words of our country—with special attention to when they were said or written and by whom—can in a small way play a part in our rediscovery of common ground.

For all of these reasons and with respect to any of the Memorable Words cited in these books, it is recognized that attribution is desired and context is useful. Every effort has been made to achieve provide such attribution and context.

These books recognize the dual inconsistencies of Memorable Words. On the one hand, knowing whence we came, whether through the study of our nation's Memorable Words or through some other approach is greatly important. On the other hand, study of these Memorable Words will never, of itself, be enough. Insufficient though it may be, however, the presentation of these Memorable Words may serve as a start for the rebuilding our national commonness; our national community.

To that end, there is great importance to knowing not only "what" was said but also by whom and in what context. These books and the Memorable Words contained herein will not untie all of the Gordian knots of American life, but they may help. Because attribution is so important and because the identification of the speaker or writer can, in itself, enhance or diminish the meaning—indeed, in some cases, even the honor—of the words so spoken or written, in nearly all cases, the identity of speaker or writer has been noted.

Apart from the book titles, movie titles, movie lines, and commercial advertising slogans, only those Memorable Words that have been spoken or written with known or traceable origin are included. Where known and in addition to the identity of the speaker, the contexts of the words are included because context can help to reveal the intent and the initial audience of the speaker.

Thus, relentless effort has been made to include attributions and reference citations. For the convenience of the reader and to assist in the reader's evaluation of the entry itself, citations, if available, are included immediately after each entry. In the case of cited writings, article titles and headings are rarely included because normally they do not of themselves assist the reader in understanding the subject, scope or even purpose of the article. In some instances, secondary attributions have been made as in the case of words spoken or written by an individual and then made public during the course of a later-published interview.

In a few rare instances, the identity of a speaker or writer and an explanation of the words' initial context are indeterminable. In these rare instances when no attribution is possible, the statement is identified as "Unknown." There are also instances in which attribution is both impossible and unnecessary, or will be left by this author to the shallow province of bored linguists.

For example, the phrase "have a nice day" was a part of this country's conversation long before the phrase was cleverly injected into the script of *Forrest Gump*. The same is true of many of the catchphrases, chants, and slogans discussed above. It is normally impossible and largely unimportant to identify exactly who originated such phrases as the words "The Whole World Is Watching" in the 1960s, or "Thank You for Your Service" in the 1970s, or "Voodoo Economics" in the 1980s, or "We Are the 1%" in the 2000s, or "Black Lives Matter" in the 2010s. In these cases, the importance of the words resides in their resonance and the duration of their repetition and echo.

Similarly, exact precision of the Memorable Words from political statements and political campaign speeches are almost beyond tracing. Such words, even though they are Memorable Words, are oftentimes used in many iterations due to the speaker's shifting intent, error or even fatigue and due to the restatement of such words at multiple sites and sometimes by multiple candidates and speakers.

There is also one matter of general historical context that is included for each year and that should be here noted. That matter of general historical context is the U.S. population as of each given year. This population number is expressed both as an absolute number and as a percentage of the U.S. population as of 1957, the beginning year of Modern America.

There are several reasons for such focus upon the American population even though, admittedly, many other aspects of American life evidence, if not in certain respects trigger, changes in the nature, strength, and unity of our national community. Such other aspects include the relative religiosity of the population, the median age of our population, the racial or ethnic composition of our population, the nature and quality of our education, the unemployment rate and the general state of our economy. However, the population data, as a ready reference point, is unique. It is presented because the numeric population and the cumulative population changes over the last six decades may be the single largest objective reference point for the changes in our society. Examples of the impact of population abound—increasing diversity, the opportunities for and the temptations of anonymity, the almost definitionally greater detachment from the mass of our fellow citizens, and diminishment of one's perception that one can make a material difference through one's behavior or efforts with respect to any aspect of societal behavior.

All citations and footnotes are included at the end of each respective volume of these books, and a listing of General Source Materials is included at Appendix B.

Limitations and Exclusions

Certain types of words and phrases are outside the scope of these books. The categories of such *non-included* words, albeit theoretically "memorable words," are described below.

Limitation to American Speakers and Writers Within the Years of Modern America

This assemblage of Memorable Words, with few exceptions, is limited to those words spoken or written by American speakers or writers[82] within the tightly defined timeframe of Modern America—those 58 years from 1957 to 2015.

Thus, even though their words may be deservingly "memorable," obviously not included in these books are the speeches of Socrates, Pericles, Cicero, Plato and the other ancient Greeks; the words of a thousand kings and queens and pontiffs; or the writings of the philosophers of the Renaissance and Reformation Periods. Closer to home but still likewise excluded, are the words of earlier Americas—Patrick Henry's Give-Me-Liberty-or-Give-Me-Death, George Washington's Farewell Address, Abraham Lincoln's Gettysburg Address, or, for that matter, the more recent inspirational speeches of Teddy Roosevelt, the comforting words of Franklin Delano Roosevelt, or even Lou Gehrig's touching words of departure to his adoring fans at Yankee Stadium on July 4, 1939.

There are only two exceptions to the exclusion of non-American speakers or writers. The first exception consists of a few instances when the words, the Memorable Words, were directed to the American community and spoken on American soil. Examples include Soviet Premier Nikita

Khrushchev's infamous "we shall bury you" remark repeated during the course of his address to the General Assembly of the United Nations in New York in 1962, and more recently, German President Angela Merkel's 2012 remarks about the role and limits of public finance. The second exception, also rare, is when the Memorable Words, although written by foreign authors, have been widely read, reviewed, and discussed in America as in the instance of the writings of French economist Thomas Piketty and the British cultural and religious theoretician Christopher Dawson.

Thus—and excepting only those few instances described above—these compilations of the Memorable Words of Modern America are limited almost entirely to the words of Americans speaking or writing during the course of Modern America. My apologies to the brilliance of the rest of the world for the narrowness of my linguistic skills and for my subservience to brevity. However, in defense, for purposes of narrowing the pool of words to be considered, and especially because one of the purposes of these books is to present a more enjoyable and approachable methodology for studying our nation's recent history, these limitations have been deemed necessary.

Legislative Excerpts

These books contain no excerpts from legislation. There are several reasons for this. First, it is a matter of volume. Every year more and more laws and regulations are enacted or promulgated by this country's many levels of government—from the legislation of the U.S. Congress to the executive orders of our country's President; from the legislative or administrative bodies and agencies of our 50 states to the ordinances of this country's nearly 3,200 counties or county equivalents and 19,500 cities,[83] not to mention the thousands of quasi-governmental bodies and regulatory authorities.

While the importance of such legislative enactments and regulatory promulgations is recognized, rarely do their words become, in and of themselves "memorable." To the contrary, most of the precise words remain forever buried amidst, for example, the 7,655,000 words now contained in the 78,691 pages of the Federal Register—which itself has expanded thirtyfold from the skimpy 2,620 pages of the Federal Register of 1936.

Similarly, all such legislation and pronouncements are literally too wordy. Consider just one body of legislation—the Internal Revenue Code. As of 2015, it consisted of 2,412,000 words, and this number ignores the millions more words contained in the thousands of tax-related case opinions.[84] The sheer volume of such words is, to a degree, incomprehensible. Many would argue that there is a problem when the words of a country's tax code are a multiple of the 788,280 words of the *King James Bible* or even the 560,000 words of Tolstoy's weighty *War and Peace*. The volume of such words in its own way forms a triumvirate of I's—Impressive, Intimidating, and Insulting—or is perhaps just silly. But more importantly in the context of these books, though legislation and regulations are certainly important, rarely do their stilted words stand out individually, in any way or to any degree, as "memorable."

For this reason, words are not excerpted from legislation or regulations. In a few instances, however, there are references to certain Memorable Words spoken or written in the context of the enactment of certain key acts of legislation such as the 1965 Civil Right Act and the revolutionary adoption of Medicare.

Campaign Gaffes and Personal Blunders

The object of these books is not to ridicule any person, party, or association. Even though campaign gaffes and personal blunders are a common staple of headlines and news cycles, they are normally soon forgotten. They are rarely of lasting and historical significance. Such gaffes or blunders, no matter how humorous and no matter how important they may seem at the moment are rarely included as Memorable Words. The few exceptions are those instances when such gaffes or personal blunders are particularly revealing or consequential such as Republican Presidential candidate Gerald Ford's 1976 remark during his Presidential debate with Jimmy Carter that "there is no Soviet domination of Eastern Europe" or Gary Hart's imprudent 1987 challenge to the press to come "follow me around"—after which they did and which, in turn, led to Hart dropping from the Presidential race.

As suggested by the reference to "campaign" gaffes, this limitation is especially relevant in the context of American political elections where candidates are expected to speak endlessly and ad nauseum. In these contexts, many misstatements are made. Many off-the-cuff comments, of at best passing interest and with only momentary significance, are reported by the press. Again, neither such campaign gaffes and personal blunders nor the responses of other candidates or the comments of news reporters are included unless they became uniquely consequential and cataclysmic to the candidate's ideas or campaign or unless the statement encapsulates a wide consensus of perception about a candidate or movement.

This author recognizes that it is arguably unfair even in these few instances to include these consequential and cataclysmic words as Memorable Words due to the relentless and onerous scrutiny and reporting of nearly every utterance of major candidates during the course of long and grueling campaigns. Nevertheless, some such statements are included below, whether fairly or unfairly, because they can have a significant and lasting impact upon political discussions and upon the success or failure of a given candidate, party, or movement.

Commentators, Columnists, Writers, Bloggers, and Secondary Source Writings

Normally, the words of commentators, columnists, writers, bloggers, and other such secondary source writers are not included, but there are exceptions—especially in those instances where such writers have presented or memorialized a line of reasoning or social position with unique clarity, brevity, and poignancy. One example of such an included writing is Harold Evans' brilliant summary of the national impact of the Vietnam War upon American life, politics, and international relations.

This general exclusion of the words of most commentators, columnists, writers, bloggers, and secondary source writings is an admittedly dangerous, but necessary, delineation since unless carefully honored, both the wisdom and babble of the millions of such parties—and especially with the splintering of the news in the 1980s and the advent of the Internet in the 1990s—could be inadvertently included, or, as the case may be, excluded.

Song Titles and Lyrics

Despite the fact that song titles and lyrics may be the poetry of Modern America, neither song titles nor lyrics are included as Memorable Words.

This is partly due, once again, to the need for brevity. But it is also due to the unique burden and preclusion of copyright restrictions.

More importantly, this exclusion is also due to the fact that the familiarity and reach of both the titles and lyrics of songs are normally generationally limited. Millions of copies of hit songs may be sold, but they are normally, almost definitionally, "*intra*-generational." There are some exceptions, but songs largely remain the separate and proud province of each generation, a part of each generation's formative and collective memory—but not beyond that. They do extend further. It may be regrettable, but it is a fact that songs normally remain, forever, separately appreciated, and separately owned by each generation.

Public Words – Not Private Words

With very few exceptions, the Memorable Words here included are only public words—words spoken, written, and delivered into and for the country's public conversation.

Private words—those spoken to only one's spouse or children, to one's small circle of friends, or to coworkers or associates—should so remain: private. Though they may be significant and revealing, by their nature and by the intent of the speaker or writer, they are not the stuff of our national conversation.

Fictional Works

The last major exclusion relates to words of fiction. As with song titles, song lyrics, and private words, the Memorable Words seldom include words excerpted from works of fiction. Although such words can obviously possess great insight, relate deep truths, have sustaining relevance, and contribute to the social discourse of our era, they are rarely included in these books.

This is an admittedly questionable line of demarcation, but such words are excluded because they are by definition "spoken" by fictional characters—and there are enough Memorable Words spoken in the realm of reality.

Linguistic Debates

The challenges of precision must also be addressed. These books are offered with a serious commitment to precision and accuracy, but the author recognizes the epistemological sleuthing that is often associated with debates about the exact wording of certain statements. While precision and accuracy are greatly desired, and certainly can be, in some circumstances, critical, some writers with far too much time on their hands engage in long debates about the insertion of "uhs" and "ahs" in a vain attempt to determine *exactly* what was said.

Thus, the last exception, or at least qualification and acknowledgement, is that although every attempt has been made to be precise about these Memorable Words, in certain instances, linguistic debates continue to swirl about the exact words spoken (and in a few rare cases, even the exact words written).

For two examples, there has been a lingering debate, first, about the exact words of Neil Armstrong as he descended upon the Moon and, secondly, about the exact wording of Rodney King's famous exhortation in the midst of the 1992 Los Angeles riots— "Can we all get along?" vs. "Can we all *just* get along" vs. "*Can't* we all *just* get along."

It is neither my place nor my desire to minimize these debates, but they are beyond the scope of these books. In those few instances where such debates exist, the most commonly accepted version of the Memorable Words are included. Every attempt has been made to assure accuracy, but the exact wording debates are happily left to someone else's writing with the use of CSI Linguistics.

Repeated or paraphrased statements present particular problems. As noted above in the context of political campaign speeches, such words are oftentimes repeated with or without minor word changes, even by the same speaker. In this context, politicians in the repetitive delivery of their campaign stump speeches deliver similar, but constantly revised, statements. In these instances, the speaker's words may slightly vary from day to day—reflecting intentional modification or tailoring for a specific speech audience or resulting from a mere instance of misspeaking and inadvertence due to the exhaustion and word fatigue of the candidate or the candidate's surrogate. In the course of this assemblage of Memorable Words, these variations are recognized and accepted; however, the essence of the statement remains and the minor word variations are not noted herein.

Closing

The next and last introductory chapter explains the format of the organization and presentation of the Memorable Words as presented in each year's chapter.

CHAPTER 6

Organization and Presentation of Memorable Words

Three Volumes –
Chronological Organization by Year

*T*he *Memorable Words of Modern America* are presented in three volumes: Volume I (1957–1976); Volume II (1977–1993); and Volume III (1994–2015).

Within each volume, the entries are organized by year. Book titles; award-winning movies; famous movie lines; the current U.S. population (both as an absolute number and as a percentage of the 1957 U.S. population of 172,000,000); the most widely-viewed or critically-acclaimed new television shows and last season television; major commercial advertising campaigns and slogans; and catchphrases, chants, and slogans are placed at the beginning of each year as shown on the Presentation Format Page at Section 6-E at the end of this chapter.

The memorable words of speakers and writers for each year are then presented in the chronological order those words were first spoken, written or published. In those few instances where anonymous entries are included, they are placed at the end of the entries for that year in which it is commonly believed such statements were first made.

Digression: The Reasons the Memorable Words Are Not Presented by Topic or Subject Matter

The original drafts of these books categorized and presented these spoken or written Memorable Words by subject category—business, commerce, and the economy; international relations and foreign policy; politics, political campaigns and governance; law, litigation and justice; health, education, and religion; and so forth. However, it was determined that in the context of especially the later years of Modern America such topical categorization is impossible. The reason for this impossibility of categorization is because for worse—*not* for better or worse—nearly everything in America has become unduly politicized.

Many Americans remain in a happy and positive spirit of disagreement about a few things such as their choice of music or their favorite sports or sports teams, but the list of such non-politicized subjects is short. Instead, most aspects of American life have been politicized—from the shows we watch to the books we read; from the friends we keep to the clubs we join; from the beers we drink to the cafe lattes we order; from burgers to sushi; from NPR to Rush Limbaugh. Americans now judge often and quickly—watching for the use of code words or the display of friend-or-enemy symbols.

Passionate opinions are held with respect to the manner of one's dress; the parenting of one's children; the exercise of one's religion. A person's opinion about medical marijuana is deemed to reflect a political view not a medical option. Right-to-life is now a matter of politics and litigation—no longer a matter of one's personal or religious beliefs. The list is endless. "Us versus Them" is the evolved mantra of Modern America.

Thus, because of the politicalization of nearly everything, topical categorization of these Memorable Words rose from a matter of challenge to one of impossibility. As a result, the Memorable Words are presented in the only way feasible—in the order they arrived—chronologically.

Information about Speakers and Writers

Immediately following the Memorable Words of speakers and writers, the identity of the speaker or writer is presented together with a brief summary about the context of the words so spoken or written and, in some cases, the consequences thereof and other related information.

All Memorable Word entries can be readily located through the use of the Reverse Index of Memorable Words—By Speaker or Writer and Key Words, which is included at Appendix A. Also included there with respect to speakers and writers is a summary description of such persons, including (i) the person's date and place of birth (and, if applicable death) so that the reader can quickly determine, if desired, the approximate age of the speaker at the time when the words were spoken or written and, relatedly, the likely generational association of the speaker or writer, and (ii) a summary identification of the person's primary profession and major public accomplishments, and, in some instances, the reason(s) for his or her fame or notoriety.

Dating of Statement or Writing

As noted above, the date when the Memorable Words of speakers and writers were first spoken or written is identified as accurately as possible since that date is used as the basis for the ordering and placement of the words. The importance of such dating also lies in the fact that when a statement was made or written is, in many cases, an integral part of the context of such words.

However, it must be noted that such dating itself presents a number of challenges. To the extent determinable, the date the statement was initially made by the speaker or the writer is the date normally used. But there are exceptions.

Excerpted statements from articles are included based upon the date of the article's original publication. Similarly, titles and excerpts from books are included based upon their year of publication, and titles and quotes from movies are included based upon their year of release.

In a few instances, such as in the case of remembrances of an event or a period of time, the statement is included in the year of the occurrence of the event to which it refers (or in a few cases, at the beginning of the decade such as remarks about the 1960s.) The reasoning is that when a statement is made—even if years —about a specific earlier event or period, the statement is in some instances more appropriately entered in the year of such event or period.

For example, the words of Franklin McCain, one of the Greensboro Four, speaking years later about the civil rights sit-ins that he, with others, initiated in 1960, are included in the early 1960s. Similarly, the later-year words of the Olympic athlete John Carlos discussing his and his teammate Tommie Smith's raising of Black Power salutes at the 1968 Olympics are included in the year 1968 rather than the year of his quoted remembrance.

The Appendices and Format of Each Year's Chronological Presentation Sources and Citations, Abbreviations, and Additional Information

A considerable collection of supporting materials, details, and information are set forth in the Appendices. Parallel appendices are included in each of the volumes of this series.

The Appendices are set forth below.

Appendix A: A Reverse Index of Memorable Words—By Speaker or Writer and Key Words. (1957–1976).

Appendix B: General Source Materials sets forth a listing of most of the general sources used in assembling these Memorable Words.

Appendix C: Schedule of Abbreviations defines those abbreviations that are used in multiple instances in these books.

Appendix D: Grammy Award Winners for Best Spoken Word Album (1959–1976) is a list of the winners, by year, of the Grammy Award for Best Spoken Word Album.

Appendix E: Seminal Books (1957–1976).

Appendix F: Pulitzer Prize-Winning Books for History, General Nonfiction, and Fiction (1957–1976).

Appendix G: *The New York Times* Best Sellers Lists.

Part 1: *The New York Times* Best Sellers List (Nonfiction) (1957–1976)

Part 2: *The New York Times* Best Sellers Lists (Adult Fiction) (1957–1976)

Part 3: *The New York Times* Best Sellers Lists for Adult Fiction - An Analysis of America's Reading (1957–2015)

Appendix H: The Best and Worst Book Titles of Modern America (1957–1976).

Appendix I: The 25 Books Most Widely Held in U.S. Libraries.

Appendix J: The Books Most Frequently Banned or Challenged in Modern America.

Appendix K: Presidential Campaign Themes and Identification Slogans (1960–1976).

Appendix L: Corporate Slogans and Advertising Taglines—A Selection of the Most Famous (1957-2015).

The format for the chronological presentation of each year's Memorable Words is set forth on the following page.

Format
(Subject Year)

<u>Seminal Books</u>

<u>Pulitzer Prize for Fiction</u>

<u>Pulitzer Prize for General Nonfiction</u>

<u>Pulitzer Prize for History</u>

<u>*The New York Times* Best Sellers List (Adult Nonfiction) –</u>
Book with Most Weeks as No. 1 Best Seller

<u>*The New York Times* Best Sellers List (Adult Fiction) –</u>
Book with Most Weeks as No. 1 Best Seller

<u>Academy Awards Best Picture</u>
Winner:

Other Nominees:

<u>*PrettyFamous'* Best Movie of the Year</u>

<u>Best Movie Line(s) of the Year</u>

<u>*(Year)* U.S. Population: ______________</u>
(Compared as a Percentage to the U.S. 1957 Population of 172,000,000: ____%)

<u>Television Shows</u>

Most Widely-Viewed Television Shows

Rank	Show Name	Years of Series (Excluding Reruns)	Show Type	Estimated Audience (In MMs)	Audience as Percentage of U.S. Population
___	*(Name of Show)*	*(Years)*	*(Genre)*	*(Audience)*	*(Percentage)*
	Cast:	*(Names of Primary Cast Members)*			
___	*(Name of Show)*	*(Years)*	*(Genre)*	*(Audience)*	*(Percentage)*
	Cast:	*(Names of Primary Cast Members)*			
___	*(Name of Show)*	*(Years)*	*(Genre)*	*(Audience)*	*(Percentage)*
	Cast:	*(Names of Primary Cast Members)*			

Widely-Viewed or Critically-Acclaimed New Television Show(s)

(Name of Show) - (Years)—(Genre)
(Names of Primary Cast Members)

Last Season Television

(Name of Show) - (Years)—(Genre)

<u>Major Commercial Advertising Campaigns and Slogans</u>

<u>Catchphrases, Chants, and Slogans</u>

<u>Memorable Words from Speeches, Books, Writings, and Other Sources</u>

PART II

The Memorable Words
of Modern America
(1957–1976)

CHAPTER 7

1957–1959

The End of the 1950s
and
The Beginning of Modern America

Year 1957

Seminal Books

Atlas Shrugged
by Ayn Rand

Rand's fourth, last, and longest novel advocates reason, individualism, capitalism, and—possibly most important historically—the assertion of the counter-productivity of governmental regulation and coercion. These themes are presented in the context of a mystery thriller and through the use of the memorable character of John Galt—or more precisely, the question of "Who is John Galt?," the book's mysterious protagonist. The exploration of why some of society's most prominent industrialists have abandoned their fortunes in a futile response to aggressive governmental regulations is one of the most notable and fascinating components of the story. But Rand also addresses sobering personal questions about motive and truth. In the work, "[t]welve years in the making," Rand delves deeply into personal and philosophical questions such as whether "the pursuit of profit (is) a noble enterprise or the root of all evil… (and) whether reason (is)… absolute (and) (whether) faith (is) an alternative source of truth."[85] Set in near-future America, *Atlas Shrugged* is presented in the format of a mystery novel about, in effect, the limits and influences upon the human spirit and the factors defining success or failure in life.

On the Road
by Jack Kerouac

Kerouac's book has come to be known as the bible of the Beat Generation of the late 1950s—in a sense, the prose accompaniment to Allen Ginsburg's epic 1955 poem, *Howl!* At the time of its publication, Kerouac's book shocked both the public and the literary establishment. Over the ensuing years, however, it came to be seen as a prescient and revealing inquiry into the struggles faced by an "outsider" finding his or her place in American society.

The Cat in the Hat
by Dr. Seuss (Theodore Geisel)

Although *Horton Hears a Who!* was written two years earlier, it was the release of *The Cat in the Hat* that first attracted wide national attention to Geisel's writings under the pen name Dr. Seuss. *The Cat in the Hat,* a children's book written and illustrated by Geisel, was written partly in response to the then-ongoing debate about the ineffectiveness of more traditional reading books for children such as William Gray and Zerna Sharp's *Dick and Jane* series, which had been used as reading primers since the 1930s. *The Cat in the Hat* was entirely different. With its repeated use of monosyllabic words and humorous illustrations, the book received immediate critical acclaim. Geisel went on to write more than 60 books, including *How the Grinch Stole Christmas* (1957) and *Green Eggs and Ham* (1960). By the time of Geisel's death in 1991, Dr. Seuss books had been translated into more than 20 languages, with more than 600 million copies sold worldwide.

The Hidden Persuaders
by Vance Packard

In *The Hidden Persuaders*, Vance Packard, a journalist and social critic, offers a sharp critique of the undue, dangerous, and increasingly sophisticated exploitation of the consumer's needs. The book also explores various psychological techniques, such as subliminal (i.e. "subthreshhold") advertising, used by businesses, advertisers, and marketers to manipulate the expectations of the consumer and to induce, enhance, and, indeed, literally create consumers' demand for products. As noted by Mark Geif in his excellent short essay written upon the 50th anniversary of the publication of Packard's "75-cent paperback," "as more goods [started coming] to the supermarket shelves [in the 1950s] advertisers decided they could no longer just sell products. Instead, they need(ed) to create brands and brand 'personalities.'"[86] Americans started identifying products by their branding —the Marlboro man, the Jolly Green Giant, and Ronald McDonald. Packard was one of the first writers to identify, with severe criticism and alarm, Madison Avenue's willingness and capacity to manipulate the buying habits of "ordinary folks." Interestingly, Packard also wrote about the application of these techniques to the political process, whereby politicians would be elected based upon their "personalities" rather than their policies. In the context of politics, just as in the context of business, messaging would devolve from focus groups, speeches would be crafted based upon market research, and even the political conventions would be carefully and skillfully choreographed.[87]

The Jacksonian Persuasion: Politics and Belief
by Marvin Meyers

The Jacksonian Persuasion is an American social and political history book focusing upon the transformative Jacksonian Age of the 1830s. The book is viewed as critical to understanding the turmoil associated with America's transformation from an agrarian society to an ever more industrial and capitalistically based society during the late 18th century and early 19th century. The book's central thesis is that the people of the Jacksonian Age "were aware of the social implications of the economic changes in which they were involved, and their reaction was ambivalent. They could not resist the new (modern) economy of corporations, credit, and financial manipulation, but neither could they abandon their image of the Old Republic … derived from the Jeffersonian idyll of a nation of yeoman farmers."[88]

Pulitzer Prize for History

Russia Leaves the War: Soviet-American Relations, 1917–1920
by George F. Kennan

The New York Times **Best Sellers List (Nonfiction)**
Books with Most Weeks as No. 1 Best Seller
The FBI Story: A Report to the People
by Don Whitehead (17 weeks)

Baruch: My Own Story
by Bernard M. Baruch (15 weeks)

<u>*The New York Times* Best Sellers List (Adult Fiction)</u>
<u>Book with Most Weeks as No. 1 Best Seller</u>

Peyton Place
by Grace Metallious (23 weeks)

<u>Academy Awards Best Picture</u>

Winner: *The Bridge on the River Kwai*

Other Nominees: *12 Angry Men, Peyton Place, Sayonara, Witness for the Prosecution*

<u>*PrettyFamous*[89] Best Movie of the Year</u>

12 Angry Men

<u>1957 U.S. Population: 172,000,000</u>

<u>Television Shows</u>

Most Widely-Viewed Television Shows

Rank	Show Name	Years of Series (Excluding Reruns)	Show Type	Estimated Audience (In MMs)	Audience as Percentage of U.S. Population
1.	*Gunsmoke*	1955–1975	Western	18.1MM	10.5%
	Cast:	James Arness - Amanda Blake - Dennis Weaver			
2.	*Danny Thomas Show*	1953–1964	Comedy	14.8MM	8.6%
	Cast:	Danny Thomas - Marjorie Lord - Annette Funicello			
3 .	*Tales of Wells Fargo*	1957–1962	Western	14.8MM	8.6%
	Cast:	Dale Robertson - Jake Ying - William Demarest			

Widely-Viewed or Critically-Acclaimed New Television Show(s)

Leave It to Beaver (1957–1963)—Family Comedy Show
Jerry Mathers – Barbara Billingsley – Hugh Beaumont - Tony Dow
American Bandstand (1957–1987) —
American Music-Performance-Dance Show
Hosted by Dick Clark

Last Season Television Show(s)

I Love Lucy (1951–1957) —Comedy
Lucille Ball - Desi Arnaz - Vivian Vance – William Frawley
(No. 2 Top TV Show of All Time—*TV Guide*)

<u>Major Commercial Advertising Campaigns and Slogans</u>

"Have a break ... Have a Kit Kat"
Kit Kat

"Look, Ma, no cavities!"
Crest Toothpaste

**<u>Memorable Words from Speeches, Books, Writings,
and Other Sources — 1957</u>**

*"This conference is called because we have no moral choice,
before God, but to delve deeper into the struggle—and to do so
with greater reliance on non-violence and with greater unity,
coordination, sharing, and Christian understanding."*

January 10, 1957. The Reverend Dr. Martin Luther King, Jr. addressing the attendees from ten states at the founding meeting of the Southern Christian Leadership Conference ("SCLC") in Atlanta, Georgia. Rev. King, Bayarde Rustin, Ella Baker, Rev. C. K. Steele, Fred Shuttlesworth, Rev. Ralph Abernathy and the other attendees sought to build upon the Montgomery, Alabama Bus Boycott victory that had ended just weeks earlier on December 21, 1956 assuring the desegregation of the Montgomery bus system. The SCLC was formed in order to coordinate nonviolent direct actions and protests across the South. At the first convention held in Montgomery, Alabama in August 1957, the name was formalized and the adoption of nonviolent mass action was selected as "the cornerstone of (the SCLC's) strategy."[90] The organization selected Rev. King as its President, and he shortly thereafter announced plans for a national tour during which he would speak at over 200 locations. Other historic events with civil rights implications were simultaneously occurring in 1957. In June 1957, Count Basie's Band became the first African

American band ever to perform at the Starlight Room at the Waldorf-Astoria Hotel in New York. In July 1957, Althea Gibson became the first African American ever to win a major tennis tournament when she won the Wimbledon Tennis champion. In August 1957, and after much heated and ponderous debate including a 24-hour, 18-minute filibuster by Senator Strom Thurmond of South Carolina, the U.S. Congress enacted a first-step Civil Rights Act. Nevertheless, it was with the formation of the SCLC that the more formal, more organized, more determined, and more coordinated civil rights movement began.

January 21, 1957
Second Inaugural Address of Dwight D. Eisenhower
(President of the United States 1953–1961)

*"We live in a land of plenty, but rarely has this earth
known such peril as today."*

•••

*"The divisive force is International Communism
and the power that it controls.
The designs of that power, dark in purpose,
are clear in practice."*

•••

*"We seek peace, knowing that peace is the climate of freedom.
And now, as in no other age, we seek it
because we have been warned,
by the power of modern weapons,
that peace may be the only climate possible
for human life itself."*

•••

*"We recognize and accept our own deep involvement
in the destiny of men everywhere.
We are accordingly pledged to honor, and to strive to fortify,
the authority of the United Nations.*

For in that body rests the best hope of our age for the assertion
of that law by which all nations may live in dignity."

...

"So we voice our hope and our belief that we can help
to heal this divided world.
Thus may the nations cease to live in trembling
before the menace of force.
Thus may the weight of fear and the weight of arms be taken
from the burdened shoulders of mankind."

January 21, 1957. From the Second Inaugural Address of Dwight D. Eisenhower. Because the constitutionally-mandated January 20th inauguration day fell on a Sunday (as it did again with Ronald Reagan's Second Inauguration in 1985), President Eisenhower took his oath of office in a private White House ceremony on January 20th and a second oath of office on this day at the U.S. Capitol as a part of the inaugural ceremonies that were commemorated before 750,000 spectators followed by a three and one-half hour parade. Eisenhower took his oath of office from Chief Justice Earl Warren, and Vice President Richard Nixon took his oath of office from U.S. Senate Minority Leader William F. Knowland.

"The aftermath of nonviolence is the creation
of the beloved community,
while the aftermath of violence is tragic bitterness."

April 7, 1957. The Reverend Dr. Martin Luther King, Jr. in his speech, *Birth of a New Nation*, delivered in Montgomery, Alabama. Rev. King was the "transcendent figure" of the civil rights movement who, with many others, shaped the early philosophy of the movement. Rev. King, following the path and tactics of Gandhi, was committed to nonviolence, and was, until the time of his assassination in 1968, the undisputed first among many dedicated equals—from clergymen such as Vernon Johns, Fred Shuttlesworth, Ralph Abernathy, Wyatt Tee Walker, James Bevel, and Jesse Jackson; to the students, organizers, activists, and protestors such as the Greensboro Four and the Freedom Riders; to the other leaders such as Julian Bond, James Farmer, Medgar Evers, James Meredith, and Roy Wilkins; and even to celebrities such as Paul Robeson, Muhammad Ali, Harry Belafonte, Dick Gregory, and Eartha Kitt—some of whom also paid dearly for their commitment and devotion to the cause of civil rights.[91]

"Rock 'n' roll"

...

"Medieval types of spontaneous lunacy"
and
"Pre-historic rhythmic trances."

May 4, 1957. The phrase "rock 'n' roll" had been introduced a year earlier by Alan Freed, the American disc jockey who is oftentimes referred to as the "father of rock 'n' roll." Although Freed's career ended abruptly as result of the payola scandal of the early 1960s, in the late 1950s Freed—like the new and emerging generation of Americans known as "teenagers" —embraced and promoted the sound of rock 'n' roll. Through his playing and promotion of this racial crossover music, Freed also helped bridge the gap of segregation by introducing the music of African American artists to young, white Americans. The ominous words about "spontaneous lunacy" and "rhythmic trances" are the warnings of a long-forgotten, but often-quoted psychologist about the powerful, presumably hypnotic influence of this new type of music.

Television Line
"Lucy, I'm home."

May 6, 1957. The signature, ritualistic announcement of Ricky Ricardo (played by Desi Arnez) upon his arrival home each day which anchored the television situation comedy *I Love Lucy*. The show first aired in 1951. It ended on this day, May 6, 1957—but has remained on television ever since. As of 2015, it remained the longest-running program to air continuously in some television markets including Los Angeles, California. The show starred Lucille Ball, Desi Arnez, Vivian Vance, and William Frawley. Along with *The Honeymooners,* the *I Love Lucy* show is often identified as one of the foundational television comedies that influenced the format and presentation of decades of situation comedies in a 30-minute time slot.

I Love Lucy, Ozzie and Harriet, Lassie, and a bit later, *Leave It to Beaver*, all presented an America that was unrecognizable by the close of the next decade, but these shows' influence upon a generation of today's older Americans remains indelible.

> ***"The central question that emerges …***
> ***is whether the White community in the South is entitled***
> ***to take such measures as are necessary to prevail, politically and***
> ***culturally, in areas where it does not predominate numerically?***
> ***The sobering answer is Yes.***
> ***The White community is so entitled because, for the time being,***
> ***it is the advanced race."***

August 24, 1957. With these disappointing words, William F. Buckley, Jr. argued in his editorial entitled "Why the South Must Prevail" that the white race should prevail as the dominant and domineering force in the South because it is the advanced, preeminent, superior, and entitled race. Buckley, who had founded the *National Review* just two years earlier, was, by many and varied accounts, a decent, well-liked, brilliant, and widely-admired man—a conservative intellectual who "gave some order and literary polish to (the) cacophonous jumble" of early conservatism. Thus, to a degree, the above statement may best be understood, albeit possibly only conveniently so, as evidence of the still-crippled ethos of the late 1950s in the context of race.[92]

"A new era of motoring has begun"

September, 1957. The words of George W. Romney, the President of the American Motor Corporation and father of 2012 Republican Presidential candidate Mitt Romney, introducing the new 1957 Rambler V8, the nation's first compact car. Although the car's name was better than its design, and although production ceased in 1969, the 1957 concept of compact and sports cars resonated with American consumers. This is further evidenced by the wild popularity of the Thunderbird, which was unveiled a year later at the International Automobile Show in New York. "Muscle cars" would remain in stable demand for decades and modern

SUVs would start to dominate the market in the 1980s, but the early era of compacts such as the Rambler foretold the demise of monster cars with huge hoods and tailfins.

"Here come the niggers."

September 23, 1957. The ugly chant of the white crowd outside of Little Rock, Arkansas' Central High School as four young African Americans approached the school's entrance for admission in September, 1957. These four young people were, in fact, journalists, but they were beaten up anyway. The diversion enabled the nine young black children to walk into school despite the blustery objections of Arkansas Governor Orval Faubus. In this sad manner, Central High School was finally integrated behind the bayonets of military troops who had been federalized by the direct order of President Dwight Eisenhower. The nation's attention was focused upon Little Rock that fall, but little more occurred. The troops were withdrawn from the city in November, and "no other racial incident occurred at the gradually integrated school."[93] However, the events at Little Rock foreshadowed the years of stubborn Southern objections to integration that were still to come. Insistent upon getting his way and reveling in his few moments on the national stage, Governor Faubus closed the high school for the entre 1958-1959 academic year on the grounds that such closure was necessary to avert further violence. Upon the petition of Governor Faubus, a federal judge later agreed to suspend the Little Rock desegregation plan for another two years, however the judge was eventually overruled by the insistent, "with-all-deliberate-speed" order of the USSC. Possibly even more telling is the fact that Governor Faubus went on to become a six-term governor of Arkansas. He did not retire from that office until 1967—a full decade later.[94]

"Beep, beep, beep…"

October 4, 1957. The simple, repetitive, lonely, and terrifying sound of the Soviet Union's Sputnik satellite as it circled the globe every 96 minutes. The beeping lasted only 21 days. Then the batteries ran out, and the sound stopped. The satellite itself, a simple 184-pound aluminum sphere with four antennae, circled the Earth for only 92 days in all before burning up upon re-entering the Earth's atmosphere. Nevertheless, the impact of the Soviet Union's successful launch of Sputnik was huge. The satellite could be seen as it passed America, and America was awakened. Almost instantly the Space Race, just one dimension of the Cold War, began. Within six months, the Eisenhower Administration formed the National Aeronautics and Space Administration (later "Agency") ("NASA"), which President Eisenhower wisely placed under civilian control. Within 18 months, NASA had selected its first seven astronauts[95] in the U.S.' contemplation of manned space flights. However, regardless of these efforts and achievements, during those weeks in October 1957 when Americans could look to the sky and see Sputnik (meaning "companion" in Russian) circling overhead, there were heightened concerns about both the intentions and the capacities of the Soviet Union—and those concerns would continue for decades.

"Say it ain't so, say it ain't so" and ***Shooting "O'Malley, Twice"***

October 8, 1957. The first chant was the reaction of thousands of Brooklyn Dodger fans to club owner Walter O'Malley's announcement that he was moving "his" baseball team to Los Angeles. The Boys of Brooklyn—Roy Campenella, Jackie Robinson, Pee Wee Reese, Gil Hodges, Don Newcombe, Duke Snider et. al. —had lost their home. The chant was a paraphrasing of the memorable headline written by Charley Owens in 1920 after a grand jury returned an indictment against "Shoeless" Joe Jackson in connection with the Black Sox World Series scandal. Brooklyn fans never forgave O'Malley's move of the Dodgers, as evidenced by the second line above the 2007 HBO documentary *Brooklyn Dodgers: The Ghosts of Flatbush.* In the movie, a Brooklyn Dodgers fan is asked who he would shoot if he were given a gun with two bullets and placed in a room with Hitler, Stalin, and O'Malley. Without hesitation, the fan said that he would shoot "O'Malley, twice." It was of little interest or comfort that O'Malley's moving of the Dodgers from Brooklyn to Los Angeles was partially due to the inadequacies of Brooklyn's Ebbets Field and O'Malley's frustrations in trying to locate another New York-area stadium site. In a larger sense as well, the move also signaled the reality that the country had gotten smaller. Non-stop transcontinental airline travel was becoming routine. The scheduling of baseball of games was no longer tied to the dictates of railroad timetables. Because of air travel and because television broadcasting and national news allowed fans to "follow" their teams everywhere, teams could be located much farther apart than ever before. But never try to tell that to a Brooklyn Dodger fan. Adding more pain and a greater sense of loss, this day, October 8, 1957, was also Brooklyn Dodger Jackie Robinson's last day in the major leagues.

"Big Atomic Plant Near Pittsburgh Supplying Power"

December 18, 1957. The above-the-fold, front-page headline of *The New York Times* announcing the opening of the world's first full-scale atomic electric power plant.[96] The Shippingport Atomic Power Station remained in operation until 1982—nearly 25 years. Including research and development, the construction of the plant cost about $120 million, with most of the initial expenses paid by the federal government. However, by the early 1970s, years before Three Mile Island (1979) and the far more serious nuclear plant disasters at Chernobyl (1986) and Fukushima (2011), it became evident that nuclear power would never constitute a major source of U.S. electrical power as was initially expected. Wholly apart from health and safety concerns (including especially nuclear waste storage issues), nuclear power was beaten back—first, by the continuing availability of relatively cheap, carbon-based alternatives, and later by the availability of natural gas resulting from technological improvements in hydraulic fracking.

Year 1958

<u>Seminal Book</u>

The Affluent Society
by John Kenneth Galbraith

One of the stunning features of John Kenneth Galbraith's book is not its correctness or lack thereof, but its continuing relevance to the issues being debated in the Modern America of the 21st century—now 50 years later. For example, one of Galbraith's themes focuses upon the meaning of economic security. He observed that certain parts of America's private sector were becoming wealthy but many Americans and certain parts of America's public sector remained poor due to the lack of needed social and physical infrastructures and the continuing burden of income disparities. Other themes of Galbraith's book, which were, in the opinion of this author, more clearly explained in his 1967 book, *The New Industrial State*, include the concepts (i) that much of American consumer demand was not organic—and, to the contrary, the new (consumer) demands within American markets were increasingly being created by the tools and machinery of advertising and marketing; (ii) that measures of production and output, such as gross national product, were poor measures of our country's social and personal well-being; and (iii) most controversially, that America must shift from a private production economy to a public investment economy by eliminating poverty, by investing in public schools, and by enhancing a "New Class" of Americans consisting of less monetarily driven citizens such as schoolteachers, professors, and surgeons. In light of the rampant consumerism and the highly competitive, even Darwinistic, markets of the early 21st century, it could be argued either that Galbraith's theories may have been correct or that his theories had limited impact upon the course of the American economy and markets.

<u>Pulitzer Prize for Fiction</u>

A Death in the Family
by James Agee (Posthumous Award)

<u>Pulitzer Prize for History</u>

Banks and Politics in America
by Bray Hammond

**<u>*The New York Times* Best Sellers List (Nonfiction) –
Books with Most Weeks as No. 1 Best Seller</u>**

Only in America
by Harry Lewis Golden (13 weeks) (Tie)

Please Don't Eat the Daisies
by Jean Kerr (13 weeks) (Tie)

**<u>*The New York Times* Best Sellers List (Adult Fiction) –
Book with Most Weeks as No. 1 Best Seller</u>**

Anatomy of a Murder
by Robert Traver (29 weeks)

<u>Academy Awards Best Picture</u>

Winner: *Gigi*
Other Nominees: *Auntie Mame, Cat on the Hot Tin Roof,
The Defiant Ones, Separate Tables*

<u>*PrettyFamous'* Best Movie of the Year</u>

Vertigo

<u>Best/Most Memorable Movie Line of the Year</u>

"Life is a banquet, and most poor suckers are starving to death!"
Rosalind Russell portraying the irrepressible Auntie Mame in the Morton
DaCosta's comedy movie of the same name.

<u>1958 U.S. Population: 174,900,000</u>

(Compared as a Percentage to the U.S. 1957 Population of 172,000,000: 101.7%)

Television Shows

Most Widely-Viewed Television Shows

Rank	Show Name	Years of Series (Excluding Reruns)	Show Type	Estimated Audience (In MMs)	Audience as Percentage of U.S. Population
1.	*Gunsmoke*	1955–1975	Western	17.4MM	9.9%
	Cast:	James Arness - Amanda Blake - Dennis Weaver			
2.	*Wagon Train*	1957–1965	Western	15.9MM	9.1%
	Cast:	Ward Bond - John McIntire			
3.	*Have Gun Will Travel*	1957–1963	Western	15.1MM	8.6%
	Cast:	Richard Boone			

Widely-Viewed or Critically-Acclaimed New Television Show(s)

The Donna Reed Show (1958–1966) – Comedy

Donna Reed – Carl Betz

Dr. Joyce Brothers Show (1958–1963) – Talk show

Host: Dr. Joyce Brothers

Memorable Words from Speeches, Books, Writings, and Other Sources – 1958

"They're going for two"

January 12, 1958. These words, sometimes heard as the most exciting words in college football, referred to the two-point conversion rule which was adopted by the NCAA on this day. This rule change was the first major rule change since 1912, and under the new rule a team can score two points after a touchdown by running the ball into the end-zone rather than (merely) kicking it through the uprights. The AFL followed this rule through the 1960s, but it was not until 1994 that the NFL finally adopted the two-point conversion rule.

"The schools are in terrible shape, what has long been an ignored national problem, Sputnik has made (education) a recognized crisis."

March 24, 1958. *Life* magazine from its five-part series (March 24 – April 21, 1958) entitled "The Crisis in U.S. Education." Over the course of these issues, *Life* compared U.S. teenagers and their Russian counterparts. In the first issue, the article addressed the need for more and better teachers. In the second issue, noting that "U.S. teachers are too few and too hard-pressed to do a nation-size job,"[97] the article insisted that more emphasis be placed upon meeting the needs of exceptional students. The series also examined alternative ideas for the teaching of math and science and closed with a focused argument outlining the need for greater involvement of and commitment from parents in sharing the tasks of education. A *Life* editorial written later in the year commented that "(U.S.) schools are in terrible shape ... the Spartan Soviet system is producing many students better equipped (to address) the technicalities of the Space Age."[98] This series of articles and editorial were merely the beginning of a long line of commissions, reports, papers, and commentaries written over the course of Modern America about the importance of education and the failures of the U.S. public school system. Each report was dutifully written and delivered sometimes with considerable fanfare, attention and alarm—such as with the release of the 1983 "Nation at Risk" report.[99] However, in the end, it is not clear that anything has dramatically changed. Increasingly over the later years of Modern America, more parents have turned to home schooling and to charter, alternative, and parochial schools. More alarming, however, is the fact that more than ever, wealthy Americans have both the means and the inclination to redirect their children away from public school systems and into private schools.

"To reach for new heights and reveal the unknown so that what we do and learn will benefit all humankind"

July 29, 1958. The gently stated purpose of the National Aeronautics and Space Administration ("NASA") which was formed this day by the signing of legislation by President Dwight Eisenhower. NASA was, however, a direct response to the Soviet Union's launch of Sputnik the prior fall and was a dimension of the Cold War. Founded just months after America's launch of the U.S.'s first earth satellite, Explorer 1, on January 31, 1958, NASA was wisely created as a non-military agency and was separated from the Department of Defense (the "DOD") in order to at least lessen the military focus of its objectives and to lessen the interservice rivalries which may have otherwise been asserted. It is not mere coincidence that just months after the formation of NASA, the U.S. Congress also enacted the National Defense Education Act—"the first general American education law since the mid-1800s" [100]—which encouraged the teaching of science, mathematics, and languages.

"The Premium Card"
(For Just $6.00 Annual Fee)

October 1, 1958. The name of American Express' initial travel and entertainment card, which was first made available to customers on this date. The first cards were merely made of paper. By the next year, American Express ("AmEx") shifted to embossed plastic cards—an industry first. In 1966, AmEx introduced the Gold Card, and in 1984, the Platinum Card. Diners Club cards had been offered since March 1950, and their success was certainly one of the motivating forces behind AmEx's development of its own card—intentionally offered at an annual rate of $1.00 *more* than Diners Club. In 1958, Bank of America ("BofA") introduced its first consumer credit card program "for middle-class consumers and small- to medium-sized merchants." BofA's credit card introduced the "revolving credit" concept. Through the combination of AmEx' Premium Card and BofA's revolving credit card program, the "cashless revolution" began. In 1974, BofA expanded its credit card services internationally, and two years later changed its card name to "Visa" — "a name that sounds the same in all languages."[101]

- The Debut of the Trans-Atlantic Jet Age -
"2 DeHavilland Comets depart London and New York,
each bound for the other city."

October 4, 1958. On this day, these two 46-passenger planes, flying for British Overseas Airways Corporation, became the first regularly-scheduled airplanes to provide Trans-Atlantic service. While such travel would be routine within just a few years, the initial offering of such scheduled flights drew the attention of the country and dramatically underscored the geo-political (and military) proximity of other continents and nations.[102]

Partially in response to the increasing number of domestic and international commercial passenger flights, Congress had formed the Federal Aviation Agency just two months earlier in August 23, 1958. Regularly-scheduled transcontinental jet passenger service from Los Angeles to New York commenced just three months later on January 25, 1959.

"To bring about less government, more responsibility, and—with God's help—a better world...."

December, 1958. The stated mission of the John Birch Society,[103] formed on this date by a small group of business leaders that interestingly included Fred C. Koch, founder of Koch Industries. The leader of the group was Robert W. Welch, Jr., a retired candy manufacturer from Belmont, Massachusetts. The initial focus of the Society was its adamant advocacy of limited government and anti-communism. Over the years, however, it has also advanced numerous conspiracy theories involving, for example, the international conspiracy and objective of the Trilateral Commission and the Council on Foreign Relations to achieve a one-world order through the guise and vehicle of the United Nations. As early as 1965, just seven years after its formation, the Society was denounced even by leading conservatives such as William F. Buckley, who characterized it as a radical, far-right organization whose beliefs were "far removed from common sense." At various times, the Society also opposed the civil rights movement, which it characterized as part of an international communist conspiracy, objected to international trade agreements, and espoused numerous immigration reduction positions. Originally based in Belmont, Massachusetts, the Society remained tightly under the leadership of Welch until his death in 1985, at which point its headquarters were moved to Appleton, Wisconsin. At its height, the Society claimed to have over 100,000 members, but its influence and membership have waned over the years. As stated by one author in a fine but wide-ranging article about Glenn Beck and the seed traces of the John Birch Society in the founding of the Tea Party, "wherever [Welch] looked, [he] saw Communist forces manipulating American economic and foreign policy on behalf of totalitarianism...., [and he concluded that] government [was] always and inevitably an enemy of individual freedom."[104]

Year 1959

Pulitzer Prize for Fiction

The Travels of Jamie McPheeters
by Robert Lewis Taylor

Pulitzer Prize for History

The Republican Era: 1869–1901
by Leonard D. White and Jean Schneider

**The New York Times Best Sellers List (Nonfiction—
Books with Most Weeks as No. 1 Best Seller**

The Status Seekers
by Vance Packard (17 weeks)

Only in America
by Harry Lewis Golden (14 weeks)

**The New York Times Best Sellers List (Adult Fiction)—
Book with Most Weeks as No. 1 Best Seller**

Exodus
by Leon Uris (20 weeks)

Academy Awards Best Picture

Winner: *Ben Hur*
Other Nominees: *Anatomy of a Murder, The Diary of Anne Frank,
The Nun's Story, Room at the Top*

PrettyFamous' Best Movie of the Year
North by Northwest

<u>1959 U.S. Population: 177,800,000</u>

(Compared as a Percentage to the U.S. 1957 Population of 172,000,000: 103.4%)

<u>Television Shows</u>

Most Widely-Viewed Television Shows

Rank	Show Name	Years of Series (Excluding Reruns)	Show Type	Estimated Audience (In MMs)	Audience as Percentage of U.S. Population
1.	*Gunsmoke*	1955–1975	Western	18.4MM	10.3%
	Cast:	James Arness - Amanda Blake - Dennis Weaver			
2.	*Wagon Train*	1957–1965	Western	17.6MM	9.9%
	Cast:	Ward Bond - John McIntire			
3.	*Have Gun Will Travel*	1957–1963	Western	15.9MM	8.9%
	Cast:	Richard Boone			

Widely-Viewed or Critically-Acclaimed New Television Show(s)

Bonanza (1959–1973) – Western Drama
Lorne Greene - Dan Blocker - Michael Landon - Pernell Roberts

Rawhide (1959–1965) – Western Drama
Eric Flemming and (Introducing) Clint Eastwood

The Twilight Zone (1959–1964) – Science Fiction
Rod Serling – Creator, Writer, and Voice-Over Host

<u>Major Commercial Advertising Campaigns and Slogans</u>

"Let Hertz put you in the driver's seat."
Hertz Rental Car

"Rice-A-Roni, the San Francisco Treat"
Rice-A-Roni

"Think small"
Volkswagen

<u>Memorable Words from Speeches, Books, Writings, and Other Sources – 1959</u>

"Motown"

January 12, 1959. On this date Barry Gordy, Jr., with $800 of borrowed money, founded his first recording company in Detroit, Michigan. Taking its name from Detroit's fame as the "motor" capital of America, the Motown label was for decades one of the most successful African American businesses in the U.S. Motown Records' first commercially successful songs, which were recorded at its small Hitsville, U.S.A. recording studio, were *Shop Around* by The Miracles and *Please Mister Postman* by The Marvelettes. Over the course of the next 15 years, Motown generated an astounding 110 Top 10 Hits, including 57 Billboard Number One singles. Motown artists included The Supremes (initially including Diana Ross), The Four Tops, The Jackson 5, Stevie Wonder, Smokey Robinson (who was also Vice President of Motown Records), and Marvin Gaye. Part of Motown's historical importance lies in the fact that many of its songs were popular amongst both African American and white audiences—and especially teenagers. Although Motown Records and Hitsville U.S.A. are correctly associated with Detroit, Michigan, Gordy relocated his operation to Los Angeles after the Detroit riots of July 1967 (43 dead, 1,189 injured, 7,200 arrests, and more than 2,000 buildings destroyed). Motown Records continued as an independent company until it was sold by Gordy and the other owners in 1988.

"Mature, middle-class Americans,
average in height and visage, family men all."
(NASA Comments)

- - -

"Some fine early morning before another summer has come,
one man chosen from the calmly intent seven …
will embark on the greatest adventure man has ever dared to take.
Dressed in an all-covering suit to protect him from explosive
changes in pressure, strapped into a form-fitting couch to cushion
him against the crushing forces of acceleration, surrounded in his

> *tiny chamber by all manner of instruments ...*
> *he will catapult upward at the head of a rocket."*
>
> *...*
>
> *"If he survives,*
> *he will become the heroic symbol of a historic triumph ....*
>
> *If he does not survive,*
> *one of the six remaining will go next."*
> (*Life* Magazine Comments)

April 9, 1959. NASA and *Life* Magazine's description of the America's seven Mercury astronauts as first introduced to the nation by the still-new NASA. The second, more dramatic, indeed sobering, introduction above is from *Life* magazine's issue on this date about the astronauts and their families. It is hard to imagine in the news- and data-packed world of the 21st century, but it was only when this Life magazine issue came out that millions of Americans learned the astronauts' names: John Glenn, Alan Shepard, Scott Carpenter, Gordon Cooper, Gus Grissom, Wally Schirra, and Deke Slayton. Many American children—especially at that time, boys—had a "favorite" astronaut. The Mercury Seven were some of America's original celebrities, and arguably among the most deserving of that status. In 1957, President Dwight Eisenhower had insisted that all candidates be test pilots. Over the course of months and from an initial pool of 500 candidates, the final seven were selected to pilot NASA's first manned spaceflights of its Mercury program. Most of the members of this initial Mercury Seven flew on all classes of NASA's manned orbital space-craft in the 20th century—Mercury, Gemini, Apollo and even the Space Shuttle. Two years later, in January 1961, Alan Shepard touched the edge of space with a terrifying 15-minute ride in which he soared 115 miles above Earth. Then, in February 1962, John Glenn became the first American to orbit the Earth. All of the original seven astronauts survived their missions except for Gus Grissom, who died during the horrific launch pad explosion of the Apollo 1 rocket in 1967. In 1979, Tom Wolfe re-introduced these men to America in his book, *The Right Stuff,* which served as the basis for Philip Kaufman's 1983 movie of the same name.

"To be as real women is to bring out the best in a man."

April 10, 1959. The philosophy of life and the words on the wall of the movie character Gidget, in the movie of the same name, which was released on this date and which starred Sandra Dee as Gidget. These words were still widely believed by many women in the late 1950s and are here included only to illustrate the stark contrast of philosophies held by women in the late 1950s and those a decade later as evidenced by any number of books and speeches about the role (and oppression) of women and what came to be known as the women's or feminist movement.

"Any literary merit the book may have is far outweighed by the pornographic and smutty passages."

June 11, 1959. U.S. Postmaster General Arthur E. Summerfield's self-righteous condemnation of D. H. Lawrence's *Lady Chatterley's Lover,* which Summerfield had banned from delivery by the U.S. Postal Service. Because it could still be legally sold in bookstores and because of the attention brought to it as a result of the Postal Service's ban, the book became an instant best seller. Shortly thereafter, a federal judge overruled Summerfield's ban, noting that "the Postmaster General [had] no special competence" to determine that which is or is not pornography, and that "a work of literature published…by a reputable publisher stands on quite a different footing from hard core pornography furtively sold for the purpose of profiting by the titillation of the dirty minded."[105] The issue of defining pornography has continued for decades. For example, in addition to *Lady Chatterley's Lover,* other books such as Henry Miller's *Tropic of Cancer,* John Cleland's *Fanny Hill* (the commonly used title for *"Memoirs of a Woman of Pleasure"*), and the *Kama Sutra* all were, at one time or another during this period, defined as obscene and pornographic. The challenge of defining pornography was not helped several years later when USSC Associate Justice Potter Stewart concluded in the 1964 case of *Jacobellis v. Ohio* that although he couldn't define pornography, "he knew it when he saw it" (paraphrased).[106]

"Isn't it better to talk about the relative merits of washing machines
than the relative strength of rockets?
Isn't this the kind of competition you want?"

July 24, 1959. Then Vice President Richard M. Nixon, in his remarks to Soviet Premier Nikita Khrushchev during the course of a series of impromptu exchanges that came to be known as the "Kitchen Debate." The encounter took place at the opening of the U.S. National Exhibition in Moscow that featured, among other things, a model American home including all forms of modern technologies and gadgets. Referring to the exchange as a debate is actually a misnomer because, in fact, Nixon and Khrushchev merely "volleyed more insults than thoughts, (each) jabbing each other with a finger in the chest" to make their respective points.[107] Khrushchev insisted that he was not impressed and that "the Russian people will (not) be astonished to see these things" since they too had modern conveniences. The political and lasting significance of the exchange lay in the fact that Khrushchev came to view Nixon as a staunch and strong-willed supporter of capitalism. More immediately, Nixon's bold push-backs to the Soviet Premier played a role in assuring Nixon's nomination as the Republican Presidential nominee the next year. Only about three months later, Khrushchev visited the U.S. and presented himself as a happy and gregarious man—even cleverly suggesting that the two countries find "…more and more use(s) for the short American word 'O.K.' "

Hawaii—Our Last State
"The State of Hawaii shall consist of all islands,
together with their appurtenant reefs and territorial waters,
included in the Territory of Hawaii …
but said state shall not be deemed to include the Midway Islands, …."

August 21, 1959. With the passage of the Hawaii Admission Act, Hawaii became the second state admitted to the Union in 1959 after Alaska's admission on January 3, 1959. Thus, Hawaii and Alaska became the first states admitted to the Union since the admission of Arizona and New Mexico in 1912 and Oklahoma in 1907. No new states have been admitted since 1959, and President John F. Kennedy, upon his victory over

Richard Nixon in 1960, thus became the first President elected by a nation composed of all 50 states.

"*I've had a helluva lot of fun, and I've enjoyed every minute of it.*"

October 14, 1959. Errol Flynn's last words upon his death. The notorious actor "died of a heart attack … (unsurprisingly, offensively, and illegally) in the arms of his 15-year-old girlfriend."[108] The actor was known for his romantic and swashbuckling movie scenes. While at times tremendously popular within the U.S., the controversial Flynn was also known for his womanizing and hard drinking. It has been suggested that even the phrase "in like Flynn" is derived from Errol Flynn's life and is meant to suggest that a person has a particular ease at getting what or whom they wanted. Humorously, Flynn was reported as having also said that "any man who dies with more than $10,000 in the bank didn't plan his life right."

CHAPTER 8

1960–1969

The Sixties:
The Years of Kennedy,
Johnson and Nixon;
Vietnam and Civil Rights;
The Great Society; and
The Counterculture of the Sixties

1960s

Catchphrases, Chants, and Slogans

"If it feels good, do it."

This common saying embodied the liberation of the 1960s youth from the sexual and social mores and behavioral boundaries of preceding generations. However, even in the 1960s, many young Americans adopted neither the saying nor its spirit, and over the ensuing decades this ethos of the 1960s/Woodstock generation somehow morphed in American culture. In fact, by the beginning of the 21st century, American culture had become an almost fearful society. The vague, individualistic philosophy of "live and let live" had been replaced by collegiate fears of micro-aggressions and a society where "excessive prudery and exaggerated warnings … (came) to surround our every indulgence…witness alcohol, tobacco, cannabis, fat, ….."[109] As stated by one observer, the modern ethos may be closer to "if it feels good, it must be risky and bad, immoral and dangerous to your health."[110]

"Tune in, Turn on, Drop out"

The mantra and words of encouragement (but not wisdom) offered by Timothy Leary, a lecturer in clinical psychology at Harvard University until his termination in 1963 and one of the fathers of the LSD/psychedelic lifestyle of the 1960s. The decades-later descendant of this slogan is the well-meaning, but for some ominously accurate, mantra that "if you remember the '60s, you weren't there."

"We shall overcome."

The key phrase and unofficial anthem of the African American Civil Rights Movement. The history of the phrase and the many songs that use the phrase have a long history, going back to Charles Tindley's first publication of a hymn entitled *"I'll Overcome Some Day."* The phrase was adapted for the Civil Rights Movement and as early as 1959 it rose again to national prominence especially after Pete Seeger, Joan Baez and others sang various adaptations of the song at rallies, festivals, and marches, including a stirring performance by the then 22-year-old Baez at the Lincoln Memorial during the August 1963 March on Washington. Later, the phrase was invoked by President Lyndon Johnson in his speech to Congress on March 15, 1965 after the "bloody Sunday" attacks on civil rights demonstrators in Selma, Alabama. The phrase was even recited in Rev. Martin Luther King Jr.'s last sermon, delivered in Memphis, Tennessee on March 31, 1968, just four days before his assassination.

"Power to the People!"

A popular anti-establishment expression and political slogan used by many groups, in many contexts, and at many protests throughout the 1960s. In 1966 and thereafter, the saying became particularly associated with the newly formed and far more radical civil rights group, the Black Panthers, founded in that year in Oakland, California by Bobby Seale and Huey Newton. The Black Panthers initially won relatively widespread support within some parts of urban black communities through their community assistance programs such as their Breakfast for Children program. However, they also embodied a far more militant and demanding course of action than the nonviolence espoused by Rev. Martin Luther King Jr. and his followers.[111] Remnants of the Black Panthers existed throughout the 1970s, but the organization was in reality short-lived, partly due to the aggressive reactions of the FBI and other law enforcement organizations. Less than six years after the group's formation, Huey Newton stated that they had "rejected the rhetoric of the gun" partly in light of the fact that "it got about 40 of us killed and sent hundreds (of my fellow Black Panthers) to prison."[112]

<u>Memorable Words from Speeches, Books, Writings,</u>
<u>and Other Sources About the Decade of the 1960s</u>

"They were the largest, the best educated,
and the wealthiest generation in American history ... (and)
many believed they had stopped a war, changed American politics,

> ***and liberated the country from the inhibited—
> and inhibiting—sensibilities of their parents."***

Tom Brokaw describing the Sixties generation in his book *Boom!* (2007). As he notes in his book, some Baby Boomers almost "defensive(ly) and a little defiant(ly)" insist that they, the Baby Boomers, were "the Greatest Generation"—a term Brokaw had applied in his crowning of the prior generation in his 1998 book of the same name. Correctly in the opinion of this author, Brokaw observed that Baby Boomers were "the largest, the best educated, and the wealthiest generation," but it was indeed the prior generation that uniquely deserved the title of "The Greatest Generation." They had survived the Great Depression, fought World War II, and created the wealth that made possible the education in the 1950s and 1960s.

> ***"I think all the troubles in the country began in the Sixties."***

Dick Army, the former House of Representatives Majority Leader), expressing a widely shared belief held by many Americans—and especially conservative Americans. While dangerously simplistic, this belief summarizes one perspective held by many Americans who, over the course of the ensuing half-century, came to wish that there was a road "back" to the quieter time before the 1960s; to a time when various institutions of Americans life—family, community, church, and law —were held in higher regard. While this belief, even longing, is widely shared in America, as is always the case about recollections of the "good old days," those days weren't good for all Americans. To the contrary, the 1950s and previous decades were extremely difficult, for example, for racial and ethnic minorities, for members of the LGBT community, for women, for the disabled and mentally ill, and in many cases for the uninsured and financially unprotected seniors.

> ***"If you thought something good came out of the Sixties,
> you're probably a Democrat;
> if you thought the Sixties were bad, you're probably a Republican."***

Former President Bill Clinton, probably correctly, albeit again unduly simplistically, summarizing the two major and differing perspectives held by Americans.[113]

> *"The '60s was only two years: '65-'67. That was it.*
> *That was the pure across-the-board renaissance*
> *of music, art and film before it got co-opted,*
> *the assassinations started and Vietnam polarized everything."*[114]

John Densmore, the drummer and one of two surviving members of the Sixties rock group, The Doors, reflecting upon the Sixties many years later. Many commentators might insist that any real discussion of the Sixties would have to include 1968, the decade's biggest and, in some ways, the most tragic year when it everything seems to come to a head, and 1969, with the almost surreal inauguration of Richard M. Nixon as President followed by the summer of Woodstock. On the other hand, Densmore indirectly reminds us that no matter how the Sixties are measured, it all happened fast – indeed, looking back from the distance of the 21st Century, it seemed like it all happened at once.

> *"There's a big 'what if' over the Sixties …*
> *Who knows what would have happened*
> *if King and Kennedy were alive?"*

Tom Hayden, a social and political activist and politician, noting the obvious and as quoted in Tom Brokaw's *Boom!* The assassinations of King and Kennedy were devastating to our society and to millions of Americans. The collision of generations that occurred in the Sixties was unique in its own way. Nevertheless, there is a certain myopia embedded in this remark as well. Every decade and every generation could lay claim to similar "what if" thoughts. If Lenin had not taken the train back to Russia, if Hitler had remained a little known postcard painter in Austria, if Lincoln had not been assassinated, if FDR had not been President, if the mongering of McCarthyism had not been stopped, if Nixon had stayed in retirement … and on and on. Consider, for example, any of Robert Cowley's fine series of "What If?" books and essays and his assembled "What If" works of other historians.[115]

Year 1960

Seminal Books

The Conscience of a Conservative
by Barry Goldwater

This book is one of the bedrock early writings of the modern American conservative movement that began its resurgence in the late 1950s and 1960s. Patrick Buchanan, a conservative columnist, television political commentator, and 1992 Republican Party Presidential hopeful, identified the book as the conservatives' "New Testament," and many American conservatives would agree. Although Senator Barry Goldwater is credited as the author, the book was actually ghostwritten by Goldwater's speechwriter and brother-in-law, L. Brent Bozell, Jr., a fellow conservative activist and a close friend and former Yale debating partner of William F. Buckley, Jr. *The Conscience of a Conservative* was not widely distributed at first. Then Bozell attended a meeting of the John Birch Society, where he persuaded Fred Koch (father of Charles and David Koch) to buy 2,500 copies for distribution. Thereafter, the book's circulation and influence continued to grow. Two years later the book contributed to Goldwater making the cover of *Time* magazine, and three years later Goldwater was selected as the Republican Presidential nominee. Although he was badly defeated by President Lyndon Johnson in the 1964 election, Goldwater had served and later continued to serve as a powerful U.S. Senator for many years (1953-1965 and 1969-1987), and the influence of his book continued to grow over the ensuing decades. During the years immediately following the book's release and following the reasoning presented therein, Goldwater and others asserted seemingly extreme positions such as suggesting that the USSC's 1954 school integration decision, *Brown v. Board of Education,* was unconstitutional and "call(ing) for the elimination of social security, federal aid to schools, federal welfare and farm programs…"[116] Some political commentators believe that the book contributed to the founding of the Tea Party movement in the early 21st century in that the book, correctly or otherwise, identified the government as "the enemy of liberty …"[117]

The Purpose of American Politics
by Hans J. Morgenthau

This book was written by author and international political relations commentator Hans J. Morgenthau. Morgenthau served in both the Kennedy and Johnson administrations—until President Johnson dismissed him due to Morgenthau's opposition to the continuance of the Vietnam War. Morgenthau, along with George Kennan and Reinhold Niebuhr, is viewed as one of the founders of the "realist school" of political thought. This now relatively obscure book has lasting relevance to 21st century in that it asserts that one of the purposes of American politics is "equality in freedom." While this concept is not itself stunning, Morgenthau argues "with subtlety and sophistication" and "impl(ies) that, in spite of frantic efforts (of our political representative bodies and governmental agencies) to adapt our policies to the demands and conditions of contemporary civilization, we fail mainly 'because we are no longer sure … what America stands for…' " [118]

To Kill a Mockingbird[119]
by Harper Lee

This Pulitzer prize-winning novel is about courage and racial inequality within the setting of a small town in the South during the Great Depression. Today, "53 years later, it remains a global blockbuster, having sold more than 30 million copies in 40 languages and still selling 750,000 copies a year, according to HarperCollins, the publisher."[120] It has even been called America's "national novel."[121] This belief is widely shared, and the 1962 movie by the same name, starring Gregory Peck, remains an American classic as well. Until the shocking discovery and the 2015 release of Ms. Lee's second book, *Go Set a Watchman,* it was thought that *To Kill a Mockingbird* was the only book she had ever written.

Pulitzer Prize for Fiction

Advice and Consent
by Allen Drury

Pulitzer Prize for History

In the Days of McKinley
by Margaret Leech

The New York Times Best Sellers List (Nonfiction) – Books with Most Weeks as No. 1 Best Seller

May This House Be Free from Tigers
by Alexander King (21 weeks)

Born Free: A Lioness of Two Worlds
by Joy Adamson (13 weeks)

The New York Times Best Sellers List (Adult Fiction) – Book with Most Weeks as No. 1 Best Seller

Hawaii
by James Michener (37 weeks)

Academy Awards Best Picture

Winner: *The Apartment*

Other Nominees: *The Alamo, Elmer Gantry, Sons and Lovers, The Sundowners*

PrettyFamous' Best Movie of the Year

Psycho

Best/Most Memorable Movie Lines of the Year

"A boy's best friend is his mother."

Anthony Perkins' frightening line from Alfred Hitchcock's psychological horror film *Psycho*. The presumably equally frightening line is Perkins' response to Janet Leigh's inquiry as to whether or not there was a vacancy at The Bates Motel—*"Oh, we have 12 vacancies: 12 cabins, 12 vacancies."*

> ***"I am more interested in the 'Rock of Ages'***
> ***than I am in the age of rocks."***

Actor Fredric March portraying William Jennings Bryant in the movie *Inherit the Wind* and here speaking in response to the famous trial lawyer, Clarence Darrow, portrayed by Spencer Tracy, as Darrow cross-examines him in this historical movie based upon the 1925 Scopes "Monkey" Trial.

> ***"Sin. Sin. Sin. You're all sinners. You're all doomed to perdition.***
> ***You're all goin' to the painful, stinkin', scaldin', everlastin' tortures***
> ***of a fiery hell, ... unless you repent."***

The fiery words of Burt Lancaster as a con man evangelist in the film version of *Elmer Gantry,* based upon Sinclair Lewis' 1927 novel.

> ***"I'm Spartacus! ... I'm Spartacus ... I'm Spartacus!"***

The words from the closing scene of the epic historical film, *Spartacus,* directed by Stanley Kubrick (who, in a wildly diverse decade, went on to produce *Lolita* in 1962 and *2001: A Space Odyssey* in 1970). The calls of *"I'm Spartacus"* are the brave responses of recaptured slaves who had been asked by the Romans to identify the real Spartacus in exchange for leniency.

<u>1960 U.S. Population: 180,700,000</u>

(Compared as a Percentage to the U.S. 1957 Population of 172,000,000: 105.0%)

<u>Television Shows</u>

Most Widely-Viewed Television Shows

Rank	Show Name	Years of Series (Excluding Reruns)	Show Type	Estimated Audience (In MMs)	Audience as Percentage of U.S. Population
1.	*Gunsmoke*	1955–1975	Western	17.6MM	9.7%
	Cast:	James Arness - Amanda Blake - Dennis Weaver			
2.	*Wagon Train*	1957–1965	Western	16.1MM	8.9%
	Cast:	Ward Bond - John McIntire			
3.	*Have Gun Will Travel*	1957–1963	Western	14.6MM	8.1%
	Cast:	Richard Boone			

Widely-Viewed or Critically-Acclaimed New Television Show(s)

The Andy Griffith Show (1960–1968) - Comedy
Andy Griffith - Ron Howard - Don Knotts
(No. 9 Top TV Shows of All Time – *TV Guide*)

<u>Major Commercial Advertising Campaigns and Slogan(s)</u>

"The quicker picker upper"[122]
Bounty

<u>Memorable Words from Speeches, Books, Writings, and Other Sources – 1960</u>

Presidential Campaign Themes, Slogans and Results
(Both Official and Unofficial)
(Only Major Presidential Party Nominees and Candidates Listed)

John F. Kennedy (and Lyndon B. Johnson) (Democratic Party)

A Time for Greatness	*Let's Get America Moving Again.*
The Man for the 60s	*Prosperity for All*
We Can Do Better	

Richard M. Nixon (and Henry Cabot Lodge) (Republican Party)

Click with Dick	*Experience Counts*
For the Future	*Keep the Peace*
Without Surrender	

Election Results:

Party	Nominees Presidential	Vice-Presidential	Electoral Vote		Popular Vote	
Democratic	John F. Kennedy	L. B. Johnson	303	56.4%	34.2MM	49.7%
Republican	Richard M. Nixon	H. C. Lodge	219	40.8%	34.1MM	49.5%
Democratic	Harry F. Byrd	S. Thurmond	15	2.8%	0	0%

"We had no notion that we'd even be served."

...

"What we wanted to do was to serve notice ...
that we were going to (try) to achieve
some of the rights and privileges we were due as citizens of this country."

February 1, 1960. Franklin McCain, one of the so-called Greensboro Four, a group of four young students attending North Carolina A&T, an all-black college. The above words are McCain's reflections on the day when he and his companions decided it was time to act against segregation and initiated what came to be called a "sit-in" at the all-white lunch counter of F.W. Woolworth in Greensboro, North Carolina. They did not get served that day or on any of the other days that they went back to that lunch counter. But their actions were among the early sparks of the Civil Rights Movement of the 1960s, and their sit-in inspired others to take action as well. On the next day, 23 students showed up at the counter asking to be served. Within a month, "thousands of mainly black students in seven states and 31 communities were similarly engaged. There were read-ins at public libraries, stand-ins at theaters, paint-ins at public art galleries, wade-ins at segregated public beaches, and kneel-ins at white churches."[123] And as for the lunch counter where it all began, approximately six months later Woolworth in Greensboro (finally) served its first black customer.

"If you give me a week, I might think of one."

August 24, 1960. President Dwight D. Eisenhower, speaking at one of his last news conferences as President. Eisenhower made the statement in response to a reporter who had asked him to name a "major idea" that his Vice President, the then-GOP Presidential nominee Richard Nixon, had proposed over the previous eight years. Eisenhower's devastating and insulting statement reflected the "awkward relationship" that existed between Eisenhower and Nixon. In 1962—just two years after Nixon lost his Presidential bid to John F. Kennedy, Nixon wrote his book *Six Crises*. In the initial draft of the book, the still-bitter Nixon wrote that "Eisenhower was one of the most devious men I've ever met." However, in the final edition, this statement was watered down and cleaned up so as to merely state that "(Eisenhower) was a far more complex and devious man than most realized, and in the best sense of those words."[124]

"I believe in an America
where the separation of church and state is absolute."

· · ·

**"If the time should ever come – and I do not concede any conflict
to be remotely possible – when my office would require me
to either violate my conscience or violate the national interest,
then I would resign the office."**

September 12, 1960. John F. Kennedy, in an address as the Democratic Presidential candidate to a group of about 300 Protestant leaders in Houston, Texas. The speech, which was largely successful, was intended to address the concerns of many non-Catholic U.S. voters that Kennedy, a Catholic, would be influenced by Papal directions. The speech was deemed necessary by the Kennedy campaign because the candidate had previously, but unsuccessfully, attempted to allay such concerns of the voters. His wife, the widely popular Jacqueline Kennedy, humorously stated at the time that she thought "it's so unfair for people to be against Jack because he's Catholic [because he's] such a poor Catholic."

**"His eyes were exaggerated, hollows of blackness,
his jaws, jowls, and face drooping with strain."**

September 26, 1960. The journalist Theodore H. White, the author of *The Making of the President* series of books, describing the tired, dark, and haggard appearance of Richard M. Nixon during the first televised Presidential debate in U.S. history on this date. Nixon had unwisely declined most makeup, and he seemed to wholly underestimate the significance of his own appearance. More importantly, Nixon seemed to underestimate the power of television itself. It was still a new medium, but the debate was watched by an estimated 70 million U.S. viewers—more than one in three Americans. Rarely does one event or appearance decide any election, but this debate accentuated and reinforced the brooding and loner aspects of Nixon's personality, especially in televised contrast to the youthful, more cheerful-appearing John F. Kennedy. Almost unsurprisingly, most of those who listened to the debate on the radio thought that Nixon had won, while most of those who viewed the debate on television thought Kennedy had won. Just six weeks later Kennedy won one of the closest Presidential elections in U.S. history. The short-lived age of Camelot began.

Year 1961

<u>**Seminal Books**</u>

The Making of the President 1960[125]
by Theodore H. White

This book was the first (and many believe the best) in a series of books by White himself (including *The Making of the President—1964, —1968, and —1972*) and by other more recent authors[126] that narrate the events and decision-making processes of presidential campaigns. Oftentimes, such coverage includes a particular focus upon persons intimately involved in the campaign. White's original book and his ensuing series served to heighten the interest of a generation of Americans in the presidential election process.

Catch-22
by Joseph Heller

Catch-22 is a satirical novel frequently cited as one of the dominant literary works of the 20th century. The book's story revolves around the life of Captain John Yossarian and takes place within the setting of a fictional U.S. Air Force squadron during World War II. The story is cleverly presented through a series of third-person narrations of the same events from the perspective of various characters. The book's title is derived from an inherently contradictory Air Force Policy that states that no airman, if he is mentally unfit, shall be required to fly. However, the "Catch-22" is that anyone who seeks such exemption is immediately deemed sane since they are showing a logical and rational concern for their own safety by merely requesting not to fly. Wholly apart from the literary genius of the book, the concept of "Catch-22 " has become part of the American vernacular for absurd, no-win, choices—of which there seem to be more and more in our Modern America. With only the possible exception of the no-good-choice phrase *"Sophie's Choice"* taken from William Styron's book and Alan Pakula's 1982 movie of the same name, the broad social adoption and use of the phrase *"Catch-22"* is unique in Modern American culture.

Stranger in a Strange Land
by Robert A. Heinlein

Heinlein uses the vehicle of this brilliant science fiction novel about a human who comes to Earth after having been raised by Martians to examine, even challenge, the social mores of American culture and to reevaluate some of its various cultural institutions such as religion, money, monogamy, and even fear of death. Heinlein's work in this book is viewed by many as especially unique because, among other reasons, it was written years before the explosion of science fiction as one of the most popular literary genres. Similarly, it was written years before the production of *Star Trek, Star Wars, Harry Potter,* and thousands of other science fiction and fantasy films. One of the terms used in Heinlein's book which should be noted is that of "Fair Witness"—a person who is trained to carefully observe and accurately report *exactly and only* that which is seen or heard without the injection of assumptions or predispositions and without the venturing of interpretation or extrapolation. In the present age of Modern America that, to a degree, is characterized by agenda reporting, compromised media, and sensationalistic journalism and in which both facts and objectivity seem elusive, Heinlein's concept of Fair Witness could have a useful, renewed utility.

Pulitzer Prize for Fiction

To Kill a Mockingbird
by Harper Lee

Pulitzer Prize for History

Between War and Peace: The Potsdam Conference
by Herbert Feis

The New York Times **Best Sellers List (Nonfiction) – Books with Most Weeks as No. 1 Best Seller**

The Rise and Fall of the Third Reich: A History of Nazi Germany
by William L. Shirer (35 weeks)

The Making of a President, 1960
by Theodore H. White (17 weeks)

***The New York Times* Best Sellers List (Adult Fiction) – Book with Most Weeks as No. 1 Best Seller**

The Agony and the Ecstasy
by Irving Stone (27 weeks)

Academy Awards Best Picture

Winner: *West Side Story*

Other Nominees: *Fanny, The Guns of Navarone, The Hustler, Judgment at Nuremberg*

***PrettyFamous'* Best Movie of the Year**

Yojimbo

Best/Most Memorable Movie Line of the Year

"Fat Man, you shoot a great game of pool."

...

"So do you, Fast Eddie."

"Fast Eddie" Paul Newman speaking to Jackie Gleason, who portrayed the fictional world-famous pool player "Minnesota Fats" in this movie, *The Hustler.* After the movie's release, a real-life pool hustler going by the nickname "New York Fats" changed his moniker and for the rest of his life played as "Minnesota Fats"—cashing in on the movie, although he had nothing to do with the film or the underlying novel.

1961 U.S. Population: 183,700,000

(Compared as a Percentage to the U.S. 1957 Population of 172,000,000: 106.8%)

Television Shows

Most Widely-Viewed Television Shows

Rank	Show Name	Years of Series (Excluding Reruns)	Show Type	Estimated Audience (In MMs)	Audience as Percentage of U.S. Population
1.	*Wagon Train*	1957–1965	Western	15.6MM	8.5%
	Cast: Ward Bond - John McIntire				
2.	*Bonanza*	1959–1973	Western	14.6MM	7.9%
	Cast: Lorne Greene - Michael Landon– Pernell Roberts – Dan Blocker				
3.	*Gunsmoke*	1955–1975	Western	13.7MM	7.5%
	Cast: James Arness - Amanda Blake - Dennis Weaver				

Widely-Viewed or Critically-Acclaimed New Television Show(s)

ABC's Wide World of Sports (1961–1998)

Jim McKay

(After 1987 - Co-hosts included Frank Gifford,
Robin Roberts, Becky Dixon and Julie Moran)

The Dick Van Dyke Show (1961–1966) – Comedy

Dick Van Dyke - Mary Tyler Moore
(No. 13 Top TV Shows of All Time – *TV Guide*)

Television Line

"The thrill of victory ... and the agony of defeat"

Excerpt from the weekly introduction to *ABC's Wide World of Sports*. This line opened every weekly show—for 37 years—from its first airing in 1961 until the last show in 1998. The sports anthology show's full introduction was *"spanning the globe to bring you the constant variety of sport ... the thrill of victory ... and the agony of defeat ... the human drama of athletic competition."* After 1971, many viewers associated the show's melodramatic narration of "the agony of defeat" with the background footage of Slovenian ski jumper Vinko Bogataj's horrific misjump and crash during a competition in West Germany. Due to the proliferation of other sports programming such as ESPN (1979) and ESPN2 (1993), *ABC's Wide World of Sports* was discontinued in the late 1990s. However, in 2007 it was named by *Time* magazine as one of the 100 best television programs of all-time.

<u>Memorable Words from Speeches, Books, Writings, and Other Sources – 1961</u>

"In the councils of government, we must guard against the
acquisition of unwarranted influence, …,,
by the military-industrial complex. The potential
for the disastrous rise of misplaced power exists and will persist
(but) we must never let the weight of this combination endanger
our liberties or democratic processes."

January 17, 1961. President Dwight D. Eisenhower's chilling (and in the opinion of some, prescient and correct) warning about the potential intrusion of the military-industrial complex upon democratic processes in his "Farewell Address to the Nation" delivered on this date.

January 20, 1961
Inaugural Address of John F. Kennedy
(President of the United States 1961–1963)

"The world is very different now.
For man holds in his mortal hands the power
to abolish all forms of human poverty and all forms of human life."

. . .

"Let the word go forth from this time and place,
to friend and foe alike, that the torch has been passed
to a new generation of Americans—born in this century,
tempered by war, disciplined by a hard and bitter peace,
proud of our ancient heritage…"

. . .

"Let every nation know …
we shall pay any price, bear any burden, meet any hardship,
support any friend, oppose any foe
to assure the survival and the success of liberty."

. . .

*"If society cannot help the many who are poor,
it cannot save the few who are rich."*

. . .

*"To that world assembly of sovereign nations,
the United Nations, our last best hope in an age
where the instruments of war have far outpaced
the instruments of peace, we renew our pledge of support...."*

. . .

*"So let us begin anew –
remembering on both sides
(amongst the two "great and powerful groups of nations")
that civility is not a sign of weakness,
and sincerity is always subject to proof.
Let us never negotiate out of fear.
But let us never fear to negotiate."*

. . .

*"The graves of young Americans
who answered the call of service surround the globe.
Now the trumpet summons us again...
to bear the burden of a long twilight struggle—
year in and year out—...
a struggle against the common enemies of man: tyranny,
poverty, disease and war itself."*

. . .

*"In the long history of the world,
only a few generations have been granted the role
of defending freedom in its hour of maximum danger.
I do not shrink from this responsibility—I welcome it.
I do not believe any of us would exchange places
with any other people or any other generation ..."*

. . .

*"And so, my fellow Americans,
ask not what your country can do for you,
ask what you can do for your country."*

January 20, 1961. From the relatively short 1,364-word Inaugural Address of John F. Kennedy. Although the approximately 15-minute address was one of the shortest in U.S. history, it is widely considered one of the best Presidential inaugural addresses. President Kennedy was both the first Catholic U.S. President and the first man born in the 20th century to hold the Office of U.S. President. Furthermore, upon his ascendancy to office he became, at age 43, the youngest elected President and simultaneously replaced President Eisenhower who was, at the age of 70, the oldest President in U.S. history. Millions of Americans were now able to watch the inauguration on television, and for many Americans, Kennedy's 1961 Inaugural Address articulated the fresh optimism, confidence, and enthusiasm that they held. During this brief period of time in the early 1960s, the prior decade of historic expansion had closed, the memories of World War II and the Korean War had started to fade, and Vietnam still remained a little-known country thousands of miles from the American shore. Kennedy took his oath of office from Chief Justice Earl Warren, and Vice President Lyndon Johnson took his oath of office from Speaker of the U.S. House of Representatives Sam Rayburn.

"To promote world peace and friendship"

March 1, 1961. The opening words of the mission statement of the Peace Corps, which was established this day by Executive Order signed by President John F. Kennedy. The concept of the Peace Corps was initially dismissed by some as a naïve and worthless gesture to the world, but over the course of the more than five decades between 1961 and 2015, nearly 220,000 Americans have served two-year, voluntary terms in the Peace Corps. The Peace Corps itself has, in turn, provided development services and aid to more than 141 countries. President Kennedy is almost universally credited with the creation of the Peace Corps, but actually the concept was initially proposed several years earlier by Senator Hubert Humphrey (D-MN) when he first introduced legislation for the creation of such a corps in 1957.

<u>U.S. Constitutional Amendment—23rd Amendment</u>

"The District (of Columbia) ... shall appoint ...
(a) number of electors of President and Vice President
equal to the whole number of Senators and Representatives ...
to which the District (of Columbia) would be entitled
if it were a state,
but in no event more than the least populous state ...."

March 29, 1961. This amendment extends the right to vote in the Presidential elections to U.S. citizens residing in the District of Columbia. The most surprising aspect of this 23rd Amendment was that it was needed at all. Until the political discussion and debates about granting Washington, D.C. residents the "right to vote" commenced, most Americans had assumed that they already had such a right to vote. However, they did not. Instead, the right of Washington, D.C. residents to vote in Presidential elections was established only upon the ratification of the 23rd Amendment on this date. Congress proposed the amendment to the states on June 16, 1960, and ratification by the requisite 38 states (two-thirds of the state legislatures) came quickly, within less than a year. But some states did object. Because a disproportionate percentage of Washington, D.C. residents were black and voted Democratic, Arkansas rejected the amendment and nine other states—all Southern states—chose to take no action. Nevertheless, the requisite two-thirds of the states' legislatures, was achievable without Arkansas and the other southern states.

"Utter Disaster" and "Total Fiasco"
The Bay of Pigs Invasion

April 17, 1961. Rarely can phrases such as "utter disaster" and "total fiasco" be used in the context of international invasions or CIA- or State Department-led operations. Usually there are "pros and cons," "upsides and downsides," and "noble causes" to be protected at "all costs." However, the Bay of Pigs invasion, a CIA-led operation held on this date and originally known as Operation Pluto, is different. The Bays of Pigs holds the dubious distinction of have been correctly described as a "fiasco." It occurred just 90 days after the U.S. broke off diplomatic relations with Cuba on January 3,

1961 upon the orders of President Dwight Eisenhower during his last days in office. The operation was carried out by a group of 1,200 CIA-financed and -trained Cuban exiles who tried to invade Fidel Castro's Cuba. The promised CIA air cover never arrived. The hoped-for Cuban uprising was never triggered. Instead, the Cuban military immediately and easily quashed the invasion. The CIA training of the exiles had been ordered by President Eisenhower, but it was President John Kennedy, new in office, who gave the final authorization and "go" order. After the "Yankee imperialist" operation's failure had been derided by Castro to the world, it was Kennedy who was forced to accept "full responsibility." Diplomatic relations between the U.S. and Cuba would remain frozen for the next 55 years until President Barack Obama started to once again "open Cuba." However, at the time of the Bay of Pigs fiasco, the U.S. was seen as merely once again meddling in the affairs of a Latin American country as it had done in many instances in the first half of the 20th century in order to "restore order" or "protect national interest." Such interventions continued in the later decades of the 20th century as well: Guatemala (1963) (CIA-backed coup); the Dominican Republic (1965) (U.S. invasion to stop a "Communist rebellion"); Chile (1973) (U.S.-supported coup to remove President Salvador Allende); Nicaragua (1981) (funding and training of the Contras); and Grenada (1983) (U.S. invasion in support of overthrow of the socialist leader).

"I believe this nation should commit itself to achieving the goal,
before this decade is out,
of landing a man on the moon and returning him safely to earth."

...

"We choose to go to the moon ... in this decade and do other things,
not because they are easy, but because they are hard,
because that goal will serve to organize and measure
the best of our energies and skills,
because that challenge is one that we are willing to accept,
one we are unwilling to postpone,
and one which we intend to win, and the others, too."

May 25, 1961 President John F. Kennedy, making his announcement in Houston, Texas that the U.S. would go to the moon "before this decade is out." Kennedy's announcement was made just 43 days after the Soviet Union had successfully launched the first man into space and was made in retort to Soviet Premier Nikita Khrushchev's insistence that their April 21, 1961 launch of cosmonaut Yuri Gagarin had somehow proven communism's superiority over decadent capitalism.

"Converts deserts into farmlands"

June 21, 1961. The heralding announcement of the opening of the nation's first desalination plants in Freeport, Texas. The plant was built by Dow Chemical Co., which is headquartered in Freeport, in less than a year under the auspices and supervision of the curiously named Office of Saline Water, a division of the Department of the Interior. The opening occurred with great fanfare. President Kennedy pressed a special switch that had been installed in his White House office in order to celebrate the occasion. The on-site ceremony was attended by both Vice President Lyndon Johnson and Secretary of the Interior Stuart Udall. Nevertheless, a mere eight years later, America shut down this desalination plant and closed the Office of Saline Water. The U.S. landed on the moon in 1969, but it also decided that year that desalination plants were somehow unnecessary. This may have been a poor decision considering the country's continuous and growing need for potable water and in light of the years of drought that have been suffered particularly by the American West. As of January 2017, more than 24% of the lower 48 states were suffering from drought conditions affecting more than 126.6 million Americans.[127] While there are about 18,500 desalination plants around the world—from Saudi Arabia to Spain and from India to Japan, as of the early 21st century, there are only 32 such plants in the United States. Many Americans believe that this desalination brainchild of the Department of the Interior more than 55 years ago should have been allowed to grow and expand.[128]

"I am the man who accompanied Jackie Kennedy to Paris – and I enjoyed myself."

June, 1961. President John F. Kennedy after returning from his trip to Europe, where he was accompanied by his widely popular young wife, Jacqueline. While in Paris, Jacqueline Kennedy had impressed the Parisians with both by her "fashion sense and ability to speak French." [129]

"A wall is a hell of a lot better than a war."

August 13, 1961. The remark attributed to President John F. Kennedy upon his learning of the construction, started in the middle of the night, of the Berlin Wall by Communist East Germans. The 12-foot high Wall—complete with a "so-called Death Strip (of) a gauntlet of soft sand to show footprints, vicious dogs, trip-wire machine guns and patrolling soldiers"[130] stretched for more than 100 miles with only a few checkpoints through which travelers between East and West Berlin could pass. Rigidly patrolled, The Wall effectively separated the residents of West Berlin from both East Berlin and East Germany. For nearly three decades, The Wall remained one of the most visible and powerful symbols of the Cold War. It was finally brought down in 1989[131] upon the ending of the Cold War and the collapse of the Soviet Union. Memories of The Wall remain close at hand and have resurfaced in the ensuing decades in the context of the Israeli West Bank wall and, more recently, in the context of the proposed wall between the U.S. and neighboring Mexico, one of the centerpieces of Republican President Donald Trump's 2016 Presidential campaign.

"Broadcasting a message of love ... that eventually grew into a worldwide ministry to millions."

October 1, 1961. With the above-stated purpose as posted on its website, televangelist Pat Robertson on this date founded the Christian Broadcasting Network ("CBN").[132] CBN is headquartered in Virginia Beach, Virginia and uses a wide array of religious variety programming to promote Christian beliefs and understanding. CBN's longest-running and most well-known show is *The 700 Club,* a religious-based daily newsmagazine hosted by Robertson himself. Robertson, a graduate of Washington and Lee University and Yale Law School, an author, and a former Southern Baptist minister, has long promoted a conservative, religious-based political and social philosophy and in 1988 sought the Republican Presidential nomination. CBN grew and diversified over the ensuing decades of Modern America, and, as noted in a 2017 book about Evangelicals, "by the mid-1980s, only two secular networks were larger than Robertson's CBN."[133] Robertson is best known for his role as the founder of CBN, the host of *The 700 Club*, and now the chancellor and CEO of Regent University (originally "CBN University"), which he founded in 1977. After CBN's founding and sustained successful growth, Trinity Broadcasting Network, headquartered in Costa Mesa, California, was founded in 1973 by Paul and Ann Crouch. PTL (Praise the Lord) Television was founded a year later, in 1974, in Fort Mill, South Carolina by Jim and Tammy Faye Bakker—although PTL was disbanded after it filed bankruptcy in 1987 after the rape and embezzlement scandal involving Jim Bakker.[134] The combined power and influence of these religious-based broadcasting networks cannot be over-stated, and collectively, among other things, they greatly furthered the political activism and influence of Christian evangelicals throughout especially the 1970s and 1980s.

Year 1962

<u>Seminal Books</u>

Silent Spring
by Rachel Carson.

In her book, *Silent Spring,* Ms. Carson brilliantly "challeng(ed) the practices of agricultural scientists and the government and warned against overuse of synthetic pesticides (and DDT in particular)." The book was initially derided by some as an "emotional and inaccurate outburst." Others went further and accused Ms. Carson of being a communist. Yet, however it was initially received, the book had immense impact. It is now widely credited with helping inspire the global environmental movement.[135] More specifically, through the book. Ms. Carson is credited with being partially responsible for the 1972 banning of DDT by the Environmental Protection Agency (the "EPA"), which had just been formed two years earlier by the Nixon administration. Some critics still stubbornly maintain that Ms. Carson's "extreme rhetoric generated a culture of fear, resulting in policies that have deprived many people access to life-saving chemicals," such as DDT. Such assertions may be, however, at least partly disingenuous since "Carson took pains to make it clear she was not calling for the banning of all pesticides, especially those that might be able to protect (humans) against insect-transmitted diseases..." such as malaria.[136] In 1964, less than two years after the publication of *Silent Spring*, Ms. Carson died of cancer at the age of 57.

Sex and the Single Girl
by Helen Gurley Brown.

An advice book addressed to single women with chapter headings such as The Availables, Where to Meet (Men), How To Be Sexy, and Kisses and Make-Up. The book was radical for its time in that it, among other things, encouraged single women to obtain a job and have sexual affairs with different men before marriage. Although the book is modest by 21st century standards, some Americans found it shocking at the time. Even the use of the word "sex" was sometimes barred in the advertising of the book. To other Americans, the book was revolutionary both in its intent to and its consequence of introducing another wave of feminism. Nevertheless, beyond dispute and regardless of the book's purpose or the reader's interpretation, the book was widely read. It sold in 35 countries and was included in many U.S. best sellers lists. Within three years Ms. Brown became Editor-in-Chief of *Cosmopolitan* magazine—a position she held for more than three decades, until 1997.

The Other America: Poverty in the United States
by Michael Harrington.

The Other America was, as is widely noted in its marketing to this day, an explosive book which revealed how many Americans were living in poverty. Harrington argued persuasively that the conventional wisdom that the U.S. was an overwhelmingly middle-class society was wrong. He started investigating poverty in America in the late 1950s and, as he had noted in a series of articles in *Commentary* in 1959 and 1960, as many as one-third of Americans lived in some form of poverty—"below those standards which we (Americans) have been taught to regard as the decent minimums for food, housing, clothing and health."[137] The book and the data and evidence presented therein were noted by President John F. Kennedy and were influential in President Lyndon Johnson's formulation of his War on Poverty launched just several years later. Michael Harrington was a graduate of Yale Law School and a prolific writer. For many years, he was a professor at Queens College in New York. However, due to his fervent commitment to socialism (and arguably his adamant rejection of any personal religious association), there was no realistic avenue for Harrington to achieve political office or success. Nevertheless, he—especially through this book—made great contributions to America by his documentation and eloquent presentation of the existence of stubborn poverty in the nation.

The Snowy Day
by Ezra Jack Keats.

The Snowy Day is the second seminal children's book of Modern America after Dr. Seuss' 1957 book, *The Cat in the Hat*. Keats, like Dr. Seuss, was an American illustrator and a prolific writer. He wrote 22 books over his career, but it was this book, *The Snowy Day*, for which he was particularly acclaimed. The book was immediately recognized as a milestone in American life because Keats' main character in the story was a young African American child. Until this book, minority children had been included in children's books only as background characters. Keats, who had grown up in a poor Polish-Jewish immigrant family in Brooklyn, wanted minority children to appear as central characters of stories. Although it may be unlikely that he would have expressed the book's objective as such, Keats introduced multiculturalism into mainstream children's literature. The next year Keats won the 1963 Caldecott Medal[138] for his illustrations in *The Snowy Day*.

The Least Dangerous Branch: The Supreme Court at the Bar of Politics
by Alexander Bickel.

This academic book is identified as a seminal book because it brilliantly addresses the role, power, and limits of the USSC—a delicate and highly debated subject in American social and political life. Bickel, a Yale law professor, starts the book by observing that the USSC's unique power is its authority to review the laws and actions of the other branches of government—even though it must depend upon the "political branches" of government to uphold its judgments. Such power became "settled" with the court's 1803 decision in *Marbury v. Madison*, but Bickel also notes that the court's decision is sustained by logic since "to leave the decision (of constitutionality) with the legislature ... (would be) to allow those whose power is supposed to be limited themselves to set the limits—an absurd invitation to consistent abuse."[139] Bickel was highly critical of many decisions of the 1953–1969 Warren Court, but possibly his most lasting influence was his articulation and support of what he called "the passive virtue" of judicial decision-making. Under this theory, courts should always refuse to decide cases based upon substantive grounds if the case can be decided upon narrower grounds. Although there are respectable counter-arguments to this theory and there may be instances in which exceptions are necessary, the theory of the "passive virtue" of de facto narrow decision-making has been widely adopted as an integral part of jurisprudential theory. Bickel's writings continue to be cited today although, tragically, Bickel himself died in 1974 at the age of 49 years.

Pulitzer Prize for Fiction

The Edge of Sadness
by Edwin O'Connor

Pulitzer Prize for General Nonfiction

The Making of the President, 1960
by Theodore H. White

Pulitzer Prize for History

The Triumphant Empire:
Thunder-Clouds Gather in the West, 1763–1766
by Lawrence H. Gipson

The New York Times Best Sellers List (Nonfiction) – Books with Most Weeks as No. 1 Best Seller

The Rothchilds: A Family Portrait
by Frederic Morton (17 weeks)

Calories Don't Count
by Herman Taller (13 weeks)

The New York Times Best Sellers List (Adult Fiction) – Book with Most Weeks as No. 1 Best Seller

Ship of Fools
by Katherine Anne Porter (26 weeks)

<u>Academy Awards Best Picture</u>

Winner: *Lawrence of Arabia*

Other Nominees: *The Longest Day, The Music Man,
Mutiny on the Bounty, To Kill a Mockingbird*

<u>*PrettyFamous'* Best Movie of the Year</u>

Lawrence of Arabia

<u>Best/Most Memorable Movie Lines of the Year</u>

"Bond. James Bond."

Sean Connery, the original James Bond, identifying himself in the movie *Dr. No*.

***"…Made to commit acts too unspeakable to be cited here
by an enemy who had captured his mind and his soul."***

A description of Laurence Harvey in *The Manchurian Candidate*, a Cold War international conspiracy thriller, about the brainwashing of the son of a prominent right-wing political couple. In the movie, the son is turned into an unwitting assassin by a foreign government, and the story is portrayed against the backdrop of the then omnipresent Cold War. With unsettling irony, the October 1962 release of the film occurred at the same time as the Cuban Missile Crisis.

***"One time Atticus said you never really know a man
until you stood in his shoes and walked around in them,
(but) just standing on (Boo) Radley's porch was enough."***

…

"I was to think of these days many times."

Scout, the narrating character in Robert Mulligan's production of Harper Lee's *To Kill a Mockingbird,* reminiscing years later about the Mississippi summer during which her father, Atticus, had boldly represented a black man falsely accused of rape in her small and segregated Southern town. Many people equally cherish the line "Miss Jean Louise. Miss Jean Louise. Stand up. Your father's passin' ."

> *"So long as the Arabs fight tribe against tribe,*
> *so long they will be a little people,*
> *a silly people, greedy, barbarous, and cruel as you are."*

Peter O'Toole, speaking in his role as the young military officer T.E. Lawrence[140] to Omar Sharif in *Lawrence of Arabia*. The words present an almost eerie foreshadowing of the seemingly constant turmoil in the region that, though admittedly not tribal in nature and not rooted in greed, nevertheless leaves paths of regional discord, violence, and death in its wake.

> *"You listen and hear your heart beat,*
> *and you hear your life ticking away.*
> *The thing that swells in your head (is that)*
> *you know absolutely for sure what's coming next."*

Burt Lancaster, speaking in his role as inmate Robert Stroud in *Birdman of Alcatraz*. The movie is a highly fictionalized account of Stroud's 42 years in solitary confinement. Although the movie's setting is Alcatraz, Stroud was actually incarcerated for most of his years as a federal prisoner at the U.S. Penitentiary in Leavenworth, Kansas—not Alcatraz—where, in fact, he was not permitted to keep birds. Stroud died in 1963, a year after the release of this film and the same year that Alcatraz Prison was itself closed.

1962 U.S. Population: 186,500,000

(Compared as a Percentage to the U.S. 1957 Population of 172,000,000: 108.4%)

Television Shows

Most Widely-Viewed Television Shows

Rank	Show Name	Years of Series (Excluding Reruns)	Show Type	Estimated Audience (In MMs)	Audience as Percentage of U.S. Population
1.	*The Beverly Hillbillies*	1962–1971	Comedy	18.1MM	9.7%
	Cast:	Buddy Ebsen - Donna Douglas - Max Baer, Jr.			
2.	*Candid Camera*	1960–1967	Reality-Humor	15.6MM	8.4%
	Cast/Host:	Allen Funt			
3.	*Red Skelton Show*	1951–1971	Comedy	15.6MM	8.4%
	Cast:	Red Skelton			

Widely-Viewed or Critically-Acclaimed New Television Show(s)

The Tonight Show with Johnny Carson (1962–1992)—
Late-Night Talk Show
Johnny Carson – Ed McMahon – Doc Severinsen
(No. 12 Top TV Shows of All Time – *TV Guide*)

Last Season Television Show(s)

Tales of Wells Fargo (1957–1962) —Western
Dale Robertson - Jake Ying - William Demarest

<u>Major Commercial Advertising Campaigns and Slogans</u>

"Let your fingers do the walking"
Yellow Pages

"We try harder"
Avis Rent-a-Car

<u>Memorable Words from Speeches, Books, Writings, and Other Sources – 1962</u>

"Guitar groups are on their way out."

January 1, 1962. Dick Rowe, an important and talented British record producer. Rowe made this remark, possibly one of the most inaccurate predictions in the history of music, immediately after the Beatles' 15-song audition with Decca Records in London on this New Year's Day in 1962. Over the next eight years, the Beatles would lead the "British invasion" of rock music into the United States and would become one of the preeminent bands in modern music history. Rowe, to his credit, adjusted his opinion and went on to sign the Rolling Stones, Them (Van Morrison), the Moody Blues, the Zombies, and even Tom Jones.

"Boy, that was a real fireball."

February 20, 1962. Astronaut John Glenn's welcomed voice and first words coming across the radio after his re-entry and splashdown landing on Earth. Glenn, one of the original "Right Stuff" Mercury Seven astronauts, orbited the Earth for only 55 minutes and 23 seconds, but with this ride he became the first American to do so. The "fireball" to which Glenn referred was his rocket's heat shield, which came loose from the force of re-entry. Years later during an interview with a reporter from *The Washington Post,* Glenn calmly stated that "as I got into the heat of reentry, I glanced out the window, and there were big flaming chunks (of the heat shield) coming back by the window…." Space launches and space travel in the 21st century now border upon the routine. It is too early to determine whether they will become events of routine commerce and travel, but unquestionably they are no longer matters of announcement, news, and celebration. In the late 1950s and 1960s, however, space travel took courage beyond description. Each launch was a major event. Americans said their prayers and held their breath for the astronauts. At the time of Glenn's launch, even the NASA engineers watched his liftoff through a periscope and from a bunker—1,000 feet away.

Television Line
"And that's the way it is, Tuesday, April…."

April 16, 1962. Walter Cronkite's nightly sign-off as anchor of the *CBS Evening News* from this date and for another 18 years, until 1981. Almost from the outset and especially after Cronkite's able and sober reporting of national events such as John F. Kennedy's assassination in 1963, Cronkite was sometimes referred to as "the most trusted man in America."[141] This reference was even supported by Gallup Polls during the period from the Kennedy years to the rise of Reagan. In a sense, Cronkite became one of the chief narrators of the emergence and transformations of Modern America. For example, when Cronkite started in 1962, the *CBS Evening News* was transmitted in black and white. It was not until January 1966 that the show's transmission switched permanently to a color format.

"…The soldier, above all other people, prays for peace,
for he must suffer and bear the deepest wounds and scars of war.
But always in our ears ring the ominous words of Plato,
that wisest of all philosophers:
'Only the dead have seen the end of war.'"

· · ·

"The shadows are lengthening for me.
The twilight is here.
My days of old have vanished, tone and tint.
They have gone glimmering through the dreams of things that were.
Their memory is one of wondrous beauty, watered by tears,
and coaxed and caressed by the smiles of yesterday.
I listen vainly, but with thirsty ears,
for the witching melody of faint bugle blowing reveille,
of far drums beating the long roll …
But in the evening of my memory,
always I come back to West Point."

· · ·

"Always there echoes and re-echoes:
Duty, Honor, Country."

May 12, 1962. General Douglas MacArthur, addressing the cadets of West Point and speaking in acceptance of the Sylvanus Thayer Award for outstanding service to the nation. General MacArthur was increasingly frail at the time of this speech, delivered just two years before his death at age 84, but he spoke gallantly and ably as he communicated his theme of Duty, Honor, Country. Regardless of one's opinion of General MacArthur, this speech resonates for its beauty. It remains one of the most eloquently written and touchingly delivered speeches in American history.

"Almighty God, we acknowledge our dependence upon Thee,
and we beg Thy blessing upon us,
our parents, our teachers and our country."

- - -

"The constitutional prohibition against laws respecting the
establishment of religion must at least mean that…
it is no part of the business of government
to compose official prayers for any group of the American people
to recite as a part of a religious program
carried on by the government."

June 25, 1962. On this date, the USSC, in a strong 6-1 majority decision in the case of *Engel v. Vitale*,[142] ruled that any prayersuch as the one first quoted above was violative of the Establishment Clause. This subject prayer was promulgated by the State of New York for recitation by students at the beginning of each school day. Because recital of the prayer was merely a recommendation and not a mandate and because the State believed the prayer to be non-denominational, the State argued that such prayer and recommendation for recital thereof did not violate the Establishment Clause of the U.S. Constitution. The Establishment Clause merely states that the government "shall make no law respecting an establishment of religion," and this school prayer question was a matter of first impression before the USSC. With the language set forth above, the USSC effectively barred "school prayers" in the U.S. A year later, the court in the case of *Abington Township School v. Schempp*[143] expanded its prior ruling by declaring that school-sponsored Bible-reading and the recitation of the Lord's Prayer were also violative of the Establishment Clause. Nevertheless, the rulings in these cases should not be overstated. Neither case prohibits individual students from reciting prayers, the study of religion as an academic study, or even the formation of and use of school property for Bible-study clubs or associations.

> ***"I once said 'We will bury you,' and I got into trouble with it.***
> ***Of course we (the Soviet Union) will not bury you with a shovel.***
> ***Your own working class will bury you."***

August 24, 1962. Soviet Premier Nikita Khrushchev, attempting to clarify, indeed change, the words he had spoken nearly seven years earlier when he asserted that history was "on the side" of the Soviet Union and that communism and that capitalism cannot long survive. The push and shove and ebb and flow of the superpowers during the course of the Cold War came to be tolerated, if not almost accepted. And Khrushchev himself changed his tone over the years. In 1960, just two years earlier than the above remark, Khrushchev even introduced the concept of "peaceful coexistence" between the East and the West. But thinly below the suggestions of peaceful coexistence, there remained a fierce and relentless tension. In the midst of the Cold War and especially in the age of the space race, nuclear missiles and duck-n-cover, every utterance of the Communist leaders—and especially those referencing being "buried"—was closely weighed and cautiously considered by the West.

Television Line
"Heeeeere's Johnny!!"

October 1, 1962. Ed McMahon's nightly greeting of host Johnny Carson on *The Tonight Show*. McMahon started using this opening shortly after Johnny Carson took over the show from Jack Paar on this date in 1962. Carson's guests on this first evening were 72-year-old Groucho Marx, Tony Bennett, Joan Crawford, Rudy Vallee, and the then-young comedy writer Mel Brooks. He hosted the show for the next three decades—until May 22, 1992. The show was broadcast from New York City until Carson moved it to Burbank, California in 1972. Over the course of the show's 4,531 episodes, Johnny Carson, along with his sidekick Ed McMahon, his bandleader Doc Severinsen and the NBC orchestra, became an American institution.

"We're eyeball to eyeball,
and I think the other fellow just blinked."

October 24, 1962. Secretary of State Dean Rusk's supposed remark in the midst of the Cuban Missile Crisis. Rusk supposedly said these words to National Security Director McGeorge Bundy upon their being informed that the 23 Russian freighters heading towards Cuba had stopped dead in the water. Although there is debate about the historical accuracy of this remark,[144] it does accurately reflect the fact that President John Kennedy's gamble of insisting upon the absence of nuclear weapons in Cuba (together with the U.S.'s agreement to remove certain of its missiles from Turkey) may have been the key to averting a nuclear ending to the crisis and to bringing to an end the horrific 13 Days in October. Upon Soviet Premier Nikita Khrushchev's orders, the Soviet missiles in Cuba were dismantled in exchange for a non-invasion pledge from the U.S. As the crisis wound down, the 156 intercontinental missiles which the U.S. had readied and armed were defused. The 54 Strategic Air Command bombers, which the U.S. had scrambled, came home. And finally, the U.S. again lowered its alert level from DefCon 3 to DefCon 5.

> ***"I leave you gentleman now.***
> ***You will now write it; you will interpret it; that's your right.***
> ***But as I leave you, I want you to …***
> ***just think how much you're going to be missing (me).***
> ***You won't have Nixon to kick around anymore,***
> ***because, gentlemen, this is my last press conference …"***

November 7, 1962. Richard M. Nixon at his "last press conference" after losing the election for the Governor of California to Democratic incumbent Edmund G. "Pat" Brown, Sr. Just as had been the case in his quest for the U.S. Presidency in 1960, Nixon had been projected to win this gubernatorial race. However, he was again rejected by the voters. This time Nixon lost by a nearly 5% margin: 51.9% for Brown, 46.9% for Nixon. Despite Nixon's implication in this statement that he was withdrawing from politics and despite his broad disfavor in the U.S. press, he was elected President of the United States just six years later.

"Good girls go to heaven, bad girls go everywhere."

1962. Helen Gurley Brown, author of the 1962 book *Sex and the Single Girl*[145] and Editor-in-Chief of *Cosmopolitan* magazine for 32 years. This phrase had been introduced years earlier by Mae West, but in Modern America it is more widely attributed to Ms. Brown and was, in fact, a "watchword" saying of Ms. Brown. Ms. Brown went so far as to have it "embroidered on a pillow she kept in her pink-walled *Cosmopolitan* editorial office."[146]

"Good Homes Building Good Citizens"

1962. The banner under which Chicago Mayor Richard J. Daley stood as he proudly opened the city's Robert Taylor Homes, the largest public housing project in the world at that time. It consisted of 28 high-rise buildings—each 16 stories tall. Nearly 38 years later, Mayor Daley's son, Mayor Richard M. Daley "looked at the sorry state of the city's public housing (also including ... the (now) infamous Cabrini-Green projects) —neglected physical plants beyond repair, rampant drug dealing, gang wars —and concluded that his father's ballyhooed concept for providing affordable housing for the city's poor had failed."[147, 148]

"The best and the brightest" vis-à-vis
"Nine millionaires and a plumber"

1962. The "best-and-brightest" phrase was originally coined by Sargent Shriver to describe the cabinet assemblage of his brother-in-law, President John F. Kennedy (although Shriver, in turn, may have adapted it from a poem by Shelley or from several other sources). President Kennedy's cabinet was composed of 16 Phi Beta Kappas, four Rhodes Scholars, and a Nobel Prize winner, and the phrase as applied to the cabinet was later immortalized as the title of the 1972 bestselling book by David Halberstam. Even by the end of the decade, some commentators had come to believe that "the best and the brightest" may have been neither.[149] The phrase has also been juxtaposed by some writers with the above-included phrase "nine millionaires and a plumber" which had been used to describe President Eisenhower's very different cabinet.[150] Because Eisenhower had assembled his cabinet "to carry out his mandate for moderation, he appointed a Cabinet composed largely of pragmatic businessmen. A notable exception was his Secretary of Labor, Martin P. Durkin, a Democrat and president of the plumbers and steamfitter's union." Variations of "Nine millionaires and a plumber" such as "Nine billionaires and a ..." have also surfaced in the context of President Donald Trump's 2016 formation of his cabinet which, like Eisenhower's cabinet, is composed mostly of highly successful and wealthy businessmen.

Year 1963

<u>Seminal Books</u>

Anti-Intellectualism in American Life[151]
by Richard Hofstadter

The role and relevance of anti-intellectualism in any society—especially a democratic society—is a uniquely complicated subject. Even the word itself is prone to subjective definition. Nevertheless, anti-intellectualism has always been a powerful presence in American society—a "virulent strain … in American life."[152] Hofstadter himself is widely recognized as one of America's greatest historians who, in the words of one writer, achieved "the trifecta of scholarly importance, popularity outside the (academic community), and unquestioned intellectual integrity"[153] In this book, Hofstadter identified the many groups, such as business and evangelical religious groups, that historically have been sources of anti-intellectualism. He addresses the role of education as a countervailing force, but he notes with concern how, especially in American society, the purposes of education have been narrowed, if not driven, by demands of "practicability and utility." Although the book is thick and has been criticized for being "long and dense,"[154] it remains a powerful and brilliantly thoughtful book with, at least in the opinion of liberal commentators, particular relevance to the early 21st century, with the rise of the Tea Party and the sustained elevation of anger in American politics. Hofstadter was a Professor at Columbia University for many years. He was the recipient of two Pulitzer Prizes books—one for this book and one for *The Age of Reform*. In the midst of writing his planned three-volume history of the United States, he died in 1970 at the age of 54.

On Revolution
by Hannah Arendt

After contrasting the two major revolutions of the 18th century, the French and American Revolutions, Arendt concludes that while the French

Revolution was the focus of far greater study and even supposed emulation, it was the American Revolution that was the success. Arendt taught at a number of American universities including Notre Dame, UC-Berkeley, and Northwestern, and in 1959 became the first female lecturer at Princeton University. Drawing upon this academic background and through her comparative examination of the French and American Revolutions, she makes in this book a series of penetrating observations about Modern America. Her other major books include *The Origins of Totalitarianism* (1951) and *The Human Condition* (1958).

The Feminine Mystique
by Betty Friedan

This book is widely cited as one of the first of a series of writings that served as the textual basis for the emerging feminist movement of the 1960s and early 1970s. Betty Friedan wrote this book after conducting a survey of her classmates at her 1957 Smith College 15-Year Class Reunion. In 1966, Ms. Friedan became one of the founders and served as the first President of the National Organization for Women. In 1971, she helped establish the National Women's Political Caucus and was a steadfast proponent of the Equal Rights Amendment (the "ERA") which, in 1972, passed both the House of Representatives (354-24) and the Senate (84-8) and was even endorsed by President Nixon. Nevertheless, the ERA failed to be ratified by two-thirds of the states, even by the extended deadline of June 30, 1982.

The Fire Next Time
by James Baldwin

This book consists of two lengthy essays relating to racial relations in the U.S. in the early 1960s—or "the Negro problem" as it was then called. Baldwin's book, which became an immediate national best seller, gave passionate voice to the still young and emerging Civil Rights Movement. The first essay, "My Dungeon Shook..." was written on the 100th Anniversary of Lincoln's signing of the Emancipation Proclamation and was written in the form of a letter to Baldwin's teenage nephew. The second essay addressed the complicated relationship between race and religion in America. Through this book and other writings, Baldwin "masterful(ly) presents the corrosion of hate, the taste of fear (and) the misery of humiliation"[155] that were components of the lives of most African Americans at this time. Although Baldwin spent much of his life as an expatriate, he was deeply involved with the Civil Rights Movement in the early 1960s, and, in the opinion of many Americans, was one of its most prominent spokesmen for a period of time. He was also one of the few prominent gay men in the Civil Rights Movement, which was largely hostile to gays at that time. Courageously, Baldwin traveled throughout the South and wrote about the impact of racial discrimination and the need for civil rights and civil respect. He described the violence in Birmingham, Alabama. He registered voters in Selma, Alabama. He stood with Harry Belafonte and his friends Sidney Poitier and Marlon Brando at the 1963 Civil Rights March in Washington, D.C. But his most lasting contribution may still be the brilliant, poignant, and timely writing of *The Fire Next Time.*

Where the Wild Things Are
by Maurice Sendak

Sendak's book is the third and last children's book of Modern America that is here identified as a seminal book.[156] Consisting of only 338 words, *Where the Wild Things Are* incorporated extraordinary illustrations and introduced, in effect, a new subject into the genre of children's books. Just as *The Snowy Day* had for the first time introduced a young black child as the lead character, Sendak's book for the first time deliberately presented a story about a child's emotions. While the book focuses on a child's anger, it also explores how children learn to grapple with and master similar emotions such as fear, danger, and even frustration and jealousy. The book initially received poor reviews. It was even banned in many libraries. However, the popularity of the book increased steadily. In 1964, the book was awarded the prestigious Caldecott Medal. By 2009, nearly 20 million copies of *Where the Wild Things Are* had been sold worldwide, and it had been adapted both as an opera and a film.

<u>Pulitzer Prize for Fiction</u>

The Reivers
by William Faulkner (Posthumous Award)

<u>Pulitzer Prize for General Nonfiction</u>

The Guns of August
by Barbara W. Tuchman

<u>Pulitzer Prize for History</u>

Washington, Village and Capital, 1800–1878
by Constance McLaughlin Green

<u>*The New York Times* Best Sellers List (Nonfiction)— Books with Most Weeks as No. 1 Best Seller</u>

Travels with Charley: In Search of America
by John Steinbeck (22 weeks)

The Fire Next Time
by James Baldwin (12 weeks)

<u>*The New York Times* Best Sellers List (Adult Fiction)— Book with Most Weeks as No. 1 Best Seller</u>

The Shoes of the Fisherman
by Morris West (14 weeks)

<u>Academy Awards Best Picture</u>

Winner: *Tom Jones*

Other Nominees: *America America, Cleopatra, How the West Was Won, Lilies of the Field*

<u>*PrettyFamous'* Best Movie of the Year</u>

The Birds

<u>Best/Most Memorable Movie Line of the Year</u>

"Let's get our shoelaces untied. Whaddya Say?"

. . .

"I'd say I've been asked with a little more finesse in my time."

Paul Newman's suggestion and Patricia Neal's sarcastic response in Martin Ritt's western film *Hud* and based upon Larry McMurtry's book, *Horseman, Pass By.*

<u>1963 U.S. Population: 189,200,000</u>

(Compared as a Percentage to the U.S. 1957 Population of 172,000,000: 110.0%)

<u>Television Shows</u>

Most Widely-Viewed Television Shows

Rank Show Name	Years of Series (Excluding Reruns)	Show Type	Estimated Audience (In MMs)	Audience as Percentage of U.S. Population
1. *The Beverly Hillbillies*	1962–1971	Comedy	20.2MM	10.7%
Cast: Buddy Ebsen - Donna Douglas - Max Baer, Jr.				
2. *Bonanza*	1959–1973	Western	19.0MM	10.0%
Cast: Lorne Greene - Michael Landon – Pernell Roberts – Dan Blocker				
3. *Dick Van Dyke Show*	1961–1966	Comedy	17.2MM	9.1%
Cast: Dick Van Dyke - Mary Tyler Moore				

Last Season Television Show(s)

Have Gun Will Travel (1957–1963) – Western – Richard Boone

Leave It to Beaver (1957-1963) – Family Comedy Show

Jerry Mathers - Barbara Billingsley - Hugh Beaumont - Tony Dow

<u>Memorable Words from Speeches, Books, Writings, and Other Sources – 1963</u>

"The problem that has no name."

. . .

"The problem lay buried, unspoken,
for many years in the minds of American women."

. . .

"It was a strange stirring, a sense of dissatisfaction, a yearning ...
that women suffered
in the middle of the 20th century in the United States.
Each suburban wife struggled with it alone.
As she made the beds, shopped for groceries ...
she was afraid to ask even of herself the silent question—
'Is this all?'"

February 19, 1963. Excerpt from Betty Friedan's book, *The Feminine Mystique,* which was released on this date. After conducting a survey of her Smith College classmates at their 15ᵗʰ reunion in 1957, Freidan was surprised to find how many of her classmates were unhappy and dissatisfied. Many of her classmates felt unfulfilled in their lives despite their being married, having children, and living in material comfort—the then widely accepted and articulated definition of a female's role in society at the time. After Friedan was unable to get any article published by any national magazine about this subject, she wrote *The Feminine Mystique.* As noted above, this book helped spark the beginning of the second wave of feminism in the country—the first being the women's suffrage movement of the late 19ᵗʰ and early 20ᵗʰ century, which led to the 1920 adoption of the 19ᵗʰ Amendment granting women the right to vote.

> ***"I draw the line in the dust and***
> ***toss the gauntlet before the feet of tyranny,***
> ***and I say segregation now, segregation tomorrow, segregation forever."***

January 4, 1963. The words of George Wallace during his initial inaugural address as Governor of Alabama. He had appeared more politically and socially moderate in the 1950s when he served as an Alabama judge, but he became—and for most of his life remained—an ardent segregationist. With the above line, he also provided the repugnant chant that would be repeated by segregationists for the next decade. Wallace's most lasting influence may be the ways in which he framed the issues of civil rights and integration. First, he asserted that these issues were matters of supposed "personal liberties" and suggested that people should be allowed "racial and cultural freedom." Second, he framed segregationist arguments in the context of an anti-federal government stance. By this reasoning, he argued that his belief in segregation was a matter of states' rights, and he passionately opposed the imposition of integration by the federal government and the USSC. By structuring the debates in this manner and by his derisive references to "pointy-headed intellectuals" and "Ivy League elites," Wallace became one of the first prominent politicians to exploit the ideological link between conservatives in the North and in the South. In later years, this new majority of conservative votes would be used strategically and effectively by Republican Presidential candidates. As a passionate segregationist, Wallace sought the Democratic Presidential nomination three times (1964, 1972, and 1976). In addition, he ran for President in 1968 on the American Independent ticket, where he (with retired four-star Air Force General Curtis LeMay as his Vice-Presidential running mate) received 9.9 million votes (13.5% of all votes) and 45 electoral votes, thus becoming the only third-party candidate in Modern America to ever receive any electoral votes. After an assassination attempt against him in May 1972, Wallace spent the rest of his life in a wheelchair. To his honorable credit, late in life he recanted many of his racist views, apologized to the African American community, and was accepted and even embraced by many members of that community.

"The right to be heard would be, in many cases, of little avail if it did not comprehend the right to be heard by counsel."

March 18, 1963. With these words contained in its unanimous ruling on the case of *Gideon v. Wainwright*, the USSC extended the Sixth Amendment right to counsel to all criminal cases in state courts as well as federal courts. While the Sixth Amendment provides for the right "to have the Assistance of counsel for his defense," there had been—until *Gideon*—a question as to whether this right also applied to the states. In response to the pencil-written petition written by Clarence Gideon, who had been convicted of burglary in Florida and was serving a five-year sentence, the USSC took up the case and resoundingly decided that Gideon should have been provided counsel. As a result of the USSC's ruling, Gideon was retried. After a mere one hour of deliberation, the jury found him innocent of all charges. Gideon died about eight years later. On his headstone are inscribed the following words taken from a letter he wrote to Abe Fortas, the attorney appointed to represent him in his USSC case, *"Each era finds an improvement in law for the benefit of mankind."* This case expanding the right of counsel to state criminal cases had a huge impact throughout the United States because most criminal cases are tried in the state, not the federal, courts.

"Alcatraz was never no good for nobody"

March 21, 1963. The words of Frank Weatherman, the last convict to leave Alcatraz Prison, as he and the other final 27 prisoners walked down the gangplank to board the prisoner ship and left the island prison. Alcatraz, known as "The Rock," had been a prison since 1858 and a federal maximum-security prison since 1934. In that time, it had been the home to such prisoners as Al Capone, Baby Face Nelson, Machine Gun Kelly, and Robert Stroud, the Birdman of Alcatraz. However, by 1963, Alcatraz had deteriorated so badly that it was no longer deemed safe for either prisoners or staff. Most of the prisoners were eventually transferred to the newly constructed and more centrally located federal maximum-security prison in Marion, Illinois about 300 miles south of Chicago.[157]

"I would rather be governed by the first two thousand names in the Boston telephone directory than the Harvard faculty."

April 28, 1963. William F. Buckley, Jr. writing in a book review published in *The New York Times* and as paraphrased by L. Edwards in his 2010 book *William F. Buckley Jr.: The Maker of a Movement*. Buckley himself used variations of this statement on numerous occasions including, for example, in 1965 during his appearance on *Meet the Press*. The line is clever and humorous, although it should be noted that he normally chose to reference Harvard University rather than Yale University, his alma mater. The historical significance of the line is that it reinforces one consistent narrative of the resurgent conservative movement that the federal government and the media especially are controlled, or at least unduly influenced, by detached, out-of-touch, liberal, Eastern academics and elites. While there may be some merit to this position, Buckley seems to be an inappropriate communicator of this theory since he himself was, by almost any measure, the very embodiment of a highly-educated, pretentious, Eastern intellectual. Furthermore, he was himself a part of the media through his editorship of the conservative magazine *National Review,* which he started in 1955, and as host of the television show *Firing Line,* which aired for nearly 33 years from 1966 to 1999.

"Ich bin ein Berliner."
("I am a Berliner")

June 26, 1963. President John F. Kennedy in West Berlin, Germany, two years after the construction of The Wall[158] that severed West Berlin from East Berlin and East Germany. By this statement to an estimated crowd of 450,000 Germans, Kennedy intended to underscore America's continuing commitment to West Germany—and particularly to the West Berliners living in the shadow of The Wall.

> *"We cannot walk alone.*
> *And as we walk, we must make the pledge*
> *that we shall always march ahead.*
> *We cannot turn back."*
>
> …
>
> *"Let us not wallow in the valley of despair.*
> *I say to you today, my friends,*
> *… even though we face difficulties of today and tomorrow,*
> *I still have a dream.*
> *It is a dream deeply rooted in the American dream.*
> *I have a dream that one day this nation will rise up*
> *and live out the true meaning of its creed:*
> *'We hold these truths to be self-evident, that all men*
> *are created equal.' "*
>
> …
>
> *"I have a dream that one day on the red hills of Georgia,*
> *the sons of former slaves and the sons of former slave owners*
> *will be able to sit down together at the table of brotherhood.*
> *I have a dream that one day even the state of Mississippi,*
> *a state sweltering in the heat of injustice,*
> *sweltering with the heat of oppression,*
> *will be transformed into an oasis of freedom and justice."*
>
> …
>
> *"I have a dream that my four little children*
> *will one day live in a nation*

where they will not be judged by the color of their skin
but by the content of their character."
...
"I have a dream ... !
I have a dream that one day down in Alabama,
with its vicious racists,
with its governor having his lips dripping
with the words of interposition and nullification ....
little black boys and black girls will be able to join hands
with little white boys and white girls as sisters and brothers."
...
"I have a dream today... !
I have a dream that one day every valley shall be exalted,
and every hill and mountain shall be made low ...
This is our hope.
This is the faith that I go back to the South with.
With this faith we will be able
to hew out of the mountain of despair a stone of hope.
With this faith we will be able to transform the jangling discord
of our nation into a beautiful symphony of brotherhood.
With this faith we will be able to work together,
to pray together, to struggle together, to go to jail together,
to stand up for freedom together,
knowing that we will be free one day."
...
"This will be the day ...
when all of God's children will be able to sing with new meaning
'My country 'tis of thee, sweet land of liberty, of thee I sing.
Land where my fathers died, land of the Pilgrim's pride,
from every mountain, let freedom ring'
And if America is to be a great nation,
this must become true."

August 28, 1963. The Reverend Dr. Martin Luther King, Jr., speaking
on the occasion of the March on Washington. The speech was delivered

shortly after the cries of singer Mahalia Jackson exhorted the Rev. King to "tell 'em about the dream, Martin, tell 'em about the dream." Her exhortations referred to the passages that the Rev. King had been working into his speeches earlier that summer. And with that, he did so in an "impromptu peroration" that contained the powerful rhetoric and reflected the deep passion of his beliefs.[159] The speech remains one of the greatest speeches in American social and political life. The Rev. King carried nine riffs to the "I have a dream" theme and forever emblazoned the phrase into the American consciousness. Almost exactly 50 years later on what is now the January national holiday celebrating the Rev. King, the public inauguration of President Barack Obama, a black man, was held in Washington, D.C., with President Obama sitting with his wife and their two children.

> *"A Negro mother wept in the street Sunday morning*
> *in front of a Baptist church in Birmingham.*
> *In her hand she held a shoe, one shoe,*
> *from the foot of her dead child.*
> *We hold that shoe with her.*
> *Every one of us in the white South*
> *holds that small shoe in his hand."*
>
> *...*
>
> *"Only we can trace the truth, Southern – you and I.*
> *We broke those children's bodies.*
> *We watched the stage set without staying it.*
> *We listened to the prologue unbestirred.*
> *We saw the curtain opening with disinterest.*
> *We have heard the play....*
> *We—the heirs of a proud South,*
> *who protest its worth and demand its recognition—*
> *we are the ones who have ducked the difficult,*
> *skirted the uncomfortable,*
> *caviled at the challenge, resented the necessary,*
> *rationalized the unacceptable,*
> *and created the day surely when these children would die."*

September 16, 1963. Eugene Patterson, an American journalist and the Pulitzer Prize-winning editor of *The Atlanta Constitution*. This column is widely viewed as his most famous writing. It was entitled "A Flower for the Graves" and was written in the immediate aftermath of the racist bombing of the 16th Street Baptist Church in Birmingham, Alabama. Deeply moved by the column's capturing eloquence, CBS News Anchor Walter Cronkite had Patterson read his column on his *CBS Evening News* on this date. Many Americans viewed the killing of these four young girls as one of the turning points in the Civil Rights Movement of the 1960s. Patterson "used his daily column to force Southerners (of which he was one), 'a people with traditions of decency' to face up to the horrors of racism."[160] He was known "for his fairness and integrity as the nation confronted racial turmoil, divisions over the Vietnam War and ethical challenges in journalism."[161] At varying times in his career, he also served as vice chairman of the U.S. Commission on Civil Rights (from 1964 to 1968), as the Managing Editor of *The Washington Post,* and later as the Editor of *The St. Petersburg Times* (now *The Tampa Bay Times*).[162]

> **"President Kennedy died at 1:00PM Central Standard Time,**
> **2:00 Eastern Standard Time, some 38 minutes ago.**
> **Vice President Lyndon Johnson has left the hospital in Dallas,**
> **but we do not know to where he has proceeded.**
> **Presumably, he will be taking the oath of office shortly**
> **and will become the 36th President of the United States."**

November 22, 1963. Walter Cronkite, broadcasting from his desk at the CBS Newsroom in New York. It was by this announcement that most Americans first learned that President John F. Kennedy had died. Surrounded by rotary telephones and wire machines, Cronkite's voice cracked with sadness and disbelief. The announcement came about an hour after a brief CBS News Bulletin had interrupted the network's regular airing of the soap opera, *As the World Turns*. Immediately after Cronkite's broadcast, all regular television show broadcasting was suspended for days —not hours, but days. In its place, all television programming was devoted solely to news about the assassination and to a national sharing of the late President's funeral. For days and weeks thereafter, the nation remained in somber shock, and this date is emblazoned in the memories of a generation of Americans.

> ***"This is a sad time for all people.***
> ***We have suffered a loss that cannot be weighed. ...***
> ***I will do my best. That is all I can do.***
> ***I ask for your help—and God's."***

November 22, 1963. President Lyndon Johnson, upon landing at Andrews Air Force Base at 6:10PM on that fateful day. Johnson had just been sworn in as President amidst a broken, tense, and despondent crowd of 27 people crammed inside the tiny conference room aboard Air Force One. The newly sworn-in President Johnson spoke in a sad and uncharacteristically humble tone—presumably still trying to comprehend the events of that tragic day and trying to absorb the responsibilities which had been placed before him.

> ***"We have talked long enough in this country about equal rights.***
> ***We have talked for one hundred years or more.***
> ***It is time now to write the next chapter,***
> ***and to write it in the books of law."***

November 27, 1963. President Lyndon Johnson, speaking in his address to a joint session of Congress just five days after the assassination of John F. Kennedy and just five days after being sworn in as President. As noted by one reporter, in this speech "sympathy for the martyred President was enlisted to advance the cause (of civil rights), as was America's desire for continuity, for stability, (and) for reassurance that the government was holding a firm course...."[163]

> ***"Just get me elected, and then you can have your war."***

December 24, 1963. The cold, cynical and calculating remark of President Lyndon Johnson made to a group of military service chiefs at a Christmas Eve reception at the White House. From the moment of President Johnson's ascendancy into office, the Vietnam War entangled his Presidency. Fairly or otherwise and despite his massive domestic agenda, by

1968, it was the Vietnam War that consumed his Presidency, defined his legacy, and negated any reasonable expectations of his re-election.

Year 1964

<u>Seminal Book</u>

One-Dimensional Man:
Studies in the Ideology of Advanced Industrial Society
by William Marcuse

Despite being written in thick prose and engulfed in theories, isms, and ologies and despite being dated due its comparisons between capitalistic and communistic societies, Marcuse's book remains critical to understanding Modern America. The book was often cited as the Bible of the New Left and the radicalism of the Sixties. Partly, this is due to the book's attack on the shallow, but controlling and dominant, consumerism and materialism of post-war America. More importantly, however, Marcuse articulated the concern that the industrial working class had been integrated into and made a part of modern capitalistic society. Marcuse argued that as an inevitable result of such integration, the avenues for and the risks of radical and challenging thought had been stifled. This theory of materialistic sublimation was simultaneously clever and alarming, since "(t)he pure form of servitude (of an individual to a society) is to exist as an instrument" of such society.[164] Marcuse did not appear to "foresee that (later) social movements … might have a transformative effect" leading to a time "when women became CEOs of major corporations, same-sex marriage rites became common, … and an African American family occupied the White House…,"[165] but Marcuse's concerns about the addictive and controlling powers of consumerism remain relevant to Modern America. In addition, one of the components of "seminal" is that of influence, and Marcuse's book had a profound and lasting influence on at least one generation of Americans.

Pulitzer Prize for General Nonfiction

Anti-Intellectualism in American Life
by Richard Hofstadter

Pulitzer Prize for History

Puritan Village: The Foundation of a New England Town
by Sumner Chilton Powell

The New York Times Best Sellers List (Nonfiction)— Books with Most Weeks as No. 1 Best Seller

A Moveable Feast
by Ernest Hemingway (19 weeks)

Four Days: The Historical Record of the Death of President Kennedy
Compiled by United Press International and
American Heritage Magazine (12 weeks)

The New York Times Best Sellers List (Adult Fiction)— Book with Most Weeks as No. 1 Best Seller

The Spy Who Came in from the Cold
by John le Carre (34 weeks)

Academy Awards Best Picture

Winner: *My Fair Lady*
Other Nominees: *Becket, Dr. Strangelove or:*
How I Learned to Stop Worrying and Love the Bomb,
Mary Poppins, Zorba the Greek

PrettyFamous' Best Movie of the Year

Dr. Strangelove or: How I Learned to Stop Worrying and Love the Bomb

Best/Most Memorable Movie Lines of the Year

"Gentleman, you can't fight in here! This is the War Room!"
George C. Scott's ironically absurd line in Stanley Kubrick's *Dr.*
Strangelove or: How I Learned to Stop Worrying and Love the Bomb.

*"I can no longer sit back and allow Communist infiltration,
Communist indoctrination, Communist subversion, and the
international Communist conspiracy to sap and impurify
all of our precious bodily fluids."*

Sterling Hayden explaining his obsession against the rampant spread of communism to a perplexed and frightened British military officer brilliantly portrayed by Peter Sellers in *Dr. Strangelove or: How I Learned to Stop Worrying and Love the Bomb.*

"A martini. Shaken, not stirred."

Sean Connery classic (and many times repeated) statement of his drink preference in *Goldfinger,* the follow-up to 1962's classic introductory line of *"Bond. James Bond."*

"My name is Pussy Galore."

...

"I must be dreaming."

The uniquely named actress, Honor Blackman, introducing herself to Sean Connery in his role as James Bond in *Goldfinger*—and Sean Connery's (understandable) response.

"Supercalifragilisticexpialidocious"

The unforgettable word of Julie Andrews in her role as Mary Poppins in Robert Stevenson's musical-fantasy film of the same name.

"The rain in Spain stays mainly in the plains."

...

"I think she's got it. I think she's got it…."

The adorable Audrey Hepburn articulating her proper English in George Cukor's film *My Fair Lady* and Rex Harrison's expressions of surprise and joy.

1964 U.S. Population: 191,900,000

(Compared as a Percentage to the U.S. 1957 Population of 172,000,000: 111.6%)

Television Shows

Most Widely-Viewed Television Shows

Rank	Show Name	Years of Series (Excluding Reruns)	Show Type	Estimated Audience (In MMs)	Audience as Percentage of U.S. Population
1.	*Bonanza*	1959–1973	Western	19.1MM	10.0%
	Cast: Lorne Greene - Michael Landon – Pernell Roberts – Dan Blocker				
2.	*Bewitched*	1964–1972	Comedy	16.3MM	8.5%
	Cast: Elizabeth Montgomery - Dick York - David White				
3.	*Gomer Pyle U.S.M.C.*	1964–1969	Comedy	16.2MM	8.4%
	Cast: Jim Nabors - Frank Sutton - Ronnie Schell				

Last Season Television Show(s)

Danny Thomas Show (1953–1964) - Comedy

Danny Thomas - Marjorie Lord - Annette Funicello

Major Commercial Advertising Campaigns and Slogans

"Does she or doesn't she?"

Clairol

"Please don't squeeze the Charmin."

Proctor & Gamble's Charmin

"Put a tiger in your tank"

Esso

Memorable Words from Speeches, Books, Writings, and Other Sources – 1964

Presidential Campaign Themes, Slogans and Results
(Both Official and Unofficial)
(Only Major Presidential Party Nominees and Candidates Listed)

Barry Goldwater (and William E. Miller) (Republican Party)

A Choice, Not an Echo   AUH2O.   In Your Heart, You Know He's Right

Anti-Republican Slogans

"In Your Heart, You Know He Might"—A Democratic response slogan alluding by implication to Goldwater's expressed willingness to use atomic weapons in Vietnam

and

"In Your Guts, You Know He's Nuts"

Lyndon B. Johnson (and Hubert Humphrey) (Democratic Party)

All The Way With LBJ   LBJ for the U.S.A.   Let's Back Johnson
My Brand Is LBJ   The Stakes Are Too High for You to Stay at Home

Election Results:

Party	Nominees		Electoral Vote		Popular Vote	
	Presidential	Vice-Presidential				
Democratic	Lyndon B. Johnson	H. Humphrey	486	90.3%	43.1MM	61.1%
Republican	Barry Goldwater	W. E. Miller	52	9.7%	27.2MM	38.5%

> ***"Let us carry forward the plans and programs of John Fitzgerald Kennedy—not because of our sorrow or sympathy, but because they are right."***
>
> **...**
>
> ***"This administration today, here and now, declares unconditional war on poverty in America. I urge this Congress and all Americans to join with me in that effort."***

January 8, 1964. President Lyndon Johnson, speaking in his first State of the Union Address before a Joint Session of Congress less than two months after his ascent to the Presidency upon the assassination of President John Kennedy. With fanfare and hope, President Johnson signed his initial War on Poverty legislation about 14 months later.[166]

> ***"Cigarette smoking is a cause of lung cancer and laryngeal cancer in men, a probable cause of lung cancer in women, and the most important cause of chronic bronchitis."***

January 11, 1964. The summary of the major conclusions of the Surgeon General's Advisory Committee on Smoking and Health,[167] which was released on this day.[168] This report and its conclusions dominated the press and television news cycles for days after the report's release. Within a year, the U.S. Congress enacted the Federal Cigarette Labeling and Advertising Act of 1965 which required that a health warning be imprinted on all cigarette packages. Several years later and in response to a growing demand for the curtailing or elimination of cigarette smoking in the U.S., Congress adopted legislation in 1969 which prohibited the advertising of cigarettes in all U.S. broadcast media. Many cities and states had already or would later enact minimum age legislation (normally ages 18 or 21) barring the sale of cigarettes to minors, but it was not until 1997 that the federal government finally made it illegal for anyone to sell cigarettes to anyone under the age of 18. In 1998 and after decades of litigation, the Tobacco Master Settlement Agreement was signed between the four major U.S. tobacco companies and the attorneys general of 46 states. At the time of the settlement, it was the largest such class action settlement in the history of the U.S., and the participating tobacco companies agreed to pay not less than $206 billion over the first 25 years of the agreement.

U.S. Constitutional Amendment – 24th Amendment

"The rights of citizens ... to vote (in any Federal election)
shall not be denied ...
by reason of failure to pay any poll tax or other tax."

January 23, 1964. This amendment prohibits the federal government from conditioning the right of a citizen to vote upon the payment of a poll tax or any other tax. Such taxes had been adopted by many Southern states in the late 19th century as a means of preventing African Americans and often poor whites from voting. The necessity of the constitutional amendment was due to the USSC's regrettable 1937 holding in *Breedlove v. Suttles* that such poll taxes were constitutional. At the time of this 1964 amendment, five Southern states still had a poll tax—Virginia, Alabama, Texas, Arkansas, and Mississippi. While the amendment itself only prohibits the imposition of a poll tax in federal elections, the prohibition was extended by the USSC in 1966 to apply equally to state elections as well.[169]

"I don't have to be what you want me to be."

February 26, 1964. Cassius Clay, at age 22, speaking on the day after he did indeed "float like a butterfly and sting like a bee" and upset Sonny Liston in a highly-contested fight for the World Heavyweight Championship in Miami Beach, Florida.[170] The next day he followed his father's lead and joined the Nation of Islam (although in 1975 he converted to Sunni Islam). Then, to the surprise and confusion of millions of adoring Americans, Clay changed his name to Muhammad Ali. Three years later, he refused conscription into the Army both as a conscientious objector and in opposition to the war in Vietnam.[171] He was convicted and stripped of his title and not allowed to fight until four years later when his conviction was overturned by the USSC in 1971. Ali, nicknamed "The Greatest," went on to win the World Heavyweight Championship two more times—in 1974 and again in 1978. He is widely considered to be one of, if not *the* greatest, heavyweight champions in history. In December, 1999, he was named "Sportsman of the Century" by *Sports Illustrated.* Over the many decades preceding his death in 2016, Ali became widely admired throughout the world, not only for his boxing talents but also for his humanity and for the passion of his beliefs in religious freedom and racial justice. As suggested by this quote and as noted by the famous writer Joyce Carol Oates, Ali also was one of the few athletes (indeed, public figures in modern life) who had the determination and ability to "define the terms of his public reputation." Ali's passion for self-definition is honorable and is similar to that of other leaders such as—albeit in the context of a profession far, far removed from professional boxing—Steve Jobs when he said, about 40 years later in the course of his address to the graduating class at Stanford University, "don't let the noise of others' opinion drown out your own inner voice, and most important, have the courage to follow your heart and intuition."[172]

"Guilty"
Jimmy Hoffa

March 1, 1964. Jimmy Hoffa, the President of the International Brotherhood of Teamsters (the "Teamsters"), was found guilty on multiple charges of jury tampering and bribery. Hoffa served as President of the Teamsters from 1958 until 1971. The 1964 convictions were the result of many prior investigations – several of them led by tenacious Teddy Kennedy, the U.S. Attorney General under President John Kennedy. In a separate trial later in 1964, Hoffa was also found guilty of misuse of union funds. After a series of lengthy appeals, Hoffa began serving a 13-year prison term in 1967. After about five years in prison, he was pardoned by President Richard Nixon with the condition that he resign as head of the Teamsters. In 1975, he vanished without a trace [173]and was declared legally dead in 1982.

"If we don't cast a ballot, it's going to end up in a situation where we're going to have to cast a bullet."

April 3, 1964. Excerpted from Malcolm X's "The Ballot or the Bullet" speech in Cleveland, Ohio. The 1964 speech, delivered less than a year before Malcolm X's assassination on February 21, 1965, was made in the year and context of the 1964 Presidential election. According to Malcolm X and as stated in the speech, "all the white political crooks will be right back in your and my community…with their false promises which they don't intend to keep." This and similar speeches evidenced the splitting of the Civil Rights Movement between those following the nonviolent path of the Rev. Dr. Martin Luther King, Jr. and those insisting upon a more aggressive and confrontational course.

"I don't think it's worth fighting for and I don't think we can get out."

May 1964. President Lyndon Johnson, speaking with his mentor Senator Richard Russell (D-GA) about the president's perception of the implacable quandary of Vietnam. Although there had been U.S. "military advisors" in South Vietnam for a number of years, this statement was made "nearly a year before (Johnson) committed U.S. combat troops."[174] The war was later justified upon the intertwining rationales that America must remain steadfast in its support of its allies and that if South Vietnam fell, then other nations in Southeast Asia would, in a "domino effect," also fall under the oppression of Communism.

"Will you join in the battle
To give every citizen an escape from the crushing weight of poverty?
....
To make it possible for all nations to live in enduring peace ..."
...
"To build the Great Society,
To prove that our material progress is only the foundation
on which we build a richer life of mind and spirit?
There are those timid souls
who say this battle cannot be won;
That we are condemned to a soulless wealth.
I do not agree.
We have the power to shape the civilization that we want."

May 22, 1964. President Lyndon Johnson, speaking at the University of Michigan and presenting the theoretical, if not spiritual, hopes upon which he proposed to construct his Great Society plans and to thereby address the many and tumultuous issues of poverty, education, and civil rights.

"One man, one vote"
- - -
"Legislatures represent people, not trees or acres.
Legislators are elected by voters,
not farms or cities or economic interests."

June 15, 1964. The "one man, one vote" principle (or, in the more appropriate and modern phraseology, "one person, one vote") is a phrase used in many countries in the context of campaigns for universal suffrage. Variant aspects of this principle had been argued before the USSC in a litany of cases, but the court's ruling two years earlier in the 1962 case of *Baker v. Carr* opened the door to finally adjudicate questions about voter redistricting. The court in that case set forth criteria for the judiciability of "political questions." On this date in 1964, Chief Justice Earl Warren, writing the majority decision in this 8-1 case, concluded, using the words set forth above, that "legislatures (are intended to) represent people, not trees or acres." Thus, the USSC finally held in *Reynolds v. Sims* that under the principle of "one man, one vote," both chambers of state legislatures had to represent districts that were established in a manner so that the legislators represented at least a roughly equal percentage of the state's population. Obviously, this ruling unintentionally encouraged the notorious use of gerrymandering in the drawing of state legislative districts, but the principle of "one man, one vote" was here finally confirmed as a constitutional right.

"No army can withstand the strength of an idea whose time has come."

June 16, 1964. Senator Everett Dirksen (R-IL), speaking on the Senate floor in support of passage of the Civil Rights Act of 1964. This phrase, based upon a Victor Hugo remark, has been used by many politicians, on many occasions, and in many contexts from same-sex marriage to making community colleges free, from requiring the teaching of ethnic studies to support of workspace flexibility.[175] Dirksen is also widely known for supposedly having said "a billion here, a billion there, pretty soon, you're talking real money."[176]

"I know it when I see it."

June 22, 1964. Potter Stewart, Associate Justice of the USSC, writing in his concurring opinion in the USSC case of *Jacobellis v. Ohio* on how pornography and obscenity could be identified even if they were terms beyond meaningful definition.

"We declare our right on this earth to be a man, to be a human being, to be respected as a human being, to be given the rights of a human in this society, on this earth, in this day, which we intend to bring into existence by any means necessary."

June 28, 1964. Malcolm X, a Muslim minister and civil rights activist who believed in the necessity of a more militant course of action than that espoused by the Rev. Dr. Martin Luther King, Jr. These words were spoken by Malcolm X at the founding rally of the Organization of Afro-American

Unity (the "OAAU") in New York, NY. The OAAU's purpose was to fight for the rights of African Americans and to promote cooperation between Africans and people of African descent in the United States. Only five days later, FBI Director J. Edgar Hoover described the OAAU as a threat to the country's "national security," and less than nine months later, Malcolm X was assassinated in New York, NY, at the hands of three members of Elijah Muhammad's Nation of Islam.[177]

"Extremism in defense of liberty is no vice, and moderation in the pursuit of justice is no virtue."

July 16, 1964. Republican Presidential candidate Barry Goldwater, in his acceptance speech at the Republican National Convention at the Cow Palace in San Francisco. The "extremism" here referenced is partially evidenced by Goldwater's promises that, as President, he would use atomic weapons in Vietnam, resume nuclear testing, and break off relations with the Soviet Union. Of more lasting significance than these words or even Goldwater's Presidential campaign was Goldwater's broader articulations of the emerging conservatism in America. Among other things, Goldwater proposed a re-direction and de facto diminishment of the role of the government by, for example, severely limiting the federal government's role in civil rights, selling off the TVA, and even privatizing Social Security—an idea that would re-surface nearly 40 years later during the presidency of George W. Bush (2001-2009).

"We still seek no wider war."
and
Authorization "to take all measures necessary"

August 4, 1964. The contradictory messages to the American people delivered in the summer of 1964. The first statement is that of President Lyndon Johnson, reassuring the American people that the war in Southeast Asia would not be expanded. This statement was made shortly after what came to be known as the Gulf of Tonkin incident, in which the U.S. military claimed that, without provocation, U.S. vessels had been attacked by North Vietnamese warships.[178] Within days thereafter,

Congress passed what came to be known as the Gulf of Tonkin Resolution, pursuant to which the President, in his capacity as Commander in Chief, was authorized "to take all necessary measures, including the use of armed force" against North Vietnam. Despite this grant of seemingly unlimited authority, President Johnson at first hesitated, indeed recoiled, at the thought of a deeper war. But he found that "they (the Kennedy men) were all hawks, they were all incisive and they had the lethal gift of certitude." Furthermore, "the voices of the Kennedy knights were amplified by the (military) Chiefs...."[179] And thus the Vietnam War was soon widened. But the war, which was soon to become the longest war in American history, or at least until the Afghanistan War, was fought without a formal declaration of war. Many believed that the Congressional passivity was a wrongful abdication of power by the Congress itself in that it allowed, at least theoretically, an assertion and exercise of presidential authority to use troops without a formal declaration of war, as contemplated by the Constitution. This granting of unparalleled authority to the presidency led to Arthur Schlesinger, Jr.'s coining of the phrase "imperial presidency." It also led Congress in 1973 to adopt the War Powers Resolution (more commonly known as the "War Powers Act"), which was intend to check, or at least restrain, the President's power to commit military forces without express Congressional approval and authority.

> *"There is a time when the operation of the machine becomes so odious,*
> *makes you so sick at heart, that you can't take part;*
> *... and you've got to put your bodies upon the gears*
> *and upon the wheels, upon the levers, upon all the apparatus*
> *and you've got to make it stop."*

October 2, 1964. Mario Savio, speaking from the top of a campus security car to an assembled group of students in Sproul Plaza at the University of California at Berkeley. The triggering event for this speech and rally was the university's banning of political activity earlier that fall and its failure to change that ban despite months of negotiations. With Savio's speech, the Free Speech Movement at Berkeley and the student protest era of America began.

Author's Note and Disclosure:
This author arrived at the University of California at Berkeley a year after Savio's speech. Four years later, in 1969 and upon his graduation, the author was selected to give one of the commencement addresses. Thus, the author was present and active at Berkeley during the years 1965-1969. Like most other students at the time, the author during this period was politically active but neither broke any laws nor was arrested at any protes. Nevertheless, he was still presumably one of "those bastards at Berkeley" referred to by Ronald Reagan during his candidacy for Governor in 1966. Three years later, the author also entered military service where he served more than four years in the Army.

The protests were not limited to Berkeley or, for that matter, to college campuses. Throughout the decade of the 1960s, protests became a staple of American life. Each protest was to a degree unique—a street march, a gathering, a boycott, a sit-in, a take-over, or a walk-out. Although each protest had its own specific purpose, there was a constant overlapping of the multiple campaigns of the 1960s – the anti-war movement, the civil rights movement, the push for individual freedoms and liberties, the emergence of America's counterculture, sex, drugs and rock 'n' roll, and on and on. While there is no easily identifiable date on which the era of protests ended, it is respectfully suggested that the era started coming to an end on May 4, 1970—the day of the shootings at Kent State. By then, the nation was exhausted. Richard Nixon was in the White House. Watergate was on the horizon. Cynicism was everywhere. Especially within the younger generations, disillusionment was prevalent because there was little hard evidence that anyone was listening; that anyone cared; that any difference was being made. The generation of Baby Boomers started to graduate. As stated by their parents, they started entering the "real world"—the world of families to care for, jobs to find, and bills to pay. It is unsurprising that many protestors started blending back into society. Whether or not the decade of the 60s made a difference is still the subject of fierce, albeit tired, debate. Some commentators suggest that America thereafter was never the same. But America never is the same. Events occur. Demographics change. Time goes on.

> ***"We are not about to send American boys***
> ***nine or ten thousand miles away from home***
> ***to do what Asian boys ought to be doing themselves."***

October 21, 1964. President Lyndon B. Johnson, speaking at Akron University in Ohio in his disingenuous attempt to reassure Americans that the war in Southeast Asia would not be expanded. There is valid and continuing debate about Johnson's actual plans in 1964, but without dispute —and greatly contributing to the growing anger and cynicism of many Americans—within 12 months of President Johnson's statement, American troop levels steadily and substantially increased. At the end of 1964, there were only 23,300 U.S. troops in Vietnam. By 1965, there were 184,300 U.S. troops in Vietnam. This number increased every year throughout Johnson's Presidency until 1968, the peak year, when there were 536,100 U.S. troops in Vietnam. Troops started to be withdrawn in 1969, but it was not until 1973—a full nine years later after the date of this speech—that all U.S. troops were withdrawn from Vietnam[180] and not until 1975 when all U.S. personnel left Vietnam upon the fall of Saigon.

> ***"This is the issue in this election:***
> ***Whether we believe in our capacity for self-government or***
> ***whether we abandon the American revolution***
> ***and confess that a little intellectual elite in a far-distant capital***
> ***can plan our lives for us better than we can plan them ourselves.***
> ***You and I are told … we have to choose between a left or right.***
> ***Well, I'd like to suggest there is no such thing as a left or right.***
> ***There's only up or down – …***
> ***man's old-old-aged dream, the ultimate in individual freedom***
> ***consistent with law and order,***
> ***or***
> ***down to the ant heap of totalitarianism."***

October 27, 1964. Ronald Reagan, in an excerpt from his famous, nationally-televised "A Time for Choosing" speech, delivered in support of Republican Presidential Candidate Barry Goldwater. The speech raised a substantial amount of money for the Goldwater Campaign (as much as

$8 million, according to The Ronald Reagan Foundation[181]). More importantly, many people view this speech as the singular event that launched Reagan's political career. Two years later, Reagan was elected Governor of California on the increasingly popular campaign themes of limiting the role and budget of government and, in Reagan's words, "send(ing) the welfare bums back to work" and "clean(ing) the mess up at Berkeley."

> ***"To regulate Commerce with foreign nations,***
> ***and among the several States ...."***
>
> ...
>
> ***"(I)f its operations affect commerce."***

December 14, 1964. The Commerce Clause of the U.S. Constitution, as first set forth above, grant to Congress the enumerated right to regulate commerce "among the several States." In 1964, the Civil Rights Act was passed by the U.S. Senate by a vote of 73 to 27, and the historic legislation, enacted 101 years after the end of the Civil War, provided that it was unlawful to "discriminate based upon race, color, religion, sex, or national origin." One of the constitutional bases for this legislation was the above-cited Commerce Clause; however, the extension of such laws to an individual's supposed "private conduct" was questioned. In the famous case of *Heart of Atlanta Motel v. United States* (and the case of *Katzenbach v. McClung*), the USSC unanimously held on this date that Congress' powers under the Commerce Clause did extend to a private business "if its operation affects commerce." Arguably in this case, such a holding was especially appropriate since 75% of the clientele of the plaintiff's motel came from out of state, and thus the motel's whites-only restriction of its accommodations clearly impacted interstate commerce. On the other hand, many commentators argued that this case wrongfully and unduly expanded the federal government's powers under the Commerce Clause. Over the ensuing decades, a number of cases have whittled back the reach and scope of the federal government's powers under the clause.[182]

Year 1965

Seminal Books

The Autobiography of Malcolm X: As Told to Alex Haley
by Malcolm X *(Published posthumously)* and Alex Haley

This book was a collaborative effort between black rights activist Malcolm X and journalist Alex Haley. There have been some challenges to Haley's memorialization of his 1963–1965 in-depth interviews with Malcolm X, which were the basis of the book, but the book remains an extraordinary autobiography of this outspoken leader. It does not specifically address Malcolm X's perception of the advised path of the Civil Rights Movement as distinguished from that of the Rev. Dr. Martin Luther King, Jr., but the book well outlines Malcolm's X's powerful philosophy of black pride and black nationalism. The book was published shortly after Malcolm X's assassination by three members of Elijah Mohammad's Nation of Islam, and was immediately recognized as an important and powerful work. As well said by one writer 25 years later, the book presented "a double message of anger and love."[183] In 1998, *Time* magazine named the book as one of the ten "required reading" nonfiction books, and 15 years later *Time* magazine selected it as one of the 100 "best and most influential books" written in English since 1923—the year of the magazine's founding.[184]

The Negro Family: The Case for National Action
(commonly referred to as the 1965 Moynihan Report)
by Daniel Patrick Moynihan

This report was written by then Assistant Secretary of Labor Moynihan, a sociologist and later U.S. Senator (D-NY). It has been highly criticized by some black leaders as an example of white patronization and cultural bias, but for many Americans its contents were both alarming and informative. The Report focused upon black poverty, the reasons behind it, and its potential consequences. It noted that within the black community there were many reasons for the growing disintegration of the nuclear family and that such disintegration, unless addressed, would have long-lasting, severe, and adverse consequences. Such consequences would range from increases in the rates of divorce, out-of-wedlock births, and child abandonment by fathers to impaired systems and patterns of education. Almost self-perpetuating, another consequence would be the inability of more and more males to find suitable employment. Despite great advances in the context of civil rights and the social and economic treatment of African Americans, multiple race-centered problems continue to exist within American society. This is evidenced, for example, by the continued economic inequities faced by many African Americans, by the growing recognition of disparate sentencing within the criminal justice system, and more recently by the rise of the Black Lives Matter movement in the early 21st century.

Unsafe at Any Speed:
The Designed-In Dangers of the American Automobile
by Ralph Nader

This was the first major book asserting a sense of consumer rights. It was delivered in the form of an indictment of the American automobile industry for failing to produce a safer automobile. The book was written by Ralph Nader when he was just 31 years of age. Nader, a "secular monk," has continued to be a powerful consumer rights and environmental advocate. Some writers attribute Nader's long and sustained focus to his reading, wherein even by the age of 14 he had read many books written by the early muckrakers such as Lincoln Steffens, Ida Tarbell, and Upton Sinclair.[185] Possibly more revealing, however, was his quandried observation "that they (the early protest writers and muckrakers) stopped with exposure. They didn't follow thought by politically mobilizing a concerned constituency."[186]

Pulitzer Prize for Fiction

The Keepers of the House
by Shirley Ann Grau

Pulitzer Prize for General Nonfiction

O Strange New World - American Culture: The Formative Years
by Howard Mumford-Jones

Pulitzer Prize for History

The Greenback Era
by Irwin Unger

The New York Times Best Sellers List (Nonfiction) – Books with Most Weeks as No. 1 Best Seller

Markings
by Dag Hammarskjold (30 weeks)

The Making of a President, 1964
by Theodore H. White (12 weeks)

The New York Times Best Sellers List (Adult Fiction) – Book with Most Weeks as No. 1 Best Seller

The Source
by James Michener (22 weeks)

Academy Awards Best Picture

Winner: *The Sound of Music*
Other Nominees: *Darling, Doctor Zhivago,
Ship of Fools, A Thousand Clowns*

PrettyFamous' Best Movie of the Year

For a Few Dollars More

Best/Most Memorable Movie Line of the Year

"The Von Trapp children don't play. They march."
Julie Andrews in Robert Wise's *The Sound of Music* and noting, boldly and with seeming surprise, if not offense, the manner in which the Von Trapp children didn't seem to yet know how to "play."

<u>1965 U.S. Population: 194,300,000</u>

(Compared as a Percentage to the U.S. 1957 Population of 172,000,000: 113.0%)

<u>Television Shows</u>

Most Widely-Viewed Television Shows

Rank	Show Name	Years of Series (Excluding Reruns)	Show Type	Estimated Audience (In MMs)	Audience as Percentage of U.S. Population
1.	*Bonanza*	1959–1973	Western	17.1MM	8.8%
	Cast: Lorne Greene - Michael Landon – Pernell Roberts – Dan Blocker				
2.	*Gomer Pyle U.S.M.C.*	1964–1969	Comedy	15.0MM	7.7%
	Cast: Jim Nabors - Frank Sutton - Ronnie Schell				
3.	*The Lucy Show*	1962–1968	Comedy	14.9MM	7.7%
	Cast: Lucille Ball - Vivian Vance - Gale Gordon				

Last Season Television Show(s)

Wagon Train (1957–1965)—Western
Ward Bond - John McIntire

Rawhide (1959–1965)—Western
Eric Flemming - Clint Eastwood

<u>Catchphrases, Chants, and Slogans</u>

"Body Counts"

With the increased war reporting from Vietnam, America starting hearing more and more about the meaning of "body counts"—the cold measure used by some military and public spokespersons to track victories and measure defeats. Just a few years later, the psychic distance allowed by the use of numeric body counts collapsed for many Americans when on June 27, 1969 *Life* Magazine published "The Faces of the American Dead in Vietnam: One Week's Toll." In this issue *Life* presented, without comment or editorial, the pictures of every American killed in a single week in Vietnam. It was received by a sobered and increasingly restless public.

"Burn, baby, burn"

This phrase arose from the ashes of the violent riots that took place in the Watts neighborhood of Los Angeles in August 1965. The riots lasted for six days and resulted in 34 deaths, 1,032 injuries, and 3,438 arrests. The riot was quelled only after Governor Pat Brown called out more than 4,000 California National Guard troops. The Watts Riots would remain the most violent race riots in Southern California for nearly 30 years—until the Rodney King riots of 1992. In response to the Watts Riots and after they ignited protests in Harlem, Newark and Detroit, former CIA Director John A. McCone headed a commission to investigate the Watts riots. It issued its report, commonly referred to as the McCone Commission Report, 18 months later in December 1965. The Report identified, unsurprisingly, that the root causes of these riots were high unemployment, poor schools, and the general inferior living conditions of "Black Americans" in Watts. Regardless of the conclusion of the Report or the substantiating data contained in it, almost nothing changed. One writer in 1995 looked back to determine whether the recommended issues were addressed and correctly noted that very little had been done and very little changed in those ensuing 30 years.[187] The chant of "burn, baby, burn" was thereafter repeated in the midst of the many other urban disturbances which rocked the 1960s. It also became the title of several songs, television show episodes, and even a 1966 book by Messrs. Jerry Murphy and William S. Cohen.

"Hell no, we won't go."

This was a common chant of antiwar protestors. It was used in protest of both the continuation of the Vietnam War and the military draft. Some writers ascribe its first use to the nationwide "Stop the Draft" week protests of 1968, but it was in use long before then. The frequency of its use increased as the war and draft continued and after more and more politicians and other leaders spoke out against the war. Conscription itself was not new in American history. It had been used by the federal government at least four times—during the Civil War, World War I, World War II, and the Cold War era (including both Korea and Vietnam). However, as noted above, part of the basis for the chant was objection to the Vietnam War itself, and it was also used as an expression of the constant subcurrent of objections resulting from the myriad of built-in draft exemptions, deferments (many of which eventually became de facto exemptions), and disqualifications. Such exemptions, deferments, and even disqualifications were seen as unfairly and disproportionately used by wealthier and better-educated young men and their families. For example, initially there were exemptions for married men. Then, there were exemptions for married men with children. Then, there were exemptions for members of the National Guard and Reserves.[188] At various times, there were also exemptions for college students and even graduate students. Others were (or arranged to have themselves) disqualified for medical or mental reasons. Of the nearly 8.7 million service members between 1964 and 1975, only about 500,000 (about 5.7%) were disqualified for criminal convictions. Although many American leaders constantly vocalized their contempt for draft evaders, in fact, only about 10,000 young men (about 0.01% of those called for active duty) were convicted of draft violations. As a course of last resort, some young men chose expatriation. It is estimated that about 100,000 draft-eligible young men left the country—most often for Canada. However, over the objections of many Americans, these expatriates received amnesty during the Carter Administration. Thus, despite the "we won't go" adamancy of the chant, most draft-eligible young men did not refuse enlistment. Instead, they were never drafted and/or despite their protests, they sought—and often achieved —alternative ways to avoid military service. A "lottery system" was initiated in December 1969, and after campaigning with a pledge to "eliminate the draft," President Richard Nixon finally did so on July 1, 1973.[189] It was replaced with what is loosely-called an "all-volunteer military," but some believe that this term is itself a misnomer and that the "all-volunteer army" should more accurately be referred to as an "all-recruitment" army.[190]

"Hey, Hey, LBJ / How many kids did you kill today?"

This cruel antiwar chant was commonly heard at protests throughout the middle and late 1960s. It became even more well known to the general public when it was heard (along with the "The Whole World Is Watching" chant) on television during coverage of the raucous anti-protests at the Democratic Party convention in Chicago, Illinois in August 1968.

<u>Memorable Words from Speeches, Books, Writings,</u>
<u>and Other Sources – 1965</u>

January 20, 1965
Inaugural Address of Lyndon B. Johnson
(President of the United States 1963–1969)

"For every generation there is a destiny.
For some, history decides.
For this generation the choice must be our own."

...

"Ours is a time of change ...
Our destiny ... will rest on the unchanged character of our people
and on our faith."

...

"In a land of great wealth,
families must not live in hopeless poverty.
In a land rich in harvest, children must not go hungry.
In a land of healing miracles,
neighbors must not suffer and die untended.
In a land of great learning and scholars,
young people must be taught to read and write."

...

"We aspire to nothing that belongs to others.
We seek no dominion over our fellow man,
but man's dominion over tyranny and misery."

...

"But more is required.
Men want to be part of a common enterprise,
a cause greater than themselves.
And each of us must find a way to advance
the purpose of the Nation, thus finding new purpose for ourselves.
Without this, we will simply become a nation of strangers."

...

"No longer need capitalist and worker, farmer and clerk,

> *city and countryside, struggle to divide our bounty.*
> *By working shoulder to shoulder together*
> *we can increase the bounty of all.*
> *We have discovered that every child who learns,*
> *and every man who finds work, and every sick body*
> *that is made whole—like a candle added to an altar—*
> *brightens the hope of all the faithful."*
>
> ...
>
> *"In each generation, with toil and tears,*
> *we have had to earn our heritage again ....*
> *And the judgment of God is hardest on those who are most favored."*
>
> ...
>
> *"If we succeed it will not be because of what we have,*
> *but it will be because of what we are;*
> *not because of what we own,*
> *but rather because of what we believe."*

January 20, 1965. From the 23-minute Inaugural Address of Lyndon B. Johnson, marking the commencement of his only full term in office. The inauguration was attended by an estimated 1.2 million people, which, at that time, was the record for any event held at the National Mall. This record would stand intact until the Presidential Inauguration of Barack Obama nearly 44 years later. The assassination of President Kennedy had itself changed the nature and tone of Johnson's inauguration as well. More than 5,500 police, military, and security forces were in full force[191] as Secret Service helicopters for the first time flew over the Inaugural Parade. President Johnson took his oath of office outdoors "but only behind bullet-proof glass." It wasn't obvious to everyone that the country was experiencing "seismic changes in the American culture"[192] or, in the words of Bob Dylan, that *the times they (were) a-changin'*," but some conservatives criticized the seeming informality of some of the dress. Upon reflection, it was more ominous that The Brothers Four delivered a "poignant rendition" of the song *"Where Have All the Flowers Gone"*—a song which in just a couple of years would be heard at antiwar protests all across the country. But on this day in 1965, the Vietnam War, the rise of the counterculture, and even the Civil Rights Movement had not yet come to fully dominate the news. The 1960s had not yet taken shape, and thus on this day, President Johnson took his oath of office from Chief Justice Earl Warren. Vice President Hubert H. Humphrey, Jr. took his oath of office from Speaker of the U.S. House of Representatives John McCormick, thereby filling the office that had been vacant for 14 months since Johnson ascended the Presidency upon the assassination of John F. Kennedy.

"Let's cool it, brothers."

February 21, 1965. The last words of Malcolm X who was assassinated on this date in New York City at the age of 39. His killers, three Nation of Islam members, were convicted and sentenced to jail for life. In many respects, by the time of his death, Malcolm X's role as a civil rights leader was already starting to fade and to become lost amidst the froth of militants like Stokely Carmichael (and later Eldridge Cleaver, Huey Newton, and even H. Rap Brown) and the sustained adherence of many African Americans to the nonviolent message of the Martin Luther King, Jr. The nature of Malcolm X's impact is hard to define. It may "lie in his personification of a radical new consciousness of pride and self-respect" and even confidence bordering on an almost deserved arrogance among many blacks. While his idea of black nationalism never approached fruition, he became—almost more in death than in life and certainly with the 1965 publication of *The Autobiography of Malcolm X*—a symbol of a stronger, more adamant approach to the many valid demands and aspects of the civil rights movement.

"(It was) Malcolm X's town, not King's."

1965. The Reverend Al Sharpton, speaking years later about the black community in New York City in the mid-1960s.[193] Today, Sharpton is, by any measure and in almost any crowd, viewed from many conflicting perspectives. However, in 1965, Sharpton was a precocious, but unrelentingly energetic and deeply committed, black child living in the projects with a single parent. During this period – the early/mid-1960s—the anger within the black community was brewing but still largely disorganized and unfocused. The sparks had not yet ignited nationwide as they had in the Watts neighborhood of Los Angeles the year before.[194] Sharpton's remark here about Malcolm X and the Rev. Dr. Martin Luther, King, Jr. describes just one of the many splits within the civil rights movement, which, like all movements, had within its ranks persons of different temperaments and varying levels of tolerance and degrees of remaining patience.

> *"This legislation marks the end of an era of partisan cynicism*
> *towards human want and misery.*
> *The dole is dead. The pork barrel is gone.*
> *Federal and state, liberal and conservative,*
> *Democrat and Republican,*
> *Americans of these times are concerned*
> *with the outcome of the next generation, not the next election ...."*

March 9, 1965. President Lyndon Johnson in the Rose Garden of the White House, upon the signing of the War on Poverty Appalachia Bill. Evaluating the failure of Johnson's War on Poverty in the context of just one sector of America, Kevin D. Williamson brilliantly presents a narrative about current-day Appalachia— "stretching from northern Mississippi to southern New York." Williamson explains that "(t)hinking about the future here and its bleak prospects is not much fun ... instead you have the pills and the dope, the morning beers, the endless scratch-off lotto cards, healing meetings up on the hill, the federally-funded ritual trading of food-stamp Pepsi for ... cigarettes and good old hard currency, tall piles of gas station nachos, the occasional blast of meth, Narcotics Anonymous meetings, petty crime, the draw (i.e. monthly welfare checks that supplement dependents' earnings in the black-market Pepsi economy), the recreational making and surgical unmaking of teenage mothers, and death. Life expectancies are short ... and getting shorter... If people here weren't 98.5 percent white, we'd call it a reservation." People move out, and "as they go, businesses disappear, institutions fall into decline, social networks erode, and there is little or nothing left for those who remain."[195] While there is now a more widespread acknowledgement of the existence and extent of poverty in America, contentious debate continues about how to address this complicated subject, and, more specifically, about the proper role of government in this context. Johnson's War on Poverty is seen by many as having been, at best, honorable in spirit, but unduly optimistic about the power of government. Others use Johnson's War on Poverty as a cruel example of the misguided role of government itself. Still, it is without dispute that urban and rural poverty continue in the U.S. Even 45 years later, the poverty rate in America was at 13.5%. In other words, although the U.S. median household income as of 2015 was $56,516, approximately 43.1 million Americans are still living under the poverty line, which is defined as a family of four individuals with an annual household income of $24,230.[196]

*"At times history and fate meet at a single time in a single place
to shape a turning point in man's unending search for freedom.
So it was at Lexington and Concord.
So it was a century ago at Appomattox.
So it was last week in Selma, Alabama."*

...

*"There is no Negro problem.
There is no southern problem.
There is no northern problem.
There is only an American problem."*

...

*"Many of the issues of civil rights
are very complex and most difficult.
But about (the right to vote)
there can be and should be no argument.
Every American citizen must have an equal right to vote."*

...

*"Their cause must be our cause too,
because ... it is all of us who must overcome
the crippling legacy of bigotry and injustice.
And we shall overcome."*

March 15, 1965. President Lyndon Johnson, in his address to a joint session of Congress, encouraging Congress to pass the Voting Rights

Act. In his speech, the President invoked the civil rights battle cry of "we shall overcome" in addressing the problem of disenfranchisement and in articulating his hope that the Voting Rights Act would help assure that especially the Southern states would thereafter be barred from their strident imposition of various restrictions on and barriers to voting by members of the black community. Although the Act was opposed by most Southern legislators and many political leaders (including future presidents Ronald Reagan (then Governor of California) and even Richard Nixon and Gerald Ford (albeit more "ambiguously")), the Voting Rights Act was passed with the overwhelming and bipartisan support of both the House (333 to 48) and the Senate (77 to 19). It was signed into law on August 6, 1965. The legislation remained the centerpiece of voting rights protections for the next nearly 50 years. However, the Voting Rights Act was severely compromised in 2013 when the USSC in the case of *Shelby County v. Holder* eviscerated the use of what is known as the "coverage formula." This formula was designed to identify those jurisdictions that had engaged in egregious voting discriminations at the time of the Act's passage in 1965 (with Congressional modifications in 1970 and 1975). In this 2013 case, the USSC struck down the coverage formula based upon the Court's conclusion that the formula was no longer responsive to current conditions. Thus, while the Court did not strike down the Act itself, without the coverage formula, most other meaningful provisions of the Voting Rights Act have become de facto, if not de jure, unenforceable.[197]

"I know you are asking today, 'How long will it take?' "

…

"How long will prejudice blind the missions of men,
darken their understanding,
and drive bright-eyed Wisdom from her sacred throne?"

….

"When will wounded Justice,
lying prostrate on the streets of Selma and Birmingham
and communities all over the South, be lifted from this dust of shame?"

…

"How long will Justice be crucified, and Truth bear it?"
...
"I come to say to you this afternoon, ... it will not be long ...
How long? Not long, because no lie can live forever.
How long? Not long ... because the arc of the moral universe is long,
but it bends towards justice."

March 25, 1965. The Reverend Dr. Martin Luther King, Jr., speaking on the steps of the Alabama State Capital upon the conclusion of the 8,000-person march from Selma to Birmingham. The speech is often-times referred to as the "How Long, Not Long" speech, or, alternatively the "Our God Is Marching On" speech since it ended with the words of "The Battle Hymn of the Republic." The phrase about the "arc of the moral universe" paraphrases the 19th century words of Theodore Parker (1810–1860), a Unitarian minister, reformer, and abolitionist. President Lincoln also used Parker's words when, for example, he adapted Parker's 1850 phrase "(a) democracy—of all the people, by all the people, for all the people" into his 1863 Gettysburg Address. Over the years the phrase "arc of the moral universe" became a common abolitionist's cry, and Rev. King used it on numerous occasions—even in his early writings in 1958; later while marching in Selma, Alabama; and in his famous "Where Do We Go From Here?" speech delivered to the Southern Christian Leadership Conference in August 1967, just eight months before his assassination in Memphis, Tennessee. The phrase was also used by President Obama when he selected it as one of the quotes sewn into the new oval rug in the White House.[198]

"Freedom is not enough.
You do not take a man who, for years, has been hobbled by chains
and liberate him, bring him to the starting line of a race
and then say 'You are free to compete with all the others,'
and still justly believe you have been completely fair."
....
"It is not enough just to open the gates of opportunity.
All citizens must have the ability to walk through those gates."

June 4, 1965. President Lyndon Johnson, in his Commencement Address at Howard University, speaking about his signing of an Executive Order mandating that federal contractors identify and eliminate any barriers to employment of minorities. While the first affirmative action policies were adopted as far back as 1943 by President Franklin D. Roosevelt, and while the term "affirmative action" was first used by President John Kennedy in an Executive Order relating to the hiring requirements of federal contractors, this Executive Order by President Johnson greatly expanded the concepts and requirements of affirmative action policies. The order, in effect, memorialized his belief that, as here stated, "freedom (alone) is not enough;" that "affirmative" action was necessary. In this manner, Johnson advocated "not just equality as a right and a theory, but … as a fact and as a result."[199] Four years later, President Richard Nixon "built on Johnson's legacy with the 'Philadelphia Order,' which set specific goals and timetables for federal contractors to hire shares of minorities reflecting the racial makeup of their local area." There has been a consistent tailoring and narrowing of affirmative action programs by the courts, but many affirmative action programs have been repeatedly upheld by the courts as well. Nevertheless, and despite the USSC's relatively consistent upholding of affirmative action programs, many Americans believe that America should (simply) be a "colorblind society" and that all affirmative actions programs should be ended.[200]

"The right of privacy"

* * *

"The specific guarantees in the Bill of Rights have penumbras, formed from emanations from those guarantees that help give them life and substance."

June 7, 1965. In an arguable departure from any notion of original intent or strict constructionism, the USSC on this date found within the U.S. Constitution and here articulated for the first time a "right of privacy." The Court in this case of *Griswold v. Connecticut* overturned an archaic state law which forbade the use of contraception by even married couples. With a 7-2 decision, the Court acknowledged that a "right of privacy" was not expressly set forth in the Constitution, but the Court's majority concluded that such a right of privacy, like the right of travel, was implicit within various other guaranties in the Bill of Rights." The significance of this case expanded greatly when just eight years later the USSC in the case of *Roe v. Wade* based that case's "right to choose" upon a woman's inherent right to privacy.

> ### *"The number of elderly citizens*
> ### *lacking access to hospitals and doctors plummeted."*
>
> ### ...
>
> ### *"The passage of Medicare and Medicaid ...*
> ### *shattered the barriers that had separated*
> ### *the federal government and the health-care system...."*

July 30, 1965. The words of Julian E. Zelizer, writing about the enactment of Medicare and Medicaid. These programs became law upon the signing of the act by President Lyndon Johnson on this day. The act was signed in Independence, MO. in the presence of former President Harry Truman, who had proposed a form of national health insurance 20 years earlier and who was issued the first Medicare card in the United States.[201] The primary significance of Medicare is its provision of medical care for seniors. As of 2014, as many as 49.4 million Americans were on Medicare.[202] However, almost of equal importance, especially in the context of the heated debates about the wisdom and feasibility of the Affordable Care Act enacted during the Presidency of Barack Obama, is the fact that Medicare and Medicaid work. Despite protestations from some opponents of national health care regarding the claimed superiority of the "free-market" and "private enterprise" and the asserted ills of "socialized medicine," and despite the insistence by some that such a program is beyond the capabilities of the government to run, Medicare works. The mechanics, the questions relating to scope of coverage, and the funding issues are complicated. Indeed, these are important issues that need close and methodical attention. However, national health insurance is administered every day to senior Americans. It has worked for decades. It is literally the medical care "lifeline" for millions of older Americans. Politics aside, this seemingly obvious conclusion can be easily confirmed the old-fashioned way—by just asking any American senior citizen.

> ***"At any given moment, public opinion is a chaos***
> ***of superstition, misinformation, and prejudice."***

Summer, 1965. Gore Vidal, decrying the "chaos" that constitutes the concept of "public opinion." Especially in the divisive American society of the early 21st century, the phrase "public opinion" should, at a minimum, be modified to the use of the phrase "public opinions." [203]

> ***"It's silly talking about how many years***
> ***we will have to spend in the jungles of Vietnam***
> ***when we could pave the whole country***
> ***and put parking stripes on it,***
> ***and still be home by Christmas."***

October, 1965. Ronald Reagan, speaking as Republican California Gubernatorial candidate, and seeming to express his sense of unbridled, albeit dark, confidence in the capacities of the U.S. military. In the opinion of many war critics, the statement evidenced hard (and blind) optimism and reflected a dangerously certain "arrogance of power," in the words of J. William Fulbright. Fulbright and other early critics of the Vietnam War felt that such "arrogance" could itself be both deadly and wrong. These early critics, including Senator Fulbright, John Kenneth Galbraith, columnist I.F. Stone, and Noam Chomsky, may have, at first, constituted a small group, but the crowd of critics grew as Reagan himself would soon see in his then-new capacity as Governor of California. To his displeasure, during his tenure, anti-war protests spread from campus to campus, from street to street in his state.

Year 1966

Seminal Books

In Cold Blood

by Truman Capote

Truman Capote's book is often cited as America's first "nonfiction novel," a phrase which is itself baffling and intriguing. The book narrates, in chilling and gruesome detail, the 1959 murders of a family in a small farming community in southwest Kansas. The murderers were soon caught and were executed by the state of Kansas in 1965, just a year before Capote's book was released. Capote wrote the book after years of research (sometimes with the help of his then neighbor and lifelong friend Harper Lee, the author of *To Kill a Mockingbird). In Cold Blood* is a distant work from Capote's other best known writing, the novella *Breakfast at Tiffany's,* but it was an instant success and remains (second only to Vincent Bugliosi's 1974 book, *Helter Skelter,* about the Charles Manson murders) one of the bestselling true crime books ever published. The brilliance of the book lies in Capote's "ability to fuse fact with ... fiction."[204] As stated by the reviewer who offered those words, "put simply, the book was of journalism and born of a novelist" in which "tenses and time frames are intercut and slippery (and the multiple) perspectives are distorted...."[205] As summarized years later by fellow writer Tom Wolfe in his collection of essays, *Mauve Gloves & Madman, Clutter & Vine, In Cold Blood* "...is neither a who-done-it nor a will-they-be-caught, since the answers to both of these questions are known from the outset... Instead, the book's suspense is based largely (upon) ... the promise of gory details, and the withholding of them until the end."[206] This storytelling technique has been widely adapted over the years in books, films, and television.

Situation Ethics: The New Morality
by Joseph Fletcher

Both the reasoning and the title of Joseph Fletcher's book served as the ethical bible and basis, or at least the convenient reasoning, for many members of especially the Sixties generation. While it is an honorable book, it dangerously suggests that one's actions cannot be judged according to absolute moral standards. Instead, the context and circumstances surrounding one's actions must be simultaneously considered. More specifically, the book argues that actions must be considered in relation to their furtherance of what is referred to as "agape love," the Greek word used to describe "love" in the Bible. By this reasoning, by this construct of ethical behavior, "laws and rules and principles and ... norms, are ... contingent, only valid if they ... serve love" in a particular situation.[207] The concept of "situation ethics" was not new and had been long debated by a number of philosophers and theologians. However, this book came at a convenient time. It quickly came to serve an entire generation of Americans, especially the Baby Boomers, as an alternative to the black-and-white, right-and-wrong ethos of prior generations. Careless readers allowed the book to infuse the concepts of "gray area," "no harm, no foul," "if it feels good, do it, and "why not" into every debate. The book and its reasoning are sober and thoughtful, but the concept of situation ethics was too tempting to resist for the restless generation of the Sixties and thereafter. Arguably, the entire concept of situation ethics is too simplistic in that it was easily used—and continues to be easily used—to justify acts of defiance, protest, civil disobedience, changes in lifestyles and personal habits. American societal ethics have never been the same. In the opinion of many Americans, situation ethics and variants thereof (such as utilitarianism's concept of "the greatest good for greatest number") have substantially and dangerously overtaken strict adherence to laws and codes of social conduct. It is beyond the scope of this book to comment on the wisdom of this choice, but it is a reality which was well-articulated and, for many, first introduced by this book.

The Arrogance of Power
by Senator J. William Fulbright

Senator Fulbright's book was the first major and widely circulated book written in opposition to the Vietnam War. Fulbright carefully presents two Americas, two paths charted in our history: "The America of ... Theodore Roosevelt (and those whom Fulbright sometimes refers to as the "super-patriots") proud, self-confident, convinced of the blessing of providence on a power that requires only to be exercised, and the America of..., an essentially magnanimous society." In this manner, Fulbright essentially compares the respective powers of humility and force as exercised by a nation. Fulbright, the long-standing Chairman of the powerful Senate Foreign Relations Committee from 1959 to 1974, openly worried about the reckless exercise of power underlying American's assertion of military force in Vietnam. He noted that "power confuses itself with virtue and tends also to take itself for omnipotence." Despite the wonders and diversity of this nation and its preserved freedom of expression, this book remains a lonely counterweight to the endless stream of books that have been written especially over the last two decades espousing American exceptionalism.[208] The book also contains prescient reasoning and a conclusion that "pre-emptive war in 'defense' of freedom would surely destroy freedom." [209]

Pulitzer Prize for Fiction

The Collected Stories of Katherine Anne Porter
by Katherine Anne Porter

Pulitzer Prize for General Nonfiction

Wandering Through Winter: A Naturalist's Record of a 20,000-Mile Journey Through the North American Winter
by Edwin Way Teale

Pulitzer Prize for History

The Life of the Mind in America
by Perry Miller

The New York Times Best Sellers List (Nonfiction) – Books with Most Weeks as No. 1 Best Seller

How to Avoid Probate
by Norman F. Dacey (17 weeks)

In Cold Blood
by Truman Capote (14 weeks)

The New York Times Best Sellers List (Adult Fiction) – Book with Most Weeks as No. 1 Best Seller

Valley of the Dolls
by Jacqueline Susann (28 weeks)

Academy Awards Best Picture

Winner: *A Man for All Seasons*
Other Nominees: *Alfie, The Russians Are Coming, The Sand Pebbles, Who's Afraid of Virginia Woolf?*

PrettyFamous' Best Movie of the Year

Who's Afraid of Virginia Woolf?

1966 U.S. Population: 196,600,000

(Compared as a Percentage to the U.S. 1957 Population of 172,000,000: 114.3%)

Television Shows

Most Widely-Viewed Television Shows

Rank	Show Name	Years of Series (Excluding Reruns)	Show Type	Estimated Audience (In MMs)	Audience as Percentage of U.S. Population
1.	*Bonanza*	1959–1973	Western	16.0MM	8.1%
	Cast: Lorne Greene - Michael Landon – Pernell Roberts – Dan Blocker				
2.	*Red Skelton Show*	1951–1971	Comedy	15.5MM	7.9%
	Cast: Red Skelton				
3.	*Andy Griffith Show*	1960–1968	Comedy	15.1MM	7.7%
	Cast: Andy Griffith - Ron Howard - Don Knotts				

Widely-Viewed or Critically-Acclaimed New Television Show(s)

Firing Line (1966–1999) – Conservative Public Affairs Interview Show
Host: William F. Buckley, Jr.
(One of the longest-running public affairs shows in television history)

Star Trek (1966-1969) – Science Fiction and Adventure Show
William Shatner – Leonard Nimoy – DeForest Kelley
(Forerunner of the *Star Trek* media franchise of
television shows, films, and even a brief animated series)

Last Season Television Show(s)

The Adventures of Ozzie and Harriet (1952–1966) –
Family Situation Comedy
Ozzie, Harriet, David, and Ricky Nelson

The Dick Van Dyke Show (1961–1966) – Comedy
Dick Van Dyke - Mary Tyler Moore
(No. 13 Top TV Shows of All Time – *TV Guide*)

<u>Major Commercial Advertising Campaigns and Slogan(s)</u>

“Fly the friendly skies.”
United Airlines

<u>Catchphrases, Chants, and Slogans</u>

“Policy of minimum candor” and “All-out limited war”

Summer, 1966. Phrases such as these reflected the circular babble speak associated with nearly all communications and debates about the Vietnam War. On the one hand, “minimum candor” became one of the models of communication by which the U.S. military and the Johnson Administration tried, with ever-lessening success, to present America's shifting positions in the Vietnam War. As a result, and in a cynical routine, American successes were reported in the cold context of body counts,[210] and American failures were buried in the deflecting jargon of press releases and military situation reports. Simultaneously, the military was itself challenged by the confusing absurdity in its instructions from U.S. political bodies and elected officials to carry out an “all-out limited war.”

<u>Memorable Words from Speeches, Books, Writings,</u>
<u>and Other Sources – 1966</u>

"If one is looking for pornography, one's going to have a long look."

January 1966. Dr. Williams Masters, explaining upon the release of his and Virginia Johnson's revolutionary book *Human Sexual Response,* the scientific—not erotic—basis, purpose, and nature of the book. Masters and Johnson soon became celebrities appearing on the cover of *Time* magazine several years later, and they married in 1971.[211] In this book, they presented a series of then-shocking conclusions about human sexuality. Such conclusions were reached after conducting groundbreaking and controversial research conducted at Washington University in St. Louis into the physiology of human sexuality. As discussed in Thomas Maier's 2013 biography of Masters and Johnson,[212] they presented in a clinical manner the four stages of sex and presented evidence that, "instead of the male being the more powerful of the sexes... women actually had a greater capacity for sex." This book furthered the open discussion of human sexuality. Although Amazon's 2016 description of the book was written with a blend of undue simplicity and marketing hyperbole, it correctly states that Masters and Johnson's book became "the Bible of the Sex Revolution of the 1960s, to such an extent that one cannot say whether this book caused the Sex Revolution or the Sex Revolution led to the creation of this book."

"The inspiration and commitment of the Great Society
have disappeared.
In concrete terms, the President simply cannot think about
implementing the Great Society at home
while he is supervising bombing missions over North Vietnam.
There is a kind of madness in the facile assumption
that we can raise the billions of dollars necessary
to rebuild our schools and cities and public transport
and eliminate the pollution of air and water

> ### *while also spending tens of billions of dollars*
> ### *to finance an 'open-ended' war in Asia."*

April 28, 1966. Senator J. William Fulbright (D-AK), an early and articulate foe of the Vietnam War, speaking of the fiscal imprudence of having the U.S. commit billions of dollars of public monies to Johnson's Great Society domestic programs while at the same time expending billions more in furtherance of what he accurately described as the "open-ended" Vietnam War in Southeast Asia. Fulbright's speech was delivered on this date before the American Newspaper Publishers Association. The speech is sometimes referred to as "The Vietnam Fallout" speech, in which he suggested that the dangers posed to American ideals would not result from a loss of faith but would stem from an arrogance of power—which was the title of Fulbright's seminal same-year book, *The Arrogance of Power*.

> ### *"You have the right to remain silent,*
> ### *Anything you say can and will be used against you in a court of law"*

June 13, 1966. With these words, the USSC in a split 5-4 decision created what have come to be known as the Miranda warning rights, which must be recited to any person arrested of a crime. Pursuant to this decision in the case of *Miranda v. Arizona*, the Fifth Amendment's protection against self-incrimination was held to include a criminal defendant's "right to remain silent." Thereafter, any person arrested of a crime also had the right to be informed (i) that "anything you say can and will be used against you in a court of law" (ii) and that he or she had a right to counsel. While the Miranda warnings are now a staple of American jurisprudence and are repeated in hundreds of television shows and movies, at the time of this ruling, the expansion of the rights of an accused were highly controversial. This ruling was one of the last major criminal law decisions of what is commonly referred to as the (Chief Justice Earl) Warren Court. Chief Justice Warren, the 14th Chief Justice of the USSC, served in that role from October 5, 1953 until his retirement on June 23, 1969. Upon his resignation, he was replaced by Chief Justice Warren E. Burger.

"Power to the People"

...

"An end of police terrorism"

...

"Patrol the pigs"

...

**"We want land, bread, housing, education, clothing, justice and peace.
And as our major political objective, a United Nations-supervised
plebiscite (of black voters only) ...
(to determine) the will of the black people as to their national destiny."**

October 15, 1966. The popular sayings, the insulting words and the stated goals of the Black Panther Party (the "BPP"), which was formed on this date by Huey Newton and Bobby Seale. Throughout its short existence, the BPP's image and reputation—enhanced by its black leather jackets, black berets, black power salute, and displays of weaponry—far exceeded both the organization's power and its influence. It was formed and centered in Oakland, CA. At its peak in 1970, just four years after its founding, the BPP claimed to have offices in 68 cities and thousands of members. Even FBI Director J. Edgar Hoover became alarmed and, in classic overreaction, called the BPP "the greatest threat to the internal security of the country." However, due to police harassments, the incarceration of many of its leaders and members, and internal disputes and discord, the BPP slowly diminished throughout the ensuing decade. By the end of the 1970s, it only had a few remaining members. Its lasting significance lies primarily in its ability to briefly bring national attention to the issue of police brutality within the black community, its symbolism of the extent of frustrations within the black community with the slow progress of civil rights, and its offering, albeit for only a brief time, of an unsuccessful alternative to the nonviolent course of the civil rights movement as charted by the Rev. Dr. Martin Luther King, Jr. and his associates and followers.

Year 1967

<u>Pulitzer Prize for Fiction</u>

The Fixer
by Bernard Malamud

<u>Pulitzer Prize for General Nonfiction</u>

The Problem of Slavery in Western Culture
by David Brion Davis

<u>Pulitzer Prize for History</u>

*Exploration and Empire: The Explorer and the Scientist
in the Winning of the American West*
by William H. Goetzmann

**<u>*The New York Times* Best Sellers List (Nonfiction) –
Books with Most Weeks as No. 1 Best Seller</u>**

"Our Crowd":- The Great Jewish Families of New York
by Stephen Birmingham (16 weeks)

Everything But Money
by Sam Levenson (13 weeks)

**<u>*The New York Times* Best Sellers List (Adult Fiction) –
Book with Most Weeks as No. 1 Best Seller</u>**

The Arrangement
by Elia Kazan (23 weeks)

<u>Academy Awards Best Picture</u>

Winner: *In the Heat of the Night*
Other Nominees: *Bonnie and Clyde, Doctor Doolittle,
The Graduate, Guess Who's Coming to Dinner*

***PrettyFamous*' Best Movie of the Year**
Cool Hand Luke

Best/Most Memorable Movie Lines of the Year
"Mrs. Robinson, you're trying to seduce me, aren't you?"

Dustin Hoffman, addressing Anne Bancroft in *The Graduate*. In addition to this line from *The Graduate*, at the time of the movie's 1967 release many college students reflected upon another line in the movie conveying adults' definition of their children's supposed future with the one word, "*Plastics.*" (The exact line being, *"I just want to say one word to you – just one word … Plastics.")*. However, in retrospect, the most interesting part of this line was that which was not said—since obviously the more prescient one-word future would have been "technology, "computers," or "microchips."

"They call me Mister Tibbs!"

Sidney Poitier's famous line from the movie *In the Heart of the Night*. Poitier portrayed a black police detective from Philadelphia who was investigating a murder in the small, racist, and fictional town of Sparta, Mississippi. This famous line was spoken by Poitier in response to the question of the local Mississippi sheriff, portrayed by Rod Steiger, when he said to Virgil Tibbs, Poitier's character, *"Virgil, that's a funny name for a nigger boy to come from Philadelphia. What do they call you up there?"*

"We find the defendants incredibly guilty."

From Mel Brooks' satirical comedy, *The Producers*, starring Zero Mostel and Gene Wilder.

"What we've got here is a failure to communicate."

Strother Martin, speaking as the sadistic prison warden to the handsome, irrepressible and lovable Paul Newman in *Cool Hand Luke*. Newman was described in the film by George Kennedy, his inmate friend, as a *"natural-born world-shaker."*

1967 U.S. Population: 198,700,000

(Compared as a Percentage to the U.S. 1957 Population of 172,000,000: 115.5%)

Television Shows

Most Widely-Viewed Television Shows

Rank	Show Name	Years of Series (Excluding Reruns)	Show Type	Estimated Audience (In MMs)	Audience as Percentage of U.S. Population
1.	*Andy Griffith Show*	1960–1968	Comedy	15.6MM	7.9%
	Cast:	Andy Griffith - Ron Howard - Don Knotts			
2.	*The Lucy Show*	1962–1968	Comedy	15.3MM	7.7%
	Cast:	Lucille Ball - Vivian Vance - Gale Gordon			
3.	*Gomer Pyle U.S.M.C.*	1964–1969	Comedy	14.5MM	7.3%
	Cast:	Jim Nabors - Frank Sutton - Ronnie Schell			

Widely-Viewed or Critically-Acclaimed New Television Show(s)

The Carol Burnett Show (1967–1978) - Variety - Sketch Comedy Show
Carol Burnett - Harvey Korman – Vicki Lawrence – Lyle Waggoner –
Tim Conway – Dick Van Dyke
(No. 16 Top TV Shows of All Time – *TV Guide*)

Last Season Television Show(s)

Candid Camera (1960–1967) – Reality - Humor
Host: Allen Funt

Major Commercial Advertising Campaigns and Slogans

"When you got it, flaunt it."
Braniff Airlines

"You don't have to be Jewish to love Levy's"
Levy's Rye Bread

Memorable Words from Speeches, Books, Writings, and Other Sources – 1967

"Green Bay Packers Over the Kansas City Chiefs"
"35-10"

January 15, 1967. The score of the first AFL-NFL World Championship, later known as Super Bowl I. The game was held at the Los Angeles Coliseum. The game featured Bart Starr as Quarterback of

Vince Lombardi's Green Bay Packers and Len Dawson as Quarterback of the Kansas City Chiefs. Super Bowl I was vastly different than today's Super Bowls. Its halftime show consisted mostly of college bands, and more significantly, the stadium was not even sold out. As many as 33,000 of the 94,000 seats at the L.A. Coliseum were empty at kickoff. Adding insult to injury, the local papers wrote editorials complaining about the exorbitant $12 game tickets ($86 in 2016 dollars). In 1967, NFL fans felt highly confident that their team would easily dominate any team of the relatively newly formed AFL. While the NFL team did win Super Bowl I, the AFL proved itself just two years later when the engaging and young Quarterback Joe Namath led the New York Jets to an upset victory over the Baltimore Colts. But even with this modest Super Bowl I, the Age of the Super Bowls had started. By 2015, the U.S. viewing audience ranged from 114 million to 120 million (whole game, halftime, final quarter) with halftime shows featuring professional performers such as Kate Perry, Lenny Kravitz, Janet Jackson, and Beyonce. Also by 2015, the average Super Bowl ticket prices were around $10,400[213] and 30-second television ads sold for about $4.5 million.[214]

"Nineteen sixty-seven: Rarely has there been a 12-month period when young American women changed as dramatically."

...

"...A new kind of woman: content to live alone but not lonely, sexually open but not 'promiscuous'...."

...

"A revolution in women's fashion, attitudes, and sexuality."

1967. From the opening of Sheila Weller's accurate and well-written description of the many dimensions of the social, political, sexual, and fashion changes that were embraced American women in the mid-1960s.[215] The transition was challenging for many women as they, apart and distancing themselves from the "traditional" roles and supposedly proper places of women, from their parents, and, in many instances, and even from their own peers. Instead, they sought out new styles and forged new roles for themselves both in society and in the American economy.

U.S. Constitutional Amendment – 25th Amendment
"Section 1. In the case of the removal of the President from office or of his death or resignation, the Vice President shall become President...."

February 10, 1967. This rather lengthy amendment resolved various succession-to-office procedures and issues relating to the President and Vice President. The amendment was deemed necessary due to ambiguities contained in Article II, Section 1 of the Constitution. The perceived need for this clarification amendment was, of course, also partly attributable to the 1963 assassination of President Kennedy and to concerns attendant to the Cold War. However, the amendment was not first utilized in the context of either assassination or the Cold War. Instead, the amendment was first utilized in the context of the 1973 resignation by Vice President Agnew and then upon the unprecedented 1974 resignation of President Richard Nixon in the wake of the Watergate scandal.

"I'm not advocating sex, drugs, alcohol and violence. I'm only saying that they've always worked for me."

Spring 1967. Hunter S. Thompson, the irrepressible and irresponsible author and Gonzo-journalist, responding to a question from a student in the audience who was trying to determine whether he understood what seemed to be Hunter's philosophy of life. The exchange occurred after Thompson's long and rambling speech at Wheeler Auditorium at the University of California at Berkeley. This author, who was in the audience that day, understood the intended humor being offered by Thompson, which was evidenced at the outset when Thompson sauntered onto the stage with a devilish grin and with his always-present bottle of Wild Turkey bourbon. The answer played well to the sex, drugs, and rock 'n' roll members of the audience. However, by 1967, the mood of many college students and much of the country had turned darker and more ominous as the Vietnam War continued, the civil rights protests and riots continued, and especially after the assassinations of The Rev. Dr. Martin Luther King and Bobby Kennedy in the spring of 1968.

Press Release
The council for the summer of love –
The Haight-Ashbury Community invites you to a Press Conference
to present the unified, positive forces
actively involved in the community.
1757 Waller   Time: 10:00AM
April 5, 1967   San Francisco, Planet Earth

April 5, 1967. The press conference haphazardly announcing the beginning of the self-styled, free-flowing phenomenon called the "Summer of Love." Two days later, the phrase first appeared in the mainstream media in an article entitled "Good Hippies' Summer Plans," which was published in the *San Francisco Chronicle*. Over the course of the summer, more than 100,000 young people arrived and stayed in the Haight-Ashbury area of San Francisco for a summer of free food, drugs, and love—all wrapped up in an environment of counterculture, flower children celebrations, and music. Although there were gatherings in other cities, San Francisco was the epicenter. The Mamas and the Papas' song *"San Francisco (Be Sure to Wear Flowers in Your Hair)"* became immortalized as the anthem of the Summer of Love even though the song was initially written to promote the June 1967 Monterey Pop Festival.

"Some of us ... have already begun to break the silence of the night"

...

"... I (have been) increasingly compelled to see the war
as an enemy of the poor and to attack it as such...
(because) the war (is) doing far more than devastating
the hopes of the poor at home."

...

"We (are) taking the black young men
who had been crippled by our society,
And sending them (8,000) miles away
to guarantee liberties in Southeast Asia
which they had not found in southwest Georgia or East Harlem
(and there is) the cruel irony

*of watching Negro and white boys on TV screens
as they die together for a nation that has been unable
to seat them together in the same school."*

April 7, 1967. The Reverend Dr. Martin Luther King, Jr., speaking at the Riverside Church in New York City and shortly after committing to participate in the Anti-Vietnam War March from Central Park to the United Nations building in New York. The speech is oftentimes referred to as the "A Time to Break Silence" or merely the "Riverside Church" speech. It is rarely considered one of King's most eloquent speeches, and it was criticized by some major civil rights leaders and even the NAACP. Nevertheless, it was powerful. It was the first time that Rev. King had come out so publicly and unequivocally against the Vietnam War—although he would also give another speech (entitled "It's A Dark Day in Our Nation") on the same subject and with the same conclusion a few weeks later at the Ebenezer Baptist Church in Atlanta, Georgia. Through both of these speeches, he effectively formed—or at least recognized— "the common link between the civil rights and peace movements."[216] In addition to calling attention to the "cruel ironies" of the war, Rev. King went on to propose "five concrete things that (the U.S.) government should do to begin the long and difficult process of extricating ourselves" from the Vietnam War. In an instance of tragic and cruel irony, Rev. King was assassinated a year to the day after giving this Riverside Church Speech. But it would be another eight years until the last Americans left the embassy in Saigon on April 30, 1975.

*"I ain't got no quarrel with them Viet Cong.
No Vietcong ever called me nigger."*

April 28, 1967. Words spoken by professional boxer Mohammed Ali explaining—just a month after he had become the world heavyweight boxing champion with a 29-0 record—the reasons for his refusing induction into the U.S. Army upon the grounds of conscientious objection.[217] Ali had shocked the nation several years earlier by announcing that he had joined the Nation of Islam.[218] At that time he had also changed his birth name, Cassious Clay, which he referred to as a "slave name," to Muhammad

Ali. As a result of this 1967 refusal of induction, Ali was widely condemned and was stripped of his title and his boxing license. He was later found guilty and sentenced to five years in prison, although he was released on appeal. Three years later, the USSC reversed his conviction. After regaining his boxing license in 1970, he twice again won and held the world heavyweight title, from 1974 to 1976 and from 1978 to 1979 before retiring in 1981. Over the course of the ensuing decades, he became an American icon. In 1999, ESPN named Ali the third greatest athlete of the 20th century—behind only Michael Jordan and Babe Ruth. In October 2003, David Granger, the editor of *Esquire* magazine, beautifully and accurately noted that Ali, "like only a very few Americans, has existed for nearly his entire life at that rare nexus of celebrity, accomplishment, and infamy...." Although suffering from Parkinson's disease, Ali, who had won the gold medal in boxing at the 1960 Olympics, was asked nearly 36 years later to light the Olympic Torch at the opening of the 1996 Olympic Games in Atlanta, Georgia. He agreed, and he did so in a manner indelibly etched into the memories of all who watched.[219]

"Tell the court I love my wife...."

June 12, 1967. The touching words of plaintiff Richard Loving which he conveyed to his lawyer shortly before Loving's case was argued before the USSC relating to the constitutionality of laws prohibiting interracial marriages. Six years earlier, Richard Loving, a 23-year-old construction worker, had lawfully married 18-year-old Mildred Jeter, a black woman, in Washington, D.C. where such interracial marriages were permitted. Shortly thereafter and after returning to Virginia, their home was raided by police. The couple was arrested for violating the state's prohibition against interracial marriages, commonly referred to as "anti-miscegenation" laws. The couple pled guilty to "cohabitating as man and wife." They were sentenced to one year in prison with the sentence suspended on the condition that they left the Commonwealth of Virginia and did not return. Several years later and as a result of their frustration of not being able to return to Virginia to see their families, they decided to appeal their conviction and to challenge the constitutionality of such statutes. In the aptly-named case, *Loving v. Virginia*,[220] the USSC in a unanimous decision concluded that such laws were violative of the U.S. Constitutions. The USSC held that "the freedom to marry, or not marry, a person of another race resides with the individual and cannot be infringed by the State." The case was immediately recognized as a landmark civil right decision especially in light of the sad fact that seventeen states banned interracial marriages at the time of the decision. Tragically, Richard Loving was killed by a drunk driver just eight years later, at the age of 41. His wife, Mildred, lost her eye in the same accident, although she lived until 2012 and was able to raise the couple's three children.[221] As of 2015, "17% of U.S. newlyweds … were of differing races or ethnicities, a fivefold increase over the 50 years" since the court's decision in this landmark case.[222]

"Long, hot summer"

July, 1967. Race or "urban" riots have occurred throughout post-bellum American history. In the 19th century, urban riots were commonly referred to as "politics out of doors," and periodically such riots would erupt during the course of the early 20th century as well. However, they became more commonplace in the 1960s. While there had been major race riots in Harlem, New York in 1964 and in the Watts area of Los Angeles, California in 1965, and while there would be riots after the assassination of the Rev. Dr. Martin Luther King, Jr. in 1968, the riots of the summer 1967 had a unique level of intensity and frequency. In the summer of 1967, the expression "long, hot summer" took on a new meaning especially after the Newark Riots began on July 12 and the Detroit Riots began on July 23, 1967. By the end of that "long, hot summer," pictures of fires and looting and National Guard and police formations became routinized on American television. By the end of that year and apart from Newark and Detroit, as many as 159 race riots had been triggered in many cities—Englewood and Plainfield, New Jersey; Rochester, New York; Flint, Grand Rapids and Pontiac, Michigan; Toledo, Ohio; Houston, Texas; Tucson, Arizona; Milwaukee, Wisconsin; Minneapolis, Minnesota; and even Portland, Oregon. To a certain extent, such riots could be attributed to the more activist political and protest culture of the 1960s. But, largely, they resulted from racial tensions. It was of little news to most Americans when the National Commission on Civil Disorder, commonly known as the Kerner Commission,[223] concluded in its 1968 Report that the race riots were a direct result of the serious, continuing and unaddressed grievances of minority racial groups, particularly African Americans.

"Admitted"
Female Students (Finally) Admitted to Harvard

Fall, 1967. Excerpted from letters of college admittance sent by Harvard University, which for the first time were sent to both men and women. In the fall of 1967 and for the first time in the 331 years since its founding in 1636, female students were admitted to Harvard University.[224] Other historically, non-co-educational universities addressed their admissions policy separately and at different times. Texas A&M had started admitting women in 1963. Vasser didn't admit men until 1969, and it was not until 1993 and 1997 that women were admitted, respectively, to The Citadel and to Virginia Military Institute. As of 2016, there were still as many as 39 American all-women's universities, but there are only three non-religious all-men's universities.

Legal Standard - "To save the life of the mother."

1967. As of this year, this was the only legal justification for abortion in any state. As a part of and in the context of the sexual revolution of the 1960s and early 1970s, increasingly heated debates continued relating to the morality and legality of what came to be referred to as "a woman's right to choose." The first legislative change occurred in New York, which in 1970 agreed to permit the lawful termination of pregnancies resulting from rape and incest. Within a year, eleven other states had enacted parallel legislation, and in 1972 the USSC ruled in the case of *Roe v. Wade* that at least during the first trimester of her pregnancy, a woman had a constitutional right to elect to terminate or continue her pregnancy.

Year 1968

<u>Seminal Books</u>

The Double Helix:
A Personal Account of the Discovery of the Structure of DNA
by James D. Watson

A controversial, autobiographical account of the discovery by Watson, Francis Crick, and Maurice Wilkins of the double helix structure of DNA. While the book has been widely criticized for Watson's self-aggrandizing presentation, it remains a classic and highly personal presentation of their 1953 groundbreaking identification of the structure of DNA – itself the physiological architecture of life's core. The book reveals the disputes, challenges and conflicts amongst the scientists and includes Watson's personal impressions as well. The significance of the discovery of the structure of DNA, the molecules of life, revolutionized biochemistry and open unlimited new pathways in the field of genetics research. In 2012, the book was selected by the Library of Congress as one the 88 "Books That Shaped America."

The Lessons of History
by William and Ariel Durant

This thin book, only 102 pages long, is a brilliant encapsulation by the Durants of what they concluded about history and philosophy after a lifetime of study and writing. Will Durant started his epic series, *The Story of Civilization,* in 1935. His initial plan was to present the world's history in a five-volume set over the course of a decade. Forty years later he completed his 11th volume—*The Age of Napoleon* (with his wife, also a historian, assisting and co-authoring the last five volumes). The brilliance and scope of the Durants' writings are, in the opinion of this author, unparalleled. *The Lessons of History* is sometimes identified as a seminal work in the place and stead of the 11 volumes as much for its brevity as its brilliance. As correctly noted in Edward Dougherty's 2015 book review, in the writing of *The Story of Civilization* the Durants were "clearly historians," but "(i) n *The Lessons*, (the Durants) are advocates, learning from history but also using history to buttress their philosophical positions."[225] The Durants retained a deep respect for the influence and powers of religion—and Will Durant, as a young man, even attended a seminary and expected to become a Catholic priest. Nevertheless, Dougherty's observation is both correct and appropriate to note because over the course of their lives, both of the Durants became atheists.

Author's Note:

I have read Durant's 11-volume The Story of Civilization *only once. I was living in a small coastal town in Spain where I had gone to live and write. Young and still naïve, I was bursting with answers and energy. But over the course of the first six months, I read all 11 volumes of Durants' series. It was their writings that, more than anything, brought me back to reality and buried me in belated humility.*

The Population Bomb
by Dr. Paul Ehrlich

This book, written by a Stanford University Professor, presented an alarmist tone and included ominous Malthusian-style warnings. The early editions of the book opened with the statement that "the battle to feed all of humanity is over. In the 1970s, hundreds of millions of people will starve …." The book also predicted inevitable societal upheavals and advocated a series of immediate actions. *The Population Bomb* became an instant best seller, and its author achieved a certain notoriety as well as a frequent guest on Johnny Carson's *The Tonight Show*. In his 1975 book, *The End of Affluence*, which was co-authored with his wife, Anne, Ehrlich doubled-down on the dire predictions he had set forth in *The Population Bomb*. In his second book, he even "outlined a Hollywood-style disaster scenario where he foresaw the President dissolving Congress during the food riots of the 1980s," followed by the U.S. suffering a nuclear attack for its mass use of insecticides."[226] As is evident, Ehrlich was a constant alarmist. He long maintained an almost stubborn insistence that the only error in the book was in the timeline, and as late as 1990—on *The Today Show*'s Earth Day special, he "predicted that 'the Supreme Court would (soon) be flooded' to such an extent that … (y)ou could tie your boat to the Washington Monument."[227] Still ignoring the lowering birthrate and other demographic changes in many parts of the world and the incredible increases in the world's food supply resulting from "agricultural savior(s)" such as Norman E. Borlaug, Ehrlich, "now 83, is not retreating from his bleak prophesies."[228]

<u>Pulitzer Prize for Fiction</u>

The Confessions of Nat Turner
by William Styron

<u>Pulitzer Prize for General Nonfiction</u>

***Rousseau and Revolution* (Vol. 10 of *The Story of Civilization*)**
by Will and Ariel Durant

<u>Pulitzer Prize for History</u>

The Ideological Origins of the American Revolution
by Bernard Bailyn

**<u>*The New York Times* Best Sellers List (Nonfiction) –
Books with Most Weeks as No. 1 Best Seller</u>**

The Money Game
by "Adam Smith" (Pseudonym for George Goodman) (25 weeks)

The Naked Ape: A Zoologist's Study of the Human Animal
by Desmond Morris (11 weeks)

**<u>*The New York Times* Best Sellers List (Adult Fiction) –
Book with Most Weeks as No. 1 Best Seller</u>**

Airport
by Arthur Hailey (30 weeks)

<u>Academy Awards Best Picture</u>

Winner: *Oliver!*

Other Nominees: *Funny Girl; The Lion in Winter;
Rachel, Rachel; Romeo and Juliet*

PrettyFamous' Best Movie of the Year
2001: A Space Odyssey

Best/Most Memorable Movie Lines of the Year
"Open the pod bay doors please, HAL."

...

"I'm sorry, Dave, I'm afraid I can't do that."

The human character speaking to HAL, his computer companion, in Stanley Kubrick's science fiction space film *2001: A Space Odyssey*. At the time of the film's release in 1968, the year 2001 seemed like a futuristic and distant year dealing with an inconceivable subject. But time passes quickly. America is now already closing its second decade of the 21st century. The inclusion of even the concept of artificial intelligence reveals the film's prescience.

"Satan is his father, and his name is Adrian.
He shall overthrow the mighty and lay waste their temples.
He shall redeem the despised and wreak vengeance
in the name of the burned and the tortured."

The chilling description of the supposed true identity of *Rosemary's Baby* in a satanic thriller by the same name. The film was directed by Roman Polanski, starred Mia Farrow and John Cassavetes, and received wide critical acclaim.

"Take your stinkin' paws off me,
you damned dirty ape."

Charlton Heston yelling in disgust and anger in *Planet of the Apes*. Although four sequels followed over the next several years, only this first film was a critical and commercial success. With a touch of appropriate selection, Rod Serling, the creator and deep-voiced narrator of the television show, *The Twilight Zone* (1959–1964), was one of the screenwriters of this original *Planet of the Apes*.

"Yeah, they're dead. They're all messed up."

While this movie line is hardly in itself memorable, this low budget, independent horror movie *Night of the Living Dead* was for many Americans the first real zombie movie and has become a cult classic.

<u>1968 U.S. Population: 200,700,000</u>

(Compared as a Percentage to the U.S. 1957 Population of 172,000,000: 116.7%)

<u>Television Shows</u>

Most Widely-Viewed Television Shows

Rank	Show Name	Years of Series (Excluding Reruns)	Show Type	Estimated Audience (In MMs)	Audience as Percentage of U.S. Population
1.	*Rowan & Martin's Laugh-In*	1967–1973	Comedy	18.5MM	9.2%
	Cast: Dan Rowan - Dick Martin - Goldie Hawn - Lily Tomlin				
2.	*Gomer Pyle U.S.M.C.*	1964–1969	Comedy	15.8MM	7.9%
	Cast: Jim Nabors - Frank Sutton - Ronnie Schell				
3.	*Bonanza*	1959–1973	Western	15.5MM	7.7%
	Cast: Lorne Greene - Michael Landon – Pernell Roberts – Dan Blocker				

Widely-Viewed or Critically-Acclaimed New Television Show(s)

60 Minutes (1968 - Present) -
News Magazine and Investigative Reporting Show
Harry Reasoner - Mike Wallace - Andy Rooney -
Steve Kroft - Lesley Stahl
(No. 6 Top TV Shows of All Time – *TV Guide*)

Mister Rogers' Neighborhood (1968-2001)[229] – Preschool Children's Show
Host: Fred Rogers
(One of three Longest-Running Children's Series)
(Along with *Captain Kangaroo* (1955-1984)
and *Sesame Street* (1970 to Present))

Last Season Television Show(s)

The Andy Griffith Show (1960–1968) - Comedy
Andy Griffith - Ron Howard - Don Knotts
(No. 9 Top TV Shows of All Time – *TV Guide*)

<u>Catchphrases, Chants, and Slogans</u>

"The whole world is watching"

August 1968. Chant of crowd outside the convention hall of the
1968 Democratic Convention in Chicago, Illinois. Through its first eight

months, 1968 had become the boiling point year with regard to frustrations with and protests of especially the Vietnam War, the Civil Rights movement, and the generalized conflicts between two distinct generations of Americans. This steady chant of "The Whole World Is Watching" was heard outside the convention hall as the Chicago police attempted to control the assembled crowd of nearly 10,000 people, which had been organized by the Students for a Democratic Society (the "SDS") and the Youth International Party (the "Yippies"). More importantly, the chant was also heard and the protests were also seen on television sets across America as heads shook—not so much in disbelief as in saddened acceptance of a changed nation. Observers were deeply divided about the nature of the police response. Some people concluded that the police overreacted and instigated a "police riot." The demonstrations and the ensuing riots largely buried the news of the nomination of Hubert Humphrey. Instead, the demonstrations and riots led to the formation of the Walker Commission to study the riots and the police's response. Eight of the protest leaders (Abbie Hoffman, Tom Hayden, David Dellinger, Rennie Davis, John Froines, Jerry Rubin, Lee Weiner, and Bobby Seale) were indicted on charges of conspiracy and incitement to riot. Over the course of the next 18 months, the trial attracted national attention. It came to be known as the "Chicago Seven Trial" after charges against Bobby Seale were dropped. In 1970, five of the seven were convicted on the intent to incite riot charges, but even these convictions were eventually reversed on appeal.

<u>Memorable Words from Speeches, Books, Writings, and Other Sources – 1968</u>

Presidential Campaign Themes, Slogans and Results
(Both Official and Unofficial)

Eugene McCarthy (Early Candidate for Democratic Party nomination)
Go Clean for Gene.   To Begin Anew …

Richard M. Nixon (and Spiro Agnew) (Republican Party)
He's Good Enough for Me in '68   Nixon Now   Nixon's The One.
This Time, Vote Like Your Whole World Depended On It
You Can't Lose 'Em All.

Hubert Humphrey (and Edmund Muskie) (Democratic Party)
Humphrey-Muskie, Two You Can Trust
Some People Talk Change, Others Cause It
Two Hearts Beat as One: Elect This Team!   *Unite with Humphrey*

George Wallace (and Gen. Curtis LeMay) (American Independent Party)
Send Them A Message   *Stand Up for America.*

Election Results:

Party	Nominees		Electoral Vote	Popular Vote
	Presidential	Vice-Presidential		
Republican	Richard Nixon	S. Agnew	301 55.9%	31.8MM 43.9%
Democratic	Hubert Humphrey	E. Muskie	191 35.5%	31.3MM 42.7%
Am Independent	George Wallace	C. LeMay	45 8.4%	9.9MM 13.5%

"To say that we are mired in stalemate (in Vietnam)
seems the only realistic, yet unsatisfactory, conclusion."

…

"It is increasingly clear to this reporter
that the only rational way out (of Vietnam)
will be to negotiate, not as victors,
but as an honorable people who lived up to their pledge
to defend democracy, and did the best they could."

February 27, 1968. Walter Cronkite, speaking shortly after the January 1968 Tet Offensive, which had been launched by the North Vietnamese and Viet Cong forces. Cronkite's remarks were made during the course of a special broadcast "…with a rare, brief, and potent editorial suggesting that America cease fighting the Vietnam War."[230] The influence of Cronkite's conclusion and his influence upon public opinion are hard for many older Americans to remember. It is even harder still for younger Americans who have grown up amongst the splintered media and amidst the politically-charged and partisan associations of so many media members. However, in the Sixties, there were just three dominant news voices in America: Walter Cronkite at CBS, and Chet Huntley and David Brinkley at NBC. ABC would not become a major source of news until the 1970s with the arrival of John Chancellor. The evening news did not even expand from 15 minutes to 30 minutes until 1963. However, as more and more Americans started to watch the evening national news, tried to understand the Vietnam War, and tried to fathom the rapid changes in the country during the Sixties, they still coalesced at least in their primary sources of information. The national evening news was subject to many different interpretations, but the presented facts themselves were widely accepted without great doubt, skepticism, or cynicism. People believed in the news. Uncle Walt wouldn't lie. And so it was that the cynicism wouldn't arrive until later—in the aftermath of Watergate, as more was learned and as sentiments hardened about the Vietnam War, and especially as more and more aspects of American life became encrusted and encumbered as matters of (conservative or liberal) ideology.

"If I've lost Walter Cronkite … (I)'ve lost Middle America."

February 27, 1968. President Lyndon Johnson, speaking to his aides as he watched Walter Cronkite's Special Broadcast, described immediately above, in which Cronkite suggested to the public for the first time that the Vietnam War, while possibly not lost, would not be won.

***"The summer of 1967 again brought racial disorders
to Americans cities, and with them shock,
fear and bewilderment to the nation."***

…

***"The President (Lyndon Johnson) established this Commission
and directed us to answer three basic questions:
What happened?
Why did it happen?
What can be done to prevent it from happening again?"***

…

***"We have visited the riot cities; we have heard many witnesses;
we have sought the counsel of experts across the country.
This is our basic conclusion:
Our nation is moving toward two societies,
one black, one white – separate and unequal."***

February 29, 1968. Excerpt from the opening Summary of The President's Advisory Commission on Civil Disorders, more commonly known as the Kerner Commission, after Illinois Governor Otto Kerner, who served as Chairman of the 11-member panel. The Kerner Commission was formed in response to the "more than 150 riots (including the infamous 1965 Watts riot and the 1967 Newark riots) ... between 1965 and 1968," and it was asked to make recommendations for changes in social and political policy. The 426-page report became a best seller. In a stunning show of interest and concern, more than 2.0 million Americans bought copies of the Commission's Report. The Report was highly critical of both federal and state governments for their inadequate housing, education, and social service policies; however, it was scorned by Republican Presidential nominee Richard Nixon at the time because it "refused to condemn the 'perpetrators' of (the) urban riots." Nixon also noted, arguably reasonably, that "until we have order, there can be no progress."[231] In any event and despite the dire warnings of the Kerner Commission, matters only got worse over the ensuing decades. According to the conclusions of The Millennium Breach, a review project and writing sponsored by the Eisenhower Foundation and prepared in 1998 by former Senator Fred Harris and others, between 1968 and 1998 (i) income disparities between the races had greatly increased; (ii) public appropriations for housing had decreased by more than 80%; (iii) urban public schools had continued to fail; and (iv) the U.S. child poverty rate had increased substantially and to the point that it was, as of 1998, four times greater than that of Western European countries.

"With America's sons in the fields far away,
with America's future under challenge here at home,
with our hopes and the world's hopes for peace
in the balance every day,
I do not believe that I should devote an hour or a day of my time
to any personal partisan causes or to any duties
other than the awesome duties of this office
– the Presidency of your country.

> *Accordingly,*
> *I shall not seek, and I will not accept,*
> *the nomination of my party for another term as your President."*

March 31, 1968. President Lyndon Johnson, announcing to the nation that he would not seek another term. President Johnson, like "his" war, was increasingly unpopular in the country. Nevertheless, his decision not to seek re-election stunned most Americans, despite the fact that most political observers believed that Johnson would have had no realistic chance to win. In the wake of his removal of himself from the political race, Johnson's Vice President Hubert Humphrey sought and eventually obtained the Democratic candidacy. Even after Humphrey's nomination, however, Humphrey found himself irrevocably tied to Johnson's Great Society and Vietnam War policies. Many Americans, albeit unfairly, also viewed Humphrey as almost a default nominee who had only obtained the nomination as the result of the tragic assassination of Robert Kennedy in June 1968. Humphrey lost to the phoenix-like rise of Richard Nixon in the ensuing three-way Presidential race with George Wallace. Five years later, Johnson would die of a heart attack at his Texas Ranch—and in cruel, indeed tragic, irony, just five days after Johnson's death the United States officially ended its combat role in Vietnam.

> *"We've got some difficult days ahead. But it doesn't really matter ...*
> *because I've been to the mountaintop.*
> *Like anybody, I would like to live a long life – longevity has its place.*
> *But I'm not concerned about that now, I just want to do God's will.*
> *And he's allowed me to go up to the mountain.*
> *And I've looked over, and I've seen the Promised Land.*
> *I may not get there with you,*
> *but ... we, as a people, will get to the Promised Land.*
> *And so I'm happy tonight;*
> *I'm not worried about anything;*
> *I'm not fearing any man.*
> *Mine eyes have seen the glory of the coming of the Lord."*

April 3, 1968. The Reverend Dr. Martin Luther King, Jr., speaking with a frightening prescience at the Mason Temple Church in Memphis, Tennessee just one day before he was assassinated. He was killed at the age of 39 while standing on the balcony of the Lorraine Motel by James Earl Ray, a white, racist drifter. Rev. King's last spoken words were to his musician friend Ben Branch, when he said "Ben, make sure you play 'Take My Hand, Precious Lord' in the meeting tonight. Play it real pretty."[232] Just as with the assassination of President John Kennedy, there have been many conspiracy theories about the Rev. King's assassination. Nevertheless, Ray confessed and pled guilty to the murder charge although he admittedly recanted the confession years later. Ray died in prison in 1998 at the age of 70.

> ***"White America killed Dr. King last night,***
> ***She made (it) a whole lot easier for a whole lot of black people today.***
> ***There no longer needs to be intellectual discussions,***
> ***Black people know they have to get guns.***
> ***White America will live to cry that she killed Dr. King."***

April 5, 1968. The heated and inflammatory rhetoric of Stokely Carmichael during his address at a rally at Howard University in Washington, D.C. the day after Rev King's assassination.[233]

> ***"Dr. King would be greatly distressed to find that his blood***
> ***had triggered off bloodshed and disorder."***
>
> ...
>
> ***"I think instead the nation should be quiet; black and white,***
> ***and we should be in a prayerful mood,***
> ***which would be in keeping with his life."***

April 8, 1968. James Farmer, Jr., shortly after the assassination of the Rev. Dr. Martin Luther King, Jr. Farmer's remarks were made in response to the eruption of riots in more than 100 U.S. cities, including Washington D.C., where President Johnson ordered nearly 14,000 federal troops and federalized National Guard units to control, if not calm, the rioters. Similar responses, together with the imposition of nighttime curfews and the banning of the sale of both alcohol and guns occurred across the country from Baltimore to Louisville and from Chicago to Los Angeles. Some black leaders, like the more militant Stokely Carmichael as noted above, placed blame directly upon "white America," and called for a far more violent response.

"It's on to Chicago, and let's win there."

...

"Is everybody o.k.?"

June 5, 1968. Robert F. Kennedy's last words to his crowd of supporters and his last lucid words, spoken a few moments later, after being shot by 24-year-old Sirhan Sirhan, a Jerusalem-born Palestinian Christian. Kennedy was just 42 years old. His wife, Ethel, was then pregnant with their 11th child. It had been less five years since his brother's assassination in Dallas, Texas. It had been only two months since the assassination of the Rev. Dr. Martin Luther King, Jr. in Memphis, Tennessee. In March, President Johnson had dropped out of the election race, and Kennedy, who earlier that evening had just won the California Democratic primary, was believed to be on his way to becoming the Democratic Party's Presidential nominee. Robert Kennedy was the only person killed that night at the Ambassador Hotel in Los Angeles, but five people were shot. As noted by one writer, "in many ways Bobby Kennedy was heir to Martin Luther King's legacy. He campaigned for civil rights and made urban poverty a chief tenet of his campaign. While President Johnson had escalated the number of soldiers in Vietnam, Bobby openly questioned the war. He was mobbed at rallies. Journalists compared him to a rock star."[234] But on that night, he was killed. Sirhan Sirhan, now 72 years of age, remains incarcerated in a California prison.

"If George McGovern were president ...
we wouldn't have Gestapo tactics in the streets of Chicago"

...

"F you, you Jew sonofabitch"***

August 26-29, 1968. The remark of Senator Abraham Ribicoff and the angry response of Chicago Mayor Richard J. Daley, in the midst of the tumultuous Democratic Party Convention in Chicago, Illinois. Ribicoff's remark was made during his nomination of George McGovern for President and while staring directly into the eyes of the powerful Mayor

Daley. Tensions ran high in the wake of the assassinations of both the Rev. Dr. Martin Luther King, Jr. and Bobby Kennedy just months earlier and with the chants of "The Whole World Is Watching" streaming into the convention center from the crowds outside.[235]

"You could have heard a frog piss on cotton. There's something awful about hearing 50,000 people go silent, like being in the eye of a hurricane."

October 17, 1968. John Carlos, U.S. sprinter and Olympic athlete, describing the terrifying silence that occurred when he and his teammate Tommie Smith raised their fists in a Black Power salute on the medal podium at the 1968 Mexico City Olympics. They raised their fists in the middle of the awards ceremony and shortly after winning, respectively, the bronze and gold medals in the 200-meter dash. As a result, both men "were expelled from the Olympics and suspended from the U.S. team."[236]

"The odious smell of censorship" ### and ### *"G-M-R-X"*

November 1, 1968. The summary concerns of Jack Valenti, then the President of the Motion Picture Association of America, and the initial movie ratings ("General/Mature/Restricted/X"). The movie ratings were adopted in order to avoid the imposition of government-mandated or government-directed censorship of the film industry. These rating levels replaced the earlier and long-outdated Hays Code, which had been in use since 1934. The demands for censorship, or at least the implementation of a movie ratings system, were triggered by audience reactions to, for example, the first use of the word "screw" in the recent 1966 film *Who's Afraid of Virginia Wolff* and to the first presentation of nudity in a major movie in Michelangelo Antonioni's 1966 film, *Blow Up*. Thus, under Valenti's leadership, the industry initiated a self-governing and voluntary rating system. It has been modified on several occasions over the decades. For example, the PG-13 rating was added in 1984, partially in response to the violence and intensity in *Indiana Jones and the Temple of Doom*. As of

1990, the general criteria were designated as violence, language, substance abuse, nudity, and sexual content, but the ratings remain the subject of severe criticism. Some film critics and commentators believe that the ratings place too much emphasis upon sexual content while under-recognizing the impact of gruesome violence. Others believe that the ratings focus too often upon the trivial aspects of the film (e.g. number of uses of profanity) rather than reflecting the overall and sometimes dark, intense, and violent themes—such as, to use one example, the inappropriate PG-13 rating for the widely popular and critically acclaimed *Hunger Games* films of 2012–2015).[237]

Year 1969

<u>Pulitzer Prize for Fiction</u>

House Made of Dawn
by N. Scott Momaday

<u>Pulitzer Prize for General Nonfiction</u>

*The Armies of the Night:
History as a Novel, the Novel as History* (Co-Winner)
by Norman Mailer

*So Human an Animal:
How We Are Shaped by Surroundings and Events* (Co-Winner)
by Rene Jules Dubos

<u>Pulitzer Prize for History</u>

The Origins of the Fifth Amendment
by Leonard W. Levy

**<u>*The New York Times* Best Sellers List (Nonfiction) –
Books with Most Weeks as No. 1 Best Seller</u>**

The Peter Principle: Why Things Always Go Wrong
by Dr. Laurence J. Peter and Raymond Hull (21 weeks)

The Money Game
by "Adam Smith" (Pseudonym for George Goodman) (17 weeks)

**<u>*The New York Times* Best Sellers List (Adult Fiction) –
Book with Most Weeks as No. 1 Best Seller</u>**

The Godfather
by Mario Puzo (15 weeks)

<u>Academy Awards Best Picture</u>

Winner: *Midnight Cowboy*

Other Nominees: *Anne of a Thousand Days; Butch Cassidy and the Sundance Kid; Hello, Dolly!; Z*

<u>*PrettyFamous'* Best Movie of the Year</u>
The Wild Bunch

<u>Best/Most Memorable Movie Lines of the Year</u>

"… I got vision and the rest of the world wears bifocals."

Paul Newman in George Roy Hill's *Butch Cassidy and the Sundance Kid,* explaining his capacities of thought to his partner, the Sundance Kid, as portrayed by Robert Redford. Redford's touching response to Newman, which was repeated several times in the movie, was merely, *"You keep thinkin', Butch, that's what you're good at."*

"Why, you crazy? The fall'll probably kill ya!"

Paul Newman in *Butch Cassidy and the Sundance Kid* joking to his partner, the Sundance Kid, after Redford complained that he didn't want to jump off a cliff into the river because he couldn't swim.

"I'm walking here! I'm walking here!"

Dustin Hoffman, in his classic portrayal of "Ratso" Rizzo, yelling at the driver of a car who almost hit him as he was walking across a street in New York City in John Schlesinger's *Midnight Cowboy.* The film also introduced many Americans to Jon Voight, who delivered a powerful performance as Joe Buck, the Midnight Cowboy.

"Oh, they're not scared of you.
They're scared of what you represent to 'em … (freedom!)."

Peter Fonda, aka Captain America, responding to Dennis Hopper's question of why some local men seemed afraid of their freewheeling, biker ways in the epic road film, *Easy Rider.* The movie, which was directed by Hopper, also was one of the first big films featuring Jack Nicholson.

"We've got to start thinkin' beyond our guns.
Those days are closin' fast."

Members of an aging outlaw gang including William Holden, Ernest Borgnine, and Robert Ryan, recognizing the end of an era in Sam Peckinpah's *The Wild Bunch.*

1969 U.S. Population: 202,700,000

(Compared as a Percentage to the U.S. 1957 Population of 172,000,000: 117.8%)

Television Shows

Most Widely-Viewed Television Shows

Rank	Show Name	Years of Series (Excluding Reruns)	Show Type	Estimated Audience (In MMs)	Audience as Percentage of U.S. Population
1.	*Rowan & Martin's Laugh-In*	1967–1973	Comedy	15.4MM	7.6%
	Cast: Dan Rowan - Dick Martin - Goldie Hawn - Lily Tomlin				
2.	*Gunsmoke*	1955–1975	Western	15.2MM	7.5%
	Cast: James Arness - Amanda Blake - Dennis Weaver				
3.	*Bonanza*	1959–1973	Western	14.5MM	7.2%
	Cast: Lorne Greene - Michael Landon – Pernell Roberts – Dan Blocker				

Widely-Viewed or Critically-Acclaimed New Television Show(s)

Sesame Street – (1970-Present) - Children's Education Series
Created by Joan Ganz Cooney and Lloyd Morrisett
and featuring Jim Henson's Muppets
(The Longest-Running Children's Series)
(Along with *Captain Kangaroo* (1955-1984) and
Mister Rogers Neighborhood (1968-2001))

Major Commercial Advertising Campaigns and Slogan(s)

"It's the real thing."
Coca-Cola

<u>Memorable Words from Speeches, Books, Writings,</u>
<u>and Other Sources – 1969</u>

January 20, 1969
First Inaugural Address of Richard M. Nixon
(President of the United States 1969–1974)

"For the first time, because the people of the world want peace,
and the leaders of the world are afraid of war,
the times are on the side of peace."

...

"The second third of this century has been a time of proud achievement.
We have made enormous strides
in science and industry and agriculture.
We have shared our wealth more broadly than ever.
We have learned at last to manage a modern economy....
We have given freedom new reach.
We have begun to make its promise real for black as well as for white."

...

"No people has ever been so close to the achievement
of a just and abundant society,
or so possessed of the will to achieve it."

...

"But we find ourselves rich in goods, but ragged in spirit;
reaching with magnificent precision for the Moon,
but falling into raucous discord on Earth."

...

"We are caught in war, wanting peace.
We are torn by division, wanting unity.
We see around us empty lives, wanting fulfillment.
We see tasks that need doing, waiting for hands to do them."

...

"To lower our voices would be a simple thing.
In these difficult years, America has suffered from a fever of words,
from inflated rhetoric that promises more than it can deliver;

from angry rhetoric that fans discontents into hatred;
from bombastic rhetoric that postures instead of persuading.
We cannot learn from one another
until we stop shouting at one another
—until we speak quietly enough so that our words
can be heard as well as our voices."

...

"The American Dream does not come to those who fall asleep.
But we are approaching the limits of what government alone can do."

...

"No man can be fully free while his neighbor is not.
To go forward at all is to go forward together.
This means black and white together, as one nation, not two.
The laws have caught up with our conscience.
What remains is to give life to what is in the law;
to ensure at last that as all are born equal in dignity before God,
all are born equal in dignity before man."

...

"After a period of confrontation,
we are entering a period of negotiation."

January 20, 1969. From the First Inaugural Address of Richard M. Nixon, as Nixon became the only man in the 20th century to be defeated for President (in 1960) and then later elected to the office. In the above passage, Nixon urged Americans to "lower (their) voices" and to restrain the explosive rhetoric that had come to so characterize the 1960s. The President also vowed to enter "an era of negotiations" and to bring the country together again. However, both the anger and the war continued unabated. Just two hours after the President's address, demonstrators started hurling rocks and beer cans at Nixon's Presidential limousines, and just two months later, in April 1969, the total number of Americans who died in the Vietnam War surpassed the number killed in World War II. President Nixon took his oath of office from Chief Justice Earl Warren. Vice President Spiro Agnew took his oath of office from Senate Minority Leader Everett Dirksen.

" …(A)fter 5 years in which more and more Americans have been sent to Vietnam, we finally have reached the point where we can begin to bring Americans home from Vietnam."

June 8, 1969. President Richard M. Nixon, just months after assuming office, announcing the initial withdrawal of 25,000 U.S. troops from Vietnam. During the course of the President's remarks, he also invited the leaders of North Vietnam to start withdrawing troops and to meet in Paris in order to start negotiating a final resolution of the war. Lastly, Nixon introduced the concept of what would come to be known as "Vietnamization," whereby South Vietnam troops would assume ever-increasing responsibility for the war.[238] This announcement was made after Nixon's meeting with President Thieu of South Vietnam at Midway Island, and it signaled a dramatic change of course. Some commentators suggest that the announcement was "a defining moment in modern American history" because "it marked the first recognition of a limit to American power."[239] These limits would be seen again in the context of the wars in Afghanistan and Iraq 35 years later. While many Vietnam War critics were disappointed by the small size of the announced withdrawal, the announcement was generally well, albeit cautiously, received. At the height of the U.S. involvement in April 1969, there were 540,000 U.S. troops in Vietnam. At the time of the signing of the Paris Peace Accords four years later in 1973, only 27,000 troops remained.

"The faces shown on the next pages are the faces of American men killed – in the official announcement of their deaths—
'in connection with the conflict in Vietnam.'
The names, 242 of them, were released
on May 28 through June 3 (1969), a span of no special significance except that it includes Memorial Day.
The numbers of the dead are average for any seven-day period during this stage of the war."

…

"In a time when the numbers of Americans killed in this war—36,000—

> *though far less than the Vietnamese losses,*
> *have exceeded the dead in the Korean War, ...*
> *we must pause to look into the faces.*
> *More than we must know how many, we must know who...."*

June 27, 1969. The sobering introduction in *Life* Magazine's "moving and, in some quarters, ... controversial" publication of its weekly issue, which this week was entitled "The Faces of the American Dead in Vietnam: One Week's Toll, June, 1969."[240] The above June 1969 excerpt references 36,000 American fatalities. This number would increase to 58,000 by the time all U.S. personnel (excluding POW/MIAs) were withdrawn from Vietnam in 1975. In 1972, just three years its release of this sobering issue, *Life* Magazine would cease publication due to huge changes in the advertising industry and to the growing dominance of television news coverage over print reporting.

> *"I had not given up hope all night long that, by some miracle,*
> *Mary Jo would have escaped from the car."*

July 18, 1969. Ted Kennedy, describing some of his thoughts after he had accidentally driven off a small bridge on Chappaquiddick Island, Massachusetts (near Martha's Vineyard), causing the drowning death of a young woman in his car, Mary Jo Kopechne. The tragedy came to be known as the "Chappaquiddick incident." The grand jury did not indict Kennedy, but many believe that Kennedy had received preferential leniency. Partly as a result of this event, Kennedy chose not to enter either the 1972 or the 1976 Presidential campaign. Some also believe that this Mary Jo Kopechne tragedy was a major contributing factor to Kennedy not receiving the Democratic Presidential nomination over Jimmy Carter in 1980.[241]

> *"That's one small step for a man ... one giant leap for mankind."*

July 20, 1969. Astronaut Neil Armstrong's first words as the 38-year-old set foot on the Moon. The Moon landing occurred just eight years and fifty-six days after President John Kennedy had challenged America to put a man on the Moon "before the end of the decade."[242] "Around the globe people (were) transfixed ...."[243] An estimated 600 million around the world watched the moon landing. Another nearly one million spectators "flocked to the Florida launch site"[244] and watched as the landing module, the Eagle, descended into the Sea of Tranquility and onto the Moon's surface. Moments later, Armstrong was joined by Buzz Aldrin who observed the "magnificent desolation" of the Moon's landscape. The two crew members of the Apollo 11 remained on the surface for two hours and thirty-one minutes while the third crew member, Michael Collins, piloted the command spacecraft alone in lunar orbit. In a call to Armstrong while he was still on the Moon, President Richard Nixon well summarized the impact of the Moon landing as shared by all humankind stating to Armstrong that "for one priceless moment, in the whole history of man, all the people on this Earth are truly one; one in their pride in what you have done, and one in our prayers that you will return safely to Earth." While on the lunar surface, Armstrong and Aldrin collected about 47 pounds of lunar material for return to Earth. They left behind only four things: (1) an American flag; (2) a patch honoring the fallen Apollo 1 crew (Virgil "Gus" Grissom, Edward H. White II, and Roger B. Chaffee), who had died in January 1967 in a tragic spacecraft cabin fire during a launch rehearsal test; (3) their footsteps on the lunar surface; and (4) a plaque on one of the Eagle's legs that reads "Here men from the planet Earth first set foot on the Moon. July, 1969 A.D. We came in peace for all mankind."[245] After their time on the lunar surface, Armstrong and Aldrin returned to the command spacecraft, and the three astronauts returned to Earth. Armstrong had flown 78 combat missions in Korea and had a long and distinguished career, but it is the 151 minutes that he and Aldrin spent walking on the Moon for which he will always be remembered. He died on August 25, 2012 at the age of 82 – survived by his fellow astronaut Buzz Aldrin, who upon learning of Armstrong's passing, noted that he had hoped to celebrate July 20, 2019, the 50th anniversary of their Moon walk, with Armstrong. But it was not to be. Several years earlier, in May 2014, Russia announced that it intended "to establish a permanently manned colony on the lunar surface by 2030." In the words of Russian Deputy Prime Minister Dmitry Rogozin, "we are coming to the Moon forever." Since it is generally conceded that Russia currently has "the most robust and reliable spacecraft," and because, in the opinion of some, the U.S. has lost "its ambitions in space," it is possible that Russia may realistically achieve its stated objective.[246]

"A man is not finished when he is defeated. He is finished when he quits."

August 5, 1969. President Richard M. Nixon, writing a note of encouragement to Senator Ted Kennedy shortly after the Chappaquiddick incident.[247] Nixon's note of encouragement was delivered after Kennedy, at least in part as a result of the incident, was not elected Senate Majority Leader. Because of the Watergate scandal and Nixon's ensuing fall from grace and his Presidential resignation thereafter, most people incorrectly assume that his own later struggles provided the context of this remark.

"Helter skelter"

August 9, 1969. The twisted words of warning pronounced by Charles Manson, the leader of a small cult known as "The Family" which on this date had actress Sharon Tate and four others murdered at Roman Polanski's home in Los Angeles. The words, somehow drawn by Manson from The Beatles' *White Album* and Manson's interpretation of the Book of Revelations, were intended to reference a forthcoming apocalyptic war between blacks and whites. Many Americans were tired and confused by the counterculture of the Sixties, the tragedies of the multiple assassinations, the tensions resulting from certain aspects of the Civil Rights Movement, the hostility against the Vietnam War, and the growing influx of drugs, but certainly, Manson and his craven, long-haired, drug-induced absurdities—consciously or otherwise, rightly or wrongly—contributed to the sad ending and a closing chapter to the decade. For many of those who held on to the dreams of the Sixties a little longer, the murders at Kent State —which occurred less than a year later—sealed the fate of the Sixties. Manson, together with five of his followers, were convicted of multiple murders in 1972. In 1974, the words "Helter Skelter" would become the chilling title of prosecutor Vincent Bugliosi's riveting best seller story about his prosecution of Charles Manson.

"Three Days of Peace and Music"
Woodstock
A Place, An Event, and A Generation

August 15-17, 1969. Woodstock is a small town in Southeast New York, about halfway between Poughkeepsie to the south and Albany to the north. Under the marketing banner of "Three Days of Peace and Music," on these days in 1969 Woodstock also became an event—a gathering an estimated 400,000 young people. Many of them were hippies, members of the country's counterculture. Drug use was common. The festival was chaotic. But there were few instances of violence. Instead, over three rain-soaked days, there were 32 performances—one after another—by the leading singers and bands of the generation. From Richie Havens (who, 25 years later, would perform at the Clinton inauguration) to Sly and the Family Stone; from Janis Joplin to Arlo Guthrie; from Credence Clearwater Revival to Jefferson Airplane; from The Grateful Dead to Joe Cocker; from Joan Baez to Country Joe; from The Who to The Band; from Crosby, Stills, Nash & Young to Blood Sweat & Tears, and on and on. Shortly before Woodstock began, the venue of the event was changed from the small hamlet of Woodstock to Max Yasgur's 600-acre dairy farm in Bethel, New York—nearly 50 miles from Woodstock. Nevertheless, no one knows of the event as "Bethel." Instead, the event has always been referred to exclusively as "Woodstock." In the jargon, legacy and history of that generation, the words "Woodstock" or "Woodstock Nation" soon came to simultaneously attach to and describe the entire generation of the Sixties counterculture Americans. The standing joke and open secret is that although "only" 400,000 people attended the three-day event, nearly every American over the age of 60 now claims to have attended; now claims to have seen Jimi Hendrix, the last act to perform, wearing his now iconic, blue-beaded white leather jacket with fringe and a red scarf; and now claims to have heard Hendrix's unforgettable, rambling, guitar solo performance of *"The Star-Spangled Banner."* In the opinion of most Americans, the Woodstock Generation did not long survive. Within years, most of their generation graduated to maturity and reality and families and work. Just like the rest of us. But for those brief three days….Woodstock did happen. Woodstock was real.

"An effete corps of impudent snobs who characterize themselves as intellectuals."

October 1969.[248] Vice President Spiro T. Agnew, speaking about those who participated in the October (1969) Moratorium to End the War. President Richard Nixon defined, embraced, and claimed to give voice to "the Silent Majority" and purported to encourage a renewed, more constructive, and more civil debate. However, Agnew, his Vice President, "extolled the virtues of political warfare." He did so with this remarks and through many other political attacks upon America's counterculture, the antiwar protestors, and the "tiny and close fraternity of privileged men" who controlled the national news media. Agnew became famous (or infamous, depending upon one's political leanings) for his scathing, alliterative use of words. Other examples used by Agnew (but possibly written by White House speechwriters William Safire and Pat Buchanan) include "blistering blue barnacles," "pusillanimous pussyfooters," "hopeless, hysterical hypochondriacs of history,"[249] and "nattering nabobs of negativism." Agnew continued such attacks for another four years until his resignation from office in October 1973 as the result of his pleading "No Contest" to numerous bribery and extortion charges.[250]

CHAPTER 9

1970–1976

**The End of Vietnam;
The Disgrace of Watergate;
The Spread of Disillusionment
and
The Rise of Cynicism**

Year 1970

Seminal Books

Bury My Heart at Wounded Knee:
An Indian History of the American West
by Dee Brown

This meticulously researched and brilliantly written book narrates the history of Native Americans in the last third of the 19th century. Although such a narrative history had been attempted before,[251] Brown's book was the first book on the subject that was well received and widely read. To this day, it has never gone out of print. The initial success of the book may have been partly a result of timing. Roughly paralleling and inspired by the Civil Rights Movement, the American Indian Movement ("AIM") had been formed in 1968—just three years earlier—with the stated goal of promoting Native American issues. The nation's primary attention was still focused upon the Vietnam War, the Civil Rights Movement, and other national issues, but AIM received wide publicity after some of its members occupied Alcatraz Island in the San Francisco Bay in 1969 and stayed for 19 months.[252] But timing aside, the book deserves respect for its accurate presentation of the details of the history of American westward expansionism from the perspective of Native Americans. Included amongst these details is the history of forced relocations and the litany of broken treaties and promises that accompanied them. In a 1971 interview, Ms. Brown was quoted as saying that "what surprised me most was how much the Indians believed the white man over and over again. Their trust in authority was amazing. They just never seemed to believe that anyone could lie."[253]

Vitamin C and the Common Cold
by Linus Pauling

Written by Linus Pauling, a Nobel Prize-winning chemist, the book extolled the health benefits and power of Vitamin C (and especially mega-doses thereof) in reducing the duration and severity of common colds. The lasting impact of this book is partly the powerful influence it had upon American people. To this day, Americans seek Vitamin C to counter common colds, despite the fact that multiple studies have indicated, and arguably even proven, that no correlation exists between the taking of Vitamin C and the duration or severity of the common cold. In response to the supposed extraordinary health benefits of taking Vitamin C as suggested by this book (including Pauling's claim that a daily dosage of Vitamin C could extend one's lifespan to 150 years!!), sales of U.S. vitamins soared and have continued to soar ever since. As of 2014, sales of vitamins had grown to $12.0 billion annually. Regardless of the perceived health benefits of such vitamins and minerals, under the Dietary Supplement Health and Education Act of 1994, this industry remains only lightly regulated because under this act "all supplements—including minerals, medicinal herbs, and protein powders—were categorized as food rather than drugs."[254]

Pulitzer Prize for Fiction

The Collected Stories of Jean Stafford
by Jean Stafford

Pulitzer Prize for General Nonfiction

Gandhi's Truth: On the Origins of Militant Nonviolence
by Erik H. Erikson

Pulitzer Prize for History

Present at the Creation: My Years in the State Department
by Dean Acheson

The New York Times Best Sellers List (Nonfiction) – Books with Most Weeks as No. 1 Best Seller

Everything You Always Wanted to Know About Sex (*But Were Afraid to Ask)*
by David Reuben (26 weeks)

The Sensuous Woman
by "J" (Pseudonym for Joan Garrity) (11 weeks)

The New York Times **Best Sellers List (Adult Fiction) – Book with Most Weeks as No. 1 Best Seller**

Love Story
by Erich Segal (34 weeks)

Academy Awards Best Picture

Winner: *Patton*

Other Nominees: *Airport, Five Easy Pieces, Love Story, M*A*S*H*

PrettyFamous' **Best Movie of the Year**

Patton

Best/Most Memorable Movie Lines of the Year

"Love is never having to say you're sorry."

The sappy line of Ali McGraw to her co-star Ryan O'Neill in the movie, *Love Story*. The movie was based upon Erich Segal's bestselling novel by the same name and was filmed partly at Harvard Law School in Cambridge, Massachusetts.

Author's Note:

This author, as a young man—several lifetimes ago—remembers many of us at the time trying to break through the doors of Langdell Hall, the Harvard Law School library, just in time to be caught in a background scene of this movie. It is only appropriate that on behalf of all of us (and there were many), an apology is here tendered, many years later, to the film's very patient crew.

***"… (N)ow I want you to remember that no bastard
ever won a war by dying for his country.
He won it by making the other poor dumb bastard die for his."***

…

***"Americans traditionally love to fight.
All real Americans love the sting of battle."***

…

> ***"…(W)e have the finest food and equipment, the best spirit,
> and the best men in the world.
> You know, by God, I actually pity those poor bastards
> we're goin' up against."***

George C. Scott addressing his troops before battle in his powerful performance as General George S. Patton in the Academy Award-winning movie *Patton,* directed by Franklin Schaffner.

> ***"I love it. God help me I love it so. I love it more than my life."***

George C. Scott in *Patton* soberly confessing how much he loves the anticipation and conduct of war.

> ***"Oh, Frank, Oh, Frank. My lips are hot. Oh, kiss my hot lips."***

Loreta Swit inadvertently creating her own nickname, "Hot Lips" Houlihan, in Robert Altman's comedic war movie *M*A*S*H.* The storyline was continued in the ensuing television series (1972–1983), which became one of the most popular series in television history.

1970 U.S. Population: 205,100,000

(Compared as a Percentage to the U.S. 1957 Population of 172,000,000: 119.2%)

Television Shows

Most Widely-Viewed Television Shows

Rank	Show Name	Years of Series (Excluding Reruns)	Show Type	Estimated Audience (In MMs)	Audience as Percentage of U.S. Population
1.	*Marcus Welby, M.D.*	1969–1976	Med. Drama	17.8MM	8.7%
	Cast:	Robert Young - James Brolin - Elena Verdugo			
2.	*The Flip Wilson Show*	1970–1974	Comedy	16.8MM	8.2%
	Cast:	Flip Wilson			
3	*Here's Lucy*	1968–1974	Comedy	15.7MM	7.6%
	Cast:	Lucille Ball - Lucie Arnaz			

Widely-Viewed or Critically-Acclaimed New Television Show(s)

The Mary Tyler Moore Show (1970–1977) – Comedy
Mary Tyler Moore - Edward Asner - Valerie Harper -
Gavin MacLeod - Ted Knight - Betty White
(No. 11 Top TV Shows of All Time – *TV Guide*)

<u>Catchphrases, Chants, and Slogans–1970</u>
"Let's Win or Get Out"

The challenge made by many Americans and by which they expressed their frustration with the Vietnam War and their desire to (somehow) bring it to an end. The ongoing debate was balanced between those who thought it both wrong and futile for Americans to be involved in a "civil war" thousands of miles from our shore and those who thought that American forces had been put in a definitionally untenable situation by trying to fight a "limited war."

<u>Memorable Words from Speeches, Books, Writings,</u>
<u>and Other Sources – 1970</u>

"The time may have come when the issue of race
could benefit from a period of 'benign neglect.'
The subject (of race) has been too much talked about.
The forum has been too much taken over
by hysterics, paranoids, and boodlers on all sides.
We may need a period in which Negro progress continues
and racial rhetoric fades.
The administration can help bring this about
by paying close attention to such progress...
while seeking to avoid situations in which extremists
of either race are given opportunities
for martyrdom, heroics, histrionics or whatever."

January 16, 1970. Daniel Patrick Moynihan, writing in a Memorandum to President Richard Nixon about the possible need to adopt and embrace a period of "benign neglect" in which issues of race received less focus, attention, and comment. Moynihan suggested this concept while serving as an urban affairs advisor to Nixon. Six years later, Moynihan was elected to the U.S. Senate, where he thereafter served for 24 years until 2000. Moynihan's concept of "benign neglect" was proposed as a response to the civil rights passions that had become so inflamed through especially the late 1960s. Part of the underlying significance of even the suggestion of a policy of "benign neglect" is that the phrase exemplifies (a) how long and how frequently racial issues have remained one of the central domestic issues of modern American life, and (b) how difficult the subject of race has been as a topic of discussion in American public discourse. In the 1950s, it was *Brown v. Board of Education,* Little Rock and school integration. In the 1960s, it was protests, marches, riots, MLK, the black power movement, voting rights, and related civil rights. But the issues never approached full resolution. For some Americans, racial issues continue to serve as merely another example of the limits of public policy and maybe even the appropriate boundaries of public involvement. Nevertheless, and regardless of one's conclusions about the role of government, the issue of race has been one of the perennial failures of American life. Great progress has been made including the ascent of some black Americans, such as Colin Powell and Condoleezza Rice and ultimately Barack Obama to the most senior positions of power and influence in America. However, the subject and many aspects of the issue remain unresolved. Even in the context of the 2016 Presidential election, issues of race, the alt-right and white nationalism, and the Black Lives Matter movement were central subjects of public debate. Despite the briefly tempting acceptance of ideas such as "benign neglect" as a means of lowering the voices and calming the crowd, upon reflection, it becomes obvious that the issues are too important and too deserving to be treated with a stance of "benign neglect." [255]

"The great question of the seventies is,
shall we surrender our surroundings,
or shall we make our peace with nature
and begin to make reparations for the damage we have done
to our air, to our land, and to our water?"

...

"Restoring nature to its natural state is a cause
beyond party and beyond factions.
It has become a common cause of all the people of this country."

...

"Clean air, clean water, open spaces—
these should once again be the birthright of every American.
If we act now, they can be."

January 22, 1970. President Richard M. Nixon, in his State of the Union address to Congress. While valid debates can be had regarding Nixon's personal commitment to environmental reform, Nixon deserves credit for, at a minimum, responding to the growing environmental concerns that came into focus throughout the 1960s. Just weeks after this State of the Union address, Nixon delivered a lengthy "Special Message to the Congress on Environmental Quality," which set forth a "37-point program embracing 23 major legislative proposals and 14 new measures being taken by administrative action or Executive Order" with respect to water and air pollution control, solid waste management, parklands and public recreation, and a myriad of organizational matters. Nixon at first created the cabinet-level Council on Environmental Quality. On July 9, 1970, he established the Environmental Protection Agency by Executive Order as an independent governmental organization. In June 1971, about a year later, he delivered another extensive message to Congress addressing both the environmental and energy needs of the country. Within two years, the Clean Air Act of 1972 was enacted, and many other environmental concerns began to be addressed. Nixon's legacy is tied to the ending of the Vietnam War and the opening of China, and his legacy is forever stained by his Watergate actions and the associated scandals leading to his eventual resignation, but his role in the context of environmental protection should be recognized. Nixon was the first President to seriously and aggressively address environmental issues. Questions about the level and appropriate boundaries of governmental regulation and the balancing of the needs of American business continue to be debated, but such debates do not diminish the early 1970s and Nixon's initial and far-reaching efforts.

> *"Even if he were mediocre,*
> *there are a lot of mediocre judges and people and lawyers.*
> *They are entitled to a little representation,*
> *aren't they, and a little chance?*
> *We can't have all Brandeises, Frankfurters, and Cardozos."*

March 16, 1970. Senator Roman Hruska (R-NE), speaking for the right of the mediocre to hold positions of public trust. This comment was made by Hruska in the context of the 1970 nomination by President Richard Nixon of G. Harrold Carswell to the USSC. For various reasons including Hruska's "mediocre" remark and Carswell's questionable performance as a Federal District Court Judge (with an astounding 58% reversal rate), Carswell was rejected by a bipartisan majority of the U.S. Senate. Hruska was seen by some as a skillful legislator. He was a member of both the Senate Appropriations Committee and the Senate Judiciary Committee. However, these remarks haunted him until his death in 1999, and to this day he is best remembered in U.S. political history for these ill-chosen words.[256]

> *"If you are able,*
> *have for them a place inside of you*
> *and save one backward glance when you are leaving*
> *for the places they can no longer go...."*

March 24, 1970. The gentle words of Michael Dave O'Donnell, then a young helicopter pilot from Springfield, Illinois, about a veteran's need to be remembered and respected, and about the common experience of a sense of abandonment felt by many veterans—even though all they had wanted to do was to serve their country. Shortly after writing this poem and on this date, McDonnell and his crew were shot down and killed in Vietnam—but even then, he was not officially declared dead by the Department of Defense until 1978.[257] Troops started coming home from Vietnam upon President Nixon's June 1969 announcement of the first withdrawal of troops from South Vietnam, and they kept coming home until the departure of the last troops upon the evacuation of the U.S. Embassy on April 30, 1975. For many of the returning veterans, both professional military and draftees, it was a lonely arrival home. Over the years, discussions about Vietnam had become heated. For many Americans, the subject eventually became toxic. Each side retreated to its corner in anger and frustration. And thus for decades, the nation remained immersed in its rancorous discord about the war. For some, it was about the miscalculation of entering the war. For others, it was about the failure to "win or get out."[258] Adding insult to injury and pain, many returning soldiers were disdained. Sometimes, almost worse, they were forgotten or ignored. They were rarely thanked for their service. There were few welcome home speeches except for those made by military officers on lonely military tarmacs. There were few parades. In the blinded or callous eyes of some anti-war activists, soldiers were somehow seen as willing co-conspirators in a national crime. It took years for some Americans to understand, or at least widely accept, the contributions made by these men — who were mostly conscripted themselves. And thus, once again, the return home was lonely; solitary; forgotten "by all but their families."

"An impeachable offense is whatever the House of Representatives considers it to be at a given moment."

April 15, 1970. Representative Gerald Ford (R-MI), speaking in intended furtherance of his attempt to impeach USSC Justice William O. Douglas. The probable genesis of the desire of Ford and many other conservatives for Douglas' impeachment was Douglas' long record as one of the USSC's most liberal Justices. However, the more specific allegations at the time related to Douglas' supposed ties to a private foundation and his controversially wide interpretation of the First Amendment as it related to the definition of pornography in a case relating to the Swedish film, *I Am Curious (Yellow)*. While the impeachment of Douglas never proceeded, Ford's remark about Congress' power to define the meaning of impeach-able offenses became important, indeed problematic, just several years later during the House Judiciary Committee's investigation of the Watergate offenses of President Richard Nixon and his associates.

"Houston, we've had a problem."

April 14, 1970. Jack Swigert, one of the three-man crew (with James Lovell and Fred Haise) of Apollo 13, reporting to NASA Space Headquarters in Houston, Texas that an oxygen tank on the spaceship had exploded and that the ship had lost two of its three fuel cells. The crew was nearly 200,000 miles from Earth when they came to the "slow conclusion" that the normal supply of electricity, light, and water were lost. The spacecraft and the men were brought safely home by the brilliant and creative efforts of the crew and NASA scientists, but Apollo 13 as a lunar landing mission was "a $375.0 million failure." Yet, in the clever and correct words of James Lovell, the Apollo 13 mission was a "successful failure." A slight variant of the above phrase was further immortalized in the 1995 film, *Apollo 13*, starring Tom Hanks, Kevin Bacon, Bill Paxton, Gary Sinise, and Ed Harris.[259]

"American policy has been to scrupulously respect the neutrality of the Cambodian people."

April 30, 1970. President Richard M. Nixon, presenting his explanation to the American people of the U.S.' "incursion" into and bombing of Cambodia. President Nixon maintained that the bombing of Cambodia was consistent with this respect of neutrality, and he went on to misleadingly suggest that Cambodia had placed "a call ... for assistance." Despite the horrendous challenge facing the President in trying to conclude a war and achieve the elusive, indeed impossible, "peace with honor," the speech was received by many Americans as further evidence that they had been misled. At this time and in the context of this war, many concluded that America, the world's most powerful nation, appeared to be a "pitiful, helpless giant." In response to President Nixon's Cambodian incursion disclosure, colleges erupted. Protesters filled the streets. The first national student strike was called. At Kent State University in Ohio, four unarmed students were killed by National Guardsmen, and for many Americans, the memory of seeing a young woman kneeling over the lifeless body of slain Jeffrey Miller is emblazoned in their memories. Despite the site of the war in faraway Vietnam, the Kent State deaths brought the war back home. Again. For some young Americans, wrought by exhaustion and disappointment, Kent State was later identified as the beginning of the end of the Sixties. Even H.R. "Bob" Haldeman, one of Nixon's chief aides, stated that "Kent State marked a turning point for Nixon, a beginning of his downhill slide toward Watergate."[260] Over the next year, the pushes and shoves continued. The country remained deeply—and evenly—divided about the war and the conduct of the administration. Nevertheless, within the next year, Congress repealed the Gulf of Tonkin Resolution,[261] antiwar demonstrations continued, and in June 1971 *The New York Times* started printing the Pentagon Papers.

These highly classified papers had been turned over to *The New York Times* by former intelligence adviser Daniel Ellsberg. They detailed the systematic misleading of the American people about the Vietnam War by the military and by elected officials over a number of years. Many Americans believed that the truth had (finally) surfaced. However, much of the damage had already been done. Public trust had been compromised. Public cynicism had been escalated with faith in authority never to again fully return.

"I'm not for women, frankly, in any job.
I don't want any of them around.
Thank God we don't have any in the Cabinet."

April 30, 1970. President Richard M. Nixon, speaking with his aide H.R. "Bob" Haldeman, and as quoted by John Dean in *The Rehnquist Choice*[262] and by Dahlia Lithwick in her article in *Slate*.[263] Nixon is also quoted in John Boertlein's 2010 less scholarly book, *Presidential Confidential*, as having stated that he didn't think "women should be in any government job whatsoever ... because they are erratic and emotional."[264] The flawed thinking of Nixon in this regard did not long continue. Since Nixon's Presidency, there have been women Cabinet Secretaries in every administration: Ford (2), Carter (5), Reagan (4), George H.W. Bush (3), Clinton (7), George W. Bush (7), and Obama (9). Amongst these 37 women cabinet members, the most common appointments of women have been as Secretary of the Department of Labor (7), Health and Human Services (5), State (3), and Commerce (3). However, it would not be until 1984 that a woman, Geraldine Ferraro (D-NY), would be nominated as a Vice-Presidential candidate by a major political party, and it would not be until 2016—46 years after Nixon's above remark—that Hillary Clinton would be the first woman nominated for President by a major political party.

"REPENT, MALE CHAUVINISTS"
"YOUR WORLD IS COMING TO AN END"
"DON'T COOK DINNER TONIGHT – STARVE A RAT TODAY"
"DON'T IRON WHILE THE STRIKE IS HOT"

August 26, 1970. Examples of chants, placards and signs held at rallies across the country on this day—the 50th Anniversary of the adoption of the 19th Amendment, which guaranteed a woman's right to vote. [265] To a degree and continuing throughout Modern America at least since the early 1970s, both men and women have continued to have different perceptions of the meaning, the correctness, and even the very core components—political, economic, and social—of what has, at times, been referred to as the "women's movement" or the "feminist movement. "

"Football is not a contact sport, it's a collision sport."

September 3, 1970. Vince Lombardi, a professional football player and coach, was one of the early and preeminent coaches of professional football. Lombardi was the gruff and beloved coach of the Green Bay Packers throughout most of the 1960s and was famous for some of his sayings such as "you aren't fired with enthusiasm, you will be fired with enthusiasm" and "those who invested the most are the last to surrender." Lombardi's teams won an astounding 72.8% of all their games and 90.1% of their post-season games including six NFL Championships and the first two Super Bowls in 1967 and 1968. Although Lombardi's coaching career ended relatively early in 1969 (and he died less than two years later on this date at the age of 57), the Super Bowl trophy is named after him. The above quote is most commonly attributed to Lombardi, but it has also been attributed by Duffy Daugherty, the head coach of Michigan State University from 1954 to 1972. The entire quote is also sometimes stated as "football is not a contact sport, it's a collision sport—dancing is a contact sport." In recent years, these words have received far more attention and even notoriety for their blunt accuracy, and especially as the consequences of concussions and their causation of the mind-impairing CTE (chronic traumatic encephalopathy) have become better understood. [266]

"The time has come for someone …
to represent the working men of this country,
the forgotten man of American politics, …"

September 10, 1970. Vice President Spiro T. Agnew, campaigning during the mid-year Congressional elections and several years before he was indicted for bribery and forced to resign the Vice Presidency in disgrace.

Here and in many later campaign speeches, Agnew argued for the rejection of the "radic-lib" agenda by claiming that the liberal agenda did not represent the "hard-working, family-oriented, church-going, tax-paying patriots."[267] The concept of the "forgotten men" and the need for America to somehow return itself to a prior time are repeated themes of modern American politics from Nixon's Silent Majority to Reagan's and Trump's respective variations of the "Make America Again" theme. Lest it not be obvious, such themes—however simplistic and dubious in their capacity for implementation—should not be ignored, if for no other reason politically than the fact that Nixon, Reagan, and Trump were all elected.

<u>Television Line</u>
"The Devil made me do it."

September 18, 1970. Flip Wilson's signature line from, among other shows, *The Flip Wilson Show,* which aired from this date through 1974. On January 31, 1972, *Time* Magazine featured Flip Wilson on its cover with the label of "TV's first black superstar" – even though, at least until his public disgrace of himself as revealed years later, most Americans would have bestowed this accolade upon Bill Cosby for his spy-agent role with Robert Culp in *I Spy.* The show, *I Spy,* ran from 1965 through 1968 and Cosby won three consecutive Emmy Awards for Outstanding Lead Actor in a Drama Series, becoming the first African American actor to receive such award.

"To assure as far as possible every working man and woman ... safe and healthful working conditions."

December 29, 1970. President Richard M. Nixon, upon his signing on this date of the federal (Williams-Steiger) Occupational Safety and Health Act ("OSHA"). This legislation greatly increased governmental regulation of U.S. workers and work sites, but federal and state governments had for many decades been involved in work safety and conditions legislation. For example, (i) in the latter half of the 19th century and the early 20th century, state factory and child labor laws had been adopted; (ii) following Wisconsin's lead in 1911, many states enacted workers' compensation boards; and

(iii) in 1934 and in the middle of the Great Depression, the federal government created the Bureau of Labor Standards. However, despite these early efforts, a fearsome number of workplace deaths and injuries continued. In January 1968, President Lyndon Johnson noted that more than 14,000 U.S. workers died and 2.2 *million* workers were injured *each year* in the U.S. In the opinion of many Americans, President Johnson had correctly referred to this as a "shame of (our) modern industrial nation." After three years of intense legislative negotiations, OSHA was finally enacted by a bipartisan Congressional vote in 1970. In order to achieve the goals sets forth in the Act, Congress created a federal agency empowered to regulate most U.S. businesses. In the ensuing years, the agency has grown and its regulations have multiplied greatly to the point that now the agency and its regulations are routinely cited as examples of the burdensome, over-regulation of U.S. businesses. However, it is also true that since the 1971 establishment of OSHA, workplace fatalities in the U.S. "have been cut by 62% and occupation injury and illness rates have declined 40%"—and these percentage declines have been achieved despite the fact that the number of U.S. workers and U.S. worksites have both doubled in the same period.[268]

Year 1971

Seminal Books

A Monetary History of the United States, **1867–1960**
by Milton Friedman and Anna Schwartz

In this book and as stated accurately, albeit uncritically, by the Princeton Press, the authors "marshaled massive historical data and sharp analytics to support the claim that monetary policy—steady control of the money supply —matters profoundly in the nation's economy, especially in navigating serious economic fluctuations." [269] In the context of economic theory, Milton Friedman was among the intellectual leaders of what has become known as the "Chicago School," which articulates an alternative theory of economics to that of the Keynesians. For decades, Friedman contributed to the intellectual basis for modern conservative economic theory by extolling the virtues of a free market economic system absent from nearly all governmental "intervention." In 1976, Friedman was awarded the Nobel Prize in Economics "at a time when almost all the previous prizes had gone to socialists."[270] Shortly after his 1977 retirement from the University of Chicago, Friedman became affiliated with the conservative Hoover Institute at Stanford University. In the early 1980s, he also served as an adviser to President Ronald Reagan and was appointed to the President's Economic Advisory Board. The other two companion books that could be included with Friedman and Schwartz's *Monetary History* are Friedman's *Capitalism and Freedom* (1962) and *Free to Choose* (1980). Many believe his writings contributed greatly to "saving" capitalism "by dismembering the idea of central planning (at a time when) most academia was mesmerized by the creed of government as savior."[271] Milton Friedman died in 2006 at the age of 94.

Fear and Loathing in Las Vegas:
A Savage Journey to the Heart of the American Dream
by Hunter S. Thompson

This book is widely recognized as the first (and possibly most famous) book written in the style that came to be known as "Gonzo journalism." This style of journalism is a sometimes nearly incoherent blend of fact and fiction in which the author becomes so deeply involved in the action and subject that he becomes the central figure in the story itself. *Fear and Loathing* was viewed by some readers as a creative, early and almost philosophical review of the failed counterculture of the Sixties. By others, it was scorned and dismissed for its weak writing, its meandering plot, and its constant infusion of scenes involving illegal drug usage. This author recognizes that the inclusion of this book amongst the other powerful books of the era is dubious; indeed, arguably undeserved. It is included merely because time has not easily diminished *Fear and Loathing* as one of the first tracts to explore certain aspects of the Sixties. Furthermore, despite the relatively universal scorn of other writers for the book, as noted by George Plimpton, "if people don't know much about writing, Hunter's probably the most popular American writer." Thompson's fame faded over the years, and his later books were less successful and enduring. His wild antics continued until his death in Colorado in 2005 at the age of 67. Upon Thompson's death and in keeping with the wild spirit of his life, Thompson's friend, Johnny Depp, spent more than $3 million to blast Thompson's ashes into the sky with a custom-built canon at a raucous "send-off" party which included fireworks, live music and an array of celebrity guests.[272]

Our Bodies, Ourselves: A Book by and for Women
by Boston Women's Health Book Collective

This book, a feminist classic, evolved from a 1969 meeting at a women's liberation conference at Emmanuel College in Boston. A group of 12 women decided "to research and share information about women's bodies"[273] including topics such as sexuality, menopause, birth control, gender identity, mental health and well-being. From this original meeting evolved a 193-page course booklet that was printed in 1970 "on stapled newsprint."[274] The first book-format printing occurred the next year and "quickly became an underground success." In 1973, Simon & Schuster published the first widely distributed commercial edition. Since that time, the book has been re-written, updated and expanded approximately every four to six years. 2011 was the year of the most recent edition.

The Closing Circle: Nature, Man, and Technology
by Barry Commoner

This book was published just one year after Barry Commoner was featured on the cover of *Time* magazine (with the subtitled "The Emerging Science of Survival") and one year after the first Earth Day on April 22, 1970. Commoner, a prominent ecologist, was one of the founders of the environmental movement. Through this book he introduced many Americans to the need to reshape our economy to the strictures, limitations, and demands of the environment. He argued that modern economies (and the underlying societal values they reflect) must eventually conform to what Commoner simply referred to as the four laws of ecology: *(i) Everything is connected to everything else, (2) Everything must go somewhere, (3) Nature knows best, and (4) There is no such thing as a free lunch.* As written in the Preface to the book, "Commoner (was) not so much concerned with pinpointing responsibility as with stating principles of inescapable rules of (environmental) experience and presenting concrete examples of what happens when they are ignored."[275] Commoner also helped to introduce the concept of "sustainability" and, based upon thoughtful evidence, argued that "no economy can long survive in violation of ecological principles."[276]

<u>Pulitzer Prize for General Nonfiction</u>

The Rising Sun
by John Toland

<u>Pulitzer Prize for History</u>

Roosevelt: The Soldier of Freedom
by James MacGregor Burns

The New York Times **Best Sellers List (Nonfiction) – Books with Most Weeks as No. 1 Best Seller**

Bury My Heart At Wounded Knee:
An Indian History of the American West
By Dee Brown (24 weeks)

The Greening of America
by Charles Reich (19 weeks)

The New York Times **Best Sellers List (Adult Fiction) – Book with Most Weeks as No. 1 Best Seller**

The Passions of the Mind
by Irving Stone (13 weeks)

Academy Awards Best Picture

Winner: *The French Connection*

Other Nominees: *A Clockwork Orange, Fiddler on the Roof, The Last Picture Show, Nicholas and Alexandra*

PrettyFamous' **Best Movie of the Year**

The French Connection

Best/Most Memorable Movie Lines of the Year

"Greet the dawn with a breath of fire".

...

"I understand a lot of people enjoy being dead.
But they're not dead, really.
They're just backing away from life.
Reach out. Take a chance. Get hurt even."

From *Harold and Maude,* Hal Ashby's dark comedy movie starring young Bud Cort, who is intrigued by death and who develops a close relationship with the much older Ruth Gordon. Upon its release, the movie was both critically and commercially unsuccessful, but the movie has over time developed an almost cult following. It was eventually recognized by the American Film Institute as being one of the 100 Funniest Films of all time.

> *"I was never to see her again.*
> *Nor was I ever to learn what became of her.*
> *We were different then.*
> *Kids were different.*
> *It took us longer to understand the things we felt.*
> *Life is made up of small comings and goings.*
> *And for everything we take with us,*
> *there is something we leave behind."*

The touching, almost poetic, words of young Gary Grimes in a gentler coming-of-age movie, Robert Mulligan's *The Summer of '42,* starring Jennifer O'Neill. The presentation of these young men in *The Summer of '42* brilliantly contrasts with the young, screen-addicted, and precocious boys of 21st century Modern America.

> *"You've got to ask yourself one question:*
> *'Do I feel lucky?' Well, do ya, punk?"*

Clint Eastwood, in his role as San Francisco Police Officer "Dirty" Harry Callahan, making his chilling challenge to a burglar in Don Siegel's epic crime and action thriller *Dirty Harry*

<u>1971 U.S. Population: 207,700,000</u>

(Compared as a Percentage to the U.S. 1957 Population of 172,000,000: 120.8%)

<u>Television Shows</u>

Most Widely-Viewed Television Shows

Rank	Show Name	Years of Series (Excluding Reruns)	Show Type	Estimated Audience (In MMs)	Audience as Percentage of U.S. Population
1.	*All in the Family*	1971–1979	Comedy	21.1MM	10.2%
	Cast: Carroll O'Connor - Jean Stapleton - Sally Struthers - Rob Reiner				
2.	*The Flip Wilson Show*	1970–1974	Comedy	17.5MM	8.4%
	Cast: Flip Wilson				
3.	*Marcus Welby, M.D.*	1969–1976	Med. Drama	17.3MM	8.3%
	Cast: Robert Young - James Brolin - Elena Verdugo				

Widely-Viewed or Critically-Acclaimed New Television Show(s)

All in the Family (1971–1979) —Comedy
Carroll O'Connor - Jean Stapleton - Rob Reiner - Sally Struthers
(No. 4 Top TV Shows of All Time – *TV Guide*)

Soul Train (1971–2006) —Musical Variety and Dance Show
Hosted by Don Cornelius
(One of longest-running, nationally syndicated
programs in television history)

The Waltons (1971–1981) —Rural Family Show
Richard Thomas – Ralph Waite – Michael Learned –
Mary Elizabeth McDonough

Last Season Television Show(s)

The Beverly Hillbillies (1962–1971) —Comedy
Buddy Ebsen - Donna Douglas - Max Baer, Jr.

The Ed Sullivan Show (1948–1971) —TV Variety Show
Host: Ed Sullivan
(No. 15 Top TV Shows of All Time – *TV Guide*)

The Lawrence Welk Show (1951–1971) —Musical Variety Show
Hosted by Big Band "Wunerful, Wunerful,"
"Ah-One, Ah-Two" Leader Lawrence Welk

Red Skelton Show (1951–1971) —Comedy
Red Skelton

<u>Major Commercial Advertising Campaigns and Slogans</u>

"Because you're worth it."[277]
L'Oreal

"It's Miller time!"

and

"If you've got the time. We've got the beer."
Miller Beer

<u>Memorable Words from Speeches, Books, Writings,
and Other Sources – 1971</u>

*"It is a long ways from Plains to Atlanta.
I started the trip four and a half years ago and,
with a four-year delay, I finally made it."*

...

*"I realize that the test of a man is not how well he campaigned,
but how effectively he meets the challenges
and responsibilities of the office."*

...

*"At the end of a long campaign,
I believe I know our people as well as anyone. ...
Georgians North and South, rural and urban,
liberal and conservative, (and) I say to you frankly
that the time for racial discrimination is over."*

January 12, 1971. Jimmy Carter, in his Gubernatorial Inauguration Address as the newly-elected Governor of Georgia. These remarks were made (and thus the reference to the "four-year delay") just four years after Carter lost a gubernatorial primary to the rabid racist and later governor, Lester Maddox. In 1976, Carter would defeat Gerald Ford and be elected the 39th President of the United States.

"Guilty"
Charles Manson and Three Other Members of Manson's "Family"

January 25, 1971. Charles Manson and his followers were convicted of 27 separate felony counts based upon, among other crimes, the gruesome 1969 murders of actress Sharon Tate and others at the Los Angeles, California home of film director Roman Polanski. Manson and all the implicated members of his "family" remain in prison or have died. The only exception was Lynette "Squeaky" Fromme, who, after serving 34 years for her 1975 conviction for pointing a gun at then-President Gerald Ford, was released on parole in 2009. In April 2016 and after 19 previous parole denials, a parole board panel recommended the release of Manson

Family member Leslie Van Houten, now 66 years of age.[278] However, on July 23, 2016, California Governor Jerry Brown overruled the board and denied parole for Houten, who at the age of 19 was the youngest member of Manson's murderous cult.[279] In December 2016, another cult member, Patricia Krenwinkel, appeared before the California Parole Board for the 16th time. Charles Manson died in prison in 2017 at the age of 83.

"Enemies list"

January 25, 1971. The date on which an aide of H.R. "Bob" Haldemann, President Nixon's Chief of Staff, first started to assemble the names of those persons deemed unfriendly to the Nixon White House and Administration. Over the next months, two senior aides, Special Counsel Charles Colson and White House Counsel John Dean greatly expanded the list to include hundreds of names—from the usual suspects (Teddy Kennedy, Walter Mondale, John Kenneth Galbraith, Dick Gregory) to the more surprising (The Presidents of Yale, Harvard, and MIT, and even Gregory Peck, Bill Cosby, and Paul Newman). The illegal and unethical concept of the list was devised so that agents of the White House in the various federal agencies could target individuals and torment them by denying grants, initiating investigations, delaying petitions or approvals, or initiating tax audits. The existence of the enemies list was revealed by John Dean in the course of his testimony before the Senate Watergate Committee on June 25, 1973. The actual use and impact of the enemies list remained the subject of lengthy dispute and disagreement, although it was soon confirmed that a disproportionate number of persons on the list had, for example, been subjected to IRS audits. Over time and especially after the eventual resignation of Nixon, the inclusion of one's name on the list was almost seen as a badge of honor. For example, CBS reporter Daniel Schorr was one of the first reporters to obtain a copy of the released list. Upon receiving it and while live on television, Schorr started reading the names on the enemies list until, to his own shock, he came upon own name.

U.S. Constitutional Amendment – 26th Amendment

"The right of citizens ... who are eighteen years of age or older,
to vote shall not be denied ...
by the United States or any State on account of age."

March 23, 1971. This amendment lowered the voting age to 18 from 21. Many perceive this amendment as an indirect result of the broad political activism of students during the 1960s and the fact that 18-year-old men were subject to the draft and were being required (or, in the case of enlistees, allowed) to fight in the Vietnam War despite the fact that they were not yet permitted to vote.

"I was ordered to go in there and destroy the enemy.
That was my job that day."
...
"I did not sit down and think in terms of
men, women, and children.
They were all classified as the same,
and that's the classification that we dealt with over there,
just as the enemy."
...
"Guilty"
Lt. William Calley

March 29, 1971. The personal statement of Lt. William Calley, who was convicted on this date of the premeditated murder of 22 Vietnamese civilians whom he, together with other members of his platoon, massacred in the village of My Lai in March 1968. Though Calley was initially sentenced to life imprisonment, by a series of sentence reductions and an eventual Presidential pardon by Richard Nixon, Calley served only 3½ years of house arrest. Fourteen other servicemen were charged, but all had their charges dismissed or were acquitted. Most Americans disagreed with the Calley verdict, especially in light of the well documented cover-up that had been perpetrated by a number of more senior officers within the military chain of command. Some military investigators recommended a lengthy list of charges be brought against numerous military personnel including two generals and four full colonels. But America was tired of war. And it had become cynical. As a result, most Americans believed that Lt. Calley, just a young 24-year-old officer at the time of massacre, had been made a scapegoat. Most believed that what came to be known as the "My Lai Massacre" was little more than another tragedy of policy and behavior and another instance of misreporting by the military about its actions in Vietnam. The cluttered and confused emotions of most Americans in the context of the subject of Vietnam were well summarized in *Time* magazine's article about Lt. Calley, when the article noted that "Vietnam is the wound of American life that will not heal."[280]

"Too Big To Fail"

August 9, 1971. On this date, the federal government established the Federal Emergency Loan Guarantee Board for the purpose and benefit of Lockheed Aircraft. After the presentation of the normal litany of horrific consequences of doing nothing, the House and the Senate—both by razor-thin voting margins—authorized the federal guarantee of approximately $250 million for the troubled aircraft company. The historical significance of this acceptance of Lockheed's "too big fail to fail" argument was that over the course of Modern America—and despite rabid and oftentimes highly justified criticism[281]—the concept of "too big to fail" became established precedent. Bailouts became a hotly debated, but periodically accepted, part of role the federal government. Without the establishment of even basic criteria for defining the circumstances in which government bailouts should be considered, bailouts continued. As a result, they altered the trajectory of modern capitalism. Rather than allowing the markets both to reward and to punish, the government in politically selected instances seemed to haphazardly respond to the probabilities of large job losses and to bold assertions (if not veiled threats) of global economic consequences. After the 1971 Lockheed bailout, the federal government stepped in to bail out Franklin National Bank just three years later. The 1980s were no different. In 1980, Chrysler was bailed out by the Carter administration through the provision of $1.5 billion in federal loan guarantees. This was followed by the Reagan administration's 1984 bailout of Continental

Illinois National Bank and then the costly, multi-year absurdity of the federal savings and loan debacle.[282] However, nothing compares in size, reach or policy significance to the 2008 Great Recession bailouts of AIG, Citibank, General Motors, and Fannie Mae and Freddie Mac. Throughout most of Modern America, the role of the federal government has been constantly and aggressively debated in the context of the provision of welfare and human services, in the support and administration of public education, and amidst a lengthy litany of social matters ranging from abortion to right-to-marry laws. Yet arguably, the public use of billions of dollars of taxpayer monies to bailout private, for-profit enterprises remains inadequately questioned and debated. Such questioning is exacerbated by the consistent absence of personal or corporate accountability and by the conspicuous lack of criminal prosecutions or demands for financial claw backs or other forfeitures by at least amongst the senior management of the recipient corporations.

"No thoughtful person can question
that the American economic system is under attack."

. . .

"The overriding first need is for businessmen to recognize
that the ultimate issue may be survival –
survival of ... the free enterprise system"

. . .

"Yale, like every other major college,
is graduating scores of bright young men ...
who despise the American political and economic system"
(Citing columnist Stewart Alsop)

. . .

"The American business executive is truly the 'forgotten man'
(in American life)."

. . .

"Political power is necessary; ... (and)
such power must be assiduously cultivated;
and ... when necessary, it must be used
aggressively and with determination—

***without embarrassment and without the reluctance
which has been (to date) so characteristic of American business."***

August 21, 1971. Lewis Powell, writing in a Confidential Memorandum to the Chairman of the U.S. Chamber of Commerce. The Memorandum, which was later leaked to the press, was entitled "Attack of American Free Enterprise System." It encouraged U.S. businesses, individually and through lobbyists, organizations, and funded institutions, to start aggressively defending the American economic system. The Memorandum cited a wide array of "broadly based and consistently pursued" attacks on America's system of justice throughout the Sixties (i) by socialists and Communists; (ii) by other individuals, such as radical lawyer William Kuntsler, Professor Herbert Marcuse of the University of California at San Diego, consumer advocate Ralph Nader (identified in the Memorandum as the "single most effective antagonist of American business"), and Yale Professor Charles Reich, through his publication of *The Greening of America* ("a frontal assault ... on our government"), and (iii) by actions and protests such as the Bank of America bombing in Santa Barbara, California. The Memorandum help to dramatically change the relationship between business and government. Thereafter, businesses become more actively involved in the political process and much more aggressive in formulating public opinion and policy. As such, the Memorandum was one of the critical turning points in the American conservative movement. Shortly after the release and partially in response to this Memorandum, corporations also started getting more aggressively and directly involved in the political processes. They did this through their lawyers and through the retention of thousands of newly-retained lobbyists. They did this through an array of organizations such as the Chamber of Commerce. They did this through the creation of funded think tanks and other institutions dedicated to influencing public opinion. Examples of such organizations and think tanks include the Business Roundtable (founded in 1972), the Heritage Foundation (founded in 1973), the Cato Insthitute (founded in 1977), and the Manhattan Institute (founded in 1978). Businesses, individually and through trade organizations, also started pushing back against what was viewed as the left-leaning and biased academics at U.S. colleges and against the allegedly liberal and biased media. About a year after Powell wrote this Memorandum, he was appointed to the USSC by President Richard Nixon. He served honorably as a highly-respected Associate Justice of the USSC for the next 15 years.

"We are men.
We are not beasts."

September 9, 1971. The words of 21-year-old prisoner L.D. Barkley, speaking on behalf of the nearly 1,300 prisoners during the infamous Attica prison uprising, which began on this day. The revolt occurred at the maximum-security Attica Correctional Facility near Buffalo, New York. It remains the worst prison riot in U.S. history, even though the revolt lasted only four days. Despite ongoing negotiations in which the State of New York agreed to meet 28 of the prisoner's demands, the uprising ended with a bloody assault by state troopers upon the orders of Governor Nelson Rockefeller. In the end, 43 people were killed—ten correctional officers and thirty-nine prisoners. The above-quoted young L.D. Barkley was one of the prisoners killed in the retaking even though at the time of the riot he was just days away from his scheduled release date. The very word "Attica" became the chilling chant of those who demanded prison reform, and the phrase 'Attica, Attica" became immortalized several years later when it was used by the actor Al Pacino in the 1975 movie *Dog Day Afternoon*. Despite early reports of the prisoners having violently killed ten of their hostages, it was ultimately confirmed that all of the correctional officer hostages were killed by the spraying bullets of the state troopers during the retaking of the prison. Attica led to some prison reforms and even years of litigation. The litigation finally came to a close 29 years later with a $12.0 million class action settlement in 2000, payable by the State of New York to families of the slain inmates. [283]

<u>Television Line</u>

"As always in parting, we wish you love, peace, and soul."

October 2, 1971. Don Cornelius, as his weekly sign-off as the "high priest of soul, funk, and disco." The sign-off was used at the end of each taping of *Soul Train*, a dance show that Cornelius created, produced, and, until 1993, hosted. *Soul Train* premièred on this day in 1971 and continued until 2006.[284] With over 1,100 episodes, it is, by some counts, the longest-running, nationally syndicated program in television history. However, Cornelius' most significant contribution and achievement may have been his initial ability to convince major U.S. corporations to reach out to large black audiences. Unfortunately, his life later descended into turmoil including a sentence of probation for spousal battery, divorce proceedings, and significant health problems. He committed suicide in his Los Angeles home in 2012 at the age of 76.

"Upper classes are a nation's past;
the middle class is its future."

October 1971. Ayn Rand, as excerpted from *The Ayn Rand Letter*, a biweekly newsletter published from October 1971 to February 1976. After Ayn Rand's 1957 publication of *Atlas Shrugged*, Rand "turned to nonfiction, both to elaborate on the philosophy set forth in her novels, and to use her philosophy, which she named Objectivism, to explain crucial cultural events and fight the negative trends she observed." After *The Objectivist Newsletter* and *The Objectivist, The Ayn Rand Letter* was the last of three successive periodicals that she published from 1962 until 1976.[285] While a brief summary of Rand's philosophy is challenging, Rand believed that "American is no longer a capitalist society… (Instead it is) a mixed economy, i.e. 'a mixture of capitalism and statism, of freedom and controls.'" [286]

"Miss, you'd better look at that note.
I have a bomb."

November 24, 1971. D.B. Cooper's brief words, as written on a note passed by Cooper to a flight attendant aboard a Boeing 727 flight from Seattle, Washington to Portland, Oregon.[287] Upon Cooper's instructions, the flight returned to Seattle, where the plane was refueled and all 36 passengers and two flight attendants were released in exchange for $200,000 in cash ($1.17 million in 2015 dollars) and four parachutes.

Cooper then directed the pilots to chart a course to Reno, Nevada. He instructed all crew members to go into the cockpit. Shortly thereafter, the aft air stair apparatus was activated, jolting the plane severely. When the plane later landed in Reno, Nevada, the air stair was still deployed, but Cooper was not in the plane. It was concluded that he must have parachuted out of the plane at some point mid-flight. Because neither Cooper nor the money[288] was ever located, the case became the subject of urban legends and remained open for decades. The FBI still insists that it is unlikely that Cooper could have survived such a risky mid-flight exit from the plane. However, this is still unknown. His fate remains unknown, and the legend of D. B. Cooper continues. In July 2016 and noting that there were no tenable leads, the FBI finally ended the case as an "active investigation."

> ***"For the Federal Government to plunge headlong financially
> into supporting child development would commit
> the vast moral authority of the National Government
> to the side of communal approaches to child rearing
> over and against the family-centered approach."***

December 9, 1971. President Richard M. Nixon, explaining one of his primary reasons for vetoing the Comprehensive Child Development Act which had been passed by an overwhelming bipartisan Senate vote of 63 to 17. This reason was the last of nine reasons cited by Nixon for vetoing the legislation despite his earlier support for the development of a national day care system. Such a day care system was envisioned particularly to make it easier for single parents to work and to assure the safety of their children. In the ensuing years, multiple other programs such as Title XX of the Social Services Amendments of 1974 were adopted to assist low-income, working parents. However, the debate about the proper public role in the provision of child care services became a part of the continuing debate about the many welfare programs that were initiated in the 1960s and early 1970s.[289]

Year 1972

<u>Seminal Book</u>

The Best and the Brightest
by David Halberstam

This book is a thoughtful and detailed presentation about the strategic origins of the tragically misguided American foreign and war policy relating to Vietnam. Written by Pulitzer Prize-winning journalist and historian David Halberstam, it focuses on how such policies could have been formulated and promoted by a team of some of the most brilliant leaders of industry and academia—"the best and the brightest" of their generation. The team had been assembled during the Kennedy administration, and many of them continued through most or all of the Johnson administration as well. As noted in *The New York Times* 1972 review of his book, Halberstam came to conclude that Vietnam happened "because '(the best and the brightest) had, for all their brilliance and hubris and sense of themselves, been unwilling to look and learn from the past. ... They ignored Hanoi history and misunderstood Munich history. ...And they had been swept forward by their belief in the importance of anti-Communism."[290] Implicit in this biting, but accurate, criticism is the "arrogance of power" about which Senator Fulbright had written six years earlier in his book titled with that phrase. [291]

<u>Pulitzer Prize for Fiction</u>

Angle of Repose
by Wallace Stegner

<u>Pulitzer Prize for History</u>

Neither Black nor White
by Carl N. Degler

The New York Times Best Sellers List (Nonfiction) – Books with Most Weeks as No. 1 Best Seller

I'm O.K. – You're O.K.
by Thomas Harris (22 weeks)

Eleanor and Franklin
by Joseph P. Lash (11 weeks)

The New York Times Best Sellers List (Adult Fiction) – Book with Most Weeks as No. 1 Best Seller

Jonathan Livingston Seagull
by Richard Bach (27 weeks)

Academy Awards Best Picture

Winner: *The Godfather*
Other Nominees: *Cabaret, Deliverance, The Emigrants, Sounder*

PrettyFamous' Best Movie of the Year

The Godfather

Best/Most Memorable Line of the Year

"I'm going to make him an offer he can't refuse."

Marlon Brando in his portrayal of Don Corleone in Francis Ford Coppola's epic movie, *The Godfather*. The movie was based upon Mario Puzo's book by the same name. Worthy of an honorable mention from the same movie are the chilling words of Richard Castellano (portraying Clemenza) when he says *"Leave the gun. Take the cannoli."*

1972 U.S. Population: 209,900,000

(Compared as a Percentage to the U.S. 1957 Population of 172,000,000: 122.0%)

Television Shows

Most Widely-Viewed Television Shows

Rank	Show Name	Years of Series (Excluding Reruns)	Show Type	Estimated Audience (In MMs)	Audience as Percentage of U.S. Population
1.	*All in the Family*	1971–1979	Comedy	21.6MM	10.3%
	Cast: Carroll O'Connor - Jean Stapleton - Sally Struthers - Rob Reiner				
2.	*Sanford and Son*	1972–1977	Comedy	17.9MM	8.5%
	Cast: Red Foxx - Demond Wilson				
3.	*Hawaii Five-O*	1968–1980	Crime Drama	16.3MM	7.83%
	Cast: Alex O'Loughlin - Scott Caan				

Widely-Viewed or Critically-Acclaimed New Television Show(s)

*M*A*S*H* (1972–1983) – Military/Medical-Based Situation Comedy
Alan Alda – Wayne Rogers – McLean Stevenson –
Loretta Swit – Gary Burghoff – Harry Morgan
(No. 25 Top TV Shows of All Time – *TV Guide*)

Last Season Television Show(s)

Bewitched (1964–1972) - Comedy
Elizabeth Montgomery - Dick York - David White

Major Commercial Advertising Campaigns and Slogans

"Heh, Mikey … He likes it!!"
Life Cereal

"Nothing runs like a Deere."
John Deere

Memorable Words from Speeches, Books, Writings, and Other Sources – 1972

Presidential Campaign Themes, Slogans and Results
(Both Official and Unofficial)

Shirley Chisholm (Early Candidate for Democratic Nomination)

Bring Us Together   *Catalyst for Change*   *Unbought and Unbiased*

George McGovern (and Sargent Shriver) (Democratic Party)
Come Home America.   Make America Happen Again   We Luv McGuv
(Anti-Democratic Party Response Slogan: *Acid, Amnesty, and Abortion)*
Richard M. Nixon (and Spiro Agnew) (Republican Party)
Nixon Now   Now More Than Ever   Re-Elect the President
(Anti-Republican Party Response Slogan: *Don't Switch Dicks in the
Middle of a Screw, Vote Nixon in '72)*
George Wallace (Early Candidate for Democratic Nomination)
Send Them A Message
Election Results:

Party	Nominees		Electoral Vote		Popular Vote	
	Presidential	Vice-Presidential				
Republican	R.M. Nixon	S. Agnew	520	96.7%	47.2MM	60.7%
Democratic	G. McGovern	S. Shriver	17	3.2%	29.1MM	37.5%

"Of my two handicaps, being female put many more obstacles in my path than being black."

February 1972. Shirley Chisholm, as the black and female candidate for the Democratic Party Presidential nomination, reflecting upon her campaign to be the 1972 Democratic Presidential candidate.[292] This "handicap" was evidenced, for example, by Walter Cronkite's comments on the *CBS Evening News* when he said upon Representative Chisholm's entering the race that "a new hat—rather, a bonnet—was tossed into the Presidential race today." Although the above may be one of Chisholm's most frequently referenced quotes, her paraphrased statement that she "measures America not by its achievement but by its potential" may be her most inspirational.

"Ms." Recognized as a Title by U.S. Government Printing Office

February 1972. The term "Ms." was in this month first recognized as an official title by the U.S. Government Printing Office. This occurred shortly after Gloria Steinem launched *Ms.* Magazine and just before the passage of the Equal Rights Amendment by both the House and the Senate – although the ERA was never ratified by the mandated two-thirds majority of the states.

"A third-rate burglary."

June 18, 1972. The scornfully dismissive characterization by White House Press Secretary Ronald L. Ziegler of the recently reported break-in at the offices of the Democratic National Headquarters at the Watergate complex in Washington, D.C. While it is believed that Ziegler had little knowledge of most of the Watergate-related crimes, he was required to testify to Congress 33 times in the ensuing years. He was not charged with any crime, but 25 other individuals in the Nixon administration were convicted of Watergate-scandal-related crimes[293] and on August 8, 1974—about two years after this "third-rate burglary"—Nixon himself became the only President in U.S. history to resign.[294]

"No skeletons rattling in your closet?"

July 13, 1972. The question Frank Mankiewicz, Democratic Presidential candidate George McGovern's political director, posed to then-Senator Thomas Eagleton, who was being vetted to serve as candidate McGovern's Vice-Presidential running mate. After his reply of "right," Eagleton was selected as McGovern's initial running mate. Eighteen days later, Eagleton stepped down after it was learned that he "had suffered several nervous breakdowns and undergone electroshock therapy."[295]

"It ain't over till it's over."

...

"Baseball is 90% mental and the other half is physical."

...

"Nobody goes there anymore. It's too crowded."

...

"It's like déjà vu all over again."

...

"The future ain't what it used to be."

...

"If you come to a fork in the road, take it."

...

"It's tough to make predictions, especially about the future."

...
"A nickel ain't worth a dime anymore."
...
"It gets late early out there."

July 22, 1972. Yogi Berra was one of the greatest major league catchers of all time. His playing career spanned 19 years from 1946 to 1965, and every season but the last was with the New York Yankees. During his playing career, Berra played in 18 All-Star games and 10 World Series championships, and on this date his "Number 8" was retired by the New York Yankees. After retiring as a player, he went on to coach or manage the New York Yankees, the New York Mets and the Houston Astros until his final retirement in 1985. He is also famous, if not even more famous, for his endless stream of gloriously, mangled sayings—affectionately known as "Yogiisms." The above list is merely a sample of the many Yogiisms. In words that only he could have chosen, Berra insisted that "I never said most of the things I said." The readers of *The Economist* in 2005 nevertheless named Berra as the "Wisest Fool of the Past 50 Years."[296]

"We are faced with a choice between
the 'work ethic' that built this Nation's character
and the new 'welfare ethic'
that could cause that American character to weaken."

September 3, 1972. Richard M. Nixon, in his Labor Day message to the nation, which was broadcast by radio. This message presaged the concerns of many social critics and the sometimes unspoken theme of many politicians that both the "work ethic" and the "social fabric" of America had been diminished by the liberal policies emanating from, especially, President Lyndon Johnson's Great Society agenda of the 1960s.

"We believe that peace is at hand."

October 26, 1972. Henry Kissinger, President Richard Nixon's national security advisor, announcing that the end of the Vietnam War was "at hand." The announcement came after years of secret negotiations between Kissinger and North Vietnam's Le Duc Tho. Because of the timing of the announcement, just a week before the Nixon-McGovern Presidential election, Kissinger's announcement came to be referred to as an "October surprise." Yet it is relatively hard to believe that Nixon believed he would need such an "October surprise" in order to assure his re-election over George McGovern as is confirmed by the fact that Nixon defeated McGovern by a shocking 512-17 electoral vote margin and with a margin of 60.7% to 37.5% of the popular vote. At the time, more Americans were critical of the "peace at hand" statement because it turned out not to be true. Peace would not be achieved until another 100,000 bombs were dropped by the U.S. on Hanoi in December during what came to be known as the "Christmas Bombing," and the final agreement would not be signed for another three months thereafter.[297] While the "peace at hand" statement is embodied in the Vietnam narrative, its historical significance may be greater because it added the above-referenced phrase "October surprise" to America's political jargon, the very concept of "October surprise" was added to the process and planning of presidential elections. The phrase came to refer to the campaign tool whereby one party, shortly before a national election—and especially a presidential election—deliberately creates or carefully times the release of an accusation or damaging information about the other candidate or otherwise makes an announcement with the specific intention of influencing the outcome of an election. Thus, numerous variations of October surprises have become a staple of U.S. presidential elections. Some October surprises have had minimal influence, such as the release of information about George W. Bush's 1976 DUI arrest, which was made in late October 2000, just days before his election victory over Democratic Candidate Al Gore. On the other hand, other October surprises may have had momentous impacts on presidential elections such as FBI Director James Comey's October 27, 2016 announcement in the context of the Trump-Clinton election of 2016. In that case, the FBI Director announced the supposed re-opening the email case of Democratic Candidate Hillary Clinton only to withdraw the announcement a few days before the election.

"No assassin in his right mind would kill me.
They know if they did that they would wind up with Agnew!"

1972. President Richard M. Nixon, joking to his aide John Ehrlichman as to why he had decided to keep Spiro Agnew on the 1972 Republican ticket.[298] Just two years after making this statement, President Nixon himself resigned the Presidency, allowing the ascendancy of then Vice President Gerald Ford. Ford had been appointed Vice President after the resignation of Spiro Agnew resulting from federal income tax evasion charges to which Agnew pled "No Contest."

"Follow the money"[299]

1972. The famous advice allegedly given to Bob Woodward, then a young *Washington Post* reporter, by his inside source, "Deep Throat," in the midst of the Watergate scandal. The exact origin of the catchphrase appears to be unknown, but it was popularized by the 1976 drama-documentary *All the President's Men* starring Robert Redford and Dustin Hoffman. The movie was based upon the bestselling book by the same name and written by Bob Woodward and Carl Bernstein. The "follow the money" phrase was intended to suggest that the best means to unraveling a political scandal is to investigate, indeed "to follow," the proverbial money trail.

"A Mind Is a Terrible Thing to Waste"

1972. The public service campaign launched in this year by the United Negro College Fund (the "UNCF") in cooperation with the Ad Council. The popular campaign has not been changed by the UNCF for decades and has to date helped to raise more than $2.2 billion and to graduate more than 350,000 minority students from college and beyond."[300] It is believed that part of the reason for the campaign's success lies in the fact that the phrase implies and reminds listeners that there are many capable, talented, African American youth who would not be able to attend college without financial assistance. Equally importantly, the very use of the word "mind" changed the dialogue. The wording of the announcement is racially neutral and does not divert the conversation to issues of "charity, social injustice, or 'at-risk' youths."[301] Possibly most importantly, because the phrase is itself true, it has become part of the American vernacular.

Year 1973

<u>Seminal Books</u>

Fear of Flying
by Erica Jong

Upon its release, *Fear of Flying* was highly controversial due to its relentless focus upon—and almost casual narration of—female sexuality. Partly, the controversy arose because the book "chronicle(d) … the soul-searching, sensuality-seeking adventures of an intellectual young poet named Isadora Wing,"[302] but the book was also controversial because of the "frank, explicit, chatty" nature of the chronicle. It is highly likely that the book may have less resonance to younger, modern audiences who are used to the frequent portrayals of sexuality in modern films and television. However, at the time of its release, the subject and tone of *Fear of Flying* were new. It was not written or offered as a feminist writing, but it encouraged discussions and a new openness about sexuality-related subjects.

Rubyfruit Jungle
by Rita Mae Brown

The book is a coming-of-age autobiographical story, but is mostly remembered—and by some readers revered—as a revolutionary book because of its inclusion of explicit sexual accounts of lesbianism. Thus, the book's significance almost parallels that of Philip Roth's 1969 novel, *Portnoy's Complaint*, in that *Rubyfruit Jungle* also addresses the subject of non-heterosexuality. *Rubyfruit Jungle* was published in an era when the modern women's movement and feminism itself were still emerging as a political and social force. In this context, *Rubyfruit Jungle* was released amidst a wide range of fiction and nonfiction publications from Betty Friedan's 1962 *The Feminine Mystique* to Germaine Greer's 1970 *The Female Eunuch,* and from Alex Comfort's 1973 *The Joy of Sex* to Erica Jong's *Fear of Flying,* described immediately above. This book was also significant by its very title—since the phrase was 1970s lesbian slang for vagina. It is reported that Brown herself does not consider the book "seminal,"[303] even though the book was described at the time as "groundbreaking" by *The New York Times*. Some commentators have gone even further and have referred to Molly Bolt, the book's lead character, as "a genuine descendant—genuine feminine descendant—of Huckleberry Finn."[304]

Pulitzer Prize for Fiction

The Optimist's Daughter
by Eudora Welty

Pulitzer Prize for General Nonfiction

Children of Crisis (Vols. 2 and 3)
by Robert Coles

Pulitzer Prize for History

People of Paradox: An Inquiry Concerning the Origins of American Civilization
by Michael Kammen

The New York Times Best Sellers List (Nonfiction) – Books with Most Weeks as No. 1 Best Seller

Dr. Atkins Diet Revolution
by Dr. Robert C. Atkins (27 weeks)

The Joy of Sex
by Alex Comfort (10 weeks)

The New York Times Best Sellers List (Adult Fiction) – Books with Most Weeks as No. 1 Best Seller

Jonathan Livingston Seagull
by Richard Bach (11 weeks)

The Hollow Hills
by Mary Stewart (11 weeks)

<u>Academy Awards Best Picture</u>

Winner: *The Sting*
Other Nominees: *American Graffiti, Cries and Whispers,*
The Exorcist, A Touch of Class

<u>*PrettyFamous'* Best Movie of the Year</u>
The Sting

<u>Best/Most Memorable Movie Lines of the Year</u>
"Sex and death.
Two things that come once in a lifetime.
But at least after death, you're not nauseous."

Woody Allen perfecting his neurotic style of thought and his unique, stammering style of performance in the futuristic science fiction comedy, *Sleeper,* which was also written (with Marshall Brickman) and directed by Woody Allen.

"Soylent Green is people!"

The exclamation in the horrific science fiction movie, *Soylent Green,* upon the macabre discovery that the basic food of this advanced society is people. The film was directed by Richard Fleischer and starred Charlton Heston and Edward G. Robinson.

"What an excellent day for an exorcism."

The words of Max von Sydow in the bone-chilling supernatural film *The Exorcist.* Although several sequels were made and a number of similar films were inspired, William Friedkin's *The Exorcist*—and especially the performance of Linda Blair as the possessed child—is widely viewed as one of the most riveting and terrifying films in the horror genre.

"You not gonna stick around for your share?"

. . .

"Naah, I'd only blow it."

The exchange between Paul Newman and Robert Redford in *The Sting,* as endearing con men, in a follow-up movie to their 1969 film *Butch Cassidy and the Sundance Kid,* in which they played endearing outlaws.

<u>1973 U.S. Population: 211,900,000</u>

(Compared as a Percentage to the U.S. 1957 Population of 172,000,000: 123.2%)

<u>Television Shows</u>

Most Widely-Viewed Television Shows

Rank	Show Name	Years of Series (Excluding Reruns)	Show Type	Estimated Audience (In MMs)	Audience as Percentage of U.S. Population
1.	*All in the Family*	1971–1979	Comedy	20.7MM	9.8%

Cast: Carroll O'Connor - Jean Stapleton - Sally Struthers - Rob Reiner

2.	*The Waltons*	1971–1981	Family Drama	18.6MM	8.8%

Cast: Ralph Waite - Judy Norton Taylor - Earl Hammer, Jr.

3.	*Sanford and Son*	1972–1977	Comedy	18.2MM	8.6%

Cast: Red Foxx - Demond Wilson

Last Season Television Show(s)

Bonanza (1959–1973) — Western

Lorne Greene - Michael Landon - Pernell Roberts - Dan Blocker

Lassie (1954–1973) — Family drama show

Jan Clayton - George Cleveland - Tommy Rettig - Donald Keeler

<u>Major Commercial Advertising Campaigns and Slogans</u>

"Have it your way."
Burger King

"Merrill Lynch is bullish on America."
Merrill Lynch

"The Uncola"
Seven Up/7 Up

<u>Catchphrases, Chants, and Slogans</u>

"Thank you for your service."

The sincere, but wholly inadequate, hackneyed, and platitudinal phrase by which millions of even well-meaning civilian Americans blithely thank military personnel for their service. The separateness, if not isolation, of the military community from the larger national community and the too-frequent emptiness of the phrase is seen by many as being exacerbated by certain facts of American life. First, only about 0.5% of the U.S. population is now in the Armed Forces. Even at the peak of World War II, only about 9% of the U.S. population was on active duty. During the Korean and Vietnam Wars, the percentage remained close to 2%, but—especially with the introduction of the "all-volunteer army" in the 1970s—the percentage has been declining for nearly 40 years. Second, the tightness of the military community itself is evidenced by the fact that nearly 80% of military personnel already have or have had a parent or sibling in uniform, and a disproportionately high number of military personnel are from Southern or rural states.[305] Compounding the problem is that in recent years, fewer and fewer members of the Congress have served in the military. As of November, 2014, less than 18% of the members of Congress had served in the military—far, far less than, for example, 1971 when 72% of the U.S. House of Representatives and 78% of the U.S. Senate were veterans.[306] Admittedly, these percentages understate the size of the military community, since the definition of the military community should, at a minimum, include spouses and children of active-duty and even retired military personnel. The "thank you for your service" expression, though not new in American culture, is placed here in Year 1973 since that was the year of introduction of an "all-volunteer" force.[307] Therefore, since military service is no longer rooted in conscription, the phrase arguably takes on even more significance.

Memorable Words from Speeches, Books, Writings, and Other Sources – 1973

"…(N)o host, no interviews, and almost no voice-over narration"

…

"I think it may be as important for our time as were the invention of drama and the novel for earlier generations."

January 11, 1973. Respectively, (i) Public Broadcasting System's ("PBS') description of the groundbreaking "reality-television" format used in its 12-episode presentation of *An American Family,* which was first aired on this date and centered on a single American family—the upper-middle-class

Loud family of Santa Barbara, California; and (ii) the words of anthropologist Margaret Meade in her overstated recognition of the impact of this type of reality television presentation. This first instance of a reality television show tracked the tumultuous lives of "real people" over the course of seven months.[308] At the time this observational documentary series was first aired, PBS was still in its infancy. It had just been formed in October 1970 and was still "a fledging 'fourth network' joining CBS, NBC, and ABC."[309] This show immediately drew national attention. It came to attract as many as 10 million viewers a week, who watched the dramatic up-and-down events of this family unfold. Some viewed the Loud family as the very embodiment of "the trite generalizations about the American family …. affluent, …uninvolved, …(living) beyond their means and for appearances…." In that sense, the show and the family members served as "symbols of (the) disintegration and purposelessness in American life." The show almost inevitably "became swamped in controversies concerning the American family and sexuality,[310] the state of the nation, the role of television, and the representation of reality."[311] Resultant discussions also focused upon (i) what many viewed as the disintegration, or at least changes, in the family with respect to parental roles and familial influence, and (ii) the ever-increasing shift away from the simply structured, nuclear family to more and more complexly structured families of step-parents, stepchildren, half-siblings, and on and on. However, possibly the most lasting impacts of the series, *An American Family* may have been in helping to establish a degree of credibility and viability for PBS and serving as a presage of the market receptivity to reality television shows – which within two decades would start dominating television broadcasting.

January 20, 1973
Second Inaugural Address of Richard M. Nixon
(President of the United States 1969–1974)

"When we met here four years ago,
America was bleak in spirit,
depressed by the prospect of seemingly endless war
abroad and of destructive conflict at home.

As we stand here today,
we stand on the threshold of a new era of peace in the world."

• • •

"Let us resolve that this era (of peace) we are about to enter
will not be what other postwar periods have so often been:
a time of retreat and isolation that leads to stagnation at home
and invites new danger abroad."

• • •

"It is important that we understand both the necessity
and the limitations of America's role in maintaining that peace."

• • •

"We have a chance today to do more than ever before …
to make life better in America
to ensure better education, … health, … housing, …
transportation, a cleaner environment, to restore respect for law,
to make our communities more livable and
(to) ensure the God-given right of every American
to full and equal opportunity.…"

• • •

"We have lived too long with the consequences of attempting
to gather all power and responsibility in Washington."

• • •

"… I offer no promise of a purely governmental solution
for every problem.
We have lived too long with that false promise.
In trusting too much in government,
we have asked of it more than it can deliver."

• • •

"Let us remember that America was built
not by the government, but by people;
not by welfare, but by work.…"

• • •

"In our own lives,
let each of us ask not just what the government will do for me,

but what I can do for myself?"

...

"As America's longest and most difficult war comes to an end,
let us again learn to debate our differences
with civility and decency."

...

"We have endured a long night of the American spirit.
But as our eyes catch the dimness of the first rays of dawn,
let us not curse the remaining dark. Let us gather the light."

January 20, 1973. From the Second Inaugural Address of Richard M. Nixon. Despite Nixon's overwhelming November 1972 popular vote and electoral college victory over Senator George McGovern and Sargent Shriver, his Second Inauguration took place amidst rancor, protests in Washington, D.C. and other large cities, a boycott by some elected officials,[312] and even a counter-inaugural held the day prior to the inauguration. Both President Nixon and Vice President Agnew took their oaths of office from Chief Justice Earl Warren. Vice President Agnew resigned from office 263 days later. President Nixon resigned from office 1 year and 201 days later.

"The 'zone of privacy'
(is) broad enough to encompass a woman's decision
whether or not to terminate her pregnancy"

January 22, 1973. With these few and striking words, the USSC expanded its prior 1965 "right to privacy" decision in *Griswold v. Connecticut* and overturned a Texas state law that, like those of many other states, prohibited abortions except for the medical purpose of saving the mother's life. Here, the USSC in the case of *Roe v. Wade* held that "states were forbidden to outlawing or regulating any aspect of abortion performed during the first trimester of pregnancy, could only enact abortion regulations reasonably related to the mother's health in the second and third trimesters, and could enact abortion laws protecting the life of the fetus only in the third trimester."[313] The 7-2 decision was heatedly debated at the time and has remained highly controversial. To this day, abortion rights remain one of the central "culture wars" debates of Modern America.

"Peace with honor"

...

***"At 12:30 Paris time today, January 23, 1973,
the Agreement on Ending the War and Restoring Peace in Vietnam
was initialed by Dr. Henry Kissinger on behalf of the United States,
and ... Le Duc Tho
on behalf of the Democratic Republic of Vietnam."***

January 27, 1973. President Richard M. Nixon, announcing on radio and television to the American people the signing of the Vietnam Peace Accords. Despite Nixon's steadfast reference to this achievement of "peace with honor," most Americans rejected such characterization. This rejection of the "peace with honor" characterization was based in part upon the fact that more than 580 American POWs were not home yet and thousands of American MIAs were still unaccounted for. But mostly, Americans were just tired of war. There was no "peace." There was no "honor." It was merely time to end the war in Vietnam, and there were no achievable alternatives to the Accords. Thus, the war ended more from exhaustion than honor. It ended more in sadness than celebration. It is not coincidental that President Nixon in his Second Inaugural Address, which had been delivered just a week earlier, re-defined the limits of American power when he stated that "the time has passed when America will make every other nation's conflict our own, or make every other nation's future our responsibility....." The debate regarding the U.S.'s world policing responsibility was temporarily settled for many Americans with this closing of the Vietnam War. However, the lessons of Vietnam quickly faded. The debate about the U.S.'s role and responsibilities within the world community would soon be reopened again, first upon the demise of the Soviet Union in the early 1990s, and again with the rise of international terrorism in the 21st century.

Wounded Knee Siege, the Occupation of Alcatraz, and the Trail of Broken Promises

February 27, 1973. On this day, the 71-day Wounded Knee Siege began when about 200 Oglala Lakota Sioux and followers of the American

Indian Movement (AIM) seized and occupied the small town of Wounded Knee on the Pine Ridge Indian Reservation in South Dakota. The siege eventually became one of the longest such sieges in U.S. history. The selection of this site was symbolic since it was here in 1890 that members of the U.S. 7th Cavalry had committed one of the worst Native American massacres in history. News of the siege briefly occupied the national headlines and attracted the interest of some members of the general public, but in the end little changed. The Wounded Knee Siege came to be viewed as another sad and symbolic act that, once again, merely reminded Americans how the U.S. continued to disgracefully treat Native Americans. AIM itself had been founded in the late 1960s in a manner and with objectives that paralleled those of the Black Panthers with respect to the black community—as a political and civil rights organization that could more militantly assert the demands of Native Americans. The Wounded Knee Siege itself followed the months-long occupation by members of AIM of Alcatraz Island in California in 1971 and the Trail of Broken Treaties protest culminating in Washington, D.C. in the fall of 1972. The naming of The Trail of Broken Treaties obviously was intended to echo the Trail of Tears, which had occurred nearly 150 years earlier when Native Americans were forcibly relocated off of their native lands. The 1972 protest was co-sponsored by eight separate Native American organizations and assembled the largest gathering ever of Native Americans in Washington, D.C. for the purpose of presenting what came to be known as the Twenty-Point Position Paper.[314] But just as the Alcatraz occupation and the Trail of Broken Treaties protest achieved little, so it was with the Wounded Knee Siege. The siege ended after two Sioux men were shot dead by federal agents and several more wounded. Two of the leaders, Russell Means and Dennis Banks, were arrested and charged with conspiracy, but those charges were dismissed the next year due to U.S. prosecutorial misconduct.[315] Despite sustained Presidential and Congressional inaction, Native Americans have almost curiously achieved the most for their communities through a series of major litigation settlements with both the federal and state governments.

"The day I screwed up baseball...."

April 6, 1973. Ron Blomberg, nicknamed "Boomer," on this date became the first Designated Hitter ("DH") in professional baseball. Years later, he remarked about this day at Fenway Park in Boston when he first stepped up to bat as a DH. Although he walked in that first at-bat, Blomberg's DH bat was still promptly sent to the Baseball Hall of Fame in Cooperstown, Ohio. DHs are still only a part of the rules of the American League but not the National League, and the rules are shunned by some baseball purists because the rules of baseball are, to some, sacred. In comparison, the National Basketball Association added the three-point shot in 1979 with little fanfare. In comparison, NCAA football banned targeting in 2013 with little fanfare. But, again, the rules of baseball, America's game, are seen as more sacred. Nothing is supposed to change—except maybe in 2016 when the Chicago Cubs won the World Series for the first time in 108 years! Nevertheless, DHs have slowly become a fixture of Major League Baseball over the last 40 years, and some DHs have earned extraordinary salaries, such as David Ortiz of the Boston Red Sox ($14.5 million in 2012) and Travis Hafner of the Cleveland Indians ($13 million in 2013). There has been a growing acceptability and even prestige of DHs, but they are still well-meaningly ridiculed by some fans. As one commentator noted, "imagine a job that pays full-time wages for part-time work; ... involves first class travel ...; ... attracts cheers, albeit with some jeers; and ... features about three to four months off a year. Oh, and it even comes with a uniform."[316]

"I'm just an old country lawyer,
and I don't know the finer ways to do it.
I just have to do it my way."

May 17 – August 7, 1973. Senator Sam Ervin (D-NC), Chairman of the Senate Watergate Committee, responding to the objections of witnesses and their counsels during the course of the Committee's investigations and the televised hearings that began on May 17, 1973. The Watergate hearings focused the attention of the riveted nation. Approximately 320 hours of live hearings were televised, and it is estimated that 85% of all U.S. households watched at least a portion of the hearings.[317] Although it is true that Senator Ervin was "just an old country lawyer" and a folksy and charming man by nature, he was also a graduate of Harvard Law School. Like nearly all Southern politicians, Senator Ervin had opposed *Brown v. Board of Education* and opposed racial integration, but he was respected for his integrity and determination, and he had come to be especially so respected by many of his peers after helping bring down Senator Joe McCarthy in 1954. He chose not to seek re-election and withdrew from the Senate on December 31, 1974—about 18 months after the Watergate hearings.

"What did the President know and when did he know it?"

May 17 – August 7, 1973. Senator Howard Baker's (R-TN) repeated inquiry to witnesses appearing before the Senate Watergate Committee, on which he served as the Ranking Minority Chairman. The question by Senator Baker, often known as the "Great Conciliator," was tendered in his attempt to identify if and how President Richard Nixon was himself directly involved in the many wrongdoings associated with the Watergate scandal.

TAPS (Trans-Alaska Pipeline System)

...

(Upon the discovery of oil in Prudhoe Bay)
"Alaska seems to be transformed
from a frozen Appalachia to a frozen Kauai."[318]

...

"I can guarantee that we will not approve any design (of a pipeline)
based on the old and faulty concept of 'build now, return later.'"[319]

July 17, 1973. On this date, the U.S. Senate by a vote of 50 to 49 (with Vice President Spiro Agnew casting the deciding vote) approved construction of the 800-mile, 48-inch diameter pipeline from Prudhoe Bay to Valdez, Alaska. The Prudhoe Bay oil field had been discovered in 1968 by the Atlantic Richfield Company, and the size and potential of the oil field were immediately recognized despite the challenges associated with the extraction costs. It took nearly five years to get approval of the pipeline, but the construction of the pipeline became a "major turning point in the struggle ... for low cost energy."[320] The challenges of the environment, logistics, and politics had to be overcome especially in light of the 1969 January 1969 Santa Barbara, California oil spill; the 1970 passage of the National Environmental Policy Act; and the burgeoning environmental movement as evidenced by the holding of the first Earth Day in May 1970. Nevertheless, with the assurance of men such as Secretary of the Interior Walter Hickel regarding the use of careful construction of the pipeline, on this date the pipeline was approved—albeit by a tight vote. Many Americans continued to object to the extraordinarily challenging construction of the pipeline through some of the world's most remote country, but the project was soon widely approved by the public. This approval became especially widespread after the OPEC oil embargo which commenced just four months later and led to a horrendous spike in gas prices and long lines at gas stations across the country. Pipeline construction began in March 1975—less than two years after its approval. It involved nearly 70,000 workers and the building of 31 construction camps. It cost 8 billion dollars, but upon the pipeline's completion in May 1977, oil started flowing. By 1988, the peak year of Alaska's oil production, 737 million barrels of oil went through the Alaska pipeline— "about 25% of U.S. oil production."[321]

> *"...I think that the Watergate tragedy is the greatest tragedy*
> *this country has ever suffered.*
> *I used to think that the Civil War*
> *was our country's greatest tragedy,*
> *but ... there were some redeeming features in the Civil War*
> *in that there was some spirit of sacrifice*
> *and heroism displayed on both sides.*
> *I see no redeeming features in Watergate."*

July 23, 1973. Senator Sam Ervin (D-NC), reacting to President Richard Nixon's decision to refuse to turn over presidential tape recordings to either his Senate Watergate committee or (Watergate) Special Prosecutor Archibald Cox. The tapes were believed to hold recorded conversations between Nixon and his assistants relating to the Watergate break-in and subsequent efforts to cover up those crimes and other related events. The resultant constitutional confrontation between the Nixon and the Senate Committee was resolved and the suspicions of Nixon's deep involvement were confirmed upon the eventual release of the tapes, pursuant to the order of the USSC.

Author's Note:

Archibald Cox was a Professor at Harvard Law School when I attended. It was a standing tradition for a group of us students to have lunch with Professor Cox about once a week at the Harkness Commons, the law student center. One week in 1972, he announced to us that he would no longer be able to join us for lunch. When we asked him why, he stated, very solemnly, that it appeared that "it was necessary for me to go to Washington (D.C.) to put some people in jail." All of us looked at one another in puzzlement. Professor Cox's appointment as Special Prosecutor had not yet been publicly announced. I later graduated, and sadly, I never had the chance to see Professor Cox again.

"I'll play her on clay, grass, wood, cement, marble or roller skates."

...

"Straight Sets: 6-4, 6-3, 6-3"

September 20, 1973. The first above quote is the taunting remark from 55-year, former tennis star and 1939 Wimbledon Champion, Bobby Riggs to 29-year-old Billie Jean King, in anticipation of their "Battle of the Sexes"[322] tennis match held on this day. The second quote is the result—the final straight-set victory score won by Billie Jean King. Just three months earlier and in the same type of "Battle of the Sexes" match, Riggs had trounced 30-year-old Margaret Court on Mother's Day and before a measly 5,000 fans in Ramona, California. Unlike the Riggs-Court match, however, this Riggs-King match was far better planned and promoted. As a result, it was played before 30,000 fans at the Houston Astrodome—at the time the largest crowd ever to watch a tennis match. It is estimated to have been also watched by an astounding 90 million people worldwide.[323] The match is frequently cited as accelerating worldwide interest in women's tennis and even 40 years later Billie Jean King reminded her fans that she knew that her win over the misogynistic Riggs would be a major step forward for women's tennis. She added that she had "also wanted the attention for … Title IX." The (anti-gender-discrimination) legislation, which had been passed just a year earlier, was straightforward and, as summarized by King, "its 37 words … basically say 'no sex discrimination',… (and) it guaranteed equal protection if you received federal funds – high school, colleges, universities … the first time a girl could receive an athletic scholarship."[324] But despite the motivations behind and implications of the match, it is best remembered for the cheering crowds, for Riggs' yellow jacket with the "Sugar Daddy" logo on the back, and for Billie Jean King's humorous presentation to Riggs of a squealing pig before the match.

"Saturday Night Massacre"

October 20, 1973. This was the phrase used to describe the historically unique events that occurred on this day when, in a clumsy panic, President Richard M. Nixon attempted to unilaterally order the firing of Archibald Cox, the Watergate Special Prosecutor. Nixon was first thwarted by Attorney General Elliot Richardson and then by Deputy Attorney General William Ruckelshaus. Both refused Nixon's order and resigned. The next-in-command, Solicitor General Robert Bork, finally agreed to implement the order and fired Cox. The "minute-by-minute events of the Saturday Night Massacre were covered live by stunned reporters on all major television networks."[325] After his firing, Cox correctly stated that "whether ours shall continue to be a government of laws and not of men is now for Congress and ultimately the American people"[326] to decide. Many Americans believed that Cox's question was answered nine months later when, on July 27, 1974, the House Judiciary Committee passed three Articles of Impeachment[327] which in turn led to Nixon's resignation a mere two weeks later.

"No Contest"
Spiro T. Agnew

October 1973. The plea of U.S. Vice President Spiro Agnew to federal income tax evasion charges. Additional bribery and extortion charges from his earlier tenure as the Governor of Maryland were dismissed concurrently therewith, but one of the conditions of the prosecutor's approval of his plea agreement was that Agnew would immediately resign his Vice Presidency. Upon sentencing, Agnew received three years' probation and was disbarred from the practice of law. Gerald Ford was appointed as the new Vice President, and, as noted below, a mere eight months later, Ford assumed the Presidency upon Nixon's resignation on August 8, 1974.

> *"Let us unite in committing the resources of this Nation*
> *to a major new endeavor, an endeavor that in this Bicentennial Era*
> *we can appropriately call 'Project Independence.'*
> *Let us set as our national goal, in the spirit of Apollo,*
> *with the determination of the Manhattan Project.*
> *That by the end for this decade …*
> *we shall be able to meet America's energy needs*
> *from America's own energy resources."*
>
> *…*
>
> *"The United States will not be dependent*
> *on any other country for the energy we need."*

November 7, 1973. President Richard M. Nixon, announcing Project Independence and proclaiming that through a national commitment to conservation and the development of alternative sources of energy, America would be energy-independent by 1980. Nixon noted America's extraordinarily high use of energy—6% of the world's population consuming 30% of the world's energy production, but this Project Independence announcement also came in the context of the 1973-1974 oil embargo.[328] The embargo had been announced a month earlier by members of the Organization of Petroleum Exporting Countries ("OPEC") in retaliation for the U.S.'s assistance to Israel during the Yom Kippur War and as a long-expected, push-back to the depletion of OPEC's resources by the world oil companies. While nothing close to Nixon's ambitious goal was ever reached (and, in fact, oil imports nearly doubled by the end of the decade), the initiative is often credited for a number of developments. Examples of such developments include the lowering of federal highway speeds to 55 miles per hour, the conversion of a number of power plants from coal to other energy sources, the re-allocation of some federal highway funds to urban mass transit projects, and, possibly most importantly, the accelerated approval and completion of the 800-mile Trans-Alaska Pipeline System between 1974 and 1977. During this late 1973 Presidential address, the clouds of Watergate were also present, with Nixon reiterating that he had no intention of quitting due to the "deplorable Watergate matter" and that he had "no intention whatever of walking away from the job I was elected to do." Despite this adamant assurance, Nixon did resign—also exactly nine months later.

> ### *"... (P)eople have got to know whether or not their President is a crook. Well, I am not a crook."*

November 17, 1973. President Richard M. Nixon's infamous denial of any involvement in the Watergate scandal that was encircling his Presidency. This statement, made 18 months after the Watergate break-in, was made by a frustrated, indeed furious, Nixon during an appearance before 400 Associated Press managing editors in Florida. Almost simultaneously, Nixon and his advisors were seeking to avoid compliance with the subpoena of 42 tapes of his conversations in the Oval Office of the White House. The tapes were eventually released, and just nine months after this "I am not a crook" statement, Nixon resigned the Presidency in disgrace.

> ### *"I am a Ford, not a Lincoln.*
> ### *My address will never be as eloquent as Mr. Lincoln's.*
> ### *But I will do my very best*
> ### *to equal his brevity and his plain speaking."*

December 6, 1973. Gerald Ford, upon being sworn in as Vice President after his appointment to replace Spiro Agnew, who resigned in October 1973.[329] Prior to the appointment, Ford had served in the House of Representatives for nearly 25 years. With his elevation to the Vice Presidency, Ford became the first person ever to be appointed under the provisions of the 25th Amendment that had just been adopted six years earlier in 1967.[330] A mere eight months later, Vice President Ford assumed the Presidency upon President Nixon's resignation on August 8, 1974. Despite the furor that arose over Ford's subsequent pardon of Nixon, President Ford was largely welcomed into the office. By broad consensus, it is now recognized that he served honorably and helped to restore a sense of honor and of dignity to the Office of Presidency. However, Ford lost the 1976 Presidential election to Jimmy Carter, and thus Gerald Ford to this date holds the dubious, or at least curious, honor of being the only person in American history to hold both the office of President and Vice President without ever having been elected to either office.

Year 1974

Seminal Books

Helter-Skelter: The True Story of the Manson Murders
by Vincent Bugliosi and Curt Gentry

This book was co-written by Vincent Bugliosi, who successfully prosecuted Charles Manson and four members of Manson's "Family" for the infamous 1969 Tate-LaBianca murders— "a series of brutal, seemingly random murders (that) captured the headlines across America."[331] The book traces with chilling precision the investigation, arrests, and successful prosecution of Manson and his followers. The murders and the bizarre details that surfaced at the trial revealed the dark side of the American counterculture of the 1960s. Some believe that Manson's actions and the highly publicized trial further contributed to the already growing rejection of the counterculture movement itself. No trial until the trial of O.J. Simpson nearly 20 years later —also in Los Angeles—riveted the country like the Manson trial. *Helter Skelter* sold over 7.0 million copies. It remains today the bestselling true crime book in history. The book's title derives from the apocalyptic race war envisioned in the twisted mind of Manson.[332]

Why Survive? Being Old in America[333]
by Robert Neil Butler

Many consider Robert Butler, through his life's work as a psychiatrist and as the result of his analysis and recommendations as set forth in this Pulitzer Prize-winning book, to be the founder of the field of geriatrics. For a multitude of reasons—some of them personal and resulting from his being raised by his grandparents—Butler devoted his life to uncovering and giving voice to the problems faced by older Americans. On the same day that Butler's book received the Pulitzer Prize for General Nonfiction, Butler started his career as the founding Director of the National Institute of Aging at the National Institute of Health. Especially because life expectancy of Americans increased by 30% in the 20th century alone and because of the number of Baby Boomers now reaching old age each month, the book's poignancy remains. However, Butler noted in 1988, 15 years after his book was first published, that "the portrait of old age in America circa 1975 … is unfortunately not so different from the one" today.[334] Nevertheless, the contributions of Butler and his book remain unaltered as well. Butler died at the age of 83. Almost as one may have expected, he worked until three days before his death from acute leukemia.[335]

The Glory and the Dream
A Narrative History of America 1932-1972
by William Manchester

Although several other of Manchester's books may be more famous (e.g. *The Death of a President* (1963), *American Caesar: Douglas MacArthur 1880-1964* (1978), and even *The Last Lion: Winston Spencer Churchill* (1983 and 1988)), this book, *The Glory and the Dream*, is offered as Manchester's seminal work. In the course of the nearly 1,400 pages of this *New York Times* Best Seller, Manchester encapsulates in narrative form the many aspects of American life during these four decades. His presentation of history was "not in black and white as so many histories are, concerned mostly with names, dates, and battles, but in full living Technicolor. A rainbow of information of what life was like."[336] Manchester's cogency and style of writing is rarely imitated by other historians. He had the unique ability to simultaneously focus not only upon that which happened but also upon why things mattered and how life was lived. In this manner, Manchester presents a brilliant admixture of both hard history and personal tales.

Author's Note:

If I were given the impossible challenge and opportunity to recommend only one book about American history, it would be this book—even though it was written nearly 40 years ago; even though it only traced American life from the beginning of the Great Depression to the fall of Nixon.

Pulitzer Prize for General Nonfiction

The Denial of Death
by Ernest Becker

Pulitzer Prize for History

The Americans: The Democratic Experience
by Daniel J. Boorstin

The New York Times Best Sellers List (Nonfiction) – Books with Most Weeks as No. 1 Best Seller

All the President's Men
by Carl Bernstein and Bob Woodward (20 weeks)

Plain Speaking: An Oral Biography of Harry S. Truman
by Merle Miller (12 weeks)

The New York Times Best Sellers List (Adult Fiction) – Book with Most Weeks as No. 1 Best Seller

Burr
by Gore Vidal (17 weeks)

Academy Awards Best Picture

Winner: *The Godfather - Part II*
Other Nominees: *Chinatown, The Conversation, Lenny, The Towering Inferno*

PrettyFamous' Best Movie of the Year

Chinatown

Best/Most Memorable Movie Lines of the Year

***"Course I'm respectable. I'm old.
Politicians, ugly buildings, and whores all get respectable
if they last long enough."***
John Huston in Roman Polanski's last U.S.-directed film, *Chinatown*, which also starred young Jack Nicholson and Faye Dunaway.

"How about some more beans, Mr. Taggert?"

...

"I'd say you'd had enough."
The question to and the response of the actor Slim Pickens in the famous "farting scene" in Mel Brooks' satirical western film, *Blazing Saddles*.

"Keep your friends close, but your enemies closer".

This line has been attributed to many writers, but it was here repeated in *The Godfather - Part II,* which like its predecessor, *The Godfather,* was directed by Francis Ford Coppola based upon Mario Puzo's book

1974 U.S. Population: 213,900,000

(Compared as a Percentage to the U.S. 1957 Population of 172,000,000: 124.4%)

Television Shows

Most Widely-Viewed Television Shows

Rank	Show Name	Years of Series (Excluding Reruns)	Show Type	Estimated Audience (In MMs)	Audience as Percentage of U.S. Population
1.	*All in the Family*	1971–1979	Comedy	20.7MM	9.7%
	Cast: Carroll O'Connor - Jean Stapleton - Sally Struthers - Rob Reiner				
2.	*Sanford and Son*	1972–1977	Comedy	20.3MM	9.5%
	Cast: Red Foxx - Demond Wilson				
3.	*Chico and The Man*	1974–1978	Comedy	19.5MM	9.1%
	Cast: Freddie Prinze - Jack Albertson				

Memorable Words from Speeches, Books, Writings, and Other Sources – 1974

"If fate had been looking for one of the powerhouses of Congress, it wouldn't have picked me"

February 6, 1974. The humble comment of Congressman Peter W. Rodino (D-NJ) as he began his able service as the Chairman of the House Judiciary Committee investigating the Watergate scandal.[337] At the time the hearings began, Rodino had been Chairman for only a few months, but over the course of the Committee's hearings he was widely praised for his insistence upon confidentiality, discipline, respect, decorum, and even bipartisanship. In July 1974, the Committee, on a bipartisan basis, approved three Articles of Impeachment against President Nixon. During this period, young Hillary Rodham (just a year out of Yale Law School where she had started dating Bill Clinton) served as a member of the impeachment inquiry staff, which advised the House Judiciary Committee with respect to impeachment procedures, historical grounds, and standards for impeachment.

"No, Mr. President, are you?"

March 19, 1974. Dan Rather, then CBS's White House Correspondent, in a brief, terse, and in the opinion of some disrespectful retort to President Richard Nixon's joking inquiry of Dan Rather as to whether Rather was "running for something." The exchange triggered both jeers and applause. After the retort, Rather asked a question that was seen as accusing Nixon of failing to cooperate with an empanelled grand jury and the House Judiciary Committee investigating Watergate-related matters. The exchange was, in and of itself, largely insignificant except as further evidence of the increasing degeneration of protocol and respect between the President and members of the press. The media's cynicism of many leaders and branches of government had begun during the Vietnam War era and continued as a result of the deliberate obfuscations made by many members of the White House staff in the context of Watergate. Dan Rather was frequently thereafter cited as an example of media bias itself, but he went on to become the news anchor of the *CBS Evening News*, a position in which he served from 1981 to 2005. He also appeared frequently on CBS' *60 Minutes*.

"…(P)robably the only laugh that man will ever get in his life is by stripping off and showing his shortcomings."

April 2, 1974. David Niven, the ever-suave and ever-unflappable British actor, speaking at the Academy Awards and upon seeing a naked man streak past him while flashing (among other things) a peace sign. The *Los Angeles Times* later wrote that the entire stunt, including the above quip, was staged, but this has never been proven. Streaking—the act of running naked through a public place or at a public event as a prank, dare, or act of protest—was nothing new to American society by 1974. The popularity of streaking may have peaked in the years 1973-1974, but it continues to this day, especially on or around college campuses. For example, there was a streaking event at the 1976 Summer Olympics, at the 1996 Wimbledon's singles tennis tournament, and even at the 2004 Super Bowl XXXVIII in

Houston, Texas—although in this last instance the streaker was dispatched with a $1,000 trespassing fine after a bone-crushing tackle by New England Patriots linebacker Matt Chatham.

> *"Earlier today, we heard from the beginning*
> *of the Preamble to the Constitution, …*
> *'We, the people.'*
> *It is a very eloquent beginning. But when the document*
> *was completed on the 17th of September 1787,*
> *I was not included in 'We, the people.'*
> *I felt somehow for many years that George Washington and*
> *Alexander Hamilton just left me out by mistake.*
> *But through the process of amendment,*
> *interpretation and court decision,*
> *I have finally been included in 'We, the people.'.*
> *Today, I am inquisitor. …*
> *My faith in the Constitution is whole, it is complete, it is total."*

July 25, 1974. Barbara Jordan (D-TX), speaking as a member of the House Judiciary Committee during the Watergate hearing. Citing James Madison and USSC Associate Justice Joseph Story, Rep. Jordan spoke eloquently about the structure of the Constitution, the balances of powers, the meaning of the phrase "high crimes and misdemeanors," and the permissible purposes of impeaching a public official. In 1972, Jordan became the first African American elected to Congress from Texas since Reconstruction, but she retired from the House in 1979 after just three terms in order to teach political ethics at The University of Texas. According to her students, she always kept a copy of the Constitution in her purse.[338]

> *Articles of Impeachment of Richard M. Nixon*
> *As Adopted by House Judiciary Committee*
> *Article 1*
> *"Richard M. Nixon, in violation of his constitutional oath*
> *…*

*has prevented, obstructed, and impeded
the administration of justice"*

...

*"(Nixon) engaged personally and through the use of close
subordinates and agents in a course of conduct or plan designed to*

...

obstruct the investigation (of the Watergate break-in);

...

*"to cover up ... and protect those responsible; and to conceal
the existence and scope of other unlawful covert activities."*

(Note: The House Judiciary Committee then set forth nine specific wrongdoings such as making false statements, withholding evidence, interfering with investigations, approving the surreptitious payment of money to witnesses for their silence, misusing the Central Intelligence Agency, leaking Department of Justice investigation information to prospective defendants, deceiving the American people, and endeavoring to cause prospective defendants to believe that they would receive favorable treatment in return for their silence or false testimony. Article 1 was adopted by a bipartisan vote of 27-11).

"Article 2.
*"... Richard M. Nixon, in violation of his constitutional oath ...
has repeatedly engaged in conduct violating
the constitutional rights of citizens (and)
impairing the due and proper administration of justice."*

(Note: The House Judiciary Committee then set forth five specific wrongdoings such as trying to obtain confidential information about political enemies from the Internal Revenue Service, misusing the Federal Bureau of Investigation by wiretapping individuals for reasons other than national security, and maintaining a secret investigative unit within the White House. Article 2 was adopted by a bipartisan vote 28-10).

"Article 3.
*"... Richard M. Nixon, in violation of his constitutional oath ...
has failed without lawful cause ... to produce papers ...*

> ***as directed by (multiple) duly authorized subpoenas***
> ***issued by the (House Judiciary Committee)."***

(Note: Art. 3 was adopted on a largely partisan basis by a vote of 21-17).
July 27, 1974. The above three Articles of Impeachment against President Richard Nixon were adopted by the House Judiciary Committee after eight months of hearings and investigations.

> ***"In the last few days ... it has become evident to me***
> ***that I no longer have a strong enough political base in the Congress***
> ***to justify continuing (my effort to complete***
> ***the term of office to which you elected me)."***
> ***(Therefore)***
> ***I shall resign the Presidency effective at noon tomorrow."***

August 8, 1974. President Richard M. Nixon in his resignation speech to the nation. Nixon, the only U.S. President ever to resign, referred to leaving office before the completion of his term as "abhorrent." Bafflingly concerned that some people would view this resignation as voluntary, he felt it necessary to remind the American people that he had "never been a quitter." However, he proclaimed that his resignation was necessary because "as President (he had to) put the interests of America first (and that) America needs a full-time President and a full-time Congress...." About a year earlier, in what is commonly referred to as Nixon's First Watergate Speech, he pointedly stated that "in any organization, the man at the top must bear the responsibility. That responsibility, therefore, belongs here, in this office. I accept it. And I pledge to you (the American people) tonight, ... that I will do everything in my power to ensure the guilty are brought to justice ....."[339] In the later trial of Presidential advisor H.R. "Bob" Haldeman, John Ehrlichman, and Attorney General John Mitchell, excerpts from the Nixon tapes were ordered released. On the tapes, Nixon is heard telling Haldeman "I don't give a sh*t what happens. I want you to stonewall it, let them plead the Fifth Amendment, cover up or anything else ... We're going to protect our people if we can." A mere four years later during an interview with David Frost, Nixon, in a twist of logic and law, stated that "oh, when the President does it, that means it is not illegal." Until his death two decades later in 1994, Nixon continued to provide comment and counsel about national policy—and especially about foreign policy matters. But he was never again trusted by many Americans, and he was passionately disliked and disregarded by many others. Truman's early characterization of Nixon as a "shifty-eyed goddamn liar" who could "talk out of both sides of his mouth at the same time and (be) lying out of both sides" had been partly dismissed as the rage of partisanship, but the sting of highly respected Barry Goldwater's later assessment of Nixon as "the most dishonest individual I have ever met in my life" was more politically devastating.[340] By the time the Watergate scandal came to a close, 48 officials from the Nixon administration had pled guilty or were convicted. Many of them received prison sentences. Among those who were so convicted or pled guilty were the Attorney General of the United States John Mitchell (who served 19 months in prison), three other cabinet members, and many of Nixon's most senior staff. [341]

> *"…(O)ur long national nightmare is over.*
> *Our constitution works.*
> *Our great republic is a government of law and not of men.*
> *Here, the people rule.*
> *But there is a higher power, by whatever name we honor Him,*
> *who ordains not only righteousness but love,*
> *not only justice, but mercy…"*
>
> *…*
>
> *"Let us restore the golden rule to our political process and*
> *let brotherly love purge our hearts of suspicion and hate."*

August 9, 1974. President Gerald Ford, in his Address to the Nation upon his accession to power as the country's first unelected President and the first President to assume office under the 25th Amendment. Nixon's departure and Ford's accession were widely welcomed by Americans after their prolonged endurance of the disgraces, insults and literal breadth of Nixon's Watergate scandal. Yet America's honeymoon with its new gregarious and decent President Ford abruptly ended for many Americans when he granted Nixon an unconditional pardon just one month later.[342] Many Americans at the time suspected this as a preplanned, *quid pro quo* arrangement between Nixon and Ford, and many believe it was this singular act which cost Ford the 1976 presidential election. Nevertheless, there was also a wide consensus, which has grown over the years, that such pardon was necessary in order to start closing the subject of Watergate so that the country, in turn, could start addressing other national issues. Similarly, the essential decency and unassuming modesty of Ford was needed. As was noted in one article on this date, with Ford "there is no whiff of charisma."[343] Although the statement is harsh and bordering on condescending, maybe this was exactly the type of President who was long overdue after the strong and assertive personalities of both Johnson and Nixon.

> ### *"Envy is the central fact of American life."*
>
> . . .
>
> ### *"The United States was founded by the brightest people in the country —and we haven't seen them since."*

Fall 1974. These are two statements by writer and universal critic Gore Vidal. The first statement was made during an interview of Vidal by fellow writer Gerald Clarke—author of *Capote* and a senior writer for many years at *Time* magazine."[344] The second statement was written by Vidal, in his usual acerbic style of commentary, in an essay titled *State of the Union*.[345] Vidal, along with many others such as William F. Buckley, Eric Severeid, George Kennan, Milton Friedman, Henry Kissinger, George Schultz, Francis Fukuyama, George Stigler, Paul Krugman, Lawrence Summers, and Robert Reich—the list is endless—, was one of the many of public intellectuals and commentators who regularly spoke and wrote about American society. Some of these individuals remained primarily in the world of academia. More commonly, however, they entered and left public life from time to time; tracking their political persuasions. Their perspectives and conclusions were radically different, but their commonality lies in their sometimes-adamant sense of their own correctness and, more importantly in the age of Modern America, their ready access to radio, television, or the press. As a group, they also have come to symbolize and constitute the new definition of "citizen politician." Due especially to the absence of term limits and the powerful tool—no, weapon—of gerrymandering, elected politicians in America are, commonly and dangerously, career politicians. The role of the "citizen politician" is now more often relegated to the advisors who enter and leave the political system from the ranks of academia, business, and occasionally the retired military.

> *"I have promised to uphold the Constitution,*
> *to do what is right as God gives me to see the right,*
> *and to do the very best I can for America."*
>
> *...*
>
> *"Theirs (i.e. the Nixon family) is an American tragedy*
> *in which we have all played a part.*
> *It could go on and on and on, or someone must write the end to it.*
> *I have concluded that only I can do that, and if I can I must."*
>
> *...*
>
> *"There are no historic or legal precedents*
> *to which I can turn in this matter."*
>
> *...*
>
> *"My conscience tells me it is my duty, not merely to proclaim*
> *domestic tranquility but to use every means I have to ensure it".*
>
> *...*
>
> *"Now therefore, I, Gerald R. Ford, President of the United States,*
> *pursuant to the pardon power conferred upon me*
> *by ... the Constitution,*
> *... grant a full, free, and absolute pardon unto Richard Nixon*
> *for all offenses against the United States*
> *which he ... has committed or may have committed*
> *... from January 20, 1969, through August 9, 1974."*

September 4, 1974. President Gerald Ford, in his televised speech to the American people announcing his granting of a full pardon to Richard Nixon, his predecessor. The decision and speech came just a month after Ford succeeded Nixon. The pardon instantly created a firestorm of anger and resentment among large segments of the Americans public, who felt strongly that Nixon should be prosecuted and could not be held "above the law." While seeking an "end" to Watergate was clearly one of the primary objectives of Ford, the pardon was also based upon Ford's conclusion that it was unlikely that Nixon could soon—or ever—obtain a "fair trial" because of the "bitter controversy and divisive national debate" that had encircled the Watergate scandal. As noted above, most Americans now believe upon objective reflection that Ford made the correct decision in granting this pardon. Nevertheless, the pardon was costly to Ford. It is commonly cited as one of the primary reasons Ford lost the presidential election to Jimmy Carter two years later.

> *"Float like a butterfly and sting like a bee.*
> *His hands can't hit what his eyes can't see.*
> *Now you see me, now you don't.*
> *George thinks he will, but I know he won't."*

October 29, 1974. Muhammad Ali's taunting poetics and bravado shortly before his "Rumble in the Jungle" fight with the then-undefeated World Heavyweight Champion and 1968 Olympic Gold Medalist George Foreman in Zaire (now the Democratic Republic of the Congo). Ali won by a knockout in the eighth round and continued his re-ascent as "The Greatest" after having been suspended for nearly four years as a result of his 1967 refusal to submit to the draft.[346] Foreman and Ali became friends thereafter. In a touching moment many years later, it was Foreman who helped Ali, now suffering and disabled by Parkinson's disease, walk onto the stage of the 1996 Oscar Awards Ceremony to be among those receiving the Oscar for *When We Were Kings*, a documentary of their 1974 Rumble in the Jungle.

WIN – Whip Inflation Now

October 1974. The well-meaning, but embarrassingly simplistic, government-sponsored program introduced by President Gerald Ford. WIN was offered as a way to spur grassroots support for combating inflation, curbing private spending, and conserving energy. The program accompanied the formation of the National Commission on Inflation and included a series of voluntary and mandatory measures that sought to encourage personal savings and appropriate spending habits. Supporters were encouraged to wear a "WIN" button. Such buttons could be obtained free by filling out a "WIN" form and mailing it to the President. The form stated that the sender would "enlist as an inflation fighter and energy saver for the duration (of the anti-inflation campaign)" and would "do the very best I can for America." The WIN program was immediately ridiculed. In response, some cynics chose to wear "WIN" buttons upside down so that they read "NIM"—for "No Immediate Miracles," "Nonstop Inflation Merry-go-round," or—best yet— "Need Immediate Money."

Year 1975

<u>Pulitzer Prize for Fiction</u>

The Killer Angels
by Michael Shaara

<u>Pulitzer Prize for General Nonfiction</u>

Pilgrim at Tinker Creek
by Annie Dillard

<u>Pulitzer Prize for History</u>

Jefferson and His Time
by Dumas Malone

**<u>*The New York Times* Best Sellers List (Nonfiction) –
Books with Most Weeks as No. 1 Best Seller</u>**

The Bermuda Triangle
by Charles Berlitz (18 weeks)

Breach of Faith: The Fall of Richard Nixon
by Theodore H. White (12 weeks) (Tie)

*Sylvia Porter's Money Book:
How to Earn It, Spend It, Save It, Invest It, Borrow It,
and Use It to Better Your Life*
by Sylvia Porter (12 weeks) (Tie)

**<u>*The New York Times* Best Sellers List (Adult Fiction) –
Book with Most Weeks as No. 1 Best Seller</u>**

Centennial
by James Michener (16 weeks)

<u>Academy Awards Best Picture</u>

Winner: *One Flew Over the Cuckoo's Nest*
Other Nominees: *Barry Lyndon, Dog Day Afternoon, Jaws, Nashville*

***PrettyFamous'* Best Movie of the Year**

Monty Python and the Holy Grail

<u>Best/Most Memorable Movie Lines of the Year</u>

"Attica! Attica! Attica!

The cries of a bank robber portrayed by Al Pacino in *Dog Day Afternoon,* as he frantically tries to stir the assembled crowd outside the bank he had just tried to rob. The cries of "Attica" refer to the real-life prison riot that occurred at New York's Attica State Prison four years earlier.[347]

"…(H)uman beings are divided into mind and body.
The mind embraces all the nobler aspirations,
like poetry and philosophy, but the body has all the fun"

Woody Allen in *Love and Death,* during one of his mock-serious philosophical debates with his cohort, Diane Keaton. As with nearly all Woody Allen films, Allen himself also wrote and directed the film.

"I don't want to talk to you no more,
you empty-headed animal food trough wiper!
I fart in your general direction.
Your mother was a hamster and your father smelt of elderberries."

John Cleese presenting a new form of absurdist comedy in *Monty Python and the Holy Grail.* In later years, the British slapstick comedy has become for many a cult classic.

"They … was givin' me ten thousand watts a day,
you know, and I'm hot to trot.
The next woman takes me out is gonna light up
like a pinball machine, and pay off in silver dollars."

Jack Nicholson alluding to the shock treatments his character received while being held in a mental ward in the hysterical, but at times dark, comedy *One Flew Over the Cuckoo's Nest.* This Milos Forman film was based upon Ken Kesey's 1962 novel of the same name.

"You're going to need a bigger boat."

Roy Scheider's understated admission of terror after his first sighting of the great white shark in *Jaws.* The film was directed by young Steven Spielberg and was based upon Peter Benchley's book.

<u>1975 U.S. Population: 216,000,000</u>

(Compared as a Percentage to the U.S. 1957 Population of 172,000,000: 125.6%)

<u>Television Shows</u>

Most Widely-Viewed Television Shows

Rank	Show Name	Years of Series (Excluding Reruns)	Show Type	Estimated Audience (In MMs)	Audience as Percentage of U.S. Population
1.	*All in the Family*	1971–1979	Comedy	20.9MM	9.7%
	Cast: Carroll O'Connor - Jean Stapleton - Sally Struthers - Rob Reiner				
2.	*Rich Man, Poor Man*	1975	Drama - Mini-Series	19.5MM	9.0%
	Cast: Peter Strauss - Nick Nolte - Susan Blakely				
3.	**Laverne & Shirley**	1976–1983	Comedy	19.1MM	8.8%
	Cast: Penny Marshall - Cindy Williams				

Widely-Viewed or Critically-Acclaimed New Television Show(s)

Saturday Night Live (1975 –) –

Late Night Live TV Sketch-Comedy Show

Dan Akroyd - John Belushi - Chevy Chase - Chris Farley -

Adam Sandler - Tina Fey - Amy Poehler

(No. 10 Top TV Shows of All Time – *TV Guide*)

Last Season Television Show(s)

Gunsmoke (1955–1975) —Western

James Arness - Amanda Blake - Dennis Weaver

<u>Major Commercial Advertising Campaigns and Slogans</u>

"Don't leave home without it"

American Express

"The ultimate driving machine"
BMW

Memorable Words from Speeches, Books, Writings, and Other Sources – 1975

"Abolished"

January 14, 1975. After nearly 40 years, the (infamous) House Committee on Un-American Activities ("HUAC") was abolished on this date by the House of Representatives. HUAC was originally formed as an investigative committee in 1938 for the purpose of uncovering communist and other subversives who had allegedly infiltrated the American government and society. Its primary focus was changed from time to time, and over the course of its existence HUAC investigated private citizens, public employees, and all allegedly subservice activities deemed harmful to the Unites States. HUAC rose to particular prominence in 1947 when it held hearings about President Truman's Federal Employee Loyalty Program and later in the context of its investigations of the alleged communist infiltration of the American film industry. HUAC hearings were frequently and rightly criticized by civil rights activists for the Committee's abuses resulting from its far-ranging investigations of many American's freedoms of belief and association.[348] HUAC's investigations and hearings are often associated with the actions and allegations of Senator McCarthy, however he had no direct involvement with HUAC. In 1969, the name of the Committee was changed to the House Committee on Internal Security, and its supposed focus was re-directed at matters of domestic security, but the successor committee was never able to shake the infamy of HUAC's blacklisting and other abuses especially during the McCarthy era of the mid-1950s.

"Guilty"
John Mitchell, Attorney General (Perjury)
H.R. "Bob" Haldeman, White House Chief of Staff
(Conspiracy, Obstruction of Justice, and Perjury)

John Ehrlichman, White House Counsel
(Conspiracy, Obstruction of Justice, and Perjury)
John Dean, White House Counsel (Obstruction of Justice)
Dwight Chapin, Secretary to the President (Perjury)
Charles Colson, Special Counsel to the President for Public Liaison
(Obstruction of Justice)
Egil Krogh, Undersecretary of Transportation (Conspiracy)
And At Least 41 Others

February 21, 1975. This date, the date upon which Attorney General John Mitchell was convicted for his involvement in the Watergate scandal, is used for all of the above-listed defendants, who were convicted of Watergate-related crimes. As a result of the June 17, 1972 break-in to the offices of Democratic National Committee and the ensuing cover-up and related matters, 69 government officials were charged; 48 of them eventually pled guilty or were convicted. The televised hearings of the House Judiciary Committee and the Senate Watergate Committee riveted the attention of the country. Each day more discoveries were made. Each day more dots were connected. The key investigators and targets—such as House Judiciary Committee Chairman Peter Rodino and Senate Watergate Committee Chairman Sam Ervin, H.R. Hunt and G. Gordon Liddy, the young *Washington Post* reporters Bob Woodward and Carl Bernstein, Deep Throat, Judge John J. Sirica, and Special Prosecutor Archibald Cox—all became household names. The Watergate Scandal became the focus of the nation for many months, and President Richard Nixon himself became the first U.S. President in history to resign. Especially since the Watergate scandal coincided so closely with the closing of the Vietnam Era, the nation and the press both embraced—and have now long maintained—a heightened degree of political cynicism. The hearings, prosecutions and pleas attendant to the Watergate scandal were unique. The nation's attention would not be similarly drawn again until arguably the murder trial of O. J. Simpson, nearly 20 years later.

"Today, America can regain the sense of pride
that existed before Vietnam.

> ***But it cannot be achieved by refighting a war that is finished
> as far as America is concerned."***
>
> ***...***
>
> ***"The time has come to look forward,
> ... to unify, to bind up the Nation's wounds,
> and to restore its health and its optimistic self-confidence."***

April 23, 1975. President Gerald Ford, speaking at Tulane University. A week after this speech, on April 30, 1975, the last ten American Marines were lifted off the roof of the U.S. Embassy in Saigon—thereby finally and forever concluding the U.S.'s presence in Vietnam. Ford's words, while understandable, were blind in their optimism. Most Americans had not—and many still have not—fully "bound up the ... wounds " caused by Vietnam. The stain of Vietnam has unalterably colored much of America's more recent history. Nearly 15 years after these comments by President Ford, the newly elected President George H.W. Bush, noted in his 1990 Presidential Inaugural Address that a "certain divisiveness" had existed since Vietnam and that "the war cleaves us still."

The Fall of Saigon

April 30, 1975. There is no easy definition of when the Vietnam War really ended. For the families of those who died, the war continues each day. For the nation, finding such a date is also hard—Nixon's 1969 announcement of the first withdrawal of troops, the signing of the Paris Peace accords, or this date, April 28, 1975. The date here used is because it was the day of the Fall of Saigon. On this day, the last Americans (excepting America's POWs and MIAs) and South Vietnamese were helicoptered out of Saigon, soon to be re-named Ho Chi Minh City. During the course of Operation Frequent Wind, "a fleet of 81 helicopters shuttled 2,312 Americans and 6,422 non-Americans to offshore carriers" ... some of them grabbing hands and clinging onto the helicopters as they lifted off the roof of the U.S. Embassy. Within hours of this final departure by the U.S., the North Vietnamese swarmed into Saigon. By 11:00 a.m. the red and blue Viet Cong flag flew over the city.[349] It was an ignominious ending to the Vietnam War. But at least it was, for some, an ending.

> *"It was the longest war in America's history,*
> *in the end the most unpopular war,*
> *the first modern war America lost.*
> *Vietnam was a watershed.*
> *It ended the liberal consensus that America had a duty to fight*
> *everywhere abroad for freedom.*
> *It destroyed the illusion of American omnipotence.*
> *It demoralized the armed forces.*
> *It polarized the country as nothing had since the Civil War. ...*
> *It diverted billions of dollars from education, health and welfare*
> *(and) left a legacy of inflation ...*
> *And it shattered everyone's faith in the honesty*
> *and credibility of government,*
> *since every administration involved*
> *systematically deceived the people."*

April 30, 1975. The above brilliantly articulate passage is from Harold Evans' book *The American Century*.[350] It identifies many aspects of the pervasive and complicated impact of the Vietnam War upon American society. These words were written many years later, but they are included here on this date because it was the final closing date of the Vietnam War. What arguably could be added to this broad summation is that the Vietnam War contributed heavily to the polarizing and politicizing of everything in America—including the press and the media. The passion of one's beliefs about the Vietnam War were oftentimes seen as wholly defining of one's life view; as somehow wholly reflective of one's probable beliefs about all other matters of the day. Worse than that, the scars from the Vietnam War were deep. The pain was severe. The memories lasted. Obviously, the scars, pain, and memories of World War II and the Korean War were likewise deep, but in the case of Vietnam there was never a unifying end. There was never a surrender by a unifying foe. There was never a celebration and closing as the troops came home. Thus, though rarely discussed now, the divisiveness of the Vietnam War (and, for some, the guilt, sadness, and sense of loss of the war) has for many Americans continued. Unabated.

"Last Seen"
Jimmy Hoffa

July 30, 1975. Jimmy Hoffa, the former President of the Teamsters (1958-1971), disappeared on this date. At the time, he had been last seen outside a restaurant in suburban Detroit, Michigan. It is believed that he was meeting mobsters Anthony Giacalone and Anthony Provenzano at the restaurant. It is also believed that at the time of his disappearance, he was in a union power struggle and was trying to unseat the Teamsters' then-President Frank Fitzsimmons, a former protégé of Hoffa. Hoffa's body has never been found, although tips and claims have been made and diggings have occurred almost routinely in the ensuing decades. As a result of his disappearance without a trace, "Where's Jimmy Hoffa?" joined "What happened to D.B. Cooper?" as the crime questions of the 1970s. In a twist of curious fate, it is both strange and fitting that Jimmy Hoffa's middle name was "Riddle."

"The Helsinki (Accords) involve political and moral commitments
aimed at lessening tension and
opening further lines of communication
between the peoples of East and West."

...

"History will judge this conference not by what we say here today
but by what we do tomorrow—
not by the promises we make but by the promises we keep"

August 1, 1975. President Gerald Ford, upon his signing of the ominously titled Helsinki Final Act, which came to be more commonly known as the Helsinki Accords.[351] The Helsinki Accords were signed by all European nations (excepting Albania), the U.S., and Canada. They were intended to address a number of post-World War II issues and were hoped to further "détente" —the lessening of tensions between the U.S. and the Soviet Union. Although their direct impacts are difficult to track, many commentators conclude that especially the provisions involving the recognition of human rights emboldened dissenters in the Soviet Union and helped served as a basis for Mikhail Gorbachev's policy of closer and friendlier relations with the U.S. in the 1980s. It is certainly impossible to say that the Accords led to the collapse of the Soviet Union in the late 1980s, but they may have contributed to, at least, internal dissension within the Soviet Union's that, in turn, led to the final dissolution of the Soviet Union and the freeing of Eastern European nations.

"A government big enough to give you everything you want,
is a government big enough to take from you everything you have."

...

"Today's mounting danger is from mass government."

...

"Never forget that in America our sovereign is the citizen ...
The state is a servant."

September 13, 1975. President Gerald Ford, speaking at a Southern Methodist Convocation on this date and echoing the "smaller, more limited government" theme that was articulated by more and more members of the Republican Party in the early and mid-1970s. Ford reiterated variations of these statements repeatedly and as early as his address to a Joint Session of Congress in mid-1974.[352] The statements are included here because they collectively reflect one of his party's dominant themes during the course of his Presidential bid in 1976 and Ronald Reagan's Presidential bid and election in 1980. What may be most striking is the speed with which this demand for a smaller government arose—less than a decade after the enactment the President Lyndon Johnson's Great Society legislation.

"I want him, boss."

October 1, 1975. Joe Frazier's yelling plea to his trainer, Eddie Futch, as Futch threw in the towel at the end of the 14th Round of the Joe Frazier—Muhammad Ali "Thrilla in Manila" fight. Futch tried to console Frazier by assuring him that "no one will ever forget what you did her today." Even Muhammad Ali later admitted that the fight was "the closest thing to dying I know of." [353]

Year 1976

Pulitzer Prize for Fiction

Humboldt's Gift
by Saul Bellow

Pulitzer Prize for General Nonfiction

Why Survive? Being Old in America
by Robert Neil Butler

Pulitzer Prize for History

Lamy of Santa Fe
by Paul Horgan

The New York Times Best Sellers List (Nonfiction) – Books with Most Weeks as No. 1 Best Seller

The Final Days
by Bob Woodward and Carl Bernstein (18 weeks)

Passages: Predictable Crises of Adult Life
by Gail Sheehy (14 weeks)

The New York Times Best Sellers List (Adult Fiction) – Book with Most Weeks as No. 1 Best Seller

Trinity
by Leon Uris (22 weeks)

Academy Awards Best Picture

Winner: *Rocky*
Other Nominees: *All the President's Men,*
Bound for Glory, Network, Taxi Driver

PrettyFamous' **Best Movie of the Year**

Taxi Driver

Best/Most Memorable Movie Lines of the Year

"Follow the money ... Just follow the money."

The whispered advice given by the character "Deep Throat" to newsman Robert Redford, portraying *Washington Post* reporter Bob Woodward in the movie *All the President's Men.* The movie is based upon the real-life investigative actions of Woodward and his fellow reporter, Carl Bernstein, which a few years earlier had helped bring down the Presidency of Richard Nixon.

"Things have got to change. But first, you've gotta get mad!"

...

"You've got to say
'I'm mad as hell, and I'm not going to take it anymore'."

Peter Finch's portrayal of the outraged news reporter, Howard Beale, in Sidney Lumet's *Network,* a satirical, dark comedy about a fictional television network

"I'm not sure she's capable of any real feelings.
She's television generation.
She learned life from Bugs Bunny.
The only reality she knows comes to her from over the TV set."

Peter Finch in his role as Howard Beale describing a character portrayed by Faye Dunaway in *Network.*

"Is it safe?"

The simple, but terrifying, question repeatedly asked of Dustin Hoffman by a sadistic, former Nazi chillingly portrayed by Laurence Olivier in John Schlesinger's classis suspense thriller, *Marathon Man.*

"Yo, Adrian."

Sylvester Stallone's frequently uttered line calling out the name of his girlfriend, Adrian, while in his role as the underdog fighter, Rocky Balboa, in John Avildsen's movie, *Rocky.* Stallone, who also wrote the *Rocky* story went on to portray Balboa in the next four *Rocky*-franchise films as well.

"You talkin' to me?"

Robert de Niro's famous ad-libbed line as the scary, out-of-control lead character in Martin Scorsese's psychological thriller *Taxi Driver,* which also starred Jodie Foster and Harvey Keitel.

<u>1976 U.S. Population: 218,000,000</u>

(Compared as a Percentage to the U.S. 1957 Population of 172,000,000: 126.7%)

<u>Television Shows</u>

Most Widely-Viewed Television Shows

Rank	Show Name	Years of Series (Excluding Reruns)	Show Type	Estimated Audience (In MMs)	Audience as Percentage of U.S. Population
1.	*Happy Days*	1974–1984	Comedy	22.4MM	10.3%
	Cast:	Henry Winkler - Ron Howard			
2.	*Laverne & Shirley*	1976–1983	Comedy	19.1MM	8.8%
	Cast:	Penny Marshall - Cindy Williams			
3.	*ABC Monday Night Movie*	1966–1998	Various	18.5MM	8.5%

Widely-Viewed or Critically-Acclaimed New Television Show(s)

Charley's Angels (1976–1981)

Kate Jackson – Farrah Fawcett – Jaclyn Smith – David Doyle

(Later seasons – Cheryl Ladd – Shelley Hack – Tanya Roberts)

<u>Major Commercial Advertising Campaigns and Slogans</u>

"The Citi never sleeps"
Citibank

<u>Memorable Words from Speeches, Books, Writings, and Other Sources - 1976</u>

Presidential Campaign Themes, Slogans and Results
(Both Official and Unofficial)

(Only Major Presidential Party Nominees and Candidates Listed)

Jimmy Carter (and Walter Mondale)

A Leader, For a Change   Challenging Leadership for Challenging Times

Get America Moving Again   I'm Jimmy Carter and I'm Running for President

*J.C. Can Save America   Not Just Peanuts**
　　　 * Republican Party Response Slogan: *Don't Settle for Peanuts.*

Gerald Ford (and Robert Dole)

Experience Counts　　　　　　　　　*He's Making Us Proud Again*
I'm a Ford, Not a Lincoln　　　　　*I'm Voting for Betty's Husband*
Let's Make America Great Again　　*Look at the Record – Ford-Dole*
　　　　　　　The Time Is Now

Election Results:

Party	Nominees		Electoral Vote	Popular Vote
	Presidential	Vice-Presidential		
Democratic	J. Carter	W. Mondale	297 55.2%	40.8MM 50.1%
Republican	G. R. Ford	R. Dole	240 48.0%	39.1MM 48.0%

"The Right of Privacy and The Right to Die"

· · ·

"(There is) no compelling interest of the state (to) compel Karen to endure the unendurable"

March 31, 1976. The conclusion of the New Jersey Supreme Court in authorizing the parents of Karen Ann Quinlan to disconnect Ms. Quinlan's ventilator after she had fallen into a persistent vegetative state nearly a year earlier. The Quinlan case raised a horrific array of issues of moral theology, bioethics, and even legal guardianship and civil rights. It had been nearly 20 years since Pope Pius XII implied that there may be a "right to die" when he pronounced that "there is no moral requirement for doctors ... (to) provide 'extraordinary medical treatment' in the care and treatment of those who are approaching death,"[354] but here a U.S. judicial court, the New Jersey Supreme Court, for the first time determined in this case of first impression that based upon one's right to privacy, a person holds an associated "right to die." To the dismay of her loved ones, Ms. Quinlan continued to breathe on her own even after the removal of her breathing ventilator. In that state of being, she never regained consciousness and was thereafter fed by artificial nutrition. She lived for nearly another decade until she died in June 1985 from respiratory failure. Within the next few years after this 1976 case of Ms. Quinlan, 18 states enacted right to die legislation, but right to die issues continued to be hotly debated. From time to time thereafter, such issues would again arise in the context of national debate. One example is the case of Terri Schiavo nearly 30 years later in 2005. In this case, doctors finally unplugged Ms. Schiavo's feeding tube over the passionate objections of some social and religious leaders and despite the arguably intrusive and insensitive governmental intervention through the enactment of emergency congressional legislation.

"I can't type. I can't file, I can't even answer the phone."

May 23, 1976. The words of 33-year-old Elizabeth Ray in response to a reporter's question about what services she provided to her "employer," Rep. Wayne L. Hays (D-OH), the then-powerful chairman of the House Administration Committee. Hays had been in the House of Representatives since 1948, and by 1976 was one of the most powerful Congressman in the House of Representatives. However, neither this tenure nor his chairmanship could protect the 64-year-old Congressman from the scandal of having Ms. Ray on his payroll for what appeared to be the sole purpose of providing sexual relations. After his initial denials, he soon admitted the arrangement, and within about three months resigned from the House rather than face an Ethics Committee investigation. Ray's statement and this scandal are here included because they exemplify what seems to be a too-frequent pattern of public official misbehavior. This pattern started to become more recognizable, or possibly just more frequently reported by the press, after the Watergate scandal. Even this Wayne Hays scandal followed on the heels of the pathetic absurdity of the November 1974 scandal involving Wilbur Mills (D-AR). At the time, Mills was the powerful Chairman of the House Ways and Means Committee, and he had even sought the presidential nomination for a brief period in 1972. However, in 1974, it was revealed that Mills had an ongoing affair with the soon-to-be infamous Annabelle Battistella, better known by her stripper stage name of Fanny Fox. These two events—Wilber Mills and Wayne Hays—like the many that followed over the ensuing years, helped reinforce the new cynicism and disillusionment (bordering sometimes on contempt) held by both the public and members of the press for both politicians and political office.

"(The) common wisdom of the day pictures Americans as a people sunk in malaise (in which) they see themselves

as a nation born perfect and aspiring to progress ...
a nation haunted by a dream of excellence"

July 4, 1976. Seven writers of *Newsweek* writing in the magazine's Special Bicentennial Edition. While most Americans attribute the description of America's "malaise" to President Jimmy Carter from a speech he gave about a year later,[355] the term was first used here in 1976. It was used to describe what for many American's was the awkward, almost ill-timed, American Bicentennial. Well-deserved and honorable celebrations and parades were held in recognition of the nation's achievements and greatness, but they were held amidst the fresh memories of the disillusioning events of recent years: Vietnam, the hostile debates about Civil Rights, the protests and riots of the 1960s, the lingering stench of Watergate, the decline on civility, and the loss of trust in authority, and – although not referenced in this article - the newly encrusted cynicism of the American press itself. It was in these years—the mid-1970s—that, intentionally or otherwise, some Americans started viewing overt expressions of patriotism and displays of the American flag as almost partisan acts. Some Americans felt—and continue to do so—that the Republican party laid almost peculiar claim to "law and order." Then to national defense. And then to the flag and all overt displays of "patriotism" itself. Such perceptions have arguably only increased with the heightened rise of both ideology and anger as component parts of the American political system.

"I will never lie to you."

July 12,1976. The excerpted words of Jimmy Carter's repeated assurance to the American people which he made during the course of his campaign for the presidency in the summer of 1976. An adaptation of these words served as the title to Robert W. Taylor's book entitled *"I'll Never Lie to You" – Jimmy Carter in His Own Words,"* which was released on this date. The campaign phrase and pledge was first made by Carter in early 1975 while campaigning in Iowa. Carter's campaign noticed how the "pledge of honesty resonated with the small audience," and the pledge of honesty eventually became one of Carter's dominant campaign themes. Throughout the campaign, Carter was one of the first candidates in modern times to run as an outsider – "he was not Nixon. He was not a lawyer. He had never held office in Washington … He would tell the truth—always."[356]

"(The American people) deserve and …
want more than a recital of problems.
We are a people in a quandary about the present.
We are a people in search of our future.
We are a people in search of a national community."

. . .

"This is the question which must be answered in 1976:
Are we to be one people bound together by common spirit,
sharing in a common endeavor;
or will we be a divided nation?
For all its uncertainty, we cannot flee the future …
(and)
There is no executive order; there is no law that can require
the American people to form a national community.
This we must do as individuals …."

July 12, 1976. Barbara Jordan (D-TX), from her brilliant and widely noted keynote address at the Democratic National Convention delivered on this date. In her address, Jordan spoke articulately about the need for a national community and the critical role each American has in achieving such a community. After the acrimonious, highly partisan decades of the 1990s and the early 21st century, these remarks seem distant. They seem almost quaint—maybe to some, even naïve. However, in 1976, the wisdom of her words was recognized. Those words resonated with many Americans, even at the moment when voters chose between two very different, but both honorable, men, Gerald Ford and Jimmy Carter.

"I believe the Republican Party has a platform
that is a banner of bold, unmistakable colors,
with no pastel shades."

August 19, 1976. Ronald Reagan, during his well-received, impromptu concession speech, delivered at the Republican National Convention in

Kansas City, Missouri. Reagan delivered the speech shortly after losing the Republican Presidential nomination to Gerald Ford. Several months later, Ford lost the presidential election to Jimmy Carter. Ford's loss to Carter was seen by many Republicans as confirmation that even in 1976 Reagan would have been the better candidate to articulate the Republicans' perceived need to reject liberalism and to lead the ascendant conservatism in America. The growing rejection of liberalism in the mid- and late-1970s encompassed far more than Reagan's simplified "the-government-is-not-the-solution-but-the-problem" theme. In response to growing concerns about the "fraud, waste, and abuse" within the federal government, many Americans tried to elevate the roles of state and local government. Others turned to grassroots political and social organizations and community action programs. In addition, there was a rise of various "direct government" actions, such as public initiatives and referenda. One dominant example is the 1978 passage of California's Proposition 13, which radically altered—indeed, radically limited—the power of government to raise money through property taxation reassessments. These changes in the mechanics of democracy coincided with the ascendancy of political conservatism and free-market economics. Doubting the wisdom, efficiency, or even constitutional right of experts and bureaucrats to address national problems, conservative economics spurned most governmental supervision and regulation. Instead, faith was placed in the unfettered and non-interfered-with growth of industry as the best distributor and arbiter of income, wealth and long-term public welfare. Lastly, there was the parallel ascendancy of the religious right and the drumbeat assertions of America's "exceptionalism." There was an increased politicalization of many aspects of American life—from education to right-to-life; from sexual preference and activity to whom one may marry; from television programming to the banning of books in public and school libraries. Most significant and worst of all was the politicization of religion itself through the burgeoning Christian media and through the efforts of increasingly powerful religious leaders such as Jerry Falwell, Pat Robertson, James Robison, and Jim Bakker. The very words "family values" and "traditional beliefs" were politicized. The fact that the Republican Party platform had, as Reagan said, "no pastel shades" offered a certain simplifying clarity in selecting one's political affiliation—but it did so at a high price. The price of such clarity was a decimation of any meaningful concept of national community (outside the context of national security) and the over-simplification of many of the challenges facing America. However, what may be most surprising about the timing of this conservative ascendancy and this rejection of the Great Society and the liberalism of the Sixties was the fact that the role and capacity of government were challenged so soon. As of the mid-1970s, only a decade had passed since the enactment of the Great Society legislation. Arguably, the issues should not have centered upon the role of government, but merely upon the capacity of government to take on too many disparate challenges at once.

> ***"I do not favor a blanket amnesty,***
> ***but for those who violated Selected Service Laws,***
> ***I intend to grant a blank pardon"***
> **Democratic Presidential Nominee Jimmy Carter**
>
> **. . .**
>
> ***"Let there be no confusion as to President Ford's position . . .***
> ***It is unequivocal, and applies equally***
> ***to draft evaders and deserters,***
> ***no blanket pardon, no blanket amnesty, no blanket clemency."***
> **Republican Vice-Presidential Nominee Robert Dole**

August 24-25, 1976. These two statements were made a day apart at the American Legion National Convention in Seattle, Washington. The statements predictably brought loud and diametrically opposite reactions from the crowd. Carter's attempt to draw the thin line between "amnesty" and "pardon" was widely viewed as a distinction without a difference. His remarks were instantly booed and loudly jeered even though he, too, was a veteran, and he had served on battleships and submarines for eight years. Conversely, the remarks of veteran Robert Dole were cheered and praised, and Dole received a lengthy standing ovation from the crowd. A few months later, Carter narrowly won the election, and on January 21, 1977, his second day in office, he pardoned all those who had avoided the draft by leaving the country. About 90% of them had fled to Canada (where they were, after some initial disputes, accepted as legal immigrants) while others went to, for example, Sweden. Carter's pardon did not extend to the estimated 500,000 to 1,000,000 active duty men who had deserted or gone AWOL. Those dispositions would be handled on a case—by-case basis.[357] Carter's actions were never accepted by some. To others, they were seen as appropriate and, in a rough manner, merely paralleled the actions of President Ford just a few years earlier when, to the similar anger of many Americans, he had pardoned Richard Nixon in an effort to end the "national nightmare" of Watergate.[358] The parallel—right or wrong—was that Carter's motivations were the same: to try to put an end to the other "national nightmare," Vietnam.

Author's Note:

At that time, this author was serving a four-year-plus active duty military commitment. Though I was a passionate opponent of the Vietnam War, I was (and am) also a veteran. Thus, both personally and on behalf of my best childhood friend who was killed in Vietnam and whose name remains emblazoned on "The Wall" in Washington, D.C., I was angered by what appeared to be Carter's granting of a forgive-and-forget pass to those who had escaped to Canada without serving or without being required to serve even a parallel period of public service. But it was a confusing issue. I confess I was also angered by the many Americans, oftentimes wealthy and educated Americans, who "escaped" the draft via bogus deferments and claimed physical conditions.

"It is no secret that Americans have lost faith in politics.
The retreat to purely personal satisfactions ....
is one of the main themes of the Seventies"

...

"Having no hope of improving their lives
in any of the ways that matter,
people have convinced themselves that what matters
is psychic improvement:
getting in touch with their feelings, eating health food,
taking lessons in ballet or belly dancing,
immersing themselves in the wisdom of the East, jogging,

learning how to 'relate,' overcoming the 'fear of pleasure.' "

...

"These pursuits ... signify a retreat
from the political turmoil of the recent past."

...

"To live for the moment is the prevailing passion
--- to live for yourself, not for your predecessors or posterity.
We are fast losing the essence of historical continuity,
the sense of belonging to a succession of generations
originating in the past and stretching in the future"

September 30, 1976. Christopher Lasch, writing in his article entitled "The Narcissist Society" in *The New York Review of Books*.[359] The article was written as a review of five books[360] relating to what Tom Wolfe famously referred to as the "Me" decade.[361] Lasch would soon write his own influential book, *The Culture of Narcissism*,[362] about the rising narcissism characterized by hedonism, self-focus and self-awareness, but in this article he captures the compelling "inward" shift and focus of the 1970s. This is evidenced by the fact that in the 1970s—and wholly apart from the plethora of bestselling books on the subjects of sex and sexuality—there was on average one or two relationship and self-help books amongst the Top 10 *New York Times* Best Sellers *every year* of the decade. Examples include, Thomas Harris' *I'm O.K. – You're O.K.* (1972), Gail Sheehy's admittedly brilliant *Passages* (1976), and Dr. Joyce Brothers' *How to Get Whatever You Want Out of Life* (1979). The trends continued throughout the next decade as well with the number of Top 10 *New York Times* Best Sellers in the genre of relationship and self-help books increasing from 15 in the 1970s to 23 in 1980s.[363]

"There is no Soviet domination of Eastern Europe, and
there never will be under a Ford administration."

October 6, 1976. President Gerald Ford, during his second Presidential Debate with Democratic Presidential nominee Jimmy Carter. President Ford "stuck to his guns" despite the ensuing inquiry from the "astonished" moderator Max Frankel of *The New York Times* who asked Ford if he had misspoken. Political gaffes are always and inevitably made during the course of lengthy political campaigns, but many believe that this remark, which instantly stalled Ford's campaign momentum at the time, played a material role in his election loss to Jimmy Carter a month later.[364]

"I've looked on a lot of women with lust. I've committed adultery in my heart many times."

November 1976. President-elect Jimmy Carter's unwise, indeed almost too-much-information remark, made by him in an interview he granted to Robert Scheer and published in *Playboy* magazine this month. While the substance of the remark was hardly shocking to most Americans, Carter's statement was widely ridiculed. It also underscored the perception of some Americans that Carter was unduly naïve, unsophisticated, and possibly unprepared to serve as the new President and Commander-in-Chief.

"The examples of Jimi Hendrix, Janis Joplin, Jim Morrison ... brought home the dangers of the road"

. . .

"We needed ... to get out of the line of fire for a while. ... Self-destructiveness had become the power that ruled us."

. . .

"6,000 pounds of turkey, ... a thousand pounds of potatoes and hundreds of gallons of gravy"

November 25, 1976. Robbie Robertson, lead guitarist and primary songwriter for The Band, reflecting upon the group's motivation for staging what was billed and known as "The Last Waltz" on this Thanksgiving Day, 1976.[365] Some have referred to it as one of the greatest concerts ever performed. The concert was even filmed by 34-year-old Martin Scorsese. In 1978, Scorsese released a documentary of the event, simply entitled *The Last Waltz*. The concert was to be The Band's last performance for at least an indefinite period. The concert was hosted by Billy Graham and held at San Francisco's Winterland, the former skating rink that had become the forum for many of the great concerts of the late 1960s and 1970s. With the exception of Woodstock, the audacity of the event was unparalleled.

Graham insisted that everyone in the audience be served Thanksgiving Dinner before the show— "Six thousand pounds of turkey, 200 of them! Three hundred pounds of Nova Scotia salmon, a thousand pounds of potatoes, hundreds of gallons of gravy, and 400 pounds of pumpkin pie!" were served.[366] But it was the incredible list of performers that created The Sixties "Last Waltz." For more than four hours, the amazed audience of 5,000 people watched one performer or group after another take the stage—The Band, Paul Butterfield, Muddy Waters, Eric Clapton, Neil Young, Joni Mitchell, Van Morrison, Bob Dylan, Ronnie Wood, Stephen Stills, Ringo Starr, The Staple Singers and Emmylou Harris with poetry readings by Lawrence Ferlinghetti and others interspersed between sets. Of course, the night ended with The Band playing *The Weight,* its greatest song ever. There is no remotely precise date upon which the Rock 'n' Roll Era of The Sixties came to an end, and it comforting to all music-lovers that new voices and bands were constantly premiering such as Bruce Springsteen, who had released *Born to Run* in 1975, just a year earlier. But for many younger Americans, the end of the Rock 'n' Roll Era of the Sixties came to an end in San Francisco. On this day. At the end of this concert – so appropriately named The Last Waltz.

CHAPTER 10

Closing

1957–1976
The Early Years of Modern America

By the end of 1976, the early years of Modern America had come to a close. Watergate and the Vietnam War had come to their unsettling ends. Exhausted and almost disoriented by the protests and rancor of the 1960s, America had both the desire and the need for a rest. It did not arrive.

The rights of millions of Americans had been an expanded as a result of the social, political, and environmental movements of the 1960s and early 1970s and the enactment of the far-reaching legislation of the Great Society. The comforting words and honorable style of President Gerald Ford had helped to start the healing of some of America's many wounds. But it was still a difficult time.

Still in 1976, the middle of the 1970s, the memories of the assassinations of President John F. Kennedy, Malcolm X, the Rev. Dr. Martin Luther King, Jr., and Bobby Kennedy all remained vivid and close. The Vietnam War had ignominiously ended, but many of the memories were fresh and the wounds still deep and raw. Furthermore, the economy was fragile and burdened by the heightened challenges of oil shortages and tensions with OPEC. Complicating matters, the political horizon was beyond projection or easy analysis. Widespread uncertainty was due in part to the recent election of the relatively unknown Jimmy Carter and the ascendancy of a stronger and stronger conservative movement. Few foresaw Ronald Reagan, let alone the Reagan era. No one could yet fully comprehend the go-go, boom-boom, trickle-down 1980s or the collapse of the Soviet Union. And for this reason, the latter part of the 1970s was almost an interim space; a pause before the change; and a wandering or, in the clumsy words attributed, albeit inaccurately, to President Carter, a "malaise."

But, as will be seen in Volumes II and III, the Memorable Words kept coming—words of explanation and exclamation. Some of them "dead serious." Some of them "lighthearted."

APPENDICES

APPENDIX A

Reverse Index of Memorable Words by Speaker, Writer and Key Words (1957–1976)

"Abolished"
>1975   House Un-American Activities Committee

Abbreviations, Schedule of – See Appendix C

ABC's Wide World of Sports – See Television Lines

Academy Awards – See Movies

"Admitted" - See Harvard University

Advertising Campaigns and Slogans *(See also, Corporate Slogans and Advertising Taglines at Appendix L).*
>*"Because you're worth it."* (L'Oreal) (1971)
>
>*"Does she or doesn't she?"* (Clairol) (1964)
>
>*"Don't leave home without it."* (American Express) (1975)
>
>*"Fly the friendly skies."* (United Airlines) (1966)
>
>*"Have a Break, Have a Kit-Kat."* (Kit Kat) (1957)
>
>*"Have it your way."* (Burger King) (1973)
>
>*"Heh, Mikey … He likes it!"* (Life Cereal) (1972)
>
>*"If you've got the time, we've got the beer."* (Miller Brewing Co.) (1971)
>
>*"It's Miller Time."* (Miller Brewing Co.) (1971)
>
>*"It's the real thing."* (Coca Cola) (1969)
>
>*"Let Hertz put you in the driver's seat."* (Hertz Rental Car) (1959)
>
>*"Let your fingers do the walking."* (Yellow Pages) (1962)

"Look, Ma, no cavities!" (Crest) (1957)

"Merrill Lynch is bullish on America." (Merrill Lynch) (1973)

"Nothing runs like a Deere." (John Deere) (1972)

"Please don't squeeze the Charmin." (Charmin) (1964)

"Put a tiger in your tank." (Esso) (1964)

"Rice-A-Roni, the San Francisco Treat." (Rice-A-Roni) (1959)

"The Citi never sleeps." (Citibank) (1976)

"The quick picker upper" (Bounty) (1960)

"The ultimate driving machine" (BMW) (1975)

"The Uncola" (Seven Up/7 Up) (1973)

"Think small." (Volkswagen) (1959)

"We try harder." (Avis Rent-a-Car) (1962)

"When you got it, flaunt it." (Braniff Airlines) (1967)

"You don't have to be Jewish to love Levy's." (Levy's Rye Bread) (1967)

AFL-NFL World Championship – See Super Bowl I

Agnew, Spiro T. (B: 1918, Baltimore, MD – D: 1996, Berlin, MD). U.S. Vice President (1969–1973) (R). *See also, "Guilty"; and Presidential Campaign Themes and Identification Slogans – 1960–1976 – Appendix K*

    1968   Presidential Campaign Themes, Slogans and Results

    1969   *"An effete corps of impudent snobs who characterize themselves as intellectuals."*

    1970   *"…(T)he working men of this country, the forgotten man of American politics…."*

    1972   Presidential Campaign Themes, Slogans and Results

Alcatraz, The Closing Of – See Weatherman, Frank

Alcatraz, The Occupation of – See American Indian Movement

Ali, Muhammad (B: Cassius Clay, 1942, Louisville, KY – D: 2016, Scottsdale, AZ). Olympic athlete, three-time World Heavyweight Boxing Champion (1964, 1974, and 1978), and civil rights activist.

    1964   *"I don't have to be what you want me to be."*

    1967   *"I ain't got no quarrel with them Viet Cong. No Vietcong ever called me nigger."*

    1974   *"Float like a butterfly and sting like a bee."*

"All-out limited war"

    1966   Catchphrases, Chants, and Slogans

American Express

    1958   *"The Premium Card"*

American Indian Movement

    1973   *"Wounded Knee Siege, the Occupation of Alcatraz, and the Trail of Broken Promises"*

Arendt, Hannah (B: 1906, Germany – D: 1975, New York, NY). German-born American political theorist, writer, and university professor.

1963 Seminal Book–*On Revolution*

Armstrong, Neil (B: 1930, Auglaize County, OH - D: 2012, Cincinnati, OH). American astronaut.

1969 *"That's one small step for a man, one giant leap for mankind."*

Army, Dick (B: 1940, Cando, ND). U.S. House of Representatives (1985–2003) (R-TX) (and House Majority Leader (1995–2003)).

1960 *"I think all the troubles in the country began in the Sixties."*

Arnez, Desi – See Television Lines

Articles of Impeachment – See House Judiciary Committee

Baker, Howard (B: 1925, Huntsville, TN – D: 2014, Huntsville, TN). U.S. Senator (1967–1985) (R-TN) (and Senate Majority Leader (1981–1985) and Senate Minority Leader (1977–1981)), White House Chief of Staff under President Reagan (1987–1988), and Ambassador to Japan (2001–2005).

1973 *"What did the President know and when did he know it?"*

Baldwin, James (B: 1924, Harlem, NY – D: 1987, France). African American writer, essayist, and political and social activist.

1963 Seminal Book – *The Fire Next Time*

Barkley, L.D. (B: 1950 – D: 1971, Attica, NY). American convict and prisoner.

1971 *"We are men. We are not beasts."*

Bay of Pigs

1961 *"Utter Disaster"* and *"Total Fiasco"*

"Beep, beep, beep,…" – See Soviet Union

Berra, Yogi (B: 1925, St. Louis, MO – D: 2015, West Caldwell, NJ). Professional baseball player, coach, manager, and master (mis-)wordsmith.

1972 *"It ain't over till it's over."*

1972 *"Baseball is 90% mental. The other half is physical."*

1972 *"Nobody goes there anymore. It's too crowded."*

1972 *"If you come to a fork in the road, take it."*

1972 *"It's tough to make predictions, especially about the future."*

1972 *"A nickel ain't worth a dime anymore."*

1972 *"It gets late early out there."*

Bickel, Alexander (B: 1924, Romania – D: 1974, New Haven, CT). American legal scholar and author.

1962 Seminal Book – *The Least Dangerous Branch: The Supreme Court at the Bar of Politics*

Black Panther Party

1966 *"Power to the People" - "Patrol the pigs" - "We want land, bread, housing, education …, justice… "*

Blomberg, Ron (B: 1948, Atlanta, GA). Professional baseball player, first Designated Hitter in professional baseball.

1973   *"The day I screwed up baseball...."*

"Body counts"

1965   Catchphrases, Chants, and Slogans

Book Titles

   Best and Worst Book Titles – See Appendix H

   Most Frequently Banned or Challenged in U.S. Libraries – See Appendix J

   Most Widely Held in U.S. Libraries – See Appendix I

Boston Women's Health Book Collective

1971   Seminal Book: *Our Bodies, Ourselves: A Book by and for Women*

Brokaw, Tom (B: 1940, Webster, SD). Television journalist, news anchor and managing editor of *NBC Nightly News* (1982-2004), and author.

1960s   *"They were the largest, the best educated, and the wealthiest generation in American history ..."*

Brooklyn Dodger Fans

1957   *"Say it ain't so, say it ain't so"* and Shooting *"O'Malley, Twice"*

Brown, Dee (B: 1908, Alberta, LA – D: 2002, Little Rock, AK). Historian, novelist, and author.

1970   Seminal Book – *Bury My Heart at Wounded Knee: An Indian History of the American West*

Brown, Helen Gurley (B: 1922, Green Forest, AR – D: 2012, New York, NY). Author, and Editor of *Cosmopolitan* magazine (1965–1997).

1962   Seminal Book – *Sex and the Single Girl*

1962   *"Good girls go to heaven, bad girls go everywhere."*

Brown, Rita Mae (B: 1944, Hanover, PA). Writer, activist, and feminist.

1973   Seminal Book – *Rubyfruit Jungle.*

Buckley, William F., Jr. (B: 1925, New York, NY – D: 2008, Stamford, CT). Author, commentator, founder of *National Review* magazine and long-time host of the television interview show *Firing Line* (1966–1999).

1957   *"The central question that emerges ..."* (White preeminence in the South).

1963   *"I would rather be governed by the first two thousand names in the ... telephone directory ...."*

Bugliosi, Vincent (B: 1934, Hibbing, MN – D: 2015, Los Angeles, CA). Attorney and author.

1974   Seminal Book – *Helter Skelter: The True Story of The Manson Murders* (Co-Authored with Curt Gentry)

"Burn, baby, burn"

1965   Catchphrases, Chants, and Slogans

Butler, Robert Neil (B: 1926 – D: 2010, Manhattan, NY). Physician/Psychiatrist specializing in the field of geriatrics, author, Founding Director of the National Institute on Aging.

 1975 Seminal Book – *Why Survive? Being Old in America*

Byrd, Henry F. (B: 1887, Martinsburg, WV – D: 1966, Berryville, VA). American newspaper publisher and conservative leader of Democratic Party; U.S. Senator (1933–1965) (D-VA), Governor (VA) (1926–1930).

 1960 Presidential Campaign Themes, Slogans, and Results

Calley, Lt. William (B: 1943, Miami, Florida). Former Lieutenant in U.S. Army. *See also "Guilty"*

 1971 *"I was ordered to go in there and destroy the enemy. That was my job that day. ..."*

Capote, Truman (B: 1924, New Orleans, LA – D: 1984, Los Angeles, CA). Novelist, screenwriter, and playwright.

 1966 Seminal Book – *In Cold Blood*

Carlos, John (B: 1945, New York, NY). U.S. sprinter and Olympic athlete.

 1968 *"You could have heard a frog piss on cotton. There's something awful about hearing 50,000 people go silent, like being in the eye of a hurricane."*

Carmichael, Stokely (B: 1941, Port of Spain, Trinidad and Tobago – D: 1998, Conakry, Guinea). Radical civil rights activist and one of the brief leaders of the black power movement of the late 1960s.

 1968 *"White America killed Dr. King last night.... There no longer needs to be intellectual discussions, ...",*

Carson, Rachael (B: 1907, Springdale, PA – D: 1964, Silver Spring, MD). Writer, scientist, ecologist, and early conservationist and environmentalist.

 1962 Seminal Book – *Silent Spring*

Carter, Jimmy ("The Man from Plains") (B: 1924, Plains, GA). 39th U.S. President (1977–1981) (D); Governor of Georgia (1971–1975) (D). *See also Presidential Campaign Themes and Identification Slogans (1960–1976) at Appendix K*

 1971 *" ... (T)he time for racial discrimination is over."*

 1976 Presidential Campaign Themes, Slogans, and Results

 1976 *"I'll never lie to you."*

 1976 *"I do not favor blanket amnesty ...."*

 1976 *"I've committed adultery in my heart many times."*

Catchphrases, Chants, and Slogans

 See also Presidential Campaign Themes and Identification Slogans – Presidential Elections 1960–1976 at Appendix K; and Corporate Slogans and Advertising Tag-Lines (1959–1976) at Appendix L

 1957 *"Here come the niggers."*

1957   *"Say it ain't so, say it ain't so"* and *Shooting "O'Malley, Twice"*
1960–1969
    1960s   *"If it feels good, do it."*
    1960s   *"Power to the People"*
    1960s   *"Tune in, Turn on, Drop out"*
    1960s   *"We shall overcome …"*
    1965   *"Body Counts"*
    1965   *"Burn, baby, burn"*
    1965   *"Hell no, we won't go"*
    1965   *"Hey, Hey LBJ / How many kids did you kill today"*
    1966   *"Politics of minimum candor"* and *"All-out limited war"*
    (1966 – See also Black Panther Party – "Power to the People"
    1968   *"The whole world is watching"*
1970 - 1976
    1970   *"Let's Win or Get Out"*
    1970   *"Repent, Male Chauvinists"*
    1973   *"Thank you for your service."*
CBS Evening News – See Television Lines
Chants - See Catchphrases, Chants, and Slogans
Chisholm, Shirley (B: 1924, New York, NY. – D: 2005, Ormond Beach, FL).
    Black, Female Democratic Presidential nomination hopeful (1972); U.S.
    House of Representatives (1969–1983) (D-NY).
    See also Campaign Themes and Slogans – Presidential Elections 1960–1976 at
        Appendix K
    1972   Presidential Campaign Themes, Slogans and Results
    1972   *"… (B)eing female put many more obstacles in my path than being black."*
Clay, Cassious – See Ali, Muhammad
Clinton, William J. (Bill) ("Bubba" or "The Comeback Kid") (B: 1946,
    Hope, AR). 42nd U.S. President (1993–2001) (D). *See also Presidential*
    Campaign Themes and Identification Slogans (1960–1976) at Appendix K
    1960s   *"If you thought something good came out of the Sixties, you're probably a*
        Democrat."
Commoner, Barry (B: 1917, Brooklyn, NY – D: 2012, Manhattan, NY).
    Biologist, ecologist, professor, and politician.
    1971   Seminal Book – *The Closing Circle: Nature, Man, and Technology*
Constitution and Constitutional Amendments – See U.S. Constitution
Cooper, D. B. (B: Unknown – D: Unknown). American criminal-at-large.
    1971   *"Miss, you'd better look at that note. I have a bomb."*
Cornelius, Don – See Television – 1971
Corporate Slogans and Advertising Tag-Lines – See Appendix L

Cronkite, Walter (B: 1916, Saint Joseph, MO – D: 2009, New York, NY). Broadcast journalist and news anchor.

1962 *"And that's the way it is, ...*

1963 *"President Kennedy died at 1:00PM Central Standard Time ...."*

1968 *" ...(T)he only rational way out (of Vietnam) ... negotiate, not as victors, but as...honorable people."*

Daley, Richard (B: 1902, Chicago, IL – D: 1976, Chicago, IL). Mayor of Chicago (1955–1976) (D). *See also Ribicoff, Abraham – 1968*

1962 *"Good Homes Building Good Citizens"*

"Deep Throat" (The unidentified, inside informant of *Washington Post* reporter Bob Woodward in the context of the Watergate investigations).

1972 *"Follow the money"*

Desalination Plant – U.S. Office of Saline Water

Dirksen, Everett (B: 1896, Pekin, IL – D: 1969, Washington, D.C.). U.S. Senator (1951–1969) (R-IL); U.S. House of Representatives (1933–1949) (R-IL).

1964 *"No army can withstand the strength of an idea whose time has come."*

Dole, Robert (B: 1923, Russell, KS). Politician, Republican Presidential Nominee (1996); U.S. Senator (1969–1996) (R-KS); U.S. House of Representatives (1961–1969) (R-KS); Recipient of Two Purple Hearts – World War II. *See also Campaign Themes and Slogans – Presidential Elections 1960–1976 at Appendix K*

1976 Presidential Campaign Themes, Slogans, and Results

1976 *"...(N)o blanket pardon, no blanket amnesty, no blanket clemency."*

Dow Chemical Company - See U.S. Office of Saline Water

Dr. Seuss – See Geisel, Theodore

Durant, Ariel – See Durant, Will

Durant, Will (B: 1885, North Adams, MA – D: 1981, Los Angeles, CA) and **Durant, Ariel** (B: 1898, Ukraine – D: 1981, Los Angeles, CA). American writers, historians, and philosophers.

1968 Seminal Book – *The Lessons of History*

Ehrlich, Dr. Paul (B: 1932, Philadelphia, PA). Biologist, professor, and author.

1968 Seminal Book – *The Population Bomb.*

Eisenhower, Dwight D. ("Ike") (B: 1890, Denison, TX – D: 1969, Washington, D.C.). 34th U.S. President (1953–1961) (R).

1957 (Second) Presidential Inaugural Address
"We live in a land of plenty, but rarely has this earth known such peril as today."
"The divisive force is International Communism and the power that it controls. The designs of that power, dark in purpose, are clear in practice."
"We seek peace, knowing that peace is the climate of freedom."

> *"We seek (peace) because (due to) the power of modern weapons ... peace may be the only climate possible for human life itself."*
> *"...(I)n that body (the United Nations) rests the best hope of our age for the assertion of that law by which all nations may live in dignity."*
> *"...(M)ay the nations cease to live in trembling before the menace of force."*

1960   *"If you give me a week, I might think of one."*

1961   *"...(W)e must guard against the ... military-industrial complex.".*

Engele v. Vitale – See U. S. Supreme Court

Ervin, Sam (B: 1896, Morganton, NC – D: 1985, Winston-Salem, NC). U.S. Senator (1954-1974) (D-NC).

1973.   *"I'm just an old country lawyer,...".*

1973   *"... (T)he Watergate tragedy is the greatest tragedy this country has ever suffered ..."*

Evans, Harold, Author/Editor of *The American Century* (2000).

1975   *"It was the longest war in America's history, in the end the most unpopular war, ..."*

Fall of Saigon, The

1975   *"There is no easy definition of when the Vietnam War really ended ..."*

Farmer, James (B: 1920, Marshall, TX. – D: 1999, Fredericksburg, VA). Civil rights activist and leader; 1942 co-founder of Congress of Racial Equality).

1968   *"Dr. King would be greatly distressed to find that his blood had triggered off bloodshed and disorder ...I think instead the nation should be quiet; black and white, ..."*

Federal Emergency Guarantee Board

1971   *"Too big to fail."*

Fletcher, Joseph (B: 1905, Newark, NJ – D: 1991, Charlottesville, VA). Professor, theologian, and author.

1966   Seminal Book – *Situation Ethics: The New Morality*

Flip Wilson Show – See Television Lines

Flynn, Errol (B: 1909, Australia – D: 1959, Vancouver, Canada (U.S. Citizenship – 1942)). American film actor.

1959   *"I've had a helluva lot of fun, and I've enjoyed every minute of it."*

Ford, Gerald (B: 1913, Omaha, NE – D: 2006, Rancho Mirage, CA). 38th U.S. President (1974–1977) (R); Vice President (1973–1974); U.S. House of Representatives (1949–1973) (R-MI). *See also Presidential Campaign Themes and Identification Slogans (1960–1976)at- Appendix K*

1970   *"An impeachable offense is whatever the House of Representatives considers it to be ..."*

1973   *"I am a Ford, not a Lincoln."*

1974   *"...(O)ur long national nightmare is over. Our constitution works."*

1974   *"...(P)ursuant to the pardon power conferred upon me ... I (grant) a full, free, and absolute pardon"*

1974   *"WIN – Whip Inflation Now"*

1975   *"The time has come (for the nation to again) look forward ...."*

1975   *"History will judge this (Helsinki Accords) conference not by what we say here today ...."*

1975   *"Today's mounting danger is from mass government...."*

1976   Presidential Campaign Themes, Slogans, and Results

1976   *"There is no Soviet domination of Eastern Europe ...."*

Frazier, Joe (B: 1944, Beaufort, SC – D: 2011, Philadelphia, PA). Professional boxer and World Heavyweight Champion (1970–1973).

1975   *"I want him, boss."*

Freed, Alan (B: 1921, Windber, PA – D: 1965, Palm Springs, CA). American disc jockey (aka "Moondog") and an early promoter of what he termed "rock 'n' roll"—a mix of blues, country, and rhythm and blues music.

1957   *"Rock 'n' roll"*

Friedan, Betty (B: 1921, Peoria, IL. – D: 2006, Washington, D.C.). Author, feminist leader, and co-founder of National Organization for Women.

1963   *"The problem that has no name."*

1963   Seminal Book – *The Feminine Mystique*

Friedman, Milton (B: 1912, Brooklyn, NY – D: 2006, San Francisco, CA). Economist, academician, and author.

1971   Seminal Books – *A Monetary History of the United States, 1867–1960* (Co-authored by Anna Schwartz)

Fulbright, J. William (B:1905, Sumner, MO – D: 1995, Washington, D.C.). U.S. Senator (1945–1974) (D-AK).

1966   Seminal Book – *The Arrogance of Power*

1966   *"The inspiration and commitment of the Great Society have disappeared."*

Galbraith, John Kenneth (B: 1908, Ontario, Canada – D: 2006, Cambridge, MA). Canadian/American economist, professor, public official, and diplomat.

1958   Seminal Book – *The Affluent Society*

Geisel, Theodore – (Dr. Seuss) (B: 1904, Springfield, MA – D: 1991, La Jolla, CA). American writer and cartoonist best known for series of children's books.

1957   Seminal Book – *The Cat in the Hat*

General Source Materials – See Appendix B

Gentry, Curt – See Bugliosi, Vincent

Gideon v. Wainright – See U.S. Supreme Court - 1963

Gidget- The Movie
> 1959   *"To be a real woman is to bring out the best in a man."*

Glenn, John (B: 1921, Cambridge, OH – D: 2016, Columbus, OH). Astronaut, and U.S. Senator (1987–1995) (D-OH).
> 1962   *"Boy, that was a real fireball."*

Goldwater, Barry (B: 1909, Phoenix, AZ – D: 1998, Paradise Valley, AZ). U.S. Senator (1953–1965; 1969–1985) (R-AZ); Republican Presidential nominee (1964).
> *See also Presidential Campaign Themes and Identification Slogans – 1960-1976 at Appendix K*

> 1960   Seminal Book – *The Conscience of a Conservative*
> 1964   Presidential Campaign Themes, Slogans, and Results
> 1964   *"Extremism in defense of liberty is no vice, …moderation in pursuit of justice is no virtue…"*

Grammy Awards for Best Spoken Words – See Appendix D

Greensboro Four – See McCain, Franklin

Green Bay Packers – See Super Bowl I

Griswold v. Connecticut – See U.S. Supreme Court

"Guilty" (Including Jury Convictions, No Contest/Nolo contendere Pleas)
> *See also "Revocation of Citizenship."*

> 1973   Agnew, Spiro
> 1971   Calley, Lt. William
> 1975   Chapin, Dwight
> 1975   Colson, Charles
> 1975   Dean, John
> 1975   Ehrlichman, John
> 1975   Haldeman, H. R. "Bob"
> 1964   Hoffa, Jimmy
> 1975   Krogh, Egil
> 1971   Manson, Charles
> 1975   Mitchell, John

Haldemann, H.R. "Bob" (B: 1926, Los Angeles, CA – D: 1993, Santa Barbara, CA). White House Chief of Staff for President Nixon (1969–1973) and businessman.
> *See also "Guilty."*

> 1971   *Enemies List*

Halberstam, David (B: 1934, New York, NY – D: 2007, Menlo Park, CA). Journalist, historian, and Pulitzer-Prize winning author.
> 1972   Seminal Book – *The Best and the Brightest*

Harrington, Michael (B: 1928, St. Louis, MO – D: 1989, Larchmont, NY). Author, political activist, democratic socialist, and academic.

1962   Seminal Book – *The Other America: Poverty in the United States*

Harvard University

1967   *"Admitted" (Female Students)*

Hawaii Admission Act

1959   *Hawaii – Our Last State.*

Hayden, Tom (B: 1939, Detroit, MI – D: 2016, Santa Monica, CA). Social and political activist, co-author of the 1960s Students for a Democratic Society Port Huron Statement, and California Senate (1992–2000) (D).

1960s   *"There a big 'if' over the Sixties…"*

Heart of Atlanta Motel v. United States – See U.S. Supreme Court

Heinlein, Robert A. (B: 1907, Butler, MO. – D: 1988, Carmel, CA). Science-fiction writer and author.

1961   Seminal Book – *Stranger in a Strange Land*

Heller, Joseph (B: 1923, Brooklyn, NY – D: 1999, East Hampton, NY). Author.

1961   Seminal Book – *Catch-22*

"Hell no, we won't go"

1965   Catchphrases, Chants, and Slogans

"Here come the niggers"

1957   Ugly Chant of Little Rock, Arkansas Crowd

"Hey, Hey, LBJ / How many kids did you kill today"

1965   Catchphrases, Chants, and Slogans

Hoffa, Jimmy (B: 1913, Brazil, IN – Disappeared: 1975, Bloomfield Township, MI). Labor union leader and President of the International Brotherhood of Teamsters (1958–1971).

See also "Guilty"

1975   *"Last seen."*

Hofstadter, Richard (B: 1916, Buffalo, NY – D: 1970, New York, NY). Professor of history and author.

1963   Seminal Book – *Anti-Intellectualism in American Life.*

House Judiciary Committee

1974   *Articles of Impeachment (Richard M. Nixon).*

Hruska, Roman (B: 1904, David City, NE – D: 1999, Omaha, NE). U.S. Senator (1954–1976) (R-NE).

1970   *"Even (the) mediocre …are entitled to a little representation aren't they…?"*

Humphrey, Hubert (B: 1911, Wallace, SD – D: 1978, Waverly, MN). U.S. Vice President (1965–1969) (D); U.S. Senate (1949–1964; 1971–1978) (D-MN); Democratic Presidential nominee (1968). *See also Presidential Campaign Themes and Identification Slogans – 1960–1976 at Appendix K*

    1964   Presidential Campaign Themes, Slogans and Results

    1968   Presidential Campaign Themes, Slogans and Results

"If it feels good, do it?

1960s – Catchphrases, Chants, and Slogans

John Birch Society

    1958   *"To bring about less government, more responsibility, and—with God's help—a better world...."*

Johnson, Lyndon B. ("LBJ") (B: 1908, Stonewall, TX – D: 1973, Stonewall, TX). 36th U.S. President (1963–1969); U.S. Vice President (1961–1963) (D); U.S. Senate (1949–1961) (D-TX); and U.S. House of Representatives (1937–1949) (D-TX). *See also Presidential Campaign Themes and Identification Slogans – 1960-1976 – Appendix K*

    1960   Presidential Campaign Themes, Slogans, and Results

    1963   *"I ask for your help—and God's."*

    1963   *"We have talked long enough in this country about equal rights.... It is time now to write the next chapter, and to write it in the books of law."*

    1963   *"Just get me elected, and then you can have your war."*

    1964   Presidential Campaign Themes, Slogans, and Results

    1964   *"This administration today, here and now, declares unconditional war on poverty in America.."*

    1964   *"I don't think it's worth fighting for ...."*

    1964   *"Will you join in the battle to give each citizen an escape from the crushing weight of poverty?"*

    1964   *"We still seek no wider war" "To take all measures necessary."*

    1964   *"We are not about to send American boys nine or ten thousand miles away ...."*

    1965   Presidential Inaugural Address

        "For every generation there is a destiny. For some, history decides. For this generation the choice must be our own."

        "Ours is a time of change (but) ... (o)ur destiny ... will rest on the unchanged character of our people and on our faith."

        "In a land of great wealth, families must not live in hopeless poverty... Children must not go hungry.... (N)eighbors must not suffer and die untended.... (Y)oung people must be taught to read and write."

        "We aspire to nothing that belongs to others. We seek no dominion over our fellow man...."

> *"Each of us must find a way to advance the purpose of the Nation....*
> *"Without this, we will simply become a nation of strangers."*
> *"No longer need capitalist and worker... struggle to divide our bounty....*
> *We can increase the bounty of all."*
> *"In each generation, with toil and tears, we have had to earn our heritage*
> *again.... And the judgment of God is hardest on those who are most*
> *favored."*
> *"If we succeed it will not be ... because of what we own, but rather because*
> *of what we believe."*

1965   *"This (War on Poverty) legislation marks the end of an era of partisan cynicism towards human want and misery. The dole is dead. The pork barrel is gone."*

1965   *"At times history and fate meet at a single time in a single place to shape a turning point in man's ... search for freedom."*

> *"There is no Negro problem, no southern ... northern problem ... only an American problem."*
> *"Many civil rights (issues) ... complex and ... difficult. But about (the right to vote) there can be no argument."*
> *"Their cause must be our cause, too, because ... all of us ... must overcome the crippling legacy of bigotry and injustice. And we shall overcome."*

1965   *"Freedom is not enough. ... (I)t is not enough just to open the gates of opportunity. All citizens must have the ability to walk through those gates."*

1968   *"If I've lost Cronkite, I've lost Middle America."*

1968   *"Accordingly, I shall not seek, and I will not accept, the nomination of my party ...."*

Johnson, Virginia E. – See Masters, Dr. William E.

Jong, Erica (B: 1942 – New York, NY). Novelist and poet.

1973   Seminal Book – *Fear of Flying*

Jordan, Barbara (B: 1936, Houston, TX – D: 1996, Austin, TX). U.S. House of Representatives (1973–1979) (D-TX); Member of House Judiciary Committee during Watergate impeachment hearings; Professor at University of Texas.

1974   *"... (W)hen (the Constitution) was completed ... I was not included in 'We, the people.'"*

1976   *"...(T)here is no law that can require the American people to form a national community...."*

Kansas City Chiefs – See Super Bowl I

Keats, Ezra Jack (B: 1916, Brooklyn, NY – D: 1983, New York, NY). Author and illustrator of children's books.

1962   Seminal Book – *The Snowy Day*

Kennedy, John F. ("JFK") (B: 1917, Brookline, MA – D: 1963, Dallas, TX).
35th U.S. President (1961–1963) (D); U.S. Senate (1953–1960) (D-MA);
U.S. House of Representatives (1947–1953) (D-MA). *See also Presidential
Campaign Themes and Identification Slogans (1960–1976) at Appendix K*

1960   Presidential Campaign, Themes, Slogans, and Results

1960   *"I believe in an America where the separation of church and state is
absolute."*

1961   Presidential Inaugural Address

*"The world is very different now. For man holds ... power to abolish all
forms of human poverty and all forms of human life."*

*"Let the word go forth ... that the torch has been passed to a new genera-
tion of Americans—born in this century, tempered by war, disciplined
by a hard and bitter peace ...."*

*"We shall pay any price, bear any burden, meet any hardship, support any
friend, oppose any foe to assure the survival and the success of liberty."*

*"If society cannot help the many who are poor, it cannot save the few who
are rich."*

*"To ... the United Nations, our last best hope in an age where the instru-
ments of war have far outpaced the instruments of peace, we renew our
pledge of support...."*

*"So let us begin anew – remembering ... that civility is not a sign of weak-
ness, and sincerity is always subject to proof. Let us never negotiate out of
fear. But let us never fear to negotiate."*

*"The graves of young Americans who answered the call of service surround
the globe. Now the trumpet summons us again ... to bear the burden of
a long twilight struggle ...."*

*"Ask not what your country can do for you - - ask what you can do for your
country.... (w)ith a good conscience our only sure reward...."*

1961   *"We choose to go to the moon ... in this decade ... because that goal will
serve to organize and measure the best of our energies and skills ..."*

1961   *"I am the man who accompanied Jackie Kennedy to Paris – and I enjoyed
myself."*

1961   *"A wall is a hell of a lot better than a war."*

1963   *"Ich bin ein Berliner." ("I am a Berliner")*.

Kennedy, Robert F. (B: 1925, Brookline, MA – D: 1968, Los Angeles, CA). U.S.
Senator (1965–1968) (D-NY); U.S. Attorney General (1961-1964).

1968   *"It's on to Chicago, and let's win there."*

1968   *"Is everybody o.k..?"*

Kennedy, Theodore (B: 1932, Boston, MA – D: 2009, Hyannis Port, MA). U.S. Senator (1962–2009) (D-MA).

1969   *"I had not given up hope … that, by some miracle, Mary Jo would have escaped from the car."*

Kerner Report (The President's Advisory Commission on Civil Disorders)

1968   *"Our nation is moving toward two societies, one black, one white – separate and unequal."*

Kerouac, Jack (B: 1922, Lowell, MA – D: 1969, St. Petersburg, FL). Novelist and poet, and early voice and leader of The Beat Generation.

1957   Seminal Book - *On the Road*

Khrushchev, Nikita (B: 1984, Kalinovka, Russia – D: 1971, Moscow, Russia). First Secretary of the Communist Party of the Soviet Union (1953-1964) and Premier of the Soviet Union (1958–1964).

1962   *"We will bury you."*

King, Jr., The Reverend Dr. Martin Luther (B: 1929, Atlanta, GA – D: 1968, Memphis, TN). Civil rights activist, and Recipient of 1964 Nobel Peace Prize. *See also Martin Luther King Jr. Day*

1957   *"… (W)e have no moral choice … but to delve deeper into the struggle.…"*

1957   *"The aftermath of nonviolence is … community ,… the aftermath of violence is … bitterness."*

1963   *"I Have a Dream."*

"Let us not wallow in the valley of despair, I say to you today, my friends, and so even though we face difficulties of today and tomorrow, I still have a dream. It is a dream deeply rooted in the American Dream."

"… (O)ne day on the red hills of Georgia, the sons of former slaves and the sons of former slave owners will be able to sit down together at the table of brotherhood."

"…(O)ne day even the state of Mississippi, a state sweltering in the heat of injustice, sweltering with the heat of oppression, will be transformed into an oasis of freedom and justice."

"…(T)hat my four little children will one day live in a nation where they will not be judged by the color of their skin but by the content of their character."

"With this faith we will be able to transform the jangling discord of our nation into a beautiful symphony of brotherhood. … (W)e will be able to work together, to pray together, to struggle together, to go to jail together, to stand up for freedom together, knowing that we will be free one day."

1965   *"The arc of the moral universe is long, but it bends toward justice."*

1967   *"Some of us … have already begun to break the silence of the night"*

1968   *"I've been to the mountaintop .…"*

Kissinger, Henry (B: 1923, Germany). U.S. Secretary of State (1973–1977); U.S. National Security Advisor (1969–1975); and Recipient, Nobel Peace Prize (1973).

1972　*"We have peace at hand."*

Lasch, Christopher (B:1932, Omaha, NE). Historian, moralist, social commentator, author, and academic.

1976　*"To live for the moment is the prevailing passion...."*

Lee, Harper (B: 1926, Monroeville, AL – D: 2016, Monroeville, AL). American author.

1960　Seminal Book – *To Kill a Mockingbird*

Legal Standard

1967　*"To save the life of the mother."*

"Let's Win or Get Out"

1970 – Catchphrases, Chants, and Slogans

***Life* Magazine**

1958　*"The schools are in terrible shape, ... Sputnik has made (education) a recognized crisis."*

1959　*"Some ... morning before another summer has come, one man chosen from the calmly intent seven ..."*

1969　*"The faces shown on the next pages are the faces of American men killed ... in Vietnam...."*

Lodge, Jr., Henry Cabot (B: 1902, Nahant, MA – D: 1985, Beverly, MA). U.S. Senate (1937–1944, 1947–1953) (R-MA); Ambassador to United Nations, South Vietnam, and Germany; and Republican Vice-Presidential Nominee with Richard Nixon (1960). *See also Presidential Campaign Themes and Identification Slogans – 1960-1976 at Appendix K.*

1960　Presidential Campaign, Themes, Slogans, and Results

Lombardi, Vince (B: 1913, New York, NY - D: 1970, Washington, D.C.). Professional football player and long-time coach of the Green Bay Packers.

1970　*"Football isn't a contact sport, it's a collision sport."*

"Long, hot summer" - See Summer, 1967.

Loving, Richard (B: 1933, Virginia – D; 1975, Virginia). Construction worker and plaintiff-husband in USSC case of *Loving v. Virginia.*

1967　*"Tell my court I love my wife...."*

Loving v. Virginia – See U.S. Supreme Court

MacArthur, General Douglas (B: 1880, Little Rock, AR – D: 1964, Washington, D.C.). American five-star general.

1962　*"The shadows are lengthening for me. The twilight is here. My days of old have vanished, ... Always there echoes and re-echoes: Duty, Honor, Country."*

Malcolm X (B: 1925, Omaha, NE - D: 1965, New York, NY). Muslim minister, black power spokesman, civil rights and human rights activist.

1964 *"If we can't cast a ballot, … (then) we're going to have to cast a bullet."*

1964 *"By any means necessary."*

1965 *"Let's cool it, brothers."*

1965 Seminal Book: *The Autobiography of Malcolm X: As Told to Alex Haley* (Co-authored with Alex Haley)

Manchester, William (B: 1992, Attleboro, MA – D: 2004, Middleton, CN). Historian, author, and biographer.

1974 Seminal Book – *The Glory and the Dream: A Narrative History of America – 1932–1972*

Mankiewicz, Frank (B: 1924 – D: 2014, Washington, D.C.). Journalist, author, and Democratic political advisor.

1972 *"No skeletons rattling in your closet?"*

Manson, Charles (B: 1934, Cincinnati, OH). Murderer, cult leader, and prisoner. See also *"Guilty"*

1969 *"Helter Skelter"*

Marcuse, Herbert (B: 1898, Berlin, Germany – D:1979, Germany (U.S. citizenship in 1940)). American and German philosopher, political theorist, author, and university professor.

1964 Seminal Book – *One-Dimensional Man: Studies in the Ideology of Advanced Industrial Society*

Masters, Dr. William E. (B: 1915, Cleveland, OH – D: 2001, Tucson, AZ). Gynecologist, medical researcher, and co-author with Virginia E. Johnson of books about human sexuality.

1966 *"If one is looking for pornography, one's going to have a long look."*

McCain, Franklin (B: 1941, Union County, NC - D: 2014, Greensboro, NC). Civil rights activist, member of so-called "Greensboro Four."

1960 *"We had no notion that we'd even be served … What we wanted to do was to serve notice …."*

McCarthy, Eugene (B: 1916, Watkins, MN – D: 2005, Washington, D.C.). U.S. Senate (1959–1971) (D-MN); U.S. House of Representatives (1949–1959) (D-MN); and Democratic Presidential nominee hopeful (1968). *See also Presidential Campaign Themes and Identification Slogans (1960–1976) at Appendix K*

1968 Presidential Campaign Themes, Slogans, and Results

McGovern, George (B: 1922, Avon, SD – D: 2012, Sioux Falls, SD). U.S. Senator (1963–1981) (D-SD); U.S. House of Representatives (1957–1961) (D-SD), Democratic Presidential nominee (1972). *See also Presidential Campaign Themes and Identification Slogans (1960-1976) at Appendix K*

1972 Presidential Campaign Themes, Slogans, and Results

McMahon, Ed (B: 1923, Detroit, MI – D: 2009, Los Angeles, CA). Comedian, actor, game show host, and Johnny Carson's nightly sidekick and announcer of *The Tonight Show* (1962-1992). *See also Television Lines*

1962   *"Heeeeere's Johnny" (The Tonight Show)*

Meade, Margaret (B:1901, Philadelphia, PA - D: 1978, New York, NY). Cultural anthropologist, writer, and academician. *See also Public Broadcasting System.*

1973   *"I think it may be as important for our time as were the invention of drama...."*

Meyers, Marvin, American academic and author.

1957   Seminal Book – *The Jacksonian Persuasion: Politics and Belief*

Miller, William E. (B: 1914, Lockport, NY – D: 1983 Buffalo, NY). U.S. House of Representatives (1951–1965) (R-NY) ; Republican Vice-Presidential Candidate (1964). *See also Presidential Campaign Themes and Identification Slogans – 1960-1976 at Appendix K*

1964   Presidential Campaign Themes, Slogans and Results

Miranda v. Arizona – See U.S. Supreme Court

Mondale, Walter (B:1928, Ceylon, MN). U.S. Vice President. (1977–1981); U.S. Senate (1964–1976) (D-MN); 1984 Democratic Presidential candidate. *See also Campaign Themes and Slogans – Presidential Elections 1960–1976 at Appendix K*

1976   Presidential Campaign Themes, Slogans, and Results

Morgenthau, Hans J. (B: 1904, Germany – D: 1980, New York, NY). German-American academic, commentator and author on the subject of international politics.

1960   Seminal Book – *The Purpose of American Politics*

"Motown"

1959   Barry Gordy's formation of Motown recording company and Hitsville, U.S.A. recording studio.

Movies

Best Movie of the Year (Academy Award Winner)

A Man for All Seasons	1966
Ben-Hur	1959
Gigi	1958
In the Heat of the Night	1967
Lawrence of Arabia	1962
Midnight Cowboy	1969
My Fair Lady	1964
Oliver!	1968
One Flew Over the Cuckoo's Nest	1975

Patton	1970
Rocky	1976
The Apartment	1960
The Bridge on the River Kwai	1957
The French Connection	1971
The Godfather	1972
The Godfather II	1974
The Sting	1973
The Sound of Music	1965
Tom Jones	1963
West Side Story	1961

Best Movie of the Year (*PrettyFamous*)

12 Angry Men	1957
2001: A Space Odyssey	1968
Chinatown	1974
Cool Hand Luke	1967
Dr. Strangelove	1964
For a Few Dollars More	1965
Lawrence of Arabia	1962
Monty Python and the Holy Grail	1975
North by Northwest	1959
Patton	1970
Psycho	1960
Taxi Driver	1976
The Birds	1963
The French Connection	1971
The Godfather	1972
The Sting	1973
The Wild Bunch	1969
Vertigo	1958
Who's Afraid of Virginia Woolf?	1966
Yojimbo	1961

Movie Lines

***2001: A Space Odyssey* (1973)**

"Open the pod bay doors, please HAL."

***All the President's Men* (1976)**

"Follow the money … Just follow the money."

***Auntie Mame* (1958)**

"Life is a banquet, and most poor suckers are starving to death!"

Birdman of Alcatraz (1962)

> *"You sit and listen to your heartbeat, ... your life ticking away."*

Blazing Saddles (1974)

> *"How about some more beans, Mr. Taggart?"*

Butch Cassidy and the Sundance Kid (1969)

> *"... I've got vision and the rest of the world wears bifocals."*

Butch Cassidy and the Sundance Kid (1969)

> *"Why, you crazy? The fall'll probably kill ya!"*

Chinatown (1974)

> *"Course I'm respectable. I'm old ...."*

Cool Hand Luke (1967)

> *"What we've got here is a failure to communicate."*

Dirty Harry (1971)

> *"'Do I feel lucky?' Well, do ya punk?"*

Dog Day Afternoon (1975)

> *"Attica! Attica! Attica!"*

Dr. No (1962)

> *"Bond. James Bond."*

Dr. Strangelove (1964)

> *"Gentlemen, you can't fight in here! This is the war room!"*

Dr. Strangelove (1964)

> *"I can no longer sit back and allow Communist infiltration..."*

Easy Rider (1964)

> *"... They're scared of what you represent."*

Elmer Gantry (1960)

> *"Sin. Sin. Sin. You're all sinners ..."*

Goldfinger (1964)

> *"My name is Pussy Galore."*

Goldfinger (1964)

> *"Shaken, not stirred."*

Harold and Maude (1971)

> *"Greet the dawn with a breath of fire...."*

Hud (1963)

> *"Let's get our shoelaces untied. Whaddya say?"*

Inherit the Wind (1960)

> *"I am more interested in the 'Rock of Ages' than ...."*

In the Heat of the Night (1967)

> *"They call me Mister Tibbs."*

Jaws (1975)

> *"You're gonna need a bigger boat."*

***Lawrence of Arabia* (1962)**
> "...So long as the Arabs fight tribe against tribe,..."

***Love and Death* (1975)**
> "... but the body has all the fun"

***Love Story* (1970)**
> "Love means never having to say you're sorry."

***Marathon Man* (1976)**
> "Is it safe?"

***Mary Poppins* (1964)**
> "Supercalifragilisticexpialidocius"

***M*A*S*H* (1970)**
> "Oh, Frank, Oh, Frank. My lips are hot. Oh, kiss my hot lips."

***Midnight Cowboy* (1969)**
> "I'm walking here! ..."

***Monty Python and the Holy Grail* (1975)**
> "I fart in your general direction. Your mother was a hamster..."

***My Fair Lady* (1964)**
> "The rain in Spain stays mainly in the plain...."

***Network* (1976)**
> "I'm mad as hell, and I'm not going to take it anymore."

***Network* (1976)**
> "She's television generation. She learned life from Bugs Bunny."

***Night of the Living Dead* (1968)**
> "Yeah, they're dead. They're all messed up."

***One Flew Over the Cuckoo's Nest* (1975)**
> "They ... was givin me ten thousand watts a day,..."

***Patton* (1970)**
> "No bastard ever won a war by dying for his country..."

***Patton* (1970)**
> "I love it. God help me I love it so...."

***Planet of the Apes* (1968)**
> "Take your stinkin' paws off me, you damned dirty ape."

***Psycho* (1960)**
> "A boy's best friend is his mother."

***Rocky* (1976)**
> "Yo, Adrian!"

***Rosemary's Baby* (1968)**
> "Satan is his father, and his name is Adrian...."

***Sleeper* (1973)**
> "Sex and death. Two things that come once in a lifetime."

Soylent Green **(1973)**
  "*Soylent Green is people!*"
Spartacus **(1960)**
  "*I'm Spartacus*"
Taxi Driver **(1976)**
  "*You talkin' to me?*"
The Exorcist **(1973)**
  "*What an excellent day for an exorcism.*"
The Godfather **(1972)**
  "*I'm going to make him an offer he can't refuse.*"
The Godfather: Part II **(1974)**
  "*Keep your friends close, but your enemies closer.*"
The Graduate **(1967)**
  "*Mrs. Robinson, you're trying to seduce me, aren't you?*"
The Hustler **(1961)**
  "*Fat Man, you shoot a great game of pool.*"
The Manchurian Candidate **(1962)**
  "*... (b)y an enemy who captured his mind and his soul.*"
The Producers (1968)
  "*We find the defendants incredibly guilty.*"
The Sting **(1973)**
  "*You not gonna stick around for your share?*" "*Naah, I'd only blow it.*"
The Sound of Music **(1965)**
  "*The Von Trapp children don't play. They march.*"
The Summer of '42 (1971)
  "*We were different then. Kids were different.*"
The Wild Bunch **(1969)**
  "*We've got to start thinkin' beyond our guns....*"
To Kill a Mockingbird **(1962)**
  "*One time Atticus said you never really know a man until ...*"

Moynihan, Daniel (B:1927, Tulsa, OK – D:2003, Washington, D.C.). U.S. Senate (1976–2000) (D-NY).

1965   Seminal Book – *The Negro Family: The Case for National Action*
1970   "*... (T)he issue of race could benefit from a period of 'benign neglect' ....*"

Ms.

1972   "*The term 'Ms'' was first recognized as an official title by the U.S. Government Printing Office.*"

Muskie, Edmond (B: 1914, Rumford, ME – D: 1996, Washington, D.C.). U.S. Secretary of State (1980–1981); U.S. Senate (1959–1980) (D-ME); and Democratic Vice-Presidential candidate (1968). *See also Presidential Campaign Themes and Identification Slogans – 1960-1976 at Appendix K*

    1968   Presidential Campaign Themes, Slogans, and Results

Nader, Ralph (B: 1934, Winsted, CT). Political activist, attorney, author, consumer rights and environmental activist, and perennial presidential candidate.

    1965   Seminal Book – *Unsafe at Any Speed: The Designed-In Dangers of the American Automobile*

National Aeronautics and Space Administration (NASA)

    1958   *"To reach for new heights and reveal the unknown ...."*

    1959   *"Mature, middle-class Americans, average in height and visage, family men all."* (See also *Life* Magazine)

NCAA

    1958   *"They're going for two"*

New Jersey Supreme Court

    1976   *"There is no compelling interest of the state" (Right of Privacy and Right to Die)*

Newsweek **Magazine**

    1976   *"The common wisdom of the day pictures Americans as a people sunk in malaise...."*

New York Times (The)

    See Best Seller Lists (Nonfiction and Adult Fiction) (1957–1976) at Appendix G

    1957   *"Big Atomic Plant Near Pittsburgh Supplying Power"*

Niven, David (B: 1910, England – D: 1983, Switzerland). English movie actor in both British and American films.

    1974   *"...(P)robably the only laugh that man will ever get in his life is by stripping...."*

Nixon, Richard M. ("Tricky Dick") (B: 1913, Yorba Linda, CA – D: 1994, New York, NY). 37th U.S. President 1969–1974; Vice President (1953–1961) (R); U.S. Senate (1950–1953) (R-CA); U.S. House of Representatives (1947–1950) (R-CA). *See also House Judiciary Committee – Articles of Impeachment; Presidential Campaign Themes and Identification Slogans (1960–1976) at Appendix K.*

    1959   *"Isn't it better to talk about the relative merits of washing machines than ... rockets?"*

    1960   Presidential Campaign, Themes, Slogans, and Results

    1962   *"I leave you gentleman now. ... You don't have Nixon to kick around anymore ...."*

    1968   Presidential Campaign Themes, Slogans, and Results

1969   Presidential Inaugural Address
"For the first time, ... the times are on the side of peace."
"The second third of this century has been a time of proud achievement...."
"No people has ever been so close to the achievement of a just and abundant society, or so possessed of the will to achieve it."
"We find ourselves rich in goods, but ragged in spirit, reaching with magnificent precision for the moon, but falling into raucous discord on earth."
"We are caught in war, wanting peace. We are torn by division, wanting unity."
"To lower our voices would be a simple thing.... America has suffered from a fever of words, from inflated rhetoric ... angry rhetoric ... from bombastic rhetoric that postures instead of persuading. We cannot learn from one another until we stop shouting at one another...."
"We are approaching the limits of what government alone can do."
"No man can be fully free while his neighbor is not ... This means black and white together... The laws have caught up with our conscience. What remains is to give life to what is in the law...."
"After a period of confrontation, we are entering a period of negotiation."

1969   *"We can begin to bring Americans home from Vietnam."*

1969   *"A man is not finished when he is defeated. He is finished when he quits."*

1970   *"Clean air, clean water, open spaces—these should ... be the birthright of every American."*

1970   *"I'm not for women, frankly, in any (Cabinet) job. I don't want any of them around."*

1970   *"American policy has been to scrupulously respect the neutrality of the Cambodian people."*

1970   *"To assure ... safe and healthful working conditions."*

1971   *"For the Federal government to plunge headlong into supporting child development...."*

1972   Presidential Campaign Themes, Slogans, and Results

1972   *"We are faced with a choice between the 'work ethic' ... and the new 'welfare ethic'...."*

1972   *"No assassin in his right mind would kill me.... (T)hey would wind up with Agnew!"*

1973   Presidential Inaugural Address
"When we met here four years ago, America was bleak in spirit, ... As we stand here today, we stand on the threshold of a new era of peace in the world."
"Let us resolve that this era (of peace) we are about to enter will not be what other postwar periods have so often been: a time of retreat and isolation...."

> *"It is important that we understand both the necessity and the limitations of America's role in maintaining that peace."*
>
> *"We have a chance (now) to do more than ever before ... to make life better in America...."*
>
> *"We have lived too long with the consequences of attempting to gather all power and responsibility in Washington."*
>
> *"... I offer no promise of a purely governmental solution for every problem. We have lived too long with that false promise. In trusting too much in government, we have asked of it more than it can deliver."*
>
> *"... America was built not by the government, but by people; not by welfare, but by work;...."*
>
> *"... (L)et each of us ask not just what the government will do for me, but what I can do for myself?"*
>
> *"... (L)et each of us make a solemn commitment ...: to bear his responsibility, to do his part, ..."*
>
> *"As America's longest and most difficult war comes to an end, let us again learn to debate our differences with civility and decency."*
>
> *"We have endured a long night of the American spirit. But as our eyes catch the dimness of the first rays of dawn, let us not curse the remaining dark. Let us gather the light."*

1973   *"Peace with honor."*

1973   *"The United States will not be dependent on any other country for the energy we need."*

1973   *"I am not a crook."*

1974   *"At noon tomorrow, Eastern Standard Time, I shall resign the Presidency.*

O'Donnell, Michael David (D: 1978). U.S. helicopter pilot in Vietnam.

1970   *"If you are able, have a place for them inside of you ...."*

Packard, Vance (B: 1914, Granville Summit, PA – D: 1996, Martha's Vineyard, MA). Journalist, social critic, and author of books such as *The Hidden Persuaders* (1957), *The Status Seekers* (1959), *A Nation of Strangers* (1972), and *The Ultra Rich: How Much Is Too Much?* (1989).

1957   Seminal Book – *The Hidden Persuaders*

Patterson, Eugene (B: 1923, Valdosta, GA - D: 2013, St. Petersburg, FL). Journalist and Pulitzer Prize-winning editor of *The Atlanta Constitution*.

1963   *"A Negro mother wept in the street ... . In her hand she held a shoe, one shoe, from the foot of her dead child. We hold that shoe with her".*

Pauling, Linus (B:1901, Portland, OR – D: 1994, Big Sur, CA). Chemist, biochemist, academic, author, and recipient of Nobel Prizes for both Chemistry (1954) and Peace (1962).

1970   Seminal Book – *Vitamin C and the Common Cold*

Peace Corps
    1961	*"To promote world peace and friendship"*
"Policy of minimum candor"
    1966	Catchphrases, Chants, and Slogans
Powell, Lewis (B: 1907, Suffolk, VA – D: 1998, Richmond, VA). Associate
    Justice of USSC (1972-1987); President of `American Bar Association
    (1964–1965).
    1971	*'No thoughtful person can question that the American economic system is
    under attack."*

"Power to the people"
    1960s – Catchphrases, Chants, and Slogans
*Presidential Campaign Themes and Slogans – See Presidential Elections 1960–1976
    at Appendix K*
*Presidential Election Results – See Year of Election (1960, 1964, 1968, 1972, and
    1976)*
Presidential Inaugural Addresses – See Name of Subject President
President's Advisory Commission on Civil Disorders – See Kerner Report
Public Broadcasting System. *See also Margaret Meade.*
    1973	*"…(N)o host, no interviews, and almost no voice-over narration."*
*Pulitzer Prize-Winning Books for History, General Nonfiction, and Fiction (1957–
    1976) – See Appendix F*
Rand, Ayn (B: 1905, St. Petersburg, Russia – D: 1982, New York, NY). Novelist
    and political and economic theorist.
    1957	Seminal Book – *Atlas Shrugged*
    1971	*"Upper classes are a nation's past; the middle class is its future."*
Rather, Dan (B: 1931, Wharton, TX). Journalist and television news anchor.
    1974	*"No, Mr. President, are you?"*
Ray, Elizabeth (B: 1943, Marshall, NC). Central figure in 1976 political sex
    scandal.
    1976	*"I can't type. I can't file. I can't even answer the phone."*
Reagan, Ronald ("The Gipper") (B: 1911, Tampico, IL – D: 2004, Bel Air, CA).
    40th U.S. President (1981–1989) (R); Governor of California (1967–1975)
    (R); and movie and television actor. *See also Campaign Themes and
    Identification Slogans – Presidential Elections 1960–1976 at Appendix K.*
    1964	*"There is no such thing as a left or right. There's only up or down…."*
    1965	*"We could pave the whole country (of Vietnam) … and still be home by
    Christmas."*
    1976	*"…(T)he Republican Party … platform … no pastel shades."*
"Repent, Male Chauvinists" – "Your World Is Coming to an End"
    1970 – Catchphrases, Chants, and Slogans

Reynolds v. Sims – See U.S. Supreme Court

Ribicoff, Abraham (B: 1910, New Britain, CN – D: 1998, New York, NY). U.S. Senator (1963–1981) (D-CN); Secretary of Health, Education and Welfare (1961–1962); Governor of Connecticut (1955–1961) (D); and Daley, Richard (B: 1902, Chicago, IL – D: 1976, Chicago, IL). Mayor of Chicago (1955–1976) (D).

> 1968   *Ribicoff: "If… McGovern were president…we wouldn't have Gestapo tactics in … Chicago."*
> *Daley: "F*** you, you Jew sonofabitch"*

Right of Privacy – See U.S. Supreme Court (Griswold v. Connecticut); See also New Jersey Supreme Court

Robertson, "Robbie" (B: 1943, Toronto, Canada). Canadian/American musician, songwriter, and member of The Band.

> 1976   *"The examples of Jimi Hendrix, Janis Joplin, Jim Morrison… brought home the dangers of the road."*

"Rock 'n' Roll" – See Freed, Allan

Rodino, Peter (B: 1909, Newark, NJ – D: 2005, West Orange, NJ). U.S. House of Representatives (1949–1989) (D-NJ); and Chairman of House Judiciary Committee during the Watergate scandal.

> 1974   *"If fate had been looking for one of the powerhouses of Congress, it wouldn't have picked me."*

Roe v. Wade – See U.S. Supreme Court

Romney, George W. (B: 1907, Colonia Dublan, Mexico – D: 1995, Bloomfield Hills, MI). Governor of Michigan (1963–1969) (R), businessman, and father of 2012 Republican Presidential nominee, Mitt Romney.

> 1957   *"A new era of motoring has begun."*

Rowe, Dick (B: 1921–D: 1986). British record producer and executive.

> 1962   *"Guitar groups are on their way out."*

Rusk, Dean (B: 1909, Cherokee County, GA – D: 1994, Athens, GA). U.S. Secretary of State (1961–1969).

> 1962   *"We're eyeball to eyeball, and I think the other fellow just blinked."*

"Saturday Night Massacre" - See Memorable Words – October 20, 1973.

Savio, Mario (B: 1942, New York – D: 1996, Sebastopol, CA). Political activist, leader of Berkeley Free Speech Movement, and later in life an instructor at Sonoma State University.

> 1964   *"There is a time when the operation of the machine becomes so odious …."*

"Say it ain't so, say it ain't so" – See Brooklyn Dodger Fans

Schwartz, Anna – See Friedman, Milton (1971 – Seminal Book – A Monetary History of the United States)

Seminal Books – Schedule of – See Appendix E

Sendak, Maurice (B: 1928, Brooklyn, NY – D: 2012, Danbury, CT). American writer and illustrator of children's books.

1963   Seminal Book – *Where the Wild Things Are*

Sharpton, Al (B: 1954, Brooklyn, NY). Civil rights activist, Baptist minister, television and radio show host, and political commentator.

1965   *"(It was) Malcolm X's town, not King's."*

Shooting "O'Malley, Twice" – See Brooklyn Dodger Fans

Shriver, Sargent (B: 1915, Westminster, MD – D: 2011, Bethesda, MD). Politician; first Director of Office of Economic Opportunity (1964–1968) and Peace Corps (1961–1966); Democratic Vice-Presidential nominee with George McGovern, 1972. *See also Campaign Themes and Identification Slogans – Presidential Elections 1960–1976 at Appendix K.*

1962   *"The best and the brightest" vis a vis "Nine millionaires and a plumber"*

1972   Presidential Campaign Themes, Slogans, and Results

Slogans – See Catchphrases, Chants, and Slogans

Soul Train – See Television Lines

Soviet Union (Officially "The Union of Soviet Socialist Republics" (USSR))

1957   *"Beep, beep, beep,…"*

Sputnik Satellite – See Soviet Union

Stewart, Potter (B: 1915, Jackson, MI. – D: 1985, Hanover, NH). Associate Justice of the USSC (1958–1981).

1964   *"I know it when I see it."*

Summerfield, Arthur E. (B: 1899, Pinconning, MI – D: 1972, West Palm Beach, FL). Chairman of Republican National Committee (1952–1953); U.S. Postmaster General (1953–1961).

1959   *"Any literary merit the book may have … outweighed by the pornographic and smutty passages."*

Summer of Love

1967   *"…to present the unified, positive forces actively involved in the community.*

Super Bowl I – (AFL-NFL Championship)

1967   *Green Bay Packers Over the Kansas City Chiefs*

Swigert, Jack (B: 1931, Denver, CO). NASA Astronaut, mechanical and aerospace engineer.

1970   "Houston, we've had a problem."

Television Lines

1957   ***I Love Lucy***
         "Lucy, I'm home." (Desi Arnez)

1961   ***ABC's Wide World of Sports***
         "The thrill of victory … and the agony of defeat."

1962   **CBS Evening News**
      "And that's the way it is, … ." (Walter Cronkite)

1962   **The Tonight Show**
      "Heeeeere's Johnny" (Ed McMahon)

1970   **The Flip Wilson Show**
      "The devil made me do it." (Flip Wilson)

1971   **Soul Train**
      "As always in parting, we wish you love, peace, and soul." (Don Cornelius)

Television – Most Widely-Viewed or Critically-Acclaimed, First Season Television, and Last Season. *(For the convenience of the reader, the word "The" has been removed from some of the below-listed television show titles)*

60 Minutes (1968)

ABC Monday Night Movie (1976)

ABC's Wide World of Sports (1961)

Adventures of Ozzie and Harriet (1966)

All in the Family (1971, 1972, 1973, 1974, 1975)

American Bandstand (1957)

Andy Griffith Show (1960, 1966, 1967, 1968)

Beverly Hillbillies (1962, 1963, 1971)

Bewitched (1964, 1972)

Bonanza (1959, 1961, 1963, 1964, 1965, 1966, 1968, 1969, 1973)

Candid Camera (1962, 1967)

Carol Burnett Show (1967)

Charley's Angels (1976)

Chico and the Man (1974)

Danny Thomas Show (1957, 1964)

Dick Van Dyke Show (1961, 1963, 1966)

Donna Reed Show (1958)

Dr. Joyce Brothers Show (1958)

Ed Sullivan Show (1971)

Firing Line (1966)

Flip Wilson Show (1970, 1971)

Gomer Pyle, U.S.M.C. (1964, 1965, 1967, 1968)

Gunsmoke (1957, 1958, 1959, 1960, 1961, 1969, 1975)

Happy Days (1976)

Have Gun, Will Travel (1958, 1959, 1960, 1963)

Hawaii Five-O (1972)

Here's Lucy (1970)

I Love Lucy (1957)

Lassie (1973)

> ***Laverne & Shirley*** (1975, 1976)
> ***Lawrence Welk Show*** (1971)
> ***Leave It to Beaver*** (1957, 1963)
> ***Lucy Show*** (1965, 1967)
> ***Marcus Welby, M.D.*** (1970, 1971)
> ***Mary Tyler Moore Show*** (1970)
> ***M*A*S* H*** (1972)
> ***Mister Roger's Neighborhood*** (1968)
> ***Rawhide*** (1959)
> ***Red Skelton Show*** (1962, 1966, 1971)
> ***Rich Man, Poor Man*** (1975)
> ***Rowen & Martin's Laugh-In*** (1968, 1969)
> ***Sanford and Son*** (1972, 1973, 1974)
> ***Saturday Night Live*** (1975)
> ***Sesame Street*** (1969)
> ***Soul Train*** (1971)
> ***Star Trek*** (1966)
> ***Tales of Wells Fargo*** (1957, 1962)
> ***Tonight Show with Johnny Carson*** (1962)
> ***Twilight Zone*** (1959)
> ***Wagon Train*** (1958, 1959, 1960, 1961, 1965)
> ***Waltons*** (1971, 1973)

The Tonight Show – See Television Lines

"The whole world is watching"

> 1968 – Catchphrases, Chants, and Slogans

"Thank you for your service"

> 1973 – Catchphrases, Chants, and Slogans

Thompson, Hunter S. (B: 1937, Louisville, KY – D: 2005, Woody Creek, CO). Author, journalist, and founder of Gonzo journalism movement.

> 1967   *"I'm not advocating sex, drugs, alcohol and violence … (but) they've always worked for me."*

> 1971   Seminal Book – *Fear and Loathing in Las Vegas: A Savage Journey to the Heart of the American Dream*

Thurmond, Strom (B: 1902, Edgeville, SC – D: 2003, Edgeville, SC). U.S. Senate (1956–2003) (R-SC) and influential conservative who ran for U.S. President in 1948 (States Rights Democratic Party) and received electoral votes again in 1960 as independent Vice-Presidential nominee with Henry F. Byrd.

> 1960   Presidential Campaign, Themes, Slogans, and Results

Trail of Broken Promises – See American Indian Movement

Trans-Alaska Pipeline System (TAPS)

1973   *"... Alaska seems to be transformed ..."*

Trans-Atlantic Flights

1958   *"The Debut of the Trans-Atlantic Jet Age"*

"Tune in, Turn on, Drop out"

1960s – Catchphrases, Chants, and Slogans

United Negro College Fund

1972   *"The Mind Is a Terrible Thing to Waste"*

U.S. Constitution

1961   23rd Amendment – Right of Residents of Washington, D.C. to Vote in Presidential Elections

1964   24th Amendment – Elimination of Poll Tax

1967   25th Amendment – Presidential Succession of Power

1971   26th Amendment – Age 18 for Right to Vote

U.S. Office of Saline Water, Department of the Interior

1961   *"Converts deserts into farmlands."*

U.S. Supreme Court

1962   *"The ... prohibition against laws respecting the establishment of religion..."* *(Engel v. Vitale)*

1963   *"The right to be heard would be, in many cases, of little avail ...."* *(Gideon v. Wainwright)*

1964   *"One man, one vote"* - *"Legislatures represent people, not trees ...."* *(Reynolds v. Sims).*

1964   *"If its operations affect commerce."* *(Heart of Atlanta Motel v. United States).*

1965   *"The right of privacy"* *(Griswold v. Connecticut)*

1966   *"You have the right to remain silent ..."* *(Miranda v. Arizona).*

1973   *"(The) zone of privacy"(is) broad enough to encompass a woman's decision..."* *(Roe v. Wade)*

U.S. Surgeon General Report

1964   *"Cigarette smoking is a cause of lung cancer and laryngeal cancer in men..."*

Valenti, Jack (B: 1921, Houston, TX – D: 2007, Washington, D.C.). Special assistant to President Lyndon Johnson; President of the Motion Picture Association of America (1966–2003).

1968   *"The odious smell of censorship"* and *"G-M-R-X"*

Vidal, Gore (B: 1925, West Point, NY – D: 2012, Hollywood Hills, CA). Writer, public intellectual, and social/cultural commentator..

1965   *"At any given moment, public opinion is a chaos of superstition, misinformation, and prejudice."*

1974   *"Envy is the central fact of American life."*

1974   *"The (U.S.) was founded by the brightest people in the country—and we haven't seen them since."*

Wallace, George (B: 1919, Clio, AL – D: 1998, Montgomery, AL). Governor of Alabama (1963–1967, 1971–1979, and 1983–1987), and four-time Presidential candidate (three times with Democratic Party; one time with American Independent Party). *See also Presidential Campaign Themes and Identification Slogans (1960–1976) at Appendix K*

1963   *"…Segregation now, segregation tomorrow, segregation forever…"*

1968   Presidential Campaign Themes, Slogans, and Results

1972   Presidential Campaign Themes, Slogans, and Results

Watson, James (B: 1928, Chicago, IL). Molecular biologist, geneticist, and one of the co-discoverers of DNA.

1968   Seminal Book - *The Double Helix: A Personal Account of the Discovery of the Structure of DNA*

Weatherman, Frank. Criminal and last prisoner to leave Federal Prison at Alcatraz.

1963   *"Alcatraz was never no good for nobody"*

Welch, Robert W., Jr. – See John Birch Society

Weller, Sheila. Author, journalist, and contributing writer for *Glamour, New York,* and *Vanity Fair* magazines.

1967   *"Rarely has there been a 12-month period when young American women changed as dramatically"*

"We shall overcome"

1960s – Catchphrases, Chants, and Slogans

White, Theodore H. (B: 1915, Dorchester, MA – D: 1986, New York, NY). Political journalist, historian, and author best-known for his series of books about the American culture and presidential elections—*The Making of the President –* (1960, 1964, 1968, and 1972).

1960   *"His eyes (were) exaggerated, hollows of blackness, his jaws, jowls, and face drooping with strain."*

1961   Seminal Book – *The Making of the President, 1960*

Woodstock – "Three Days of Peace and Music" - See Memorable Words - 1969.

Woodward, Bob – See "Deep Throat"

Wounded Knee Siege – See American Indian Movement

X, Malcolm - See Malcolm X

Zelizer, Julian (B: 1969, Union, NJ). Professor of History and Public Affairs, Princeton University.

1965   *"The passage of Medicare and Medicaid … shattered the barriers that had separated the federal government and the health-care system…"*

Ziegler, Ronald L. (B: 1939, Covington, KY – D: 2003, Coronado, CA). White House Press Secretary (1969–1974).

1972   *"A third-rate burglary."*

APPENDIX B

General Source Materials

Author's Note

The following is a combined list of some of the primary General Source Materials for all three volumes of *Dead Serious and Lighthearted—The Memorable Words of Modern America (Volume I—1957–1976)*; *Volume II (1977–1993)*; and *Volume 3 (1994–2015)*. Specific source references and citations are set forth in the Notes and Citations.

Adslogans.com.

Advergize.com.

afi.com. (American Film Institute's Greatest Movie Quotes of All Times).

Agel, J., *Words That Make America Great* (Timeless Documents), Random House , Inc. New York, NY (1999).

Ambrose, Stephen; Brinkley, Douglas, *Witness to History*, HarperCollins Publishers, New York, NY (1999).

Andersen, Kurt, *Reset*, Random House, Inc., New York, NY (2009)

Boller, Jr., Paul E., *Presidential Anecdotes*, Penguin Books, New York, NY (1981).

Borgen, Mack W., *The Relevance of Reason – The Hard Facts and Real Data About the State of Current America (Volume 1 – Business and Politics)*, Brody & Schmitt Publishers, Santa Barbara, CA. (2013).

Borgen, Mack W., *The Relevance of Reason – The Hard Facts and Real Data About the State of Current America (Volume II – Society and Culture)* Brody & Schmitt Publishers, Santa Barbara, CA (2013).

Boyer, Paul S. (Editor in Chief), *The Oxford Companion to United States History*, Oxford University Press, New York, NY (2001).

Brokaw, Tom, *Boom - Talking About the Sixties,* Random House, Inc., New York, NY (2007).

Browne, Ray B.; Brown, Pat, *The Guide to United States Popular Culture*, Bowling Green State University Popular Press, Bowling Green, OH (2001).

Caro, Robert A., *The Years of Lyndon Johnson: The Path to Power* (1982); *Means of Ascent* (1990); *Master of the Senate* (2002); and *The Passage of Power* (2012), Alfred A. Knopf, Inc., New York, NY.

Carroll, Peter N., *It Seemed Like Nothing Happened: The Tragedy and Promise of America in the 1970s,* Holt, Rinehart and Winston, New York, NY (1982).

Carruth, Gorton, *The Encyclopedia of American Facts and Dates, (10*th *Edition),* HarperCollins Publishers, Inc., New York, NY (1997).

Crystal, David, *The Cambridge Biographical Encyclopedia*, Cambridge University Press, Cambridge, UK (1994).

Davis, Kenneth C., *Don't Know Much About Geography*, Avon Books, New York, NY (1992).

Davis, Kenneth C., *Don't Know Much About the American Presidents,* Hyperion, New York, NY (2012).

Del Re, Gerard and Patricia, *History's Last Stand*, Avon Books, New York, NY (1993).

D'Souza, Dinesh, *Ronald Reagan–How an Ordinary Man Became an Extraordinary Leader*, Touchstone, New York, NY (1997).

Evans, Harold, *The American Century*, Alfred A. Knopf, Inc., New York, NY (2000).

Filmsite.org (Great Film Quotes by Decade).

Garner, J., *We Interrupt This Broadcast*, (2d Edition),,Sourcebooks, Inc., Naperville, IL (2000).

George-Warren, Holly; Romanowski, Patricia (Editors), *The Rolling Stone Encyclopedia of Rock & Roll*, Rolling Stone Press Book, New York, NY (2001).

Gibbs, Nancy; Duffy, Michael, *The President's Club: Inside the World Most Exclusive Fraternity*, Simon & Schuster, New York, NY (2012).

Greenfield, Jeff, *Television – The First Fifty Years,* Harry N. Abrams Publisher, New York, NY (1977).

Grun, Bernard (Based Upon Werner Stein's Kulturfahrplan), *The Timetables of History: A Horizontal Linkage of People and Events*, Simon and Schuster, Inc., New York, NY 1982.

Halberstam, David, *The Best and the Brightest*, Fawcett Publications, Inc., Greenwich, CN (1972).

Halberstam, David. *The Fifties,* Villard Books, New York, NY (1993).

hawes.com (Hawes Publications) (*New York Times* Best Sellers Lists (1957–1999)).

Hirsch, Jr., E. D.; Kett, Joseph F.; Trefil, James, *The Dictionary of Cultural Literacy: What Every American Needs to Know*, Houghton Mifflin Company, Boston, MA (1988).

iancfriedman.com. (Friedman, Ian C., *The Words That Matter*).

Jennings, Peter; Brewster, Todd, *The Century*, Doubleday, New York, NY (1998).

Kearns, Doris, *Lyndon Johnson and the American Dream*, Harper & Row Publishers, New York, NY (1976).

Kennedy, Caroline, *A Patriot's Handbook: Songs, Poems, Stories, and Speeches Celebrating the Land We Love*, Hyperion, New York, NY (2003).

Kirchon, John W. (Editor-in-Chief), *Chronicle of America*, Chronicle Publications, Inc., Mount Kisco, NY (1989) (Publication Undated).

Kleinfelder, Rita Lang, *When We Were Young: A Baby-Boomer Yearbook*, Prentice Hall, New York, NY (1993).

Knauer, Kelly (Editor), *Time—Person of the Year—75*th *Anniversary Celebration*, Time, Inc., New York, NY (2002).

Korach, Myron, *Common Phrases and Where They Come From*, The Lyons Press, Guilford, CT (2002).

Lewis, R.W.B.; Lewis, Nancy, *American Characters,* Yale University Press, New Haven, CT (1999).

Library of Congress, *Presidential Campaign Posters,* Quirk Books (2012).

MacNeil, Robert, *The Way We Were: 1963 – The Year Kennedy Was Shot,* Carroll & Graf Publishers, Inc., New York, NY (1988).

Manchester, William, *The Glory and the Dream: A Narrative History of America 1932–1972,* Little, Brown and Company, Boston, MA (1974).

Martin, Michael; Gelber, Leonard, *Dictionary of American History*, Rowan & Allanheld Publishers, Totowa, NY (1978).

McCain, John, *Character Is Destiny*, Random House, Inc., New York, NY (2005).

McKay, Brett and Kate "The 35 Greatest Speeches in History," *www. artofmanliness.com*, August 1, 2008.

Murphy, Cullen.; Purdum, Todd S., "Farewell to All That: An Oral History of the Bush White House," *Vanity Fair*, December 28, 2008.

National Geographic, *Eyewitness to the 20*th *Century*, National Geographic Society (1998).

Nelson, Rebecca (Editor), *The Handy History Answer Book* ™, Visible Ink Press, Canton, MI (1999).

Panati, Charles, *Panati's Extraordinary Endings of Practically Everything and Everybody,* Harper & Row, New York, NY (1989).

presidency.ucsb.edu (University of California at Santa Barbara, The American Presidency Project).

Presidentialcampaignselectionsreference.wordpress.com.

Ravitch, Diane (Editor), *The American Reader: Words That Moved a Nation*, HarperCollins Publishers, Inc., New York, NY (1990).

Reay-Smith, John, *The Lawyer's Quotation Book: A Legal Companion*, Barnes & Noble Books, New York, NY (1991).

Robinson, Ray (Compiled by), *Famous Last World: Fond Farewells, Deathbed Diatribes, and Exclamations Upon Expiration*, Workman Publishing, New York, NY (2003).

Safire, William; Safir, Leonard, *Words of Wisdom: More Good Advice*, Simon & Schuster, Inc., New York, NY (1989).

Schlesinger, Arthur, *A Thousand Days,* Houghton Mifflin Harcourt, Boston, MA (1965).

Schlesinger, Arthur, *The Imperial Presidency,* Houghton Mifflin Harcourt, Boston, MA (1973).

Shulman, Arthur; Youman, Roger, *How Sweet It Was – Television: A Pictorial Commentary*, Crown Publishers, Inc. New York, NY (1966).

Smith-Davies Publishing, Ltd., *Speeches That Changed the World: The Stories and Transcripts of the Moments That Made History*, Smith-Davies Publishing, Ltd., London, UK (2005).

taglineguru.com.

The Economist, Pocket World in Figures – 2016 Edition, Profile Books, Ltd., London, UK (2016).

The New York Times Guide to Essential Knowledge, St Martin's Press, New York, NY (2007).

Trachtman, Michael G., *The Supremes' Greatest Hits – The 44 Supreme Court Cases That Most Directly Affect Your Life* (2nd Edition), Sterling Publishing, New York, NY (2007).

Washington, Peter (Editor), *Comic Poems*, Albert A. Knopf, Inc., New York, NY (2001).

Webster III, Orville V., *The Book of Presidents*, Santa Monica Press LLC, Santa Monica, CA (1998).

Webster III, Orville V., *The United States of America: Reference Book*, Santa Monica Press LLC, Santa Monica, CA (1998).

Worth, Fred L., *The Trivia Encyclopedia*, Brooke House Publishers, Los Angeles, CA (1974).

APPENDIX C

Schedule of Abbreviations

Author's Note

For the convenience of the reader, the following is a combined Schedule of Abbreviations for all three volumes of *Dead Serious and Lighthearted—The Memorable Words of Modern America Volume I (1957–1976)*; *Volume II (1977–1993)*; and *Volume III (1994–2015)*.

ADA	Americans with Disabilities Act
AIDS	Acquired Immune Deficiency Syndrome
AIM	American Indian Movement
AMA	American Medical Association
AmEx	American Express
ATF	Bureau of Alcohol, Tobacco and Firearms
BB	Billion(s)
BofA	Bank of America
BPP	Black Panther Party
CDC	Center for Disease Control
CEO	Chief Executive Officer
CIA	Central Intelligence Agency
CTE	Chronic Traumatic Encephalopathy
DH(s)	Designated Hitter(s)
DJIA	Dow Jones Industrial Average
DOD	Department of Defense
DOJ	Department of Justice
ESPN	Entertainment and Sports Programming Network

ERA	Equal Rights Amendment
FAA	Federal Aviation Administration
FBI	Federal Bureau of Investigation
FCC	Federal Communications Commission
HEW	Federal Department of Health, Education and Welfare
HUAC	House Un-American Activities Committee
IPO	Initial Public Offering
MLB	Major League Baseball
MLK Day	Martin Luther King, Jr. Day
MM	Million(s)
NAFTA	North American Free Trade Act
NASA	National Aeronautics and Space Administration
NBA	National Basketball Association
NFL	National Football League
NSA	National Security Agency
NYSE	New York Stock Exchange
OAAU	Organization of Afro-American Unity
OEO	Office of Economic Opportunity
OPEC	Organization of Petroleum Exporting Countries
OSHA	Occupational Safety and Health Act
PBS	Public Broadcasting System
PGA	Professional Golfers' Association of America
PLO	Palestine Liberation Organization
PUSH	People United to Save Humanity
SCATANA	Security Control of Air Traffic and Air Navigation Aids
SCLC	Southern Christian Leadership Conference
SEC	Securities and Exchange Commission
Sec'y	Secretary
S&L	Savings and Loan
TAPS	Trans-Alaskan Pipeline System
Teamsters	International Brotherhood of Teamsters
TMI	Three Mile Island
UNCF	United Negro College Fund
USSC	United States Supreme Court
WMD	Weapons of Mass Destruction

Grammy Awards
for
Best Spoken Word Album
(1959–1976)

Introduction

The Grammy Awards are a series of awards presented by the National Academy of Recording Arts and Sciences of the U.S. The Grammy Awards are largely performance-based awards that, in effect, are based upon criteria similar to other performing arts awards such as the Emmy Awards for television, the Tony Awards for stage performances, and the Academy Awards for motion pictures.

The Grammy Award for Best Spoken Word Album has been annually awarded since the Grammy's first awards ceremony in 1959—in other words, throughout nearly all of Modern America. Over the years, there have been some minor name and eligibility changes to the award (e.g. the award category now includes audio books, poetry readings and even storytelling), but the award has consistently been presented to recognize creative and/or moving "spoken words" first presented in a qualifying format during the prior year.

As a result of the selection process, the limited size of the music industry, and arguably the political leanings of its members, there is an almost inevitable, but noteworthy, political bias that should be remembered. Many would consider there to be a strong politically liberal bias in the selection of these Best Spoken Word category winners, but this does not in itself diminish the value of giving appropriate recognition to these well-spoken words.

The winning works for the Best Spoken Word Album are set forth below:

<u>Year</u>	<u>Work of "Spoken Word"</u>
1959	***The Best of the Stan Freberg Shows*** by Stan Freberg
1960	***A Lincoln Portrait*** by Carl Sandburg
1961	***FDR Speaks* produced** by Robert Bialek
1962	***Humor in Music*** by Leonard Bernstein
1963	***The Story-Teller: A Session with Charles Laughton*** by Charles Laughton
1964	***Who's Afraid of Virginia Woolf?* written** by Edward Albee and performed by Melinda Dillon, George Grizzard, Uta Hagen, and Arthur Hill
1965	***BBC Tribute to John F. Kennedy* performed** by the cast of *That Was the Week That Was*
1966	***John F. Kennedy: As We Remember Him* produced** by Goddard Lieberson
1967	***Edward R. Murrow: A Reporter Remembers, Vol. I – The War Years*** by Edward R. Murrow
1968	***Gallant Men*** by Everett Dirksen
1969	***Lonesome Cities*** by Rod McKuen
1970	***We Love You Call Collect*** by Art Linkletter and Diane Linkletter
1971	***Why I Oppose the War in Vietnam*** by the Rev. Dr. Martin Luther King, Jr.
1972	***Desiderata*** by Les Crane
1973	***Lenny* produced by Bruce Botnick and performed** by the original Broadway cast
1974	***Jonathan Livingston Seagull*** by Richard Harris
1975	***Good Evening*** by Peter Cook and Dudley Moore
1976	***Give 'em Hell, Harry!*** by James Whitmore

APPENDIX E

Seminal Books (1957–1976)

Arendt, Hannah, *On Revolution* (1963)

Baldwin, James, *The Fire Next Time* (1963)

Bickel, Alexander, *The Least Dangerous Branch: The Supreme Court at the Bar of Politics* (1962)

Boston Women's Health Book Collective, *Our Bodies, Ourselves: A Book by and for Women* (1971)

Brown, Dee, *Bury My Heart at Wounded Knee: An Indian History of the American West* (1970)

Brown, Helen Gurley, *Sex and the Single Girl* (1962)

Brown, Rita Mae, *Rubyfruit Jungle* (1973)

Bugliosi, Vincent; Gentry, Curt, *Helter-Skelter: The True Story of the Manson Murders* (1974)

Butler, Robert, *Why Survive? Being Old in America* (1964) (Pulitzer Prize for General Nonfiction)

Capote, Truman, *In Cold Blood* (1966)

Carson, Rachel, *Silent Spring* (1962)

Commoner, Barry, *The Closing Circle: Nature, Man and Technology* (1971)

Durant, William F. and Ariel, *The Lessons of History* (1968)

Ehrlich, Dr. Paul, *The Population Bomb* (1968)

Fletcher, Joseph, *Situation Ethics: The New Morality* (1966)

Friedan, Betty, *The Feminine Mystique* (1963)

Friedman, Milton and Schwartz, Anna, *A Monetary History of the United States 1867–1960* (1971)

Fulbright, Senator J. William, *The Arrogance of Power* (1966)

Galbraith, John Kenneth, *The Affluent Society* (1958)

Geisel, Theodore under pen name Dr. Seuss, *The Cat in the Hat* (1957)

Goldwater, Barry, *The Conscience of a Conservative* (1960)

Halberstam, David, *The Best and the Brightest* (1972)

Harrington, Michael, *The Other America: Poverty in the United States* (1962)

Heinlein, Robert A., *Stranger in a Strange Land* (1961)

Heller, Joseph, *Catch-22* (1961)

Hofstadter, Richard, *Anti-Intellectualism in American Life* (1963) (Pulitzer-Prize for General Non-Fiction)

Jong, Erica, *Fear of Flying* (1973)

Keats, Ezra Jack, *The Snowy Day* (1962)

Kerouac, Jack, *On the Road* (1957)

Lee, Harper, *To Kill a Mockingbird* (1961) (Pulitzer-Prize for Fiction)

Manchester, William, *The Glory and the Dream: A Narrative History of America – 1932–1972* (1974)

Marcuse, William, *One-Dimensional Man: Studies in the Ideology of Advanced Industrial Society* (1964)

Meyers, *The Jacksonian Persuasion: Politics and Belief* (1957)

Morgenthau, Hans J., *The Purpose of American Politics* (1960)

Moynihan, Daniel Patrick, *The Negro Family: The Case for National Action* (1965)

Nader, Ralph, *Unsafe at Any Speed: The Designed-In Dangers of the American Automobile* (1965)

Packard, Vance, *The Hidden Persuaders* (1957)

Pauling, Linus, *Vitamin C and the Common Cold* (1970)

Rand, Ayn, *Atlas Shrugged* (1957)

Sendak, Maurice, *Where the Wild Things Are* (1963)

Thompson, Hunter S., *Fear and Loathing in Las Vegas: A Savage Journey to the Heart of the American Dream* (1971)

Watson, James D., *The Double Helix: A Personal Account of the Discovery of the Structure of DNA* (1968)

White, Theodore H., *The Making of the President, 1960* (1961) (Pulitzer Prize for General Nonfiction)

X, Malcolm and Haley, Alex, *The Autobiography of Malcolm X: As Told to Alex Haley* (1965)

Pulitzer Prize-Winning Books for History, General Nonfiction, and Fiction (1957–1976)

Pulitzer Prize-Winning Books for History (1957–1976)

1957 *Russia Leaves the War: Soviet-American Relations, 1917–1920* by George F. Kennan

1958 *Banks and Politics in America* by Bray Hammond

1959 *The Republican Era: 1869–1901* by Leonard D. White and Jean Schneider

1960 *In the Days of McKinley* by Margaret Leech

1961 *Between War and Peace: The Potsdam Conference* by Herbert Feis

1962 *The Triumphant Empire: Thunder-Clouds Gather in the West, 1763-1766* by Lawrence H. Gipson

1963 *Washington, Village and Capital, 1800–1878* by Constance McLaughlin Green

1964 *Puritan Village: The Foundation of a New England Town* by Sumner Chilton Powell

1965 *The Greenback Era* by Irwin Unger

1966 *The Life of the Mind in America* by Perry Miller

1967   *Exploration and Empire: The Explorer and the Scientist in the Winning of the American West* by William H. Goetzmann

1968   *The Ideological Origins of the American Revolution* by Bernard Bailyn

1969   *The Origins of the Fifth Amendment* by Leonard W. Levy

1970   *Present at the Creation: My Years in the State Department* by Dean Acheson

1971   *Roosevelt: The Soldier of Freedom* by James MacGregor Burns

1972   *Neither Black nor White* by Carl N. Degler

1973   *People of Paradox: An Inquiry Concerning the Origins of American Civilization* by Michael Kammen

1974   *The Americans: The Democratic Experience* by Daniel J. Boorstin

1975   *Jefferson and His Time* by Dumas Malone

1976   *Lamy of Santa Fe* by Paul Horgan

Pulitzer Prize-Winning Books for General Nonfiction (1962–1976)

1962   *The Making of the President, 1960* by Theodore H. White

1963   *The Guns of August* by Barbara W. Tuchman

1964   *Anti-Intellectualism in American Life* by Richard Hofstadter

1965   *O Strange New World: American Culture–The Formative Years* by Howard Mumford-Jones

1966   *Wandering Through Winter: A Naturalist's Record of a 20,000-Mile Journey Through the North American Winter* by Edwin Way Teale

1967   *The Problem of Slavery in Western Culture* by David Brion Davis

1968   *Rousseau and Revolution* (Vol. 10 of *The Story of Civilization*) by Will and Ariel Durant

1969   *The Armies of the Night: History as a Novel, the Novel as History* by Norman Mailer (Co-Winner)

1969   *So Human an Animal: How We Are Shaped by Surroundings and Events* by Rene Jules Dubos (Co-Winner)

1970   *Gandhi's Truth: On the Origins of Militant Nonviolence* by Erik H. Erikson

1971   *The Rising Sun* by John Toland

1972   (No Award Given)

1973   *Children of Crisis (Vols. 2 and 3)* by Robert Coles

1974   *The Denial of Death* by Ernest Becker

1975   *Pilgrim at Tinker Creek* by Annie Dillard

1976   *Why Survive? Being Old in America* by Robert Neil Butler

Pulitzer Prize-Winning Books for Fiction (1957–1976)

1957   (No Award Given)

1958   *A Death in the Family* by James Agee (Posthumous Award)

1959   *The Travels of Jamie McPheeters* by Robert Lewis Taylor

1960   *Advice and Consent* by Allen Drury

1961   *To Kill a Mockingbird* by Harper Lee

1962   *The Edge of Sadness* by Edwin O'Connor

1963   *The Reivers* by William Faulkner (Posthumous Award)

1964   (No Award Given)

1965   *The Keepers of the House* by Shirley Ann Grau

1966   *The Collected Stories of Katherine Anne Porter* by Katherine Anne Porter

1967   *The Fixer* by Bernard Malamud

1968   *The Confessions of Nat Turner* by William Styron

1969   *House Made of Dawn* by N. Scott Momaday

1970   *The Collected Stories of Jean Stafford* by Jean Stafford

1971   (No Award Given)

1972   *Angle of Repose* by Wallace Stegner

1973   *The Optimist's Daughter* by Eudora Welty

1974   (No Award Given)

1975   *The Killer Angels* by Michael Shaara

1976   *Humboldt's Gift* by Saul Bellow

APPENDIX G

The New York Times Best Sellers Lists

Part 1
The New York Times Best Sellers List (Nonfiction) (1957–1976)

Top Two Books with Most Weeks as Either No. 1 or No. 2:
George Goodman
The Money Game (1968–1969) (42 weeks)
William H. Shirer
The Rise and Fall of the Third Reich (1961) (35 weeks)
Authors with More Than One Book as Either No. 1 or 2:
Theodore H. White:
The Making of a President, 1960 (1961) (17 weeks)
The Making of a President, 1964 (1965) (12 weeks)
Bob Woodward and Carl Bernstein
All the President's Men (1974) (20 weeks)
The Final Days (1976) (20 weeks)

Year	Ranking	Author	Title	No. of Weeks
1957	No. 1	Whitehead, Don	*The FBI Story: A Report to the People*	17
	No. 2	Baruch, Bernard M.	*Baruch: My Own Story*	15
1958	No. 1	Golden, Harry Lewis	*Only in America*	13
	No. 1	Kerr, Jean	*Please Don't Eat the Daisies*	13
1959	No. 1	Packard, Vance	*The Status Seekers*	17
	No. 2	Golden, Harry Lewis	*Only in America*	13
1960	No. 1	King, Alexander	*May This House Be Free from Tigers*	21
	No. 2	Adamson, Joy	*Born Free: A Lioness of Two Worlds*	13
1961	No. 1	Shirer, William L.	*The Rise and Fall of the Third Reich*	35
	No. 2	White, Theodore H.	*The Making of a President, 1960*	17
1962	No. 1	Morton, Frederic	*The Rothchilds: A Family Portrait*	17
	No. 2	Taller, Herman	*Calories Don't Count*	13
1963	No. 1	Steinbeck, John	*Travels with Charley: In Search of America*	22
	No. 2	Baldwin, James	*The Fire Next Time*	12
1964	No. 1	Hemingway, Ernest	*A Moveable Feast*	19
	No. 2	UPI and American Heritage Magazine	*Four Days: The Historical Record of the Death of President Kennedy*	12
1965	No. 1	Hammarskjold, Dag	*Markings*	30
	No. 2	White, Theodore H.	*The Making of a President, 1964*	12
1966	No. 1	Dacey, Norman F.	*How to Avoid Probate*	17
	No. 2	Capote, Truman	*In Cold Blood*	14
1967	No. 1	Birmingham, Stephen	*"Our Crowd": The Great Jewish Families of New York*	16
	No. 2	Levenson, Sam	*Everything But Money*	13
1968	No. 1	Goodman, George*	*The Money Game*	25
	No. 2	Morris, Desmond	*The Naked Ape: A Zoologist's Study of the Human Animal*	11
1969	No. 1	Peter, Dr. Laurence J., and Hull, Raymond	*The Peter Principle*	21
	No. 2	Goodman, George*	*The Money Game*	17
1970	No. 1	Reuban, David	*Everything You Always Wanted to Know About Sex*	26
	No. 2	Garrity, Joan **	*The Sensuous Woman*	11
1971	No. 1	Brown, Dee	*Buried My Heart at Wounded Knee: An Indian History of the American West*	24

* Under pseudonym "Adam Smith"

** Under pseudonym "J"

	No. 2	Reich, Charles	*The Greening of America*	19
1972	No. 1	Harris, Thomas	*I'm O.K. – You're O.K.*	22
	No. 2	Lash, Joseph P.	*Eleanor and Franklin*	11
1973	No. 1	Atkins, Dr. Robert C.	*Dr. Atkins' Diet Revolution*	27
	No. 2	Comfort, Alex	*The Joy of Sex*	10
1974	No. 1	Bernstein, Carl; Woodward, Bob	*All the President's Men*	20
	No. 2	Miller, Merle	*Plain Speaking: An Oral Biography of Harry S. Truman*	12
1975	No. 1	Berlitz, Charles	*The Bermuda Triangle*	18
	No. 2	White, Theodore H.	*Breach of Faith: The Fall of Richard Nixon*	12
	No. 2	Porter, Sylvia	*Sylvia Porter's Money Book*	12
1976	No. 1	Woodward, Bob; Bernstein, Carl	*The Final Days*	18
		Sheehy, Gail	*Passages: Predictable Crises of Adult Life*	14

Part 2
The New York Times Best Sellers Lists (Adult Fiction) (1957–1976)

Top Two Books with Most Weeks as No. 1 Bestselling Book (Adult Fiction):

Richard Bach

    Jonathan Livingston Seagull (1972–1973)   (38 weeks)

James Michener

    Hawaii (1960)   (37 weeks)

Authors with More Than One No. 1 Bestselling Book (Adult Fiction):

James Michener

    Hawaii (1960)   (37 weeks)

    The Source (1965)   (22 weeks)

    Centennial (1975)   (16 weeks)

Irving Stone

    The Agony and the Ecstasy (1961)   (27 weeks)

    The Passions of the Mind (1971)   (13 weeks)

Leon Uris

    Exodus (1959)   (20 weeks)

    Trinity (1976)   (22 weeks)

<u>Year</u>	<u>Author</u>	<u>Title</u>	<u>Weeks as No. 1</u>
1957	Metallious, Grace	*Peyton Place*	23 weeks
1958	Traver, Robert	*Anatomy of a Murder*	29 weeks
1959	Uris, Leon	*Exodus*	20 weeks
1960	Michener, James	*Hawaii*	37 weeks
1961	Stone, Irving	*The Agony and the Ecstasy*	27 weeks
1962	Porter, Katherine Anne	*Ship of Fools*	26 weeks
1963	West, Morris	*The Shoes of the Fisherman*	14 weeks
1964	Carre, John le	*The Spy Who Came in from the Cold*	34 weeks
1965	Michener, James	*The Source*	22 weeks
1966	Susann, Jacqueline	*Valley of the Dolls*	28 weeks
1967	Kazan, Elia	*The Arrangement*	23 weeks
1968	Hailey, Arthur	*Airport*	30 weeks
1969	Puzo, Mario	*The Godfather*	15 weeks
1970	Segal, Erich	*Love Story*	34 weeks
1971	Stone, Irving	*The Passions of the Mind*	13 weeks
1972	Bach, Richard	*Jonathan Livingston Seagull*	27 weeks
1973	Bach, Richard	*Jonathan Livingston Seagull*	11 weeks (Tie)
	Stewart, Mary	*The Hollow Hills*	11 weeks (Tie)
1974	Vidal, Gore	*Burr*	17 weeks
1975	Michener, James	*Centennial*	16 weeks
1976	Uris, Leon	*Trinity*	22 weeks

Part 3
The New York Times Best Sellers Lists
for Adult Fiction
An Analysis of America's Reading
(1957–2015)

(Author's Note: In order to obtain a wider range of data for analysis, the following is based upon the entire era of Modern America from 1957 to 2015. This Part 3, "An Analysis of America's Reading (1957–2015)" appears in each of the three volumes of *Dead Serious and Lighthearted*.

Introduction

As evidenced by the cacophony of our recent American political and social debates, Americans are out of step with one another. Teams have been picked. Walls have been built. Distances are kept. People with different opinions are viewed with suspicion, if not disdain.

But in the quieter moments of our national conversation, there is recurring agreement that it would be good if more commonality—or at least more understanding—could be found amongst ourselves. It would be good to talk more and argue less. It would be good if our national community could be strengthened.

One place to begin may be for us to "get to know" each other better, and in a small and partial way this can be done by examining which books have been memorable to us as a nation; which books and which authors we read—as a nation.

This Appendix focuses upon of one of *The New York Times* Best Sellers Lists. In order to present a more orderly and comprehensive picture of what America has been reading and in order to present more meaningful statistical comparisons, this Appendix encompasses all 58 years of Modern America—nearly six decades, from 1957 to 2015. Therefore, as noted above, this Appendix appears in the same format in each of the three volumes of *Dead Serious and Lighthearted—The Memorable Words of Modern America (Volume I (1957-1976)*; *Volume II (1977-1993)*; and *Volume III (1994-2015)*.

Such analysis won't begin to reveal all of the answers. But it is interesting. It may help. We may come to know our own America just a bit better. We may be able to catch at least a glimpse of who we are. We may pick up a few more pieces to the American puzzle.

As explained in more detail below, the two primary reasons for my use of *The New York Times* Best Sellers Lists are (i) its authoritative dominance as one of the preeminent sources of data about the reading choices of the American public; and (ii) the statistical validity of the data, which is achievable due to the mere fact that the lists have been regularly published as national lists for nearly 75 years—since 1942.

The Background and Explanation of *The New York Times* Best Sellers Lists

The first reason for analyzing *The New York Times* Best Sellers Lists is that, despite periodic controversies, they are widely considered to be among the most authoritative national lists of bestselling books in America. The precise methodology used by *The New York Times'* staff for the compilation of the lists and rankings of books has always been and remains a carefully guarded trade secret of the publisher, but it is known that the lists are based upon weekly sales data collected by *The New York Times* from selected independent and chain bookstores and wholesale booksellers throughout the United States.

Over the years, multiple categories for fiction and nonfiction books have been added and even these categories have been subdivided and modified. For example, in 1984, the list of "Advice, How-To, and Miscellaneous" books was presented for the first time. At the time, it was conceded that this new category was added largely because the sales of these "how-to" books were crowding out the more traditional General Nonfiction books.

In the context of lists of fiction books, similar subdivisions and modifications have been made. For example, one of the more controversial changes was made in July 2000, when a list for "Children's Best Sellers" was added. This new list was added in response to the overwhelming dominance of J. K. Rowling's *Harry Potter* books, which had been monopolizing the top of the Best Sellers List for Fiction. Thus, since 2000, fiction books have been divided between Adult Fiction Best Sellers and Children's Fiction Best Sellers. Even more recently, in 2010, belated adjustments were made to the Best Sellers Lists in order to make room for and to recognize the substantial sales of ebooks.

Years of Publication and the Resultant Possibility of Statistical Validity

The second reason for analyzing *The New York Times* Best Sellers Lists is simply because there are so many of them. In the years of Modern America (1957–2015), 3,052 Best Sellers Lists for Adult Fiction have been published by *The New York Times*. The "missing" 16 weeks in that 59-year period are attributable to the fact that no lists were published during the newspaper strikes of 1962, 1963, 1965, and 1978.

Author's Note:
For an explanation of my definition of 1957 and 2015 as the boundary years of what is defined as "Modern America," see Chapter 4 above.

Thus, because of the sheer number of lists, some statistical validity is achievable. An analysis of this data reveals meaningful information (i) about America's reading habits—or at least its book purchasing and reading interests; (ii) about the prominence of certain books, types of books, and authors; and (iii) upon closer examination, about the many changes in the book publishing industry.

It is acknowledged that even with an analysis of *The New York Times* lists, a razor-accurate understanding of which books Americans buy and read is impossible. For example, urban/rural, educational level, and regional reading differences cannot be determined. Furthermore, anomalies occur and some massively successful and important books make it to the bestselling lists but never achieve a No. 1 status. The best example of this may be Harper Lee's Pulitzer Prize-winning *To Kill a Mockingbird.* Although it is one of the seminal books of Modern America and although *To Kill a Mockingbird* spent 98 weeks on the Best Sellers List, it never ranked No. 1 for any given week.

The lists also can be misleading for reasons such as "fast sales" and "double counting." "Fast sales" is a phrase used to reflect that the fact that the lists identify only top book sales in a given week, rather than total book sales overall for the month or year. "Double counting" refers to the fact that certain sales of a book may be counted twice due to the potential for overlap counting of both wholesaler and retailer sales.

Lastly, there is always the risk of rigging. Over the years and despite careful internal controls, there have been periodic attempts by authors, publishers, wholesalers, and retailers to rig the list. These attempts have been made through, for example, bulk buying (by companies, organizations, or institutions) and other forms of data manipulation. Sometimes rigging is attempted through self-buying by the author, by the author's employees, associates, or supporters, or even by the publisher. For example, in July 2015, Ted Cruz's book, *A Time for Truth,* was excluded from the Best Sellers List for Nonfiction because of "the overwhelming preponderance of evidence that the sales" of his book were made through strategic bulk purchases. As expected on both sides, Senator Cruz dismissed the claim and demanded an apology, but *The New York Times* stood by its conclusion based upon its evidence of author-directed, book-buying manipulation. It is impossible to know for certain about the existence or the depth of the Chinese Wall between *The New York Times'* editorial page and its Best Sellers Lists, but if this purchasing manipulation charge is true, the appropriateness of Senator Cruz' book title, *A Time for Truth,* is awkwardly called into question.

Nevertheless, and despite these caveats and cautions, *The New York Times* Best Sellers Lists remain one of the best ways to track America's reading habits. The data below focuses only on *The New York Times* Best Sellers List for *Adult Fiction.*

I.
The Memorable Words and Titles from *The New York Times* Best Sellers List (1957–2015)

A summary of my analysis of and conclusions relating to *The New York Times* Best Sellers List for Adult Fiction (1957–2015) (sometimes referred to hereinafter as the "BSL-Fiction") is set forth below.

Authors

Over the course of Modern America, 205 different authors have had No. 1 books on the BSL–Fiction. Of these 205 authors (including co-authors), 59% (i.e. 121 of them) have been male and 41.0% (i.e. 84 of them) have been female. Although complete gender parity has thus not yet been achieved, these percentages far exceed the level of gender parity in many other contexts of American social and economic life.

Nearly one-half of these authors (i.e. 82 of them or 42% of them) have reached No. 1 on the BSL–Fiction *only once* in their careers.

Books

Through the course of the 3,052 *New York Times* Best Sellers Lists that have been published during the years of Modern America, 647 different books have held the position of No. 1 best seller. The average time for a book to remain at No. 1 on the BSL–Fiction is 4.7 weeks.

Interestingly, the number of weeks that books have stayed as No. 1 on the BSL–Fiction has shortened over the later decades of Modern America. This may be due, in part, to changes in the book publishing market such as the proliferation of ebooks and the overall greater number of written works available as a result of, for example, print-on-demand and other self-publishing platforms.

However, in the opinion of this author, it is much more likely that the shortened period for which any book has remained at No. 1 reflects two changes in American life.

The first change is the shortened attention span of U.S. readers. In the age of the Internet, Twitter, and the many other forms of social media, the importance of the perceived need for speed, brevity, and instancy has been elevated. As result, reading itself has become, at worst, a lost art, and at best, a secondary luxury reserved for one's spare moments.

The second change is that especially starting in the 1980s, there has been a true, deep, and seemingly permanent refusal of some readers to read books written by a person known to hold countering, foreign or even discomforting beliefs. For example, the mere "liberal" or "conservative" subject of some books and/or their author, are deemed inherently offensive and off-putting to some.

In any event, the number of weeks a No. 1 book on the BSL–Fiction holds that position has decreased *greatly* over the last decades, as is evidenced by the following list:

Period	Number of Years in Period	Average Number of Books as No. 1 on List in Any Given Year
1957–1969	13	25.2 weeks
1970–1979	10	25.6 weeks
1980–1989	10	12.5 weeks
1990–1999	10	13.9 weeks
2000–2009	10	10.8 weeks
2010–2015	6	11.6 weeks

II.
The Memorable Authors
(1957–2015)

Overall Winners

Based upon the number of books written by the author in a particular decade that became No. 1 Best Sellers, the "top" and most memorable fiction writers, by decade, are as follows:

1957–1969	James Michener (2 books – *Hawaii, The Source*)
1970–1979	Richard Bach (*Jonathan Livingston Seagull*) (No. 1 Book – 2 years)
1980–1989	Robert Ludlum (3 books – *The Bourne Identity, The Parsifal Mosaic, The Aquitaine Progression*) John le Carre (2 books – *The Little Drummer Girl, The Russia House*) Stephen King (2 books – *Skeleton Crew, It*)
1990–1999	John Grisham (2 books – *The Pelican Brief, The Street Lawyer*) James Redfield (*The Celestine Prophecy*) (No. 1 Book – 2 Years)
2000–2009	John Grisham (4 books – *The Brethren, A Painted House, Skipping Christmas, The Appeal*) Dan Brown (*The Da Vinci Code* (No. 1 Book – 3 years) and *The Lost Symbol*)
2010–2015	E. L. James (*Fifty Shades of Grey*)

It is beyond the scope of this Appendix to analyze the topical subjects of the Memorable Authors or their Memorable Titles, but the last entry, E.L. James' *Fifty Shades of Grey*, deserves special note in the context of tracking and understanding America's changing society. It is revealing in and of itself that *Fifty Shades of Grey* was marketed and sold in the United States with little controversy and was widely- and well-received by the American public (29 weeks as the No. 1 Best Seller–Fiction). This alone reflects changes—for better or worse—in America's social norms.

For example, compare the relative non-controversy about *Fifty Shades of Gray* with the large and litigious controversies and social shockwaves surrounding the marketing and sale of earlier books such as *Lady Chatterley's Love, Tropic of Cancer,* and *Fanny Hill.* These books included explicit descriptions of sex and used then-unprintable words. *Lady Chatterley's Lover* was literally the subject of a U.S. Senate debate in 1930, and all three books (*Lady Chatterley's Lover, Tropic of Cancer,* and *Fanny Hill*) were banned in the United States until the intervention of the USSC in 1959. There is also the example of *Portnoy's Complaint*. Written by Philip Roth and published in 1969, *Portnoy's Complaint* caused great controversy and was also widely condemned. Although its publication was allowed in the United States, many public libraries banned the book for its explicit treatment of sexuality and depictions of masturbation.

Top 10 Fiction Writers of Modern America

Twenty-five writers have written books that have been No. 1 on the BSL–Fiction for more than 25 weeks. However, James Michener is the only writer to have had multiple books (*The Source* (1965–1966—40 weeks) and *Hawaii* (1960–1961—39 weeks)) as No. 1 on the BSL–Fiction for more than 25 weeks.

Based upon the number of weeks during which an author had one of his or her books listed as No. 1 on *The New York Times* BSL–Fiction, the following list represents the Top 10 Fiction Writers of Modern America:

Rank	Author	Years	Number of Weeks
1.	James Michener	1960–1988	200
2.	Stephen King	1979–2015	147
3.	John Grisham	1992–2015	134
4.	James Patterson (Note 1)	2001–2015	96
5.	Robert Ludlum	1978–1990	84
6.	John le Carre	1974–1991	77
7.	Dan Brown	2003–2013	75
8.	Tom Clancy	1986–2012	74
9.	Leon Uris	1959–1977	66
10.	Sidney Sheldon	1978–1992	58

Pure Volume Writing Award

The "Pure Volume Writing Award" is a measure of a writer's work *volume*. It is based upon how many of an author's books have appeared—albeit some of them for very short periods—on *The New York Times* BSL–Fiction. Some writers write a great book and then stop. The classic example is Harper Lee, author of *To Kill a Mockingbird*. Until recently, this 1960 novel was her only known writing, and, as noted above, although it won a Pulitzer Prize and has become one of America's most revered books, it has never been a No. 1 Best Seller. But unlike Harper Lee, other writers write much and publish often.

In the context of writing volume, James Patterson is in a league of his own. Sometimes by himself and sometimes with co-authors, Patterson has written an amazing 52 books that have appeared as No. 1 on the BSL–Fiction. Even though most writers think that even a piece of fiction should take longer than a weekend to write and even though most of his works stay at No. 1 for only 1-4 weeks. Patterson's capacity to generate published and commercially successful works in recent years (2001 through 2015) has been formidable and amazing.

Duration and Longevity Award

The Pure Volume Writing Award, discussed above, identifies James Patterson as the writer who has written the most BSL-Fiction No. 1 books. However, all of Patterson's BSL–Fiction books have been written (albeit amazingly) in the relatively tight 14 year timeframe of 2001-2015.

The Duration and Longevity Award identifies those writers who have had a No. 1 book on the BSL-Fiction *in the greatest number of years*. The list below identifies those nine authors who have had a No. 1 book on the BSL–Fiction in 15 or more years. Only three authors—Stephen King (29 years), John Grisham (23 years), and Danielle Steele (20 years) —have had a No. 1 book on the BSL-Fiction for 20 or more years.

In a slightly different measure of duration and longevity, Stephen King is the author with the Longest Run on the BSL–Fiction. In other words, King is the author who has the greatest number of years between his first book (1979) and his most recent book (2015) on the BSL–Fiction.

Name of Authors With Book as No. 1 on the BSL–Fiction in 15 or More Years

Author	Number of Years
Stephen King	29 years
John Grisham	23 years
Danielle Steele	20 years
Patricia Cromwell	17 years
Tom Clancy	16 years
Mary Higgins Clark	16 years
Janet Evanovich	16 years
James Michener	15 years
James Patterson	15 years

The Heartbreak Award and One-Hit Wonders

The recipient of the Heartbreak Award in the context of BSL–Fiction books is easy to identify—Steig Larsson. Larsson indisputably deserves the Heartbreak Award for the simple, but tragic, reason that all three of Larsson's bestselling Millennium Trilogy books were published after his early death in 2004.

The concept of the One-Hit Wonder Awards is more complicated. The inclusion of an author's name below is not intended to diminish their achievement. Just as every songwriter wishes they had written *American Pie* like Don McLean, every author would mortgage his dog to get a book on this BSL–Fiction list. As will be seen from the below list, the definitional sweep of the One-Hit Wonders list also dubiously includes the names of masters such as Boris Pasternak, Katherine Anne Porter, and Elia Kazan.

Nevertheless, the tracking of one-hit wonders is an American pastime. Thus (and, again, solely in the context of *The New York Times* BSL–Fiction), the ten writers who wrote *only one BSL–Fiction No. 1 book that stayed as No. 1 for 20 weeks or more are as follows:*

<u>Author</u>	<u>Title</u>	<u>Years and Number of Weeks</u>	
Richard Bach	*Jonathan Livingston Seagull*	1972–1973	(38 weeks)
Robert Traver*	*Anatomy of a Murder*	1957	(29 weeks)
James Redfield	*The Celestine Prophecy*	1994–1995	(27 weeks)
Boris Pasternak	*Dr. Zhivago*	1958–1959	(26 weeks)
Katherine Anne Porter	*Ship of Fools*	1962	(26 weeks)
James Gould Cozzens	*By Love Possessed*	1957–1958	(24 weeks)
Elia Kazan	*The Arrangement*	1967	(23 weeks)
Grace Metalious	*Peyton Place*	1957	(23 weeks)
Kathryn Stockett	*The Help*	2010–2012	(22 weeks)
Mary McCarthy	*The Group*	1963–1964	(20 weeks)

* Pen name for John D. Voelker.

III.
The Memorable Books
(1957–2015)

Most Popular, Bestselling Book For Each Year

The following is a list, by year, setting forth the books that dominated the Best Sellers Lists for Fiction. The list identifies the book's title, its author, and the number of weeks the book remained as No. 1 on the BSL–Fiction.

<u>Year</u>	<u>Author</u>	<u>Title</u>	No. of Weeks <u>As No. 1</u>
1957	Grace Metalious	*Peyton Place*	23
1958	Robert Traver*	*Anatomy of a Murder*	29
1959	Leon Uris	*Exodus*	20
1960	James Michener	*Hawaii*	37
1961	Irving Stone	*The Agony and the Ecstasy*	27
1962	Katherine Anne Porter	*Ship of Fools*	26
1963	Morris West	*The Shoes of the Fisherman*	14
1964	John le Carre	*The Spy Who Came in from the Cold*	34
1965	James Michener	*The Source*	22

1966	Jacqueline Susann	*Valley of the Dolls*	28
1967	Elia Kazan	*The Arrangement*	23
1968	Arthur Hailey	*Airport*	30
1969	Mario Puzo	*The Godfather*	15
1970	Erich Segal	*Love Story*	34
1971	Irving Stone	*The Passions of the Mind*	13
1972	Richard Bach	*Jonathan Livingston Seagull*	27
1973	Richard Bach	*Jonathan Livingston Seagull*	11
	Mary Stewart	*Hollow Hills*	11
1974	Gore Vidal	*Burr*	17
1975	James Michener	*Centennial*	16
1976	Leon Uris	*Trinity*	22
1977	Colleen McCullough	*The Thorn Birds*	15
1978	Sidney Sheldon	*Bloodline*	13
1979	Robert Ludlum	*The Martarese Circle*	14
1980	Robert Ludlum	*The Bourne Identity*	16
1981	James Michener	*The Covenant*	16
1982	Robert Ludlum	*The Parsifal Mosaic*	16
1983	John Le Carre	*The Little Drummer Girl*	12
1984	Robert Ludlum	*The Aquitaine Progression*	13
1985	Stephen King	*Skeleton Crew*	10
1986	Stephen King	*It*	12
1987	Danielle Steele	*Fine Things*	9
1988	Tom Clancy	*The Cardinal of the Kremlin*	12
1989	John le Carre	*The Russia House*	9
1990	Scott Turow	*The Burden of Proof*	11
	Jean M. Auel	*The Plains of Passage*	11
1991	Alexandra Ripley	*Scarlett*	12
1992	John Grisham	*The Pelican Brief*	12
1993	Robert James Waller	*The Bridges of Madison County*	35
1994	James Redfield	*The Celestine Prophecy*	13
1995	James Redfield	*The Celestine Prophecy*	14
1996	Anonymous**	*Primary Colors*	9
1997	Charles Frazier	*Cold Mountain*	14
1998	John Grisham	*The Street Lawyer*	9
1999	J. K. Rowling	*Harry Potter and the Philosopher's Stone*	10
2000	John Grisham	*The Brethren*	9
2001	John Grisham	*A Painted House*	4
	Mary Higgins Clark	*On the Street Where You Live*	4
	James Patterson	*Suzanne Diary for Nicholas*	4

	Clive Cussler	*Valhalla Rising*	4
	John Grisham	*Skipping Christmas*	4
2002	Alice Sebold	*The Lovely Bones*	6
2003	Dan Brown	*The Da Vinci Code*	20
2004	Dan Brown	*The Da Vinci Code*	28
2005	Dan Brown	*The Da Vinci Code*	7
2006	Mitch Albom	*For One More Day*	6
2007	Khaled Hosseini	*A Thousand Splendid Suns*	13
2008	John Grisham	*The Appeal*	5
2009	Dan Brown	*The Lost Symbol*	7
2010	Stieg Larsson	*The Girl Who Kicked the Hornets' Nest*	7
2011	Kathryn Stockett	*The Help*	15
2012	E. L. James	*Fifty Shades of Grey*	28
2013	Nicholas Sparks	*Safe Haven*	7
2014	Donna Tartt	*The Goldfinch*	4
	Gillian Flynn	*Gone Girl*	4
2015	Paula Hawkins	*The Girl on the Train*	16

* Robert Traver is the pen name for John D. Voelker.

** Anonymous" author later confirmed as political commentator and writer Joe Klein.

Books with the Greatest Number of Weeks at No. 1 on the BSL–Fiction

The following is a ranked list of the books that remained No. 1. on the BSL–Fiction for more than 25 weeks during the years of Modern America. The list sets forth the book's ranking, the number of weeks it remained as No. 1, its author, the year or years during which it was so ranked, and its title.

__Rank__	__Number Of Weeks__	__Author__	__Year(s)__	__Title__
1.	59	Dan Brown	2003–2006	*The Da Vinci Code*
2.	41	Erich Segal	1970–1971	*Love Story*
3.	40	James Michener	1965–1966	*The Source*
4.	39	James Michener	1960–1961	*Hawaii*
5.	38	Richard Bach	1972–1973	*Jonathan Livingston Seagull*
6.	38	Robert James Waller	1993–1995	*The Bridges of Madison County*
7.	36	Leon Uris	1976–1977	*Trinity*
8.	34	John le Carre	1964	*The Spy Who Came in from the Cold*

9.	30	Arthur Hailey	1968	*Airport*
10.	29	Saul Bellow	1964–1965	*Herzog*
10.	29	E. L. James*	2012, 2014	*Fifty Shades of Grey*
10.	29	Robert Traver**	1957	*Anatomy of a Murder*
13.	28	Allen Drury	1959–1960	*Advice and Consent*
13.	28	James Michener	1974–1975	*Centennial*
13.	28	Jacqueline Susann	1966	*Valley of the Dolls*
16.	27	James Redfield	1994–1995	*The Celestine Prophecy*
16.	27	J.D. Salinger	1961–1962	*Fanny and Zooey*
16.	27	Irving Stone	1961	*The Agony and the Ecstasy*
19.	26	Boris Pasternak	1958–1959	*Dr. Zhivago*
19.	26	Katherine Anne Porter	1962	*Ship of Fools*

* Pen Name for Erika Mitchell.

** Pen name for John D. Voelker.

Branding

Some authors attempt to "brand" their books by using formats or titles that come to be identified with that particular author and help readers identify their books. The following are some of the more dominant and well-known authors who always or frequently title-brand their books in the manners set forth below.

Author	Manner of Title-Branding
Janet Evanovich	Numbers: Hot Six, Seven Up, Hard Eight, To the Nines …
Sue Grafton	Letters: "L" Is for Lawless, "N" Is for Noose, "P" Is for Peril, …
Charlaine Harris	Use of the word "Dead:" – Dead and Gone, Dead in the Family, Dead Reckoning, …
Stieg Larsson	The Girl Who …, The Girl with …"
James Michener	One-word titles: Hawaii, Centennial, Chesapeake, Space, Poland, Alaska …
James Patterson's	Frequent use of Numbers: 1st to Due, 2nd Chance, 3rd Degree, 16th Seduction …
Nora Roberts	"in Death" series: Promises in Death, Fantasy in Death, Treachery in Death …
John Stanford	"Prey" series: Easy Prey, Chosen Prey, Naked Prey …"

Conclusion

The above compilations, listings and comments have been offered as only one sub-category of the Memorable Words of Modern America. This presentation of data and information about these important, popular books is here offered as merely another component of the words that encapsulate American life.

Other valuable sources of list of "memorable word" titles are included at Appendix E (Seminal Books (1957–1976)), Appendix F (Pulitzer Prize-Winning Books for History, General Nonfiction, and Fiction (1957–1976)); and Appendix H (The Best and Worst Book Titles in Modern America (1957–1976)).

APPENDIX H

The Best and The Worst Book Titles of Modern America (1957–1976)

Americans love lists. At times, it seems that the very word "Lists" should be noted as one of the most "Memorable Words" of Modern America. The Top 10 Beaches, The 10 Cures for Anxiety, The 20 Signs of Depression, The 10 Best Retirement Towns, America's Best Neighborhoods, The 10 Towns with the Best Sidewalks, The 5 Best Movies, The 20 Worst Commutes, The 100 Most Beautiful Drives, 10,000 Things We Have To Do Before (We) Die, The 10 Best Books of Lists, and on and on.

In keeping with America's love of lists and in keeping with the "Lighthearted" portion of the title of this book, the Best and the Worst Book Titles of the Years 1957-1976 are set forth below.

The words "best" and "worst" are inherently vague. Rarely can adequate definitions or guiding parameters for these words be crafted. Thus, the lists are unavoidably subjective. These book titles are included, nevertheless, because many of them have become "memorable words." The titles are a component of Modern America, and they are humbly offered for your review and consideration.

Most of the titles are drawn from a close review of *The New York Times* Best Sellers Lists, but a few books such as Peter Matthiesen's *At Play in the Fields of the Lord* and Richard Farina's *Been Down So Long It Looks Like Up to Me,* have been included in the Best Titles List because of their uniquely wonderful titles despite the fact that the books were not best sellers.

Set forth below are the following four lists:

List 1   The 25 Best Book Titles - Fiction (1957–1976)
List 2   The 25 Best Book Titles—Nonfiction (1957–1976)
List 3:   The 25 Worst Book Titles (1957–1976)—Fiction
List 4:   The 25 Worst Book Titles (1957–1976)—Nonfiction

List 1
The 25 Best Book Titles - Fiction
(1957–1976)

(Listed in Alphabetical Order)

A Second-Hand Life (Charles Jackson) (1967)

A Stranger in the Mirror (Sidney Sheldon) (1976)

At Play in the Fields of the Lord (Peter Matthiesen) (1965)

Been Down So Long It Looks Like Up to Me[367] (Richard Farina) (1966)

Heaven Has No Favorites (Erich Maria Remarque) (1961)

Man to Match My Mountain (Irving Stone) (1957)

Naked Came the Stranger ("Penelope Ashe", a pseudonym for a group of 24 journalists led by *Newsday* columnist Mike McGrady) (1969)

One Hundred Years of Solitude (Gabriel Garcia Marquez) (1967)

On the Night of the Seventh Moon (Victoria Holt) (1972)

Remember Me to God (Myron S. Kaufman (1957)

The Billion Dollar Sure Thing (Paul E. Erdman) (1973)

The Darkness and the Dawn (Thomas B. Costain) (1959)

The Gang That Couldn't Shoot Straight (Jimmy Breslin) (1970)

The Goodbye Look (Ross MacDonald) (1969)

The House of a Thousand Lanterns (Victoria Holt) (1974)

The King Must Die (Mary Renault) (1958)

The Last Angry Man (Gerald Green) (1957)

The Last Temptation of Christ (Nikos Kazantzakis) (1959)

The Man Who Loved Cat Dancing (Marilyn Durham) (1972)

The Passions of the Mind (Irving Stone) (1971)

The Spy Who Came in from the Cold (John le Carre) (1964)

The Thirteenth Apostle (Eugene Vale) (1959)

The Winds of War (Herman Wouk) (1971)

The Winter of Our Discontent (John Steinbeck) (1961)

Tinker, Tailor, Soldier, Spy (John le Carre) (1974)

When the Legends Die (Hal Borland) (1963)

List 2
The 25 Best Book Titles – Nonfiction
(1957–1976)
(Listed in Alphabetical Order)

A Long Row of Candles: Memoirs & Diaries, 1934–1954 (C.L. Sulzberger) (1969)

A Nation of Strangers (Vance Packard) (1972)

A Thousand Days: John F. Kennedy in the White House (Arthur M. Schlesinger, Jr.) (1965)

Born in a Crowd (Gloria Braggioti) (1957) (Autobiography)

Brian Piccolo: A Short Season (Jeannie Morris) (1972)

Common Stocks and Uncommon Profits and Other Writings (Philip A. Fisher) (1958)

Gentlemen, Scholars and Scoundrels: A Treasury of the Best of Harpers Magazine from 1850 to the Present (Horace Knowles) (1959)

I'd Do It Again – Autobiography of James Michael Curley (James Michael Curley) (1957)

In Cold Blood (Truman Capote) (1966)

Kids Say the Darndest Things (Art Linkletter) (1957)

Part of a Long Story (Agnes Boulton) (1958) (Wife of Eugene O'Neill)

Passages: Predictable Crises of Adult Life (Gail Sheehy) (1976)

Sex and the Single Girl (Helen Gurley Brown) (1962)

The Arrogance of Power (Senator J. William Fulbright) (1967)

The Best and the Brightest (David Halberstam) (1972)

The Boys of Summer (Roger Kahn) (1972)

The Conscience of a Conservative (Barry Goldwater) (1959)

The Day Christ Died (Jim Bishop) (1957)

The Glory and the Dream: A Narrative History of America, 1932–1972 (William Manchester) (1975)

The Longest Day: The Classic Epic of D-Day June 6, 1944 (Cornelius Ryan) (1959)

The Points of My Compass (E.B. White) (1962)

Three Saints and a Sinner: Julia Ward Howe, Louisa, Annie, and Sam Ward (Louise Hall Tharp) (1957)

Too Much Too Soon (Diana Barrymore and Gerald Frank) (1958)

When the Cheering Stopped: The Last Years of Woodrow Wilson (Gene Smith) (1964)

Zen and the Art of Motorcycle Maintenance: An Inquiry Into Values (Robert M. Pirsig) (1974)

List 3
The 15 Worst Book Titles - Fiction
(1957–1976)

(Listed in Alphabetical Order)

Come Ninevah, Come Tyre (Allen Drury) (1973)
Gabriela, Clove and Cinnamon (Jorge Amado) (1962)
Hornblower and the Hotspur (C.S. Forester) (1962)
Jonathan Livingston Seagull (Richard Bach) (1972)
Manfreya in the Morning (Victoria Holt) (1966)
Penmarric (Susan Howatch) (1971)
Rabbit Redux (John Updike) (1972)
Shardik (Richard Adams) (1975)
Taking the Pelham One Two Three (John Godey) (1973)
That Quail, Robert (Margaret A. Stranger) (1966)
The Levanter (Eric Ambler) (1972)
The Nylon Pirates (Nicholas Monsarrat) (1961)
Theophilus North (Thornton Wilder) (1973)
Tunc (Lawrence Durrell) (1968)
Uhuru (Robert Roark) (1962)

List 4
The 15 Worst Book Titles – Nonfiction
(1957–1976)

(Listed in Alphabetical Order)

Any Woman Can! (David Reuban, M.D.) (1971)
Cagney by Cagney (James Cagney) (1976)
Do You Sincerely Want To Be Rich (Charles Raw, Bruce Page, and Godfrey
    Hodgson) (1971)
*Earthly Paradise: Colette's Autobiography Drawn from Her Lifetime
    Writings* (Robert Phelps) (1966)
From Those Wonderful Folks Who Gave You Pearl Harbor (Jerry Della
    Femina) (1970)
Happiness Is a Stock That Doubles in a Year (Ira U. Cobleigh) (1967)
I Owe Russia $12.00 (Bob Hope) (1963)
Larousse Gastronomique (Prosper Montagne) (1961)
Never Trust a Naked Bus Driver (Jack Douglas) (1960)
O Ye Jigs & Juleps! (Virginia Cary Hudson) (1962)
Pentimento (Lilian Hellman) (1973)
Tarantula (Bob Dylan) (1971)

The Kandy-Kolored Tangerine-Flake Streamline Baby (Tom Wolfe) (1965)
The Last Plantagenets (Thomas B. Costain) (1962)
What Time's the Next Swan? (Walter Slevbak) (1962)

APPENDIX I

—◆—

The 25 Books Most Widely Held in U.S. Libraries

The following list has been compiled by the Online Computer Library Center (far more well-known as the "OCLC"). The OCLC is a nonprofit cooperative organization that was formed in 1967. Headquartered in Dublin, Ohio, the OCLC is now a worldwide organization. Its 23,000 library members are committed to improve "access to the information held in libraries around the globe, and find ways to reduce costs for libraries through collaboration."[368]

Based upon OCLC data, the following is a list of the 25 books that are most widely held in U.S. libraries and the number of such books (rounded to the nearest 1000).

As is evident from this list, beyond the dominance of the *Bible* and the *U.S. Census*, most of the books are pre-20th century classics. The newer books on this list are J.R.R. Tolkien's *The Lords of the Rings* (No. 8) (first published in 1954 and 1955) and Jim Davis' *Garfield* (No. 15) (first published in book format in 1980). Also, if all of the *Harry Potter* books* (the first of which was published in 1997) were counted together, then the *Harry Potter* books would have ranked 5th on the list with 44,965 libraries.

Ranking	Author	Title	Library Holdings
			(Rounded to Nearest 1000)
1.	--	*Bible*	797,000
2.	--	*U.S. Census*	461,000
3.	--	*Mother Goose*	67,700
4.	Dante Alighieri	*Divine Comedy*	62,000
5.**	Homer	*Odyssey*	46,000
6 .	Homer	*Iliad*	44,000
7.	Twain, Mark	*Huckleberry Finn*	43,000
8.	Tolkien, J.R.R.	*The Lord of the Rings*	41,000
9.	Shakespeare, William	*Hamlet*	40,000
10.	Carroll, Lewis	*Alice's Adventures in Wonderland*	39,000
11.	Cervantes, Miguel de	*Don Quixote*	38,000
12.	--	*Beowulf*	38,000
13.	--	*Koran*	37,000
14.	Moore, Clement Clarke	*Night Before Christmas*	33,000
15.	Davis, Jim	*Garfield*	33,000
16.	Twain, Mark	*Tom Sawyer*	32,000
17.	Aesop	*Aesop's Fables*	32,000
18.	--	*Arabian Nights*	32,000
19.	Shakespeare, William	*MacBeth*	30,000
20.	Swift, Jonathan	*Gulliver's Travels*	29,000
21.	Defoe, Daniel	*Robinson Crusoe*	29,000
22.	Shakespeare, William	*Romeo and Juliet*	29,000
23.	--	*Bhagavad-Gita*	29,000
24.	Dickens, Charles	*Christmas Carol*	28,000
25.	Chaucer, Geoffrey	*Canterbury Tales*	28,000

* *Harry Potter and the Philosopher's Stone* (1997), ... *and the Chamber of Secrets* (1998), ... *and the Prisoner of Azkaban* (1999), ... *and the Goblet of Fire* (2000), ... *and the Order of the Phoenix* (2003), ... *and the Half-Blood Prince* (2005), ... *and the Deathly Hallows* (2007).

** As noted above, if all of the *Harry Potter* books were counted together, then the 44,965 libraries with *Harry Potter* books would have ranked 5th on the list.

APPENDIX J

The Books Most Frequently Banned or Challenged in Modern America

The First Amendment and its articulated right of free speech and expression are sacred to American life. They are deeply embedded in American society. Nevertheless, each year various groups, for a variety of reasons, seek to ban certain books from classrooms and libraries. While a very small percentage of books are, in fact, challenged and even fewer are "successfully" banned from classrooms and libraries, the challenges from parents, families, religious groups, and other organizations still occur with almost surprising regularity.[369] Almost without exception, the public's attention is drawn to the book and sales of the book increase.

The mere fact that a book has been challenged does not, in and of itself, make the book's title a component of America's Memorable Words, deserving of inclusion in this book. However, almost curiously and counter-productively from the perspective of those persons or groups seeking to have a book banned from a school or library, the mere existence of the furor and notoriety of the challenge itself heightens the public's familiarity with the book, or at least its title. This unintended consequence is well-exemplified in the case of *Charlotte's Web*, *To Kill a Mockingbird*, *Catcher in the Rye*, and, more recently, certainly *Fifty Shades of Grey*.

As noted above, the most common sources of such challenges are parents, teachers, or religious groups seeking to have identified books banned from classrooms (37.6%), school libraries (34.1%), or public libraries (25.3%). Only a de minimus 3.0% occurred at the post-secondary level or targeted university or academic libraries.

Conversely, the most common entity approving the banning of such books has traditionally been local school boards (or their designated sub-committees) in the professed protection of Christian or, in the opinion of some, pseudo- or misrepresented Christian beliefs.

In the opinion of this author and except in rare instances involving, for example, national secrets (or specific and identifiable national interests), books should never be banned from public libraries. However, this author also believes that it could be extremely useful if authors and their publishing houses self-identified and self-rated their books in a manner similar to the voluntary (G, PG, PG-13, R and X) rating system that has been used for almost 50 years in the motion picture industry.[370] Such ratings could greatly assist children, parents, and school districts in evaluating the book's age appropriateness.

Nevertheless, at least some of the challenges have bordered upon the absurd, such as the attempts to ban Boston Women's Health Book Collective's *Our Bodies, Ourselves* (1971), Harper Lee's *To Kill a Mockingbird* (1960), and—the best/worst yet, Martin Handford's *Where's Waldo* (1987).

According to the American Library Association, there were only 464 challenges to books recorded in 2012, but there were 5,099 challenges reported from 2000 to 2009, and a rather astounding 17,700 challenges filed since 1990.[371] Each such challenge, at least for a brief period of time, attracts the public's attention and consumes the energy and resources of respondent libraries or school boards.

Based upon an analysis of the book challenges during the decade 2000-2009, the most common bases for such challenges, by percentage, were as follows:[372]

<u>Category of Objection</u>	<u>Frequency of Such Category Asserted as Basis for Challenge to Book's Availability</u>
"Sexually Explicit"	28.6%
"Offensive Language"	23.4%
"Unsuited to Age Group"	17.9%
"Violence"	11.2%
"Homosexuality"	6.5%
"Occult" or "Satanic" Themes	5.0%
"Religious Viewpoint"	5.2%
"Anti-Family"	2.2%

Other less common reasons that are sometimes cited in book challenges are racism, drugs/smoking/alcohol, political viewpoint, and suicide. Sexual-based objections, in addition to sexual explicitness and homosexuality, as noted above, have also included objections to writings about nudity and even sexual education. Certainly, the wrapped-too-tight, homerun winners, however, have to be the sought bannings of Dav Pilkey's *The Adventures of Captain Underpants* and, even better yet, the sought banning of the initial 1987 edition of Martin Handford's *Where's Waldo* for the supposedly boob-exposing wardrobe malfunction on the book's beach scene page.[373]

Even amongst the select list of the powerful and culturally influential books that were included in the Library of Congress' 2012 "Books that Shaped America" exhibit, a number of the books have been banned or challenged at one time or another in the course of Modern America. A list of such challenged books is set forth below. Where the alleged basis or bases for such challenges have been identifiable, that information is included as well.

Beloved, Toni Morrison (1987). Violence, sexual content, and discussion of bestiality.

Bury My Heart at Wounded Knee, Dee Brown (1970). Unduly controversial.

Catch-22, Joseph Heller (1961).

Charlotte's Web, E. B. White (1952). Religious objections to portrayal of animals with human abilities such as, in this case, speaking.

Fahrenheit 451, Ray Bradbury (1953). Because one of the books which get banned in this novel was The Bible.

Harry Potter Series, J. K. Rowling (1997–2007). Occult themes.

In Cold Blood, Truman Capote (1966). Sexual content, violence, and profanity.

Our Bodies, Ourselves, Boston Women's Health Book Collective (1971). Sexual content and alleged promotion of homosexuality.

Stranger in a Strange Land, Robert A. Heinlein (1961). "Too adulty themes" for classroom discussion.

Sylvester and the Magic Pebble, William Steig (1969). Presentation of anthropomorphic animals and particularly the portrayal of police as pigs.

Tarzan Series, Edgar Rice Burroughs (1912-1916). Unsuitable for children since Tarzan and Jane were not married when they started cohabitating in the trees.[374]

The Autobiography of Malcolm X: As Told to Alex Haley, Malcolm X and Alex Haley (1965). Crime and "anti-white statements."

The Dictionary (Both American Heritage and Merriam Webster). Inclusion of "objectionable" entries including, in particular, slang words such as "bed," "knockers," and "balls."

The Lorax, Dr. Seuss (1971). Objected to by logging industry for its anti-deforesting plot line.

The Words of Cesar Chavez, Cesar Chavez (2002).

To Kill a Mockingbird, Harper Lee (1960). Degrading, profane and racist work that "promotes white Supremacy."

Where's Waldo, Martin Handford (1987). Offensive partial nudity in one of the wardrobe malfunction scenes in the beach pictures.

Where the Wild Things Are, Maurice Sendak (1963). Too "dark and disturbing."

Below is an even more expansive list of books that have been challenged in the United States over the years. These are the books that have been most frequently challenged during the 13-year period 2001–2013. The years in which each book was in "the top ten list of the most challenged books" are indicated in parenthesis.

The most frequently challenged books were the newer books, such as Robert Cormier's *The Chocolate War,* Peter Parnell and Justin Richardson's *And Tango Makes Three,* and Stephen Chbosky's *The Perks of Being a Wildflower.* However, some of the classics were also frequently challenged including Mark Twain's *The Adventures of Huckleberry Finn,* John Steinbeck's *Of Mice and Men,* Harper Lee's *To Kill a Mockingbird,* and of course J.D. Salinger's *The Catcher in the Rye.*

Absolutely True Diary of a Part-Time Indian, Sherman Alexei (2013, 2012, 2011, 2010).

Adventures of Huckleberry Finn, Mark Twain (2007, 2002).

Alice (series), Phyllis Reynolds Naylor (2011, 2006, 2003, 2002, 2001).

And Tango Makes Three, Peter Parnell and Justin Richardson (2012, 2010, 2009, 2008, 2007, 2006).

Arming America: The Origins of a National Gun Culture, Michael A. Bellesiles (2004, 2003).

Bless Me, Ultima, Rudolfo Anaya (2013, 2008).

Bluest Eye, Toni Morrison (2013, 2006).

Brave New World, Aldous Huxley (2011, 2010).

Captain Underpants (series), Dav Pilkey (2013, 2012, 2005, 2004, 2002).

Catcher in the Rye, J.D. Salinger (2009, 2005, 2001).

Chocolate War, Robert Cormier (2009, 2007, 2006, 2005, 2004, 2002, 2001).

Color of Earth (series), Kim Dong Haw (2011).

Crank, Ellen Hopkins (2010).

Earth, My Butt, and Other Big Round Things, Carolyn Mackler (2009, 2006).

Fallen Angels, Walter Dean Myers (2004, 2003, 2001).

Fifty Shades of Grey, E. L. James (2013, 2012).

Forever, Judy Blume (2005).

Golden Compass, Philip Pullman (2007).

Gossip Girls (series), Cecily Von Ziegesar (2011, 2008, 2006).

Harry Potter (series), J. K. Rowling (2003, 2002, 2001).

His Dark Materials (trilogy), Philip Pullman (2008).

Hunger Games (trilogy), Suzanne Collins (2013, 2011, 2010).

I Know Why the Caged Bird Sings, Maya Angelou (2007, 2004, 2002, 2001).

It's Perfectly Normal: Changing Bodies, Growing Up, Sex, and Sexual Health, Robbie H. Harris (2005, 2003).

My Mom's Having a Baby! A Kid's Month-by-Month Guide to Pregnancy, Dory Butler (2011).

Of Mice and Men, John Steinbeck (2004, 2003, 2001).
Olive's Ocean, Kevin Hanks (2007).
Perks of Being a Wallflower, Stephen Chomsky (2013, 2009, 2008, 2007, 2006, 2004).
Scary Stories (series), Alvin Schwartz (2012, 2008, 2006).
Summer of My German Soldier, Bette Greene (2001).
Taming the Star Runner, S.E. Hinton (2002).
Thirteen Reasons Why, Jay Asher (2012).
To Kill a Mockingbird, Harper Lee (2011, 2009).
Twyla; ten, l8r, g8r (series) by Lauren Myracle (2011, 2009, 2008, 2007).
Twilight (series), Stephanie Meyer (2010, 2009).
Whale Talk, Chris Crutcher (2005).

The tug-of-war over the reach, scope, and protections of the First Amendment in the context of book publishing and book disseminations will continue unabated in Modern America. In the opinion of this author and for at least three reasons, it is highly unlikely that the number of book bannings or challenges will diminish in the forthcoming years. First, there is simply a raw increase in the number of books being published due to the growing size of America's population and to changes in the book publishing industry including, for example, the advent of self-publishing and the growth of independent presses. Second, the traditional bases for seeking the banning of books—sexual-explicitness, offensive language, etc.—are certainly not becoming less common in the varied and coarse styles of American writing and conversation. Third, with the growth and speed of the Internet, news is transmitted across the country at higher and higher speeds. Thus, the communications and de facto cross-encouragements will increase amongst those persons or groups seeking the banning of books that they deem objectionable.

APPENDIX K

Presidential Campaign Themes and Identification Slogans (1960–1976)

1960   John F. Kennedy (D) / Richard M. Nixon (R)
John F. Kennedy (and Lyndon B. Johnson)
A Time for Greatness
Let's Get America Moving Again
Prosperity for All
The Man for the '60's
We Can Do Better
Richard M. Nixon (and Henry Cabot Lodge)
Click with Dick
Experience Counts
For the Future
Keep the Peace Without Surrender

1964   Barry Goldwater (R) / Lyndon B. Johnson (D)
Barry Goldwater (and William E. Miller)
A Choice, Not an Echo
AUH2O
In Your Heart, You Know He's Right
Lyndon B. Johnson (and Hubert Humphrey)
All The Way With LBJ
LBJ for the U.S.A.
Let's Back Johnson

My Brand Is LBJ
The Stakes Are Too High for You to Stay at Home

**1968   Eugene McCarthy (D) / Hubert Humphrey (D) /
Richard M. Nixon (R) / George Wallace (American Independent
Party)**

Eugene McCarthy (Candidate for Democratic Presidential Nominee)
Go Clean for Gene.
To Begin Anew …

Hubert Humphrey (and Edmund Muskie)
Humphrey-Muskie, Two You Can Trust
Some People Talk Change, Others Cause It
Two Hearts Beat as One: Elect This Team!
Unite with Humphrey

Richard M. Nixon (and Spiro T. Agnew)
Nixon Now
Nixon's The One
This Time, Vote Like Your Whole World Depended On It
You Can't Lose 'Em All

George Wallace (and Curtis LeMay)
Stand Up for America

**1972   George McGovern (D) / Richard M. Nixon (R) /
George Wallace (D)**

George McGovern (and Sargent Shriver)
Come Home America
We Luv McGuv

Richard M. Nixon (and Spiro T. Agnew)
President Nixon – Now More Than Ever

George Wallace (Candidate for Democratic Presidential Nominee)
Send Them A Message

1976   Jimmy Carter (D) / Gerald Ford (R)

Jimmy Carter (and Walter Mondale)
A Leader for a Change
Challenging Leadership for Challenging Times
Get America Moving Again
I'm Jimmy Carter and I'm Running for President
Not Just Peanuts

Gerald Ford (and Robert Dole)
Experience Counts
He's Making Us Proud Again
I'm a Ford, Not a Lincoln
I'm Voting for Betty's Husband

APPENDIX L

Corporate Slogans and Advertising Taglines– A Selection of the Most Famous (1957–2015)

Introduction

A business or corporate slogan is essentially an advertising tagline or phrase used steadily, consistently and repeatedly in order to identify to prospective customers the nature and benefits of a given company or its products. Businesses spend billions of dollars creating and then reinforcing their business' "brand," and a tagline or slogan especially one that is clever and easily remembered—is invaluable in creating such brand awareness and reinforcing customer loyalty.

As summarized by Aurora Gatbonton[375] there are five guidelines for creating a great slogan—

1. Identification ("stay consistent with the brand name");
2. Memorable;
3. Beneficial (to reveal the "purpose and benefits of the product");
4. Differentiation (use of creativity and originality in order to stand out in "an overcrowded market"); and
5. Simplicity (through the use of "proven words and short keywords").

Dating of such slogans and taglines is difficult because variants of such slogans and taglines are oftentimes market-tested over multiple periods of several months. In other instances, earlier slogans and taglines are resurrected in later years. Nevertheless, where possible, the date of the initial market use of each slogans and taglines is indicated below in parentheses.

Because of the dating difficulties and because many of these slogans and taglines have been used throughout the years of Modern America, the below list includes all the years from 1957 through 2015 and is reproduced as an Appendix in all three volumes of *Dead Serious and Lighthearted—The Memorable Words of Modern America.*

Examples of some of the more famous and date-identifiable corporate slogans and advertising taglines are included in the text of the three volumes within the year each slogans or tagline was first introduced. They are reprinted below together with other slogans and taglines in order to present a comprehensive list of the famous corporate slogans and taglines from the years 1957 through 2015.

Lastly, some of the famous corporate slogans and taglines from the pre-Modern Era are also separately set forth below. Although they were first introduced prior to 1957, their use continued thereafter.

Corporate slogans and taglines are included in these volumes because they have, almost by design and definition, become some of the most Memorable Words of Modern America. A reader's quick recognition of such slogans and taglines also evidences the power of marketing and advertising within American society.

Ace Is the Place	Ace Hardware (1989)
Always Low Prices	Walmart (1988)
American by Birth. Rebel by Choice	Harley-Davidson
Be All You Can Be	U.S. Army (1981)
Because I'm Worth It	L'Oreal (1971)
Because So Much Is Riding on Your Tires	Michelin
Betcha Can't Eat Just One	Lay's Potato Chips (1981)
Better Living Through Chemistry	DuPont
Between Love and Madness Lies Obsession	Calvin Klein (1986)
Capitalist Tool	Forbes (1979)
Come to Marlboro Country	Marlboro Cigarettes
Connecting People	Nokia
Does She or Doesn't She?	Clairol (1964)
Don't Leave Home Without It	American Express (1975)
Eat Fresh	Subway (1978)
Everything You Always Wanted in a Beer. And Less.	Miller Lite Beer
Fly the Friendly Skies	United Airlines (1966)
Get a Piece of the Rock	Prudential Life Insurance
Grace, Space, Pace	Jaguar
Hand-Built by Robots	Fiat Strada (1979)
Have a Break. Have a Kit-Kat	Kit Kat (1957)
Have It Your Way	Burger King (1973)

Hertz Puts You in the Driver's Seat!	Hertz
Hey Mikey ... He Likes It!!	Life Cereal (1972)
How Do You Spell Relief?	Rolaids
Ideas for Life	Panasonic
I Can't Believe I Ate the Whole Thing	Alka-Seltzer
I Coulda Had a V-8!	V-8
If You've Got the Time, We've Got the Beer	Miller Brewing (1971)
Imagination at Work	General Electric
Innovation	3M
Intel Inside	Intel
Is It Live, or Is It Memorex?	Memorex
I think, Therefore IBM	IBM (1988)
It Keeps Going and Going and Going	Energizer Batteries (1989)
It's Everywhere You Want to Be	Visa (1988)
It's Miller Time!	Miller Brewing (1971)
It's the Real Thing	Coca-Cola (1969)
Just Do It	Nike (1987)
King of Beers	Budweiser
Leave the Driving to Us	Greyhound
Let Hertz Put You in the Driver's Seat	Hertz Rental Car (1959)
Let Your Fingers Do the Walking	Yellow Pages (1962)
Like a Good Neighbor, State Farm Is There	State Farm Insurance
Live In Your World. Play In Ours	PlayStation2
Look Ma, No Cavities!	Crest (1957)
Make Believe	Sony
Merrill Lynch Is Bullish on America	Merrill Lynch (1973)
Must See TV	NBC
Nationwide Is on Your Side	Nationwide Insurance
Nothing Comes Between Me and My Calvins	Calvin Klein Jeans
Nothing Outlasts the Energizer. *It Keeps Going and Going...*	Energizer Batteries
Nothing Runs Like a Deere	John Deere (1972)
Pleasure Is the Path to Joy	Haagen-Dazs
Please Don't Squeeze the Charmin	Proctor & Gamble's Charmin (1964)
Put a Tiger in Your Tank	Esso (1964)
Quality Never Goes Out of Style	Levi's
Reach Out and Touch Someone	AT&T (1979)
Reassuringly Expensive	Stella Artois (1981)
Rice-A-Roni, the San Francisco Treat	Rice-A-Roni (1959)

Ring Around the Collar	Wisk Laundry Detergent
Save Money. Live Better.	Walmart
See the USA in Your Chevrolet	Chevrolet
Solutions for a Small Planet	IBM
Stronger Than Dirt	Ajax
Tastes Great, Less Filling	Miller Lite Beer
The Antidote for Civilization	Club Med (1982)
The Beer That Made Milwaukee Famous	Schlitz
The Best a Man Can Get	Gillette (1989)
The Citi Never Sleeps	Citibank (1976)
The Happiest Place on Earth	Disneyland
The Most Trusted Name in News	CNN
There Is No Substitute	Porsche
The Quicker Picker Upper[376]	Bounty (1960)
The Uncola	Seven Up / 7 Up (1973)
The Ultimate Driving Machine	BMW (1975)
The World Is Crazy. But at least It's Getting Regular Analysis	*The Economist*
Think Big	Imax
Think Outside the Bun / Head for the Border	Taco Bell
Think Small	Volkswagen (1959)
We Bring Good Things to Life	General Electric
We Do Chicken Right	KFC
We Try Harder	Avis (1962)
We Never Stop Working for You	Verizon Wireless
What's In Your Wallet?	Capital One
When EF Hutton Talks, People Listen	EF Hutton
When It Absolutely, Positively Has To Be There Overnight	Federal Express (1982)
When There Is No Tomorrow	Fed Ex
When You've Got It, Flaunt It	Braniff Airlines (1966)
Where's the Beef?	Wendy's (1984)
You Deserve a Break Today	McDonalds
You Don't Have To Be Jewish to Love Levy's	Levy's Rye Bread (1967)
You're Going to Love the Way You Look. I Guarantee It.	Men's Warehouse, Inc
You've Got Questions, We've Got Answers	Radio Shack

Pre-Modern Era

All the News That's Fit to Print	*The New York Times* (1896)
A Diamond Is Forever	De Beers Consolidated (1948)
A Little Dab'll Do Ya	Brylcream (1949)
Breakfast of Champions	Wheaties (1935)
Finger Lickin' Good	Kentucky Fried Chicken (KFC)(1952)
Good to the Last Drop	Maxwell House (1915)
I'd Walk a Mile for a Camel	Camel (1921)
It Takes a Licking and Keeps on Ticking	Timex (1956)
Lucky Strike Means Fine Tobacco	Lucky Strike
Melts in Your Mouth, Not in Your Hand	M&Ms (1954)
M'm! M'm! Good!	Campbell Soup (1935)
Plop, Plop, Fizz, Fizz, Oh, What a Relief It Is	Alka-Seltzer (1953)
Say It with Flowers	FTD (1917)
Snap! Crackle! Pop!	Kellogg's Rice Krispies (1932)
They-re G-r-r-r-eat	Kellogg's Frosted Flakes (1952)
When You Care Enough to Send the Very Best	Hallmark (1934)
You'll Wonder Where the Yellow Went When You Brush Your Teeth with Pepsodent	Pepsodent (1956)
You're In Good Hands with Allstate	Allstate (1956)

Acknowledgements

It is not easy to know where to begin thanking those many people who have encouraged and helped me in the writing and publishing of the three volumes of *Dead Serious and Lighthearted*. I again confess that I have long believed that the very word "Acknowledgements" is too lame; too inadequate; too limited. In common parlance, it seems to suggest a mere head nod as a person "acknowledges" a friend on a crowded street or, in the world of thoughts and ideas, it seems to describe the cautioned recognition, the "acknowledgement," of another person's beliefs or the mere "acknowledgement" of the possibility as to the correctness of another person's insights, thoughts or theories.

But here the acknowledgements are so much more.

The first deserved acknowledgements are generalized and widely disbursed because in my assemblage of *The Memorable Words of Modern America* many of my friends and associates have offered to me invaluably great ideas and steady reminders of those many "memorable words" which needed to be here included.

I am a student of history, but as with all of us, it is the America which I have lived which has affected me the most. However, the way that history is received and absorbed is also relevant, and in that context I know that a special acknowledgement is owed still—and is here again willingly given—to my parents and to my sisters and brothers-in-law. My parents have both been deceased for a number of years now, but it was them, more than almost anyone, who instilled in me a certain irrepressible, almost stubborn, sense of optimism about our country and who encouraged me to look deeper and past the mere headlines about our country.

The second set of acknowledgements is also somewhat generalized—but equally important. This set of acknowledgements, especially in the edgy and coarse context of our modern American conversation, could possibly be criticized by some readers, but I hope not. The second set of acknowledgements is to the thousands of authors, writers, commentators, analysts, reporters, researchers, statisticians, investigators, and groups and associations who collectively have preserved, presented, and, in some cases, themselves helped immortalize the important words and works of others. It is here unnecessary for me to comment on their respective motives—political, social, monetary, self-serving or self-aggrandizing, but their works are too deserving of special note and thanks for they too are often overlooked; too easily discounted. However, their writings collectively allow us all to better understand our own country.

I also wish to thank my friends for having patience, for offering criticism—genuinely and gently given, and, when necessary, for encouraging me to not give up; to keep writing. As I noted with my first books, there is little doubt, at least in my own mind, that most writers write because they can't sing. As I often joked, if I could have wrapped up these entire books into a couple of great Guthrie ballads, I would have. I promise. But it was my friends who were honest enough to remind me that I couldn't sing. It was my friends who cared enough to keep me writing. However, even with the words assembled, these books could not have been finalized, organized, polished, and published without the guidance of Gail Kearns, whose talent, experience, and friendship were invaluable and who helped me assemble a team of wonderful people to see these books through to publication and release. My thanks to Al Bagdonas and Cynthia Calzone for their fine, early editing work, and my special thanks to Ben Siems, my primary editing consultant and advisor, whose steady flow of thoughtful ideas and corrections and whose detailed editing so greatly improved the final texts. I also wish to thank Ghislain Viau, who designed my page layouts with an extraordinary blend of creativity, patience, and relentless commitment; to Alan Hebel and Ian Koviak, two of America's great book cover artists, for capturing my ideas into the cover design, and to Jen Burton of the Columbia Indexing Group, for her invaluable indexing—too often an under-appreciated talent and skill—no science.

I also wish to particularly thank my informally assembled Board of Editors and those friends—Wayne Bell, Tim Bremner, Lisa Consani, Pat Gordon, Paul Hermann, Scott King, Martha Lang, Mark Levin, Reid Olson, and John Van Donge, who took the time to carefully review early excerpts and to provide early testimonials—and my special thanks to General Dulaney O'Roark, my former commanding officer, my life-long friend, and, in case he doesn't already know it, my mentor, for his review of my books, steady encouragement, and early testimonial as well.

Lastly, I want to thank my beautiful wife for allowing me both the time and the freedom to write, and my son who, when he was younger, used to ask me when he was going to be able to start reading some of my own books. Maybe now, little man. Maybe now.

Notes and Citations

1   This is the approximate U.S. population as of 2015, the last year of Modern America (1957-2015), as that phrase is defined in Chapter 4.

2.   As will be discussed more thoroughly in this book, it is acknowledged that all lists are inherently dangerous; all lists are almost definitionally imbued with the near certainty of inadvertent exclusions. The list of these dominant historians of Modern America is no different. The names here referenced such as David McCullough, Jon Meacham, William Manchester, Will and Ariel Durant, Doris Kearns Goodwin, Michael Beschloss, Howard Zinn, David Halberstam, Richard Hofstadter, and Arthur Schlesinger, Jr., are cited only as examples of the many tremendous historians who have, at least at one point in their careers, focused upon Modern America.

3.   Santayana, G., *The Life of Reason* (1905), p. 284. Although Santayana's remark is far more well-known, this author prefers the articulations of Will Durant (at times co-authoring with his wife Ariel) in his brilliant, detailed and thoughtful 11 volumes of *The Story of Civilization* that "nothing that has ever happened is quite without influence at this moment. The present is merely the past rolled up and concentrated in this second of time. You, too, are your past; often your face is your autobiography; you are what you are because of what you have been .... So (it is) with a city, a country, and race; it is its past, and cannot be understood without it." Will Durant, as quoted in *The Gentle Philosopher* (2006).

4.   Meacham, J., "Keeping the Dream Alive," *Time*, July 2, 2012, p. 26.

5.   McLaughlin, M., as quoted in *The Week*, November 18, 2011, p. 17 citing the *Chillicothe* (Ohio) *Gazette*.

6.   In recent years, about 3,000 people a year have renounced their citizenship— usually for tax-motivated reasons. However, for most Americans, expatriation, just like isolation and withdrawal, is neither a realistic nor a desired choice. Most of us wish to remain Americans. For that reason as well, the failure of our national community is not an option.

7. See, e.g. Silver, N., *The Signal and the Noise* (2012).

8.   These topical subdivisions are the same as those identified by the University of Kentucky analysis, which divided the study of history in political history (the rise and fall of governments, political leaders, electoral responsibilities, and the different types of governments, such as democratic and dictatorial); diplomatic history (relationships between nations, governments, and diplomats and the ideas shared by each); social history (cultural customs, education and demographics and including cultural history focusing upon a specific culture's languages, literature, and entertainment); economic history (different systems of markets, industries and classes of people); and intellectual history (cultural ideology and epistemology). *Uky.edu.*

9.   Almost as a matter of idle curiosity, it is interesting to note that there are also vast differences among people and among genders. As we have all endured, some people speak constantly. Others speak hardly at all. Women speak substantially more than men—roughly 20,000 words per day as compared with the estimated male average of 7,000 words per day. Amongst all people, it is estimated that people on average speak about 16,000 words per day. Using this rough average of 16,000 words per day and the average U.S. life expectancy of 78.7 years (76 years for men and 81 years for women), the average American will speak approximately 6,000,000 words a year and 459,600,000,000 words over the course of a lifetime. And although no one's really counting, some sorting out of the memorable words becomes necessary.

10.   To take just one example, in the course of research for his latest book about Thomas Jefferson, (Meacham, J., *Thomas Jefferson: The Art of Power* (2012)), writer Jon Meacham commented in his book-tour speeches how he, God bless him, read every one of the 128+ letters written between Thomas Jefferson and John Adams.

11.   Leavy, Jane, *The Last Boy: Mickey Mantle and the End of America's Childhood* (2011).

12.   *taglineguru/2016campaignslogansurvey.*

13.   *The Week,* July 18, 2014, p. 10, quoting Brownstein, R., *NationalJournal.com.*

14.   *Id.* See also McWhorter, J., *cnn.com/2016/02/13/opinions.*

15.   For a complete listing of all books referenced herein as "Seminal Books," see Appendix E.

16.   The Library of Congress, "America Reads" Introductory Brochure, as distributed at its exhibition June 16, 2016 – December 31, 2016. Other seminal books lists referenced in the Library of Congress' Exhibit include Denby, D., *Lit Up: One Reporter, Three Schools, Twenty-Four Books That Can Change Lives* (2016); Foster, T., *Twenty-Five Books That Shaped America* (2011); Nafisi, A., *The Republic of Imagination: A Life in Books* (2014); Nelson, S., *So Many Books, So Little Time: A Year of Passionate Reading* (2003); Patrick, B., Editor, *The Books*

That Changed My Life: Reflections by 100 Authors, Actors, Musicians, and Other Remarkable People (2016); Pross, F., reading *Like a Writer: A Guide for People Who Love Books and for Those Who Want to Write Them* (2006); Schwalbe, W., *The End of Your Life Book Club* (2013); and Rose, P., *The Shelf: From LEQ to LES: Adventures in Extreme Reading* (2014).

17. For more detailed information, see *pulitzer.org*.

18. The selection of these movie lines has been made by and is solely the responsibility of the author. Some of the quotes have been drawn from sources such as "The 100 Best/Most Memorable Movie Lines of All Time," *msn.com*, March 23, 2016; the "100 Greatest Movie Quotes of All Time" as chosen by the American Film Institute and listed during its television special that originally aired on June 21, 2005 and as listed at *afi.com/100 Years*; and "Great Film Quotes," which are presented by decade at *filmsite.org*. In keeping with the focus of this book upon Modern America (1957-2015), great movie lines from prior years are not included even though, for example, lines such as Clark Gable's "Frankly, my dear, I don't give a damn" (*Gone with the Wind* (1939)) and Marlin Brando's "I coulda been a contender" (*On the Waterfront* (1954)) are regularly selected as among the most famous movie lines of all time.

19. Paralleling the pronouncement of "Guilty," the phrase "Banned for Life" has been used by various sports associations with respect to individuals in response to a wide range of wrongful actions and/or statements. While the precise rules relating to the imposition of a banning for life with respect to any player, manager, or other person associated with the sport vary greatly, such bannings are seen as a means of protecting the integrity of the sport, the game, and the league. Historically, such bannings were most frequently the result of a player or coach's association with gambling, such as the case of the infamous Black Sox scandal in which nine members of the Chicago White Sox were banned for life in 1919 for throwing games in the World Series. More recently, such bannings have been based upon a wider range of reasons including doping, substance abuse, criminal convictions, and even the making of racially offensive remarks. Oftentimes, the banning coincides with a "stripping" of the individual's previously-held titles as in the case of Lance Armstrong, who was stripped of his seven Tour de France titles or barring the person from induction into a Hall of Fame, as in the case of Pete Rose. Despite the "for life" pronouncement, a number of such individuals have been reinstated.

20. In these books, the terms "Guilty" and "Acquitted" are deemed to include all of the variant forms of both words. Thus, the term "Guilty" includes both cases in which an individual has been found guilty by a judge or jury and those in which the individual has pled guilty or even entered a plea of *nolo contendre*. Similarly, the term "Acquitted," includes both cases in which an individual

has been found acquitted by a judge or jury and those in which a case has been dismissed against an individual due to, for example, a judicial ruling of a mistrial or a dismissal with prejudice.

21.   Unlike the beginning dates of an era, the ending date for Modern America as that phrase is used in this book is *neither* subjective not complicated. To the contrary, it is relatively obvious. The year 2015 was selected because any words spoken or written more recently (and especially including, for example, the plethora of words associated with the 2016 Presidential Election) have not had any time to be sorted out. Oftentimes, their importance has merely been associated with the fleeting news cycle, and they have passed no minimum tests of time and remembrance.

22.   On October 29, 1929, America incurred the most devastating stock market crash in its history, signaling the beginning of the Great Depression.

23.   On Sunday, December 7, 1941, "a day which will live in infamy," the Japanese attacked Pearl Harbor, and the formal U.S. involvement in World War II began. This phrase was used by President Franklin D. Roosevelt in his address to Congress the very next day, December 8, 1941. The speech was brilliant and short. It was a mere seven minutes in length. It was broadcast live by radio, and it is estimated that more than four out of five Americans—more than 80% of all Americans—listened to Roosevelt on that Monday at mid-day. Within an hour, 33 minutes to be precise, a formal Declaration of War was passed by Congress, and America entered World War II. The Declaration was passed nearly unanimously, with only one Representative, Jennette Rankin, the first women ever to be elected to the House of Representatives and a lifelong pacifist from Montana, voting against the Declaration. Nearly sixty years later, another "Pearl Harbor Day" struck America on 9/11. While it is still too early to know, some believe that historians will eventually reach a level of consensus that Monday, September 11, 2001 marked the beginning of a new age, the Age of Terrorism.

24.   The invasion of Normandy by the Allied Forces sealed the fate of Germany's Third Reich and the end of the war, but on that day, nearly 12,000 men died (2,700 British, 949 Canadians, and 6,600 Americans) and tens of thousands more were wounded. It was not until 1945 that Germany and, three months later, Japan, surrendered and World War II ended. VE (Victory in Europe) Day was May 8, 1945. VJ (Victory of Japan) Day was August 14, 1945, a day that is most commonly and visually remembered as a result of Alfred Eisenstaedt's famous photograph of an American sailor kissing a woman in a white dress in Times Square, New York City. After those days in 1945 and over the next eighteen months, men came home, families were re-united, and new lives began—in a sense, literally, with the arrival of the Baby Boomers.

25. The DOD reports that as of March 31, 2016, 6,706 military personnel have died in the Afghanistan War (Operation Enduring Freedom) and the Iraq War (Operation Iraqi Freedom). Another over 52,000 have been reported as wounded in action. However, these numbers materially underestimate the true scope and extent of injuries suffered by U.S. troops, their families, and their loved ones, such as psychological trauma that develops as a result of injuries incurred during military action or from the cumulative effects of multiple tours of duty.

26. From another "grassy knoll," the second "grassy knoll" in less than a decade, the Kent State Shootings occurred on May 4, 1970 at Kent State University in Ohio. On that day, students had assembled to protest America's invasion of Cambodia which President Nixon had disclosed five days earlier on April 30, 1970. In the usual ebb and flow of these types of protests, students had protested and marches had begun, and the police (and in this case, the National Guard) had been called out to preserve and protect. But this time things went wrong. The guardsman fired 67 rounds in 13 seconds. Four students were killed and nine others wounded. The political significance of the Kent State Shootings was in the nation's response. More than 4.0 million students went on strike. Hundreds of universities, colleges, and high schools were closed throughout the United States. Many believe that this was one of the turning points, one of those cathartic moments borne of both clarity and exhaustion, when public opinion coalesced even more strongly against America's role in Vietnam (and now Cambodia). Others would go further and suggest that on that day in May, at Kent State and with the wide distribution of John Filo's Pulitzer Prize winning photograph of Mary Ann Vecchio kneeling over the body of Jeffrey Miller, the 1960s ended—appropriately dazed, confused, aimless, adrift, and saddened with its dearth of achievements. See Laurant, D., "Kent State: A History Lesson That He Lives and Teaches...," *Accent on Living,* Health Publications, Spring, 2001 (Article about Dean Kahler, who has his own memory of Kent State. He was shot and was paralyzed from the chest down on that day so many years ago. To this day, he still lives and teaches in Ohio.) In October 2012, and more than forty years after the shooting, Kent State University opened a "May 4 Visitors Center" to help visitors "better understand the events of that day set against the political and cultural changes of the time." Associated Press, October 18, 2012. See also, Porter, C., "Four Decades Later ... Embracing the Tragedy as Part of University's History," *The Wall Street Journal,* November 24-25, 2012.

Author's Note:

As a result of the Kent State shootings, even Harvard Law School, my law school, suspended classes for the first time in its history. This author, like many of my fellow classmates, spread out and travelled around the Northeast organizing anti-war actions and, upon invitation, giving speeches to high schools and college student bodies. It is my not-so-funny-at-the-time remembrance that some professors, upset over the suspension of classes and cancellation of final examinations, required the completion of excruciating, weeks-long take-home examinations over the summer. Despite this author's passionate opposition to the Vietnam War, it was my honor to eventually serve in the U.S. Army for more than four years, three months, and sixteen days.

27.   The fall of Saigon occurred on April 30, 1975, almost exactly five years to the day from the tragedy of Kent State. The capture of Saigon, the capital of South Vietnam, by the North Vietnamese army led to the strangely-named Operation Frequent Wind, the largest helicopter evacuation in history. In the chaos of the last days and the last other operations such as Operations Babylift, which evacuated about 2,000 orphans from the country, and Operation New Life, which evacuated over 10,000 Vietnamese refugees), many thousands of Vietnamese were evacuated from Vietnam. But many of U.S.'s allies remained. They were left behind. Even according to the new Communist government that took over, more than 200,000 South Vietnamese government officials, military officers and soldiers were sent to deadly "re-education camps" during the ensuing years. And thus America's longest war (at least until our current, now longer Afghanistan War) ended poorly, incompletely, and with a degree of confusion, sadness and bitterness that remains with America to this day.

28.   According to Ed Feulner, who eventually served for 35 years as the President of The Heritage Foundation, there are now more than 600,000 donors. In December 2012, Senator Jim DeMint (R-SC) announced his retirement from the U.S. Senate in order to become the new President of The Heritage Foundation. Henninger, D., "A Lesson in Conservative Optimism—The Weekend Interview with Ed Fuelner," *The Wall Street Journal*, December 8-9, 2012.

29.   Henninger, D., "A Lesson in Conservative Optimism—The Weekend Interview with Ed Fuelner," *The Wall Street Journal*, December 8-9, 2012.

30.   *The Week,* May 1, 2015, p. 5.

31.   See Brokaw, T., *Boom!: Talking About the Sixties* (2008).

32.   The eloquent historian James T. Patterson in his new book, *The Eve of Destruction,* also presents a compelling case for identifying 1965 as one of the "hinge years—when history turns and goes in another direction." Patterson argues that 1965, a year of hopeful optimism, low unemployment, phenomenal economic GDP growth, and great legislative achievement (e.g. Voting Rights, Medicare and Medicaid, the formation of the Departments of Housing

and Urban Development and Transportation), was the last year before "the Sixties" began. Gordon, J., "When the Sixties Began," *The Wall Street Journal*, December 24, 2012 review of Patterson's book. See also, Patterson, James, *Restless Giant: The United States From Watergate to Bush v. Gore*, (2005), which, in effect, picks up America's story where William Manchester's magnificent *The Glory and the Dream: A Narrative History of America—1932–1972* leaves off.

33. Sean Connery, with his looks, charm and style became an instant star; a god-like hero beyond reproach. But both the times and the tolerances were different then. For example, co-star Ursula Andress caused a stir, and a Hollywood journalist wrote that "tawny 26-year-old Ursula Andress should have been billed not by her last name, but as 'Undress'." Kamp, D., The Birth of Bond, *Vanity Fair*, October, 2012, p. 249.

34. The recipients were Dr. Shinya Yamanaka of Japan and John Gurdon of Great Britain.

35. Vatter, W., *The Wall Street Journal*, September 24, 2013 (review of Audrey Petty's book, *High Rise Stories: Voices From Chicago Public Housing*, (2013) (279 pp)).

36. Walsh, B., "Rites of Spring," *Time*, October 1, 2012, p. 56. See also, Souder, W., *On a Farther Shore: The Life and Legacy of Rachel Carson*, which describes "the moment when a gentle, optimistic proposition called 'conservation' began its transformation into the bitterly divisive idea that would come to be known as 'environmentalism'."

37. General MacArthur, who would pass away just two years later, told the young cadets in the dated eloquence of his, an earlier, generation that "…in my dreams I hear again the crash of guns, the rattle of musketry, the strange, mournful mutter of the battlefield."

38. See Corbin, I. "From Port Huron to Zuccotti Park," *The Wall Street Journal*, August 3, 2012 (Reviewing *Taking It Big: C. Wright Mills and the Meaning of Political Intellectuals* by Stanley Aronowitz (2012)). Interestingly, a very different crowd made its own "statement" just a couple of years earlier, when William F. Buckley, Jr. invited about 100 conservative activists to the Buckley family estate in Sharon, Connecticut. The conference "would mark the founding of the Young Americans for Freedom" and would issue what came to be known as the "Sharon Statement." Unlike the SDS's Port Huron Statement and almost parroting the views of Buckley's relatively new conservative publication *National Review*, the Sharon Statement "affirmed the importance of limited government, the efficacy of the free market, and the need to seek victory over rather than coexistence with Communism." Edwards, L., *William F. Buckley Jr.: The Maker of a Movement*, (2010), p. 75.

39. Ms. Brown would go on the be the Editor of *Cosmopolitan* for 32 years.

40. Now, 50 years later, the soup company is "returning the favor" by changing its can design and offering its soups in various colors, just as Warhol had envisioned. *Time,* September 17, 2012, p. 52.

41. Johnny Carson aired his last show on May 22, 1992. At the end of that show, he quietly thanked Ed McMahon and Doc Severinsen "and the people watching" and closed his last show by saying "I bid you a very heartfelt goodnight." In 2005, 13 years later, Carson died at the age of 79.

42. But, as noted above, there are a number of other thoughtful opinions on the subject of which year deserves recognition as the true, most deserving transformational year. A powerful case was made by the Americana History Channel in its show, *1964* …. that this was the year deserving of the accolade "the beginning." It was the argument of the producers of this show that 1964 was the "last year" of "hopefulness and excitement." It was not just the 1964 British invasion arrival of The Beatles at the newly-named Kennedy Airport. More importantly, 1964, the year of the nomination of Barry Goldwater for President, was the year of the birth of the modern conservative movement. Drawing heavily from this show, but with a differing opinion, see *1959: The Year Everything Changed* (2009) written by the Pulitzer-prize-winning author, journalist, and cultural historian, Fred Kaplan. He argues first that that the counterculture of the 1960s changed very little in the lasting course of American history, and as suggested by the title of his book that it was 1959 that was one of the transformational years in American history.

43. Kamp, D., "The Birth of Bond," *Vanity Fair,* October, 2012, p. 243.

44. By 1947, just two years after the end of the World War II, the size of our armed forces had been cut by nearly 90%—"from their wartime strength of 12.0 million to 1.5 million." Halberstam, D., *The Fifties* (1993), p. 27.

45. The "relocation centers" were located in isolated areas in seven states and housed over 120,000 Japanese and Japanese-Americans (including about 2,200 Japanese who were transported from South America at the outbreak of the war). Adding insult to injury, most of the relocation centers were located on Native American lands. The last center at Tule Lake, California was closed on March 20, 1946, and the powers of the War Relocation Authority were officially terminated by President Truman shortly thereafter. Only two of these former camps are open to visitors: Heart Mountain, located just east of Cody, Wyoming, and Manzanar, located at the base of the Sierra Nevada Mountains between Lone Pine and Independence, California.

46. Halberstam, D., *The Fifties* (1993), p. 52.

47. The Hungarian uprising, though long inevitable, was spontaneous in origin. It lasted only 18 days, although sporadic violence and periodic economic interruptions continued through the middle of 1957. Within less than two weeks,

Soviet forces entered Budapest and other parts of the country. Within days thereafter, relative peace was imposed, and the world came to understand that the uprising never had a realistic chance of succeeding. Over 2,500 Hungarians and 700 Soviet troops were killed. More than 350 Hungarians were later executed, another 13,000 were imprisoned, and many were deported to the Soviet Union. See generally, Applebaum, A., *Iron Curtain: The Crushing of Eastern Europe 1944-1956* (2012).

48. The author here admits caution in the use of this phrasing as it relates to even the death of Stalin. Just as some Americans used this phrase in the context of the U.S.'s killing of Osama bin Laden in Abbottabad, Pakistan in 2011, it may cross the boundaries of propriety and possibly even morality to express joy or happiness in the passing of another person. However, the phrasing here seems both narratively and morally permissible when one considers the enormity of Stalin's crimes against his own people—for which he never paid and for which he was never called to atone for in any court of international jurisdiction.

49. Despite the warlike implications of this phrase and despite its widespread interpretation by most Westerners, Soviet Premier Khrushchev insisted that this was not a statement of intimidation or a nuclear threat. Instead, several months later (and again in the U.S. several years later) he stated that this phrase was merely a reference to the Marxist saying that "the proletariat is the undertaker of capitalism." Disingenuously, he insisted that the phrase was merely an expression of competing values between the worker society of the Soviet Union and the bourgeois West.

50. Halberstam, D., *The Fifties* (1993), p. 52.

51. Although the actual hostilities occurred from June 1950 until July 1953, the war period was extended until January, 1955 due to the uneasy and protracted peace negotiations. Of the 54,200 American deaths, 33,700 "were actual battle deaths." See Korean War Statistics, Veterans of the Korean War, *veteransinfo.net.*

52. Americans had no idea that they would come to care about Southeast Asia. Most Americans had never heard of Vietnam. They didn't know where it was. They had no idea that in less than a decade the new war in Vietnam would have to be fought mostly by their young sons; that the war would be shown to them in another kind of living and dying color. In 1957, Americans didn't yet have to struggle with trying to understand how a small country, so many miles away, could devastate the American psyche and community. After all, Americans had been through the Great Depression and World War II. Americans thought it was inconceivable that a distant war in a small county would, in some cases, break up Americans families and turn generation against generation.

53. It is estimated that by the time the original GI Bill ended in 1956, nearly one-half of the 16.0 million World War II veterans had taken advantage of

some of the benefits conferred by the bill. The impact of the "blandly and bureaucratically named" Servicemen's Readjustment Act of 1944 cannot be overstated. At the time of its enactment, the Congressional debate about this legislation "rarely penetrated the public awareness" because "the nation's focus was upon the daily advances, setbacks and genuine horrors of the war…." In addition, Congress had estimated that only about 7% (rather than 50%) of veterans would take advantage of the GI Bill's education benefits since college was still then viewed as a bastion of the elite. It was also believed that only a small number of GIs would take advantage of the college-access benefits if for no other reason than less than one-half of the GIs who served in World War II had even finished high school. But Congress was wrong. Millions of World War II vets came home anxious, ready, and eager to go to college. They saw the GI Bill as an opportunity to change their lives. And they took it. For millions of veterans and for their young families and their newly-built communities, everything changed. It is not easy to measure the impacts of the GI Bill— "14 … Nobel Prize winners, 3 Supreme Court Justices, 3 Presidents, a dozen Senators, 2 dozen Pulitzer Prize winners, 238,000 teachers, 891,000 scientists, 67,000 doctors, 450,000 engineers, 240,000 accountants, 17,000 journalists, 22,000 dentists…." It altered the dreams of millions of Americans—both the veterans and their families. It moved their horizon. It created their success. It generated a new kind and a new level of affluence never before experienced by any country. It changed "both the aspirations and the expectations of all Americans, veterans and nonveterans alike. A nation of renters (became) a nation of homeowners." Suburbs were built. Highways were laid. Almost unwittingly, "the Cold War (found) its warriors—not in the trenches or the barracks, but at the laboratory and the wind tunnel and the drafting table." Humes, E., *Over Here: How the G.I. Bill Transformed the American Dream* (2006), pp. 5-6 and 33.

54.   Halberstam, D., *The Fifties* (1993), p. x.

55.   Halberstam, D., *The Fifties* (1993), p. 117. Possibly more interesting and more accurate was the characterization by Maohirior Amaya, a Japanese intellectual and high-level civil servant "… that the American Century was the same thing as the Oil Century—an era in which the economy was driven by oil instead of coal and in which, for the first time, the worker became a consumer as well." *Ibid.*, p. 117. In a manner similar to that of the GI Bill, the importance of oil in the 20th Century cannot be easily overstated. It contributed, if not assured, the affluence and relative ease and mobility of life of citizens in developed nations. It fueled—both figuratively and literally—the development of the automobile industry and the construction of massive highway infrastructures. It created the possibility and cost-effectiveness of air travel. As a mere

by-product, it created the concept of tourism and the development of the worldwide hospitality industry. Oil enabled a plethora of derivative innovations and products—especially, for example, plastics. It led to the formation of OPEC. Furthermore, oil was an omnipresent influence upon international politics in general and in the enhanced geopolitical significance of the Middle East. It also was a major source of certain forms of environmental degradations such as global warming and major oil spills and resultantly, albeit indirectly, helped to trigger, especially in the last quarter of the 20th Century, the growth and importance of the environmental movement.

56. Disneyland, which had opened in Anaheim, California just a couple of years earlier in 1955, was still getting its kinks out. However, by 1957, Disneyland welcomed 4.0 million visitors with admission prices they could afford. The rest of the Disney entourage—Disneyworld in Florida (1971), the Disney TV Channel (1977), the Disney Cruises (1995), and the cross-marketing world of Disney—would be introduced to a changed nation over the next five decades of Modern America.

57. Halberstam, D., *The Fifties* (1993), p. x.

58. Noonan, P., "The I's Have It," *The Wall Street Journal*, November 17-18, 2012. Noonan laments in this column that "we are becoming a conceited nitwit society" in which we are "pushy and self-aggrandizing" and "no one is ashamed to brag now. And show off." She notes, possibly correctly, that America has lost its culture of modesty and that, in its place, there is "an epidemic of egomania (which has stricken) America's civilian and military leadership." In the context of the tragic General David Petraeus debacle, she cleverly compares, for example, how neither General Ulysses S. Grant nor General Dwight D. Eisenhower ever decorated their uniforms. Noonan notes that Grant "wore his uniform with four stars on his shoulder and nothing else. And that was "a fellow who'd earned a few medals," whereas now generals, such as General Petraeus and his fellow officers, routinely display their "fruit salad" rows and rows of awards and ribbons. These small military examples arguably pale in comparison to the rough parallels of brash self-aggrandizement and self-promotion that are now both common and even expected in American politics and business.

59. See, e.g. Kevin M. Kruse's book *One Nation Under God* (2015), as reviewed by D.H. Hart in *The Wall Street Journal*, June 10, 2015.

60. Except for a brief period during the 1953-1954 season on the long-defunct Dumont television network, the NBA was not presented on network television until the 1955-1956 season. Interest in the NBA grew steadily and eventually gained a stalwart television audience on NBC, ABC, and other network stations such as on ESPN and the NBA Network which were launched in 1979 and 1999, respectively.

61. With Bill Russell as their dominating Center, the Boston Celtics won eleven NBA titles over the next thirteen seasons. After playing for a year (1958) with the Harlem Globetrotters, 7'1", 250-pound Wilt Chamberlain joined the then-Philadelphia Warriors (the team moved to San Francisco in 1962), and thus began the Russell-Chamberlain rivalry, one of the greatest sports rivalries in history.

62. Roberts, R., "When the Bear Left for Bama," *The Wall Street Journal*, September 13, 2013.

63. By 2013, athletics coaches—and particularly football coaches—were the highest-paid public employees in 40 states. *Deadspin Report, news, msn,.com,* May 10, 2013. Addressing the question of college football coaching salaries, see generally, Gaul, G. M, *Billion-Dollar Ball: A Journey Through the Big-Money Culture of College Football* (2015).

64. Dundee, A., *Time*, December 19, 2012.

65. Leavy, J., *The Last Boy: Mickey Mantle and the End of America's Childhood*, p. 164. This wonderfully titled and brilliantly written book encapsulates the era — the last days of "America's Childhood."

66. *Ibid.*, p. 164.

67. See, e.g., Weingroff, R., "The Genie in the Bottle: The Interstate System and Urban Problems, 1939–1957," quoting Fishman, R., "The American Metropolis at Century's End: The Past and Future Influences," *Housing Facts and Findings*, Winter, 1999.

68. *The Week*, March 23, 2012, citing S. Hargreaves, *CNNMoney.com*. See also, *Time*, March 26, 2012, p. 5.

69. Holmes, M., *Ultimate Classic Cars: The World's Greatest Automobiles*, (2007), pp. 33-35.

70. Burrough, B., "Remembrance of Wings Past," *Vanity Fair*, March 2013, p. 254. This article relates the fascinating, but tragic, downfall of Merv Adelson—once one of the owners of Rancho La Costa in San Diego and one of the founders of Lorimar productions. By 2013, he was 84 years old, "broke and living in a one-bedroom apartment in Santa Monica, California."

71. George Harrison would join the group the next year, and in 1962, Ringo Starr would join The Beatles and round out the Fab Four.

72. This 122.7 birth rate at the peak of the Baby Boom compares with the more recent birth rate of 64 births per 1,000—an all-time U.S. low, as of 2007-2010. Jordan, M., *The Wall Street Journal*, November 30, 2012, citing the Pew Research Center. But see, Calfas, J., "Birthrate on Rise For First Time in 7 Years," *USA Today*, June 17, 2015 (Identifies a real, but statistically irrelevant, 1% increase in the birth rate).

73. Brokaw, T., *The Greatest Generation* (1998).

74. Halberstam, D., *The Fifties* (1993).

75. In 1963, the movie, *The Ugly American*, was also released starring Marlon Brando as Ambassador Harrison MacWhite.

76. Weintraub, J., "Paul Anka – A V.F. Portrait," *Vanity Fair*, May 2013, p. 184.

77. *American Bandstand* remained on television for 32 years until 1989. For many, Dick Clark, until almost the end of his life in April 2012, remained the ageless teenager.

78. A book of the same title by John de Graaf, David Nann, and Thomas H. Taylor was released in 2001.

79. T.J. Jemison lived until December 2013. See *Time*, December 9, 2013, p. 19.

80. Caro, Robert *The Passage of Power* (2012), p. xiv.

81. Senator Thurmond of South Carolina opened his filibuster on August 28, 1957 by denouncing the proposed Civil Rights Bill as "cruel and unusual punishment." Over the next 24 hours and 18 minutes, "the senator, armed with throat lozenges and malted milk tablets, recited the voting rights laws of every state to (supposedly) show (that) adequate protection existed. He also recited the Declaration of Independence and launched into a history of Anglo-Saxon juries to counter the bill's proposal to allow judges to punish cases of civil contempt without a jury trial." The Southerners didn't rise up and convince the other Senators to block the legislation, and thus Thurmond finally stopped his filibuster after a strong denunciation of "those nine men" on the Supreme Court who had, three years earlier in the case of *Brown v. Board of Education* outlawed school segregation. With that closing denunciation, he finally quit and left the chamber. The bill passed less than two hours later by an overwhelming vote of 62-15. *Associated Press*, June 27, 2003, quoting Nadine Cohodas' biography entitled *Strom Thurmond and the Politics of Southern Change* (1995).

82. In a few rare instances, words spoken by foreigners are included, but only in instances where (i) the words were directed to or were about the United States or about Americans, and (ii) the words, for whatever reason(s), became the subject of widespread debate and discussion with the United States. Examples include Soviet Premier Nikita Khrushchev's infamous statement addressed to Americans that "we (the Soviet Union) will bury you," and, more "lightheartedly," the unflappable British actor David Niven's wonderful remarks at the 1974 Academy Awards upon seeing a naked man streak past him on the stage.

83. The number of cities and towns (and "populated areas") is as high as 35,000 according to the U.S. Geological Survey, however this smaller number of 19,500 is used because it includes only those population centers that are incorporated and have a more formalized municipal government.

84. Greenberg, S, *taxfoundation.org*, citing word compilation data from West Publishing Company. See also Crews, W., Young, R., "The Towering Federal Register," *dailycaller.com*, May 21, 2013.

85.   *aynrand.org.*

86.   Greif, M., "The Hard Sell," *The New York Times*, December 30, 2007.

87.   *Ibid.*

88.   *jounals.cambridge.org.*

89.   PrettyFamous is a multi-source data evaluation and presentation company founded in 2010, and the films included herein are from PrettyFamous' 2016 list of Best Movies at *msn.com*, April 4, 2016.

90.   *Sclcnational.org.*

91.   Evans, H., *The American Century* (2000), p. 460; *wearethebeloveD.C.ommunity. org.*

92.   See generally, Wills, G., *The New York Review of Books*, February 11, 2016 review of E. J. Dionne's *Why the Right Went Wrong: Conservatism—from Goldwater to the Tea Party and Beyond* (2016); and Schultz, K., *salon.com*, June 7, 2015.

93.   Evans, H., *The American Century* (2000), pp. 474-475.

94.   See generally, Evans, H., *The American Century* (2000), pp. 474-475.

95.   See below, April 9, 1959 (*"Mature, middle-class Americans, average in height and visage, family men all."*).

96.   Finney, J., *The New York Times*, December 18, 1958.

97.   See, Weber, S., "Our 'Sputnik Moment:' Then and Now," February 11, 2011, *pbs.org.*

98.   *Ibid.*

99.   A Nation at Risk: The Imperative for Education Reform, a report of President Ronald Reagan's National Commission on Excellence in Education (April 1983).

100. Kleinfelder, R., *When We Were Young* (1993), p. 222.

101. *creditcardforum.com*, "History of Visa" at *usa.visa.com.*

102. See generally, Paur, J., "'Comets' Debut Trans-Atlantic Jet Age," *wired.com*, October 4, 2010.

103. *jbs.org.*

104. Wilentz, S., "Confounding Fathers: The Tea Party's Cold War Roots," *The New Yorker*, October 18, 2010.

105. Federal Judge Frederick van Pelt Bryan opining in the *Lady Chatterley's Lover* book-banning case. See generally, "Control of Obscenity," *library-cqpress.com.*

106. 378 U.S. 184 (1964).

107. Evans, H., *The American Century* (2000), p. 479.

108. Excerpted from the excellent compilation of such last words by Ray Robinson in his book *Famous Last Words* (2003).

109. Klein, R., *The New York Times*, July 28, 1996 (Review of David Shaw's *The Pleasure Police: How Bluenose Busybodies and Lily-Livered Alarmists Are Taking All the Fun Out of Life* (1996)).

110. *Ibid.*

111. See discussion of Black Panthers' statement at October 1966.

112. Carroll, P., *It Seems Like Nothing Happened: The Tragedy and Promise of America in the 1970s* (1982), p. 54, citing Wilson, W., *Power, Racism, and Privilege* (1973), p. 149.

113. This statement was made by former President Bill Clinton to Tom Brokaw and is cited by Brokaw in his book *Boom!: Talking about the Sixties* (2008).

114. Weiss, J., "The Doors Defined California Cool in the '60s. How Does Their Legacy Stack up 50 Years Later?," *thewashingtonpost.com*, October 6, 2017.

115. See, e.g.. *What If* series of books about American History such as *What If? The World's Foremost Military Historians Imagine What Might Have Been* (1999), and *What If? Eminent Historians Imagine What Might Have Been* (2001).

116. Wills, G., *The New York Review of Books*, February 11, 2016.

117. Garry Wills quoting E.J. Dionne in his review of E. J. Dionne's *Why the Right Went Wrong: Conservatism—from Goldwater to the Tea Party and Beyond* (2016)

118. Review in *Science*, March 10, 1961, a weekly publication of the American Association for the Advancement of Science.

119. See also, 1962 – Pulitzer Price for General Nonfiction.

120. Seal, M., *Vanity Fair*, August 2013, p. 109.

121. Laura Bush, the former first lady, as quoted in M. Seal's article in *Vanity Fair*, August 2013 109. See also, Trachtenberg, J., Stevens, L., *The Wall Street Journal*, February 7-8, 2015 (Referencing the worldwide sale of 40.0 million copies of *To Kill a Mockingbird*); 1961 – Books – Pulitzer Prize for Fiction.

122. *Adslogans.com* identifies 1971 for the initial use of this slogan, however variants of the slogan were used earlier.

123. Evans, H., *The American Century* (2000), p. 498.

124. See Martin, J., "Portrait of a Political Odd Couple," *The Wall Street Journal*, February 2-3, 2013 (Reviewing Jeffrey Frank's Book *Ike and Dick* (2013)).

125. See also, 1962 – Books – Pulitzer Price for General Nonfiction.

126. See, e.g., Halperin, M., Heilemann, J. *Double Down: Game Change 2012* (2012).

127. National Integrated Drought Information System at *drought.gov*.

128. *Texasarchive.org*.

129. Davis, Kenneth, C., *Don't Know Much About the American Presidents* (2012), p. 488.

130. *History.com* (Berlin Wall).

131. Officially, The Wall was removed upon the reunification of East and West Germany on October 3, 1990.

132. *cbn.com*.

133. Wills, G., "Where Evangelicals Came From," *The New York Review of Books*, April 20, 2017 (Reviewing Frances Fitzgerald's *The Evangelicals: The Struggle to Shape Americas* (2017)).

134. In 1989, Jim Bakker was found guilty on 24 counts of mail and wire fraud. Although he was originally sentenced to 45 years in prison, the sentence was reduced to eight years, of which Bakker served five years in federal prison prior to his release. Jim and Tammy Bakker were divorced in 1992.

135. See, e.g., *Rachelcarson.org.*

136. Walsh, B., "Rites of Spring," *Time,* October 1, 2012, p. 56. See also, Souder, W., *On a Farther Shore: The Life and Legacy of Rachel Carson* (2012), which describes "the moment when a gentle, optimistic proposition called 'conservation' began its transformation into the bitterly divisive idea that would come to be known as 'environmentalism'."

137. Michael Harrington, as quoted in Isserman, M., *The New York Times,* June 19, 2009.

138. See *ala.org* (Association for Library Service to Children).

139. Bickel, A., *The Least Dangerous Branch: The Supreme Court at the Bar of Politics* (1962).

140. See, generally, Anderson, S., *Smithsonian Magazine,* July, 2014 at *smithsonian. com.*

141. See February 27, 1968 (President Lyndon Johnson's remarks that "if I've lost Walter Cronkite … I've lost Middle America.").

142. 370 U.S. 421 (1962). Justice Douglas agreed with the decision via a concurring opinion. Justices Frankfurter and White did not participate in the final vote.

143. 374 U.S. 203 (1963).

144. See, e.g. Kessler, G,. *washingtonpost.com,* June 23, 2014.

145. See 1962 – Seminal Book, *Sex and the Single Girl* by Helen Gurley Brown.

146. *The Week,* August 24-31, 2012, p. 39.

147. Vatter, W., *The Wall Street Journal,* September 24, 2013 (review of Audrey Petty's book, *High Rise Stories: Voices From Chicago Public Housing,* (2013)).

148. For a possibly successful turnaround of a major public housing project, see Cousins, T., "The Atlanta Model for Reviving Poor Neighborhoods," *The Wall Street Journal,* September 14-15, 2013, discussing the highly targeted and preliminarily successful turnaround of the 1,400-resident East Lake Meadows project in Atlanta, Georgia.

149. See, e.g., Dallek, R., *Camelot's Court: Inside the Kennedy White House* (2013), as reviewed by Landers, R., *The Wall Street Journal,* November 21, 2013.

150. *Dol.gov* (Eisenhower Administration, 1953–1961).

151. See also, 1964 – Pulitzer Price for General Nonfiction.

152. Masciotra, D., *the dailybeast,* March 9, 2014.

153. Lemann, N., *Columbia Journalism Review,* September/October 2014.

154. *Ibid.*

155. Binn, S., *The New York Times,* January 31, 1963.

156. See also, 1963 – Seminal Book – *The Cat in the Hat* and 1962 – Seminal Book – *The Snowy Day.*

157. See *alcatrazhistory.com.*

158. See Memorable Words – August 13, 1961.

159. Evans, H., *The American Century* (2000), p. 464.

160. *The Week,* January 25, 2013, p. 35.

161. *Ibid.,* p. 35.

162. McFadden, R., *The New York Times,* January 13, 2013.

163. Caro, R., *The Passage of Power: The Years of Lyndon Johnson* (2012), p. xv.

164. Aronson, R., "Marcuse Today," *bostonreview.net,* November 17, 2009.

165. *Ibid.*

166. See Memorable Words - March 9, 1965.

167. "Smoking and Health: Report of the Advisory Committee to the Surgeon General of the Public Health Service "(Report Released January 11, 1964) (Surgeon General Luther L. Terry, M.D.).

168. As summarized in the Centers for Disease Control and Prevention, "History of the Surgeon General's Reports on Smoking and Health," *cdc.gov.*

169. *Harper v. Virginia Board of Elections.*

170. See generally, Lipsyte, R., "Clay Discusses his Future, Liston, and Black Muslims," *The New York Times,* February 27, 1964.

171. See Memorable Words – April 28, 1967.

172. Steve Jobs' graduation address at Stanford University, June 12, 2005 (at *news.stanford.edu*).

173. See Memorable Words - July 30, 1975.

174. Evans, H., *The American Century* (2000), p. 526. See also, Memorable Words – December 23, 1963.

175. See, Swaim, B., *The Wall Street Journal,* January 22, 2015 and his discussion of Todd Purdum's book by the same name (*An Idea Whose Time Has Come* (2014)) about the battle for the passage of the Civil Rights Act of 1964 and released on the 50th anniversary of that momentous legislation.

176. Notwithstanding the widespread attribution of this statement to Senator Dirksen, according to The Dirksen Congressional Center, a non-partisan, not-for-profit civic organization in Pekin, IL, the statement may not have ever been so made by Dirksen.

177. See Memorable Words - February 21, 1965.

178. See also, Memorable Words - October 1964.

179. Evans, H., *The American Century,* (2000), p. 528.

180. *americanwarlibrary.com.*

181. *reaganfoundation.org.*

182. See, e.g., *United States v. Lopez* (1995) (Constitutionality of Congress' Gun-Free School Zones Act of 1990) and *United States v. Morrison* (2000) (Challenge to federal law prohibiting violence against women).

183. Soloman, C., *Los Angeles Times*, February 11, 1990.

184. Gray, M., *Time*, August 17, 2011.

185. See, Evans, H., *The American Century*, (2000), p. 560.

186. *Ibid.*

187. Dawsey, D., "25 Years After the Watts Riots: McCone Commission's Recommendations Have Gone Unheeded," *Los Angeles Times*, July 8, 1990.

188. Unlike during the Afghanistan and Iraq Wars in the early 21st Century, very few National Guard or Reserves were deployed in the 1960s and 1970s to Vietnam (only about 15,000 over the course of the war). Thus, enlistment in the National Guard or the Reserves was correctly seen as a means to avoid deployment to Vietnam.

189. See *"Thank you for your service"* comments in Chapter 9 (Year 1973).

190. See the 2014 remarks of U.S. Army Col. (Ret) Lawrence B. Wilkerson set forth below.

191. At the time of President Nixon's 1969 Inauguration, this number had nearly doubled to nearly 9,000 District police, regular troops, and National Guardsman. Kilpatrick, C., Oberdorfer, D., "Richard M. Nixon Becomes President with 'Sacred Commitment' to Peace," January 21, 1969, *washingtonpost.com*.

192. *carlanthonyonline.com*, January 20, 2015. See also, Kilpatrick, C., "Johnson Takes Oath and Vows Drive for Great Society, World Without Hate," January 21, 1965, *washingtonpost.com*.

193. Andrews, S., *Vanity Fair*, April 2016, p. 161.

194. See, Catchphrases, Chants, and Slogans in Chapter 8 (Year 1965) – *"Burn baby, burn."*

195. *The Week*, January 31, 2014, p. 36 adapted from Kevin D. Williamson's re-titled article "The Big White Ghetto" about the "Appalachian towns and villages stretching from northern Mississippi to southern New York." The article first appeared in the *National Review*, December 16, 2013.

196. U.S. Census Bureau at *census.gov*; Institute for Research on Poverty (University of Wisconsin – Madison) at *irp.wisc.edu*.

197. See, Evans, H., *The American Century*, (2000), pp. 462-463.

198. Lewis, M., "Obama's Way, "*Vanity Fair,* October 2012, p. 210. See also, Scherer, M., "Barack Obama," *Time*, December 31, 2012, p. 62.

199. *The Week,* June 28, 2013, p. 9; *pbs.com*.

200. Evans, H., *The American Century*, (2000) pp. 462-463.

201. Zelizer, J., "How Medicare Was Made," *newyorker.com*, February 15, 2015. National health insurance had been proposed even earlier by President Teddy

Roosevelt as far back as 1912. As noted in the article, President Franklin Roosevelt had also considered making health care a part of his 1937 Social Security proposal but decided against trying for such inclusion, fearing that it would be "too controversial."

202. Anderson, S., *medicaresources.org.*, October 26, 2016, citing data from the Kaiser Family Foundation.

203. Vidal, G., "Sex and the Law," *Partisan Review* (Summer, 1965). Partisan Review was a small-circulation quarterly published in New York. The magazine, which focused upon literary, political, and cultural commentary, was first published in 1934. While well respected among some commentators, the magazine had a long and complicated history—from its early association with Progressive and Communist parties to the rumors of it being CIA-funded. It ceased publication in 2003.

204. Colquhoun, K., "Book of a Lifetime: *In Cold Blood,* by Truman Capote," May 12, 2011 at *independent.co.uk.*

205. *Ibid.* See also, *markmywords.blogspot.com* (1976) and *research.omicsgroup.org.*

206. Wolfe, T., *Mauve Gloves & Madmen, Clutter & Vine* (1976).

207. Fletcher, J., *Situation Ethics: The New Morality* (1966), p. 30.

208. See, e.g. Gingrich, N., *A Nation Like No Other: Why American Exceptionalism Matters* (2011). See also, Lee, T., "Newt Gingrich Best Articulates American Exceptionalism," *Human Events*, September 12, 2011.

209. Fulbright, Senator J. William, *The Arrogance of Power* (1966), pp. 4 and 154.

210. See Catchphrases, Chants, and Slogans – Chapter 8 (Year 1966) – "*Body counts.*"

211. Dr. Masters divorced his prior wife in 1971 so that he could promptly thereafter marry his co-author Virginia Johnson whom he had initially hired as a research assistant many years earlier in 1957. The marriage of Masters and Johnson itself ended in divorce in 1992.

212. Maier, Thomas, *Masters of Sex: The Life and Times of William Masters and Virginia Johnson, the Couple Who Taught America How to Love* (2013).

213. Wray, C., *The Birmingham News*, Janaury 31, 2015.

214. Smith, C., *Forbes*, January 16, 2015.

215. Weller, S., "It Happened in 1967," *Vanity Fair,* March 2017.

216. *History.com* ("April 4, 1967: Martin Luther King, Jr. Speaks Out Against the War").

217. A variation of this phrase, "*No Vietnamese Ever Called Me Nigger,*" was used a year later as the title to a documentary about the front-line lives of black soldiers in Vietnam.

218. See Memorable Words – Chapter 8 (Year 1964).

219. See *Americanswhotellthetruth.org; iancfriedman.com* (Words Matter – Muhammad Ali, April 28, 1967).

220. 388 U.S. 1 (1967).

221. Coleman, A., *Time*, June 10, 2016.

222. *The Week,* June 2, 2017, citing data from the Pew Research Center.

223. See also, Memorable Words – Chapter 7 – February 29, 1968) (Kerner Commission).

224. Despite this change in admissions protocol, the close and long-established relationship between Harvard University and Radcliffe College, which is nearly adjacent to the Harvard University, should be noted even though, admittedly, the complete merger of these two universities has taken many decades. Radcliffe College was founded in 1879. From 1879–1943, "Harvard professors repeated to Radcliffe students the lectures they gave at Harvard." *college.harvard.edu.* After World War II, the majority of Harvard classes were co-educational, but even though Harvard degrees were awarded to Radcliff students starting in 1963. The admissions protocol, as noted, was not changed until 1967, and the governing bodies of Harvard and Radcliffe was not completed until 1999.

225. Doughertty, E., Book Review, National Association of Scholars, September 9, 2015, *nas.org.*

226. *Politicaloutcast.com.*

227. *Ibid.*

228. Haberman, C., "The Unrealized Horrors of Population Explosion," May 31, 2015, *nytimes.com.* Haberman also notes (a) that "while (food) shortages persist in some regions, they were often more a function of government incompetence, corruption or civil strife than of an absolute lack of food," and (b) that in the opinion of some commentators, "the villain (of food shortages) is not over-population but, rather, overconsumption."

229. This year, 1968, is used because this was the first year in which *Mister Rogers' Neighborhood* was broadcasted nationally. The series originated in 1963, but it was only broadcasted locally and regionally between 1963 and 1968.

230. *iancfriendman.com,* February 27, 2010.

231. Carroll, P., *It Seems Like Nothing Happened: The Tragedy and Promise of America in the 1970s* (1982), p. 18, citing Congressional Quarterly, *Nixon: The Second Year of His Presidency,"* (1971), p. 67.

232. From Taylor Branch's book, *At Canaan's Edge*, the third book of his trilogy about Martin Luther King and the Civil Rights Movement. The books have won many awards, including the 1989 Pulitzer Prize for History.

233. UPI, 1968 Year in Review, *upi.com.*

234. "Assassination: The Night Bobby Kennedy Was Shot," *The Independent,* January 20, 2007, *independent.uk.co.*

235. See Catchphrases, Chants, and Slogans – Chapter 8 (Year 1968).

236. *The Week*, April 20, 2012. See also, Davis, D., *Smithsonian Magazine*, August 2008.

237. See generally, The Classification and Ratings Administration, *filmratings.com*.

238. For a transcript of the President's remarks, see *presidency.ucsb.edu*.

239. Evans, H., *The American Century*, (2000), p. 537.

240. *Time.com.*, May 15, 2014.

241. See also, Memorable Words – Chapter 8 (Year 1969 – August 5, 1969) (President Richard Nixon).

242. See Memorable Words – Chapter 8 (Year 1961 – May 25, 1961) (President John Kennedy).

243. Pastor, A., "Remembrances – Neil Armstrong 1930-2012," *The Wall Street Journal*, August 27, 2012.

244. Pastor, A., "Remembrances – Neil Armstrong 1930-2012," *The Wall Street Journal*, August 27, 2012.

245. See *nasa.gov*.

246. Bates, T., *The Week*, May 23, 2014, p. 3.

247. See Memorable Words – Chapter 8 (Year 1969 - July 18, 1969) (Ted Kennedy).

248. See also, Memorable Words – Chapter 9 (Year 1970 – September 11, 1970) (Spiro Agnew).

249. Clines, F., "Spiro T. Agnew, Point Man for Nixon Who Resigned Vice-Presidency, Dies at 77," *The New York Times*, September 19, 1996. See also, Agnew, S., *Go Quietly ... Or Else* (1980) (Agnew's memoir which is titled after the supposed threat made to Agnew by Richard Nixon's Chief of Staff Alexander Haig); Frank, J., *Ike and Dick: Portrait of a Strange Political Marriage* (2013); and Bork, Robert H., *Saving Justice* (2013) (Great, albeit short, summary of these tumultuous years of the second term of Nixon's Presidency).

250. See Memorable Words – Chapter 9 (Year 1973 – October 1973) - "No Contest" - Spiro T. Agnew.

251. See, e.g., Jackson, H., *A Century of Dishonor* (1885).

252. In addition to the occupation of Alcatraz, members of AIM were among those who took part in the 71-day occupation at the Pine Ridge Reservation at Wounded Knee, South Dakota in 1973. The tense protest was triggered by the actions of the then-chairman of the Pine Ridge Indian Reservation, which had resulted in the deaths of two Native Americans. In the 1974 trial after the occupation had ended, all charges against the Native Americans were dismissed after a number of incidents of government misconduct were disclosed.

253. Brown, Dee as quoted in Martin, D., "Dee Brown, 94, Author Who Revised Image of West," *The New York Times*, December 14, 2002 (Written at the time of her death).

254. *The Week*, July 18, 2014, p. 9.

255. See, e.g. Wilkinson, F., "Benign Neglect," *nytimes.com,* June 11, 2008 (Discussing prior administration's seeming adoption of policies of benign neglect in the context of the 2008 presidential election and the rise of Barack Obama who, at the time of this article, was a viable presidential contender.

256. See Stephens, B., *The Wall Street Journal,* February 5, 2013 (Speaking of the Hruska's defense-of-mediocrity remark in the politically-charged context of President Obama's nomination of Chuck Hagel to serve as Secretary of Defense).

257. Poem excerpted from Evans, H., *The American Century,* (2000), p. 537, citing *Dear America: Letters Home from Vietnam* (1985) edited by Bernard Edelman.

258. See Catchphrases, Chants, and Slogans – Chapter 9 (Year 1970).

259. *hq.nasa.gov.*

260. Carroll, P., *It Seems Like Nothing Happened – The Tragedy and Promise of America in the 1970s* (1982), p. 18.

261. See 1964 – Memorable Words – August 4, 1964.

262. Dean, J., *The Rehnquist Choice: The Untold Story of the Nixon Appointment That Redefined the Supreme Court* (2001).

263. Lethwick, D., *Slate.,* October 11, 2001.

264. Boertlein, J., *Presidential Confidential* (2010), p. 293.

265. Carroll, Peter N., *It Seemed Like Nothing Happened: The Tragedy and Promise of America in the 1970s* (1982), p. 34.

266. See, e.g. David Maraniss' review of Peter Landesman's documentary *Concussion,* Mark Fainaru-Wade and Steve Fainaru's book *League of Denial: The NFL, Concussions and the Battle for Truth,* and several other books in *The New York Review of Books,* February 1, 2016. See also, the 2015 movie *Concussion* starring Will Smith and Alec Baldwin.

267. See, e.g. Mason, R., *Richard Nixon and the Quest for a New Majority* (2004).

268. MacLaury, J., "The Job Safety Law of 1970: Its Passage Was Perilous," *do.gov; law.du.edu.*

269. *Press.princeton.edu.*

270. Moore, S., "The Man Who Saved Capitalism" *The Wall Street Journal,* July 31, 2012.

271. *Ibid.*

272. Upon such launching, Hunter Thompson's ashes joined those of Timothy Leary and Gene Roddenberry who had had their ashes disbursed into space eight years in 1997.

273. *Ourbodiesourselves.org.*

274. *Ibid.*

275. See Sears, P. B., Professor Emeritus of Yale University, Preface to *The Closing Circle* (1971), p. 12.

276. *Id.*, p. 13.

277. *Adslogans.com* identifies this slogan as first being used as early as 1967.

278. See Almasy, S., *cnn.com*, April 14, 2016.

279. See Associated Press, July 23, 2016 at *nbc.news.com*.

280. Hagopian, P., *The Vietnam War in American Memory: Veterans, Memorials, and the Politics of Healing* (2011).

281. See, e.g., Ritholtz, B., *Bailout Nation: How Greed and Easy Money Corrupted Wall Street and Shook the World Economy* (2009); and Gunn, D., "The Nanny Nation," *freakonomics.com*, July 8, 2009.

282. For one popularized description of the underlying crooks and causes of the savings and loan crisis, see Michael Lewis' best-selling book *Liar's Poker* (1989).

283. See generally, Wicker, T, *A Time to Due* (1975) (Written by the then young *New York Times* reporter Tom Wicker, who had participated in the negotiations) and Foreman, J., Jr., *"Blood in the Water: The Attica Prison Uprising of 1971 and Its Legacy* (2016).

284. *The Week*, February 17, 2012, p. 37.

285. *aynrand.org*.

286. *Ibid.*

287. Because the note was immediately reclaimed by Cooper, the exact wording of the note cannot be definitively ascertained. However, this is the wording as best recollected by the recipient flight attendant.

288. A young boy did find a "soiled packet of $20" bills near the Columbia River in 1980, but the bills were never positively identified as D.B. Cooper's hijack money. Del Re, G. and P., *History's Last Stand* (1993), p. 180.

289. The American Presidency Project at *presidency.ucsb.edu*. For an excellent summary of federal financing for child care, see Cohen, A., "A Brief History of Federal Financing for Child Care in the United States, *Financing Child Care*, Summer/Fall, 1966 and at *futureofchildren.org*.

290. Nvasky, V., "How We Got into the Messiest War in Our History" *The New York Times*, November 12, 1972.

291. See 1966 – Seminal Book – *The Arrogance of Power* by Senator J. William Fulbright.

292. Reported by Kisner, R., "Shirley Chisholm Kicks Off Campaign for US. Presidency," *Jet*, February 1972.

293. See Memorable Words – Chapter 9 (Year 1975 – February 21, 1975).

294. See Memorable Words – Chapter 9 (Year 1974 – July 25, July 27, and August 8, 1974).

295. Barnes, F., "The Also-Ran Who Also Ran," *The Wall Street Journal*, July 21–22, 2012, citing Glosser, J., *The Eighteen-Day Running Mate: McGovern, Eagleton, and a Campaign in Crisis* (2012).

296. *The Economist*, January 27, 2005. Berra beat out many other nominated contenders, including every eligible U.S. President (excepting John F. Kennedy), every recent President of Russia, a few businessmen (including Donald Trump), and others. The wining nominees were Berra, in first place; Yassir Arafat in second place; and Ronald Reagan and Pope John Paul II tied for third place.

297. For an excellent summary of Kissinger's "peace at hand" statement, see Ian Friedman's "Words Matter" at *ianfriedman.com*. In a cruel twist of fate, on January 23, 1973—less than three months after Kissinger's "peace at hand" statement— former President Lyndon Johnson died of a heart attack at his Texas ranch.

298. Ehrlichman, J., *Witness to Power: The Nixon Years* (1982).

299. See Best/Most Memorable Movie Lines of the Year – Chapter 9 (Year 1976).

300. *AD.C.ouncil.org*.

301. *Quora.com*. See also, *aef.com* (Advertising Educational Foundation – United Negro College Fund (1972–Present).

302. Schillinger, L., "A Woman's Fantasy in a Modern Reality by Erica Jong, 40 Years Later," *The New York Times*, December 18, 2013 at *nytimes.com*.

303. Masad, I., *bustle.com*, June 5, 2015 (Referencing her interview with Brown upon the 2015 re-release of Rubyfruit Jungle.)

304. *Penguinrandomhouse.com* citing the remark of Donna Shalala, the U.S. Secretary of Health and Human Services under President Bill Clinton from 1993 to 2001 and the current president of the Clinton Foundation.

305. See, e.g. *The Week*, June 5, 2015, p. 14, citing Zucchino, D., Cloud., D., *Los Angeles Times*.

306. Wellford, R., *pbs.org*, November 11, 2014.

307. Some people suggest that the characterization of our military as an "all-volunteer" force is itself misleading. Instead, since volunteers are oftentimes identified through the use of sophisticated advertising campaigns and are disproportionately recruited from lower income families, the more accurate characterization of today's military might be an "all-recruit" force.

308. Margaret Meade as quoted in Abigail McCarthy's article, "'An American Family' and 'The Family of Man.' '*The Atlantic*, July, 1973.

309. *pbs.org/program/American-family*.

310. During the course of the series, Lance, the eldest son, came out to his family as gay, and, thus, Lance became the first openly gay character in a continuing role on television. As a result and for some, he became an icon within the LGBT community.

311. Crawford, P., Hafsteinsson, S., "Can a Documentary Be Made of Real life?: The Reception of *An American Family*" (1996) at *dartmouth.edu*.

312. A boycott of a Presidential Inauguration by elected officials would not occur again for nearly 50 years, until the Presidential Inauguration of Donald Trump in 2017. See Zelizer, J., *thedailybeast.com*, January 19, 2017.

313. Summary of case from "The Supreme Court: *Roe v. Wade,*" *pbs.org.*

314. Upon the arrival of the protestors in Washington, D.C., the Nixon Administration refused to meet with them. Eventually, some concessions were made by the federal government through Department of the Interior negotiators, but by any reasonable measure, the protest failed to achieve any meaningful or lasting results.

315. See Chertoff, E., "Occupy Wounded Knee: A 71-Day Siege and a Forgotten Civil Rights Movement," *theatlantic.com* (October 23, 2012) (Written upon the death of former AIM leader, Russell Means, at the age of 72).

316. Ventre, M., *AA.com/Americanway*, April 1, 2013, p. 34.

317. Garay, R., Museum of Broadcast Communications at *museum.tv/archives.*

318. Zelnick, R., "The Oil Rush of '70," *The New York Times*, March 1, 1970.

319. Secretary of the Interior Walter Hickel as quoted in Simon, A., "The Trans Alaska Pipeline: A Struggle for Balance," *washingtonhistory.org.*

320. Simon, A., "The Trans Alaska Pipeline: A Struggle for Balance," *washingtonhistory.org.*

321. American Oil & Gas Historical Society, "Trans-Alaska Pipeline History," *aoghs.rg.* See also, *The American Experience – The Alaska Pipeline – Timeline, pbs.org.*

322. Over the ensuing decades, there were a number of "Battle of the Sexes" matches (e.g. Bobby Riggs and Vitas Gerulaitis v. Martina Navratilova and Pam Shriver (1985) (Doubles Match); Martina Navratilova v. Jimmy Connor (1992); and Karsten Braasch v. the Williams Sisters (1998)). However, none of them achieved the notoriety or viewership of the 1973 Bobby Riggs v. Billy Jean King Match.

323. Greenspan, J., "When Billie Beat Bobby, " September 20, 2013, *history.com.*

324. *The Week*, September 15, 2017, p. 10.

325. Summary of Presidential Impeachment Proceedings, *historyplace.com.*

326. *Ibid.*

327. See Memorable Words – Chapter 9 (Year 1974 – August 8, 1974).

328. For brief summaries of the 1973–1974 oil crisis, see *history.state.gov/1969-1976/oil-embargo* and *energytrendinsider.com/2013/10/23.*

329. See Memorable Words – Chapter 9 (Year 1973 – October, 1973).

330. See Memorable Words – Chapter 8 (Year 1967 – February 10, 1967).

331. *wwnorton.com.*

332. See Memorable Words – Chapter 8 (Year 1969 – August 9, 1969).

333. See also Pulitzer Prize for General Nonfiction – Chapter 9 (Year 1975).

334. Butler, R. N., *ISI*, November 21, 1988.

335. Martin, D., *The New York Times*, July 7, 2010, quoting Dr. David B. Reuban, chief of the division of geriatrics at the University of California, Los Angeles.

336. Grigsby, S., "Books That Changed My Life: *The Glory and the Dream*," *dailykos. com.*, December 2, 2011.

337. Quoted in Shipkowski, B., *Associated Press,* May 8, 2005.

338. Clines, F., *The New York Times*, January 18, 1996.

339. Speech of President Richard Nixon, April 30, 1973.

340. Harry S. Truman, as quoted in Merle Miller's *Plain Speaking: An Oral Biography of Harry S. Truman* (1974) and Barry Goldwater in his memoirs, *Goldwater* (1988).

341. See Memorable Words – Chapter 9 (Year 1975 – February 21, 1975).

342. See Memorable Words – Chapter 9 (Year 1974 – September 4, 1974).

343. Schenker, I., *The New York Times,* August 9, 1974.

344. Clarke, G., "The Art of Fiction: Interview with Gore Vidal," *The Paris Review*, Fall, 1974.

345. This essay was included in Vidal's book, *Matters of Fact and Fiction: Essays 1973–1976* (1977) and *The State of the Union: The Nation's Essays 1958–2008* (2013).

346. See Memorable Words – Chapter 8 (Year 1967 – April 28, 1967).

347. See Memorable Words – Chapter 9 (Year 1971 – September 9, 1971).

348. See, e.g. Schultz, B. and S., *It Did Happen Here: Recollections of Political Repression in America* (1989). (Note: The title of this book is drawn from Sinclair Lewis' 1935 semi-satirical political novel entitled *It Can't Happen Here: What Will Happen When America Has a Dictator* (1935)).

349. Evans, H., *The American Century* (2000), p. 594.

350. Evans, H., *The American Century* (2000), p. 522.

351. *History.state.gov/milestones*; Carroll, P., *It Seems Like Nothing Happened – The Tragedy and Promise of America in the 1970s* (1982), p. 165.

352. See, e.g., Federer, B., "Gerald Ford Gave Same Warning Over and Over and Over," *wnd.com,* July 13, 2016.

353. *The Week,* Obituary: "The Heavyweight Champ Whose Rivalry Defined An Era," November 18, 2011, p. 38.

354. Cited in Angell, M., "May Doctors Help You to Die?," *The New York Review of Books*, October 11, 2012, p. 39.

355. See July 15, 1977 (President Jimmy Carter).

356. *Ontheissues.org.* See also, Walker, B., "The New Jimmy Carter," *American Thinker*, March 18, 2008.

357. This number compares with and is about ten times the estimated 40,000 who deserted throughout the entire period of World War II. Giraldi, P., *huffingtonpost.com*, July 3, 2014.

358. See Memorable Words – Chapter 9 (Year 1974 – September 4, 1974).

359. Lasch, C., "The Narcissist Society," *The New York Review of Books*, September 30, 1976.

360. Hougan, J., *Decadence: Radical Nostalgia, Narcissism, and Decline in the Seventies* (1976); Rubin, J., *Growing (Up) at Thirty-Seven* (1976); Zweig, P., *Three Journeys: An Anthology* (1976); Schur, E., *The Awareness Trap: Self-Absorption Instead of Social Change* (1976); and Kernberg, O., *Borderline Conditions and Pathological Narcissism* (1976).

361. See Wolfe, T., "The 'Me' Decade and the Third Great Awakening," *New York Magazine*, August 23, 1976.

362. Lasch, C., *The Culture of Narcissism: American Life in an Age of Diminishing Expectations* (1979).

363. For a more detailed analysis of this shift in the dominate subjects of American reading by decade, see *mackwborgen.com* at Blog No. 62 (January 15, 2016).

364. Gordon, J., "A Short History of Presidential Debates," *The Wall Street Journal*, October 16, 2012.

365. Robertson, R., "We Were the Band," *Vanity Fair*, November 2016, p. 176.

366. *Id.*, p. 182.

367. As great as these words are as a book title, it should be acknowledged that they are taken from traditional blues lyrics dating back to the 1920s.

368. *Oclc.org*.

369. See generally, *ncac.org* ("The Kids' Right to Read Project" of the National Coalition Against Censorship); *bannedbooksweek.org*; Celania, M, *neatorama.com*, September 29, 2011; Bates, T., Hansen, L., *theweek.com*, September 19, 2013; and American Library Association, "Banned & Challenged Books," *ala.org*.

370. See Memorable Words – Chapter 8 (Year 1968 - November 1, 1968).

371. Bates, T., Hansen, L., *theweek.com*, September 19, 2013.

372. American Library Association, "Banned & Challenged Books," *ala.org*.

373. See Gruebel, C., "11 Books That Were Banned for Completely Ridiculous Reasons," September 29, 2015, *barnesandnoble.com*. See also, Mins, R., "Where's Waldo? Not in the Libraries Because He's Been Banned," *The Current* (University of Missouri – St. Louis), October 17, 2005, *umsl.edu*.

374. Curiously, this book banning occurred of all places at the public library of Tarzana, California.

375. *Hongkiat.com*. See also, "Ad Slogan Hall of Famc" at *adslogans.co.uk; advergive. com; brandongaile.com; fastcompany.com; taglineguru.com*.

376. *Adslogans.com* identifies 1971 as the initial use of this slogan, however variants of the slogans were used earlier.

Index and Topical Cross-References

Information in footnotes is indicated by the letter *n* in parentheses,
followed by note number.

CPSIA information can be obtained
at www.ICGtesting.com
Printed in the USA
LVHW111427111118
594875LV00001BA/1/P